FINANCE OR FOOD?

The Role of Cultures, Values, and Ethics in Land Use Negotiations

Exploring the ways in which culture, systems of value, and ethics impact agriculture, *Finance or Food?* addresses contemporary land questions and conditions for agricultural land management. Throughout, the editors and contributors consider a range of issues, including pressure on farmland, international and global trade relations, moral and ethical questions, and implications for governance.

The focus is on land use in Australia, Canada, and Norway, chosen for their commonalities as well as their differences. With reference to these specific national contexts, the contributors examine political, ecological, and ethical debates concerning food production, alternative energy, and sustainability. The volume argues that recognition of food, finance, energy, and climate crises is driving investments and reframing the strategies of development agencies. At the same time, food producers, small farmers, and pastoralists facing eviction from their land are making their presence felt, not just locally but in national policy arenas and international fora as well.

Finance or Food? investigates the cultural implications of new developments in global land use and is essential reading for both academics and policymakers.

HILDE BJØRKHAUG is an associate professor in the Department of Sociology and Political Science at the Norwegian University of Science and Technology and senior advisor at Ruralis, Institute for Rural and Regional Research.

PHILIP MCMICHAEL is a professor in the Department of Development Sociology at Cornell University.

BRUCE MUIRHEAD is a professor in the Department of History and Associate Vice President of Research Oversight and Analysis at the University of Waterloo.

Finance or Food?

The Role of Cultures, Values, and Ethics in Land Use Negotiations

EDITED BY
HILDE BJØRKHAUG, PHILIP MCMICHAEL,
AND BRUCE MUIRHEAD

UNIVERSITY OF TORONTO PRESS
Toronto Buffalo London

Chapter 7 was originally published in *Agriculture and Human Values*,
March 2017, Volume 34, Issue 1, pp. 223–35, as "Responsibility to the Rescue?:
Governing Private Financial Investment in Global Agriculture" by Jennifer
Clapp. Reprinted with permission of Springer.

ISBN 978-1-4875-0312-3 (cloth)   ISBN 978-1-4875-1724-3 (EPUB)
ISBN 978-1-4875-2247-6 (paper)   ISBN 978-1-4875-1723-6 (PDF)

Library and Archives Canada Cataloguing in Publication

Title: Finance or food? : the role of cultures, values, and ethics in land use
    negotiations / edited by Hilde Bjørkhaug, Philip McMichael, and Bruce
    Muirhead.
Names: Bjørkhaug, Hilde, editor. | McMichael, Philip, editor. | Muirhead,
    Bruce, editor.
Description: Includes bibliographical references and index.
Identifiers: Canadiana 2019017689X | ISBN 9781487503123 (hardcover) |
    ISBN 9781487522476 (softcover)
Subjects: LCSH: Land use, Rural. | LCSH: Agriculture – Economic aspects.
Classification: LCC HD111 .F56 2020 | DDC 333.76–dc23

This book has been published using funds provided by the Norwegian
Research Council.

University of Toronto Press acknowledges the financial assistance to its
publishing program of the Canada Council for the Arts and the Ontario Arts
Council, an agency of the Government of Ontario.

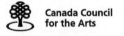 

Contents

Acknowledgments

This book emerged from research, open meetings, and workshops initiated by the project Frogs, fuel, finance or food? Cultures, values, ethics and arguments on agricultural land (FORFOOD). Contributions to the book were invited from these academic meetings.

We would like to thank the Norwegian Research Council program SAMKUL (No. 220691) for funding for the project and the University of Waterloo and its Balsillie School for International Affairs for hosting the FORFOOD workshop kicking off this book project. In conjunction with the Norwegian Research Council, UW provided funding for that meeting through its International Research Partnership grants program.

The editors of this book, Hilde Bjørkhaug, Philip McMichael, and Bruce Muirhead, have appreciated the collaboration and hard work of the authors who have contributed to the intellectual evolution of this book. We are also very grateful to Daniel Quinlan, Acquisitions Editor at the University of Toronto Press, for guiding us through the publication process, two anonymous reviewers for providing critical and helpful comments, and finally to the Manuscript Review Committee at UTP for additional valuable input and support for the publication of this book. We trust that this edited collection will provide readers with insights into rarely addressed issues focused on culture, values, and ethics.

FINANCE OR FOOD?

The Role of Cultures, Values, and Ethics
in Land Use Negotiations

1 Introduction to Cultures, Values, Ethics, and Arguments on Agricultural Land

HILDE BJØRKHAUG, PHILIP MCMICHAEL, AND BRUCE MUIRHEAD

Introduction

Agricultural land is a vital resource on which we depend for food production. While increasing numbers of people in the world find their food in the supermarket, 95 per cent of the calories we rely on for our sustenance originate directly or indirectly from agricultural land (FAO 2015). This land is in direct competition with other activities – housing, infrastructure, mining, investment, carbon offsetting, nature conservation, and industry, among other uses. And those activities seem to be winning. Every year, 50,000 square kilometres of agricultural land is lost to urbanization or industrialization (FAO 2015). Further, agricultural soil is a non-renewable resource because of the thousand-year horizon that is required to restore one centimetre of lost earth with a new, high-quality replacement. This is the result of the spatiality and the climatic, biological, and geological conditions of soil location. Hence, competition for agricultural land with non-agricultural activity has direct impacts for national and global food security.

The spectre of food insecurity is also intensified by the combination of global population growth, political unrest, environmental degradation, climate change, unfair trade practices, and market speculation of agricultural assets. These processes, and their outcomes, have heightened global interest in securing land as an asset – what has been referred to as "land grabbing." The conflicts over multiple land uses often marginalize women, Indigenous peoples, and peasants, as well as the cultural significance of land. At the same time, this asset-based view of land side-lines non-economic values and other less tangible public goods including aesthetics, maintenance of a sense of "place," and intrinsic links between humans and nature (or humans as nature). Agricultural, environmental, and financial interests imply different and potentially conflicting approaches to land. One might ask, Are endangered frogs or fuel worth more than agricultural land? And to whom, with what interest? And for what purpose?

We begin to answer those questions. This book explores the ways that culture, values, and ethics influence claims and justifications in decisions about agricultural land in the recent past, the present, and in the future, and across geographical spaces and governance structures. The book presents research from an interdisciplinary and international group of academics to offer a multidimensional analysis of the ways culture creates and transforms discourses and practices in decisions on agricultural land.

Defining Land Questions

Land and its management reflect variables that include its lived history, culture, and politics. From the first civilization in Mesopotamia, which was founded on the irrigated cultivation of land (Hole 1966), via the cultural, political, and economic dominance of landed elites (Mazoyer and Roudart 2006), to the Green Revolution of the mid-twentieth century (Smedshaug 2010), various and sometimes conflicting interests have characterized land use and management. Given the continuing modernization of farming practices, and especially the impetus to "go big or go home," the growth in international agricultural trade, and capital and resource accumulation, land is now a resource of even greater strategic importance. Questions of territorial integrity, conservation set-asides,[1] "feeding the world," protection of smallholder rights, "yield gaps" between small and large agriculture, common property resources for peasants, forest-dwellers, and fisherfolk, landscapes as carbon sinks, and new investment opportunities now occupy policy discourses and stimulate competing claims.

Land use and management generally invoke two organizing principles – sustaining *extant* small-farming systems and deploying land to meet the needs of industrial society. Each has its own cultural referent: rural values and economic value. Whereas the former may have concrete territorial and/or community significance, the latter tends to be embedded in a more abstract market culture. In the former, food anchors domestic cultural diets, whereas in the latter, food supplies standardized cross-national diets. In the former, land is a means of local livelihood, while in the latter land is a means of production for distant consumers. In the former, landscapes may serve to sustain biodiverse ecosystems, but in the latter they may offset greenhouse gas emissions in some other, distant part of the world. This division of organizing principles informs much of the contemporary contention over land use and management practices.

Where land is subjected to market rationality via the global food regime, its use is increasingly abstracted from local needs (McMichael 2009). This is evident in ubiquitous extractive agro-export operations, which promote overproduction of foodstuffs for "dumping" in third markets at the expense of small-scale farming systems, volatility in food commodity and land prices, and rising environmental degradation over the last several decades (Gardner 1996; Ball, Fanfani, and Guiterrez 2010). These developments generate contestations over land use, as diverse social actors articulate competing understandings about human–nature relationships and land-management practices. Such conflicts express powerful tensions between differing conceptions of land's value. As Polanyi (1957) reminds us, land is not produced for sale and therefore is a "fictitious commodity" – so it becomes a site of contention over its preservation as a life source (for humans and non-human species) or as an object of pricing, profit, and "biophysical override" via agro-industrialization (Weis 2007).

A key claim by agro-industrial investors and free-trade policymakers is that feeding the world requires large-scale industrial agriculture, agri-chemical input suppliers, giant processors and retailers, and an agro-export system to supply a world market for all. In 2008 the legitimacy of this claim was challenged by a severe world food crisis, generating food riots across thirty food-dependent countries, the great majority of which were in the Global South (Patel and McMichael 2009). Among several contributing factors, including price inflation of agri-inputs, was the conversion of land-for-food crops to fuel crops, mandated or subsidized by governments responding to pressures for biofuels in the midst of rising energy prices. The World Bank claimed U.S. corn ethanol mandates were responsible for 65 per cent of the food price spike (Berthelot 2008). In response, food-exporting countries blocked exports to protect their own consumers, which resulted in a doubling of food prices in just a few months (see figure 1.1) (Brobakk and Almås 2011).

This food crisis was a wake-up call, with implications far beyond the food sector alone. It also marked a radical change from the food- and crop-surplus culture of the 1980s and 1990s – when "post-productivism," "multifunctionality of agriculture," cultural landscape management, and preservation became important policy issues, especially in Europe, to the increased competition and speculation over land resources, and the subsequent decline in food stocks (Brobakk and Almås 2011). The pressures on land are multiple and complex. Certainly, a critical consideration is the imperative to feed and house a growing global population increasingly divorced from the land. As well, certain influential sectors believe that land should generate wealth through resource extraction and financial speculation, both of which are largely done by non-rural investors.

Figure 1.1. FAO Food Price Index 1961–2018

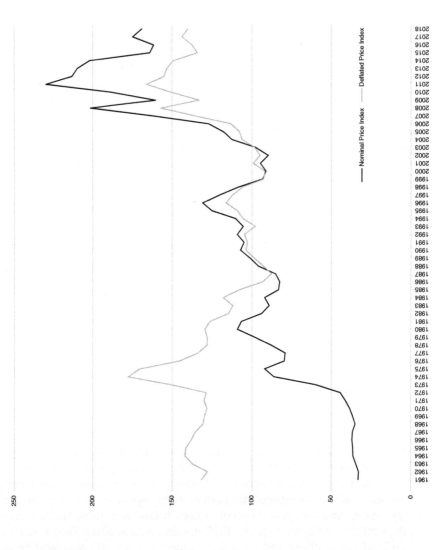

——— Nominal Price Index   ——— Deflated Price Index

Given these imperatives, the non-trade values of land, such as its cultural dimensions, are easily sidelined. If we look at financial investment, media attention, and societal upheavals (such has the food riots in 2008), the value of agricultural land and its resources now raises serious questions about the long-term viability of subordinating land to market values. In this regard, we note an emerging epistemic shift in land-use or landscape management to sustain ecosystems, rural cultures, farming knowledges, and food-producing capacity into the future (McMichael 2011).

An elemental conflict arises over the rights of agribusiness and/ or investors versus those of rural food producers, that is, land appropriation via a discourse of "global food security" or stabilization of *extant* small-farming systems that now provide food to 70 per cent of the world's people (ETC 2017). The ongoing "global land grab," which often displaces small producers, enables investors to convert land to a financial asset for "flex crops" (Borras et al. 2012), depending on whether biofuels, biomass, feed, or food crops command the highest market prices. Land is appropriated not only by private investors, as (predominantly Middle Eastern and East and South Asian) governments now bypass WTO trade rules to appropriate land offshore to ensure food and fuel supplies for their own citizens during food crises and food trade interruption (McMichael 2013).

Future research needs to address not only the political, ecological, and ethical debates over land use and food security (at different scales), but also to focus on sustainability, resilience, and rights to food, and to *produce* food in a context of the private/public enclosure of land and common property resources upon which millions of local food producers and consumers, and smallholders, across the world depend. Agricultural land is usually protected by regulation as well as protectionism that prohibits or limits financial speculation in farmland. However, states might also do one thing at home and another abroad. For example, Norway has a protectionist policy on Norwegian food production, yet it invests in agriculture abroad through one of the world's largest sovereign wealth funds, the Norwegian Government Pension Fund – Global.

In this book we explore and analyse values, arguments, and justifications that lead to the management of such investments. We address urgent ethical challenges in the governance of natural resources, particularly in view of global justice. We ask, Who should govern resources like water and soil? By what criteria and for what purpose? How should citizens balance monocropping for world markets against sustaining local multifunctional farming systems? Does land grabbing have a place, and for whom? Does food justice align with land justice? Are corporate rights equivalent to the rights of farming cultures? Is the market principle able to ensure food justice? Should all countries rich in arable land provide food according to some distributive and global principle of justice, or should they act from a primary responsibility to their own inhabitants? What are the ethical and political responsibilities of investments in agricultural land?

Background to the Book

This book project emerged from research, open meetings, and workshops initiated by the project Frogs, Fuel, Finance or Food? Cultures, Values, Ethics and Arguments on Agricultural Land (FORFOOD).[2] Contributions to the book were invited from these academic meetings, and experts outside the project enriched the FORFOOD results with research and experiences external to the project's framework. It is an interdisciplinary project that combines strengths and insights from sociology, geography, political science, history, philosophy, and cultural studies. The framework for the project was shaped by cultural studies, an innovative interdisciplinary field of research and teaching that investigates the ways in which culture creates and transforms individual experiences, everyday life, social relations, and power. By working across boundaries that often are constrained and siloed by separate academic fields, cultural studies addresses new questions and develops flexible tools that adapt to a rapidly changing world.

Finally, from the cultural studies field, FORFOOD was inspired by the situational analysis approach (Clarke 2005). Here the unit for analysis is the situation. In FORFOOD, agricultural land and research questions address elements within and around land questions, such as how the land "situation" is constructed or how it is being challenged or maintained. In this approach, agricultural land is seen as a discursive creation, existing in texts, talks, mindsets, actions, and its practical materialization. The strength of the design lies in the tools provided for mapping the situation, building on multiple types of data and allowing multiple disciplines to work together. The contributors to this book address contemporary land questions and analyse cultural conditions for agricultural land management from several sites: pressure on farmland in domestic or international relations (policy and public discourses on agricultural land and competing resources, property, and community rights); international and global trade relations (trade agreements, regulations, and certification schemes); and moral and ethical questions and governance implications. Three natural resource–dependent countries were selected for FORFOOD's empirical studies – Australia, Canada, and Norway – for commonalities and contrasts. How they respond to the central theme of the book will be brought out in those chapters. Additionally, the book focuses on the political, ecological, and ethical debates about land use for food production, providing alternative energy, and sustaining global ecosystems. The frogs, fuel, finance, and food theme is central to balancing these priorities.

Given recent trends – financialization of the global food system, the biofuels rush, and rising land acquisitions on every continent – the global land-use regime has reached a watershed. While every country has its distinctive political culture, often shaped by land settlement/use histories, all are involved in global pressures to acquire land for future security – often by foreign investment interests, as noted above. Recognition of food, finance, energy, and climate crises is driving such investments and reframing the strategies of development agencies. At the same time, food producers, small farmers, and pastoralists who face eviction from their land and/or access rights to common lands, for example, are making their presence felt in this debate, not only locally, where they are calling for a moratorium on the "global land grab," but also in national policy arenas and international forums, and particularly the UN's Food and Agriculture Organization, whose Committee on World Food Security (CFS) has recently incorporated the voice and votes of civil society organizations that represent these populations.

The newly framed debates in the CFS are giving new life to the FAO's original mandate to protect landed cultures. Currently, various CFS/High Level Panel of Experts reports are under review. Discussions of the food crisis have been taking place, including those about appropriate conduct in land acquisition as a response to current and future food and energy needs. Here, the financial impulse to secure access to (often offshore) land for food and biofuel production, as well as for conservation (Kyoto's Clean Development Mechanism [CDM] and Reducing Emissions from Deforestation and Forest Degradation [REDD] protocols), for speculation, and/or for indebted governments to defray debt, is under increasing scrutiny through the lens of sustainability of agrarian and forest cultures. In this book we investigate how this is occurring, via studies from both the Global North and the Global South to establish the cultural implications of new developments in global land use, as well as to chart the growing institutional contestation (by the FAO and World Bank, in particular) between a financial calculus and a cultural-ecological calculus as the world confronts a future of limits.

Organization

As has been shown, the overarching objective of the book is to explore how culture, what we might call natural justice, and values and ethics influence arguments and justifications for decisions on the management of agricultural land in the recent past, the present, and into the future. (Indeed, chapter 12 is focused on possibilities that await generations yet unborn.) This collection seeks to highlight tension between the international and the domestic over land purchases as well as provide insights into how "resource hierarchies" are culturally constructed, as different interests and agendas compete for land.

In order to accomplish this, chapters have been grouped by their thematic unity. For example, falling under the policy and public discourse leitmotif are chapters that include Philip McMichael, Hugh Campbell and David Reynolds, and Katrina Rønningen. These ask why some issues remain outstanding, seemingly insoluble without a more robust *public* intervention than seems possible under present circumstances. McMichael situates contemporary land questions within the current political-economic conjuncture and evaluates the political mechanisms by which it is represented and managed. Such representations include those from "above" and "below" – in particular the UN/FAO's Committee on World Food Security, and the grassroots land movements.

From both positions, actors are developing representational discourses about the role of states, markets, farmers, and investors and rights. McMichael's chapter endeavours to identify and disentangle the discourses to establish clearer understandings of the politics informing behaviours and the unfolding forms and visions of land use. It also reflects on the author's experience of local and global land management in the deliberations of the CFS, and critically evaluates the utility of the UN system in addressing land use for the future.

Campbell and Reynolds contemplate the failure of the recent Doha round of the World Trade Organization and focus on the place of agriculture in negotiations, as it has been both one of the most hotly contested elements of free trade deliberations and holds considerable significance for the future of the planet. The WTO's multilateral approach appears to be dead in the water, so what about free trade agreements (FTAs) between countries, outside of that agency?

The fate of FTAs on agriculture link to the wider themes of this book that deal with the ownership and increasingly internationalized and financialized character of markets in agricultural land. The chapter presents about twenty years of negotiations, from the conclusion of the Uruguay Round of GATT in 1995, when agriculture seemed to be moving steadily towards free trade status, to the present, with the "conclusion" of the Trans-Pacific Partnership negotiations and its transformation into the Comprehensive and Progressive TPP following the U.S. withdrawal. Campbell and Reynolds discuss how the failure to liberalize international trade in food products opens up several ways in which we might re-imagine policy futures for food and farming. Their approach also suggests that FTAs have become a cul-de-sac based upon a narrow focus on tariffs and border protections against *food* imports, which don't consider the wider realignments in the global transfer of ownership of *farms* themselves. This distinction between agriculture/food and land/farming becomes increasingly important as the liberalization of one stalls while the other gathers momentum.

For her part, Rønningen analyses developments in agricultural policies in Europe, from "multifunctionality" to the growing focus on increased food production for food security – she notes, for example, that both the European and Norwegian models of agriculture emphasized multifunctional objectives from the very outset: food security and the rural employment that prevented a rural exodus. In the process, European legislation, as well as that of Norway, secured a sustainable income level for farmers as commodities were subsidized and farmers benefited. Beginning in the later 1980s, as memories of wartime starvation faded, this situation moved away from preoccupation with food security towards environmental and rural entrepreneurship concerns about climate change. With the food crisis of 2008, however, the Continent has seen a return to food security in a neo-productivist turn, with renewed focus on production, productivity, and increased legitimacy for "sustainable intensification," which means neo-productivism. Developments on that front are characterized by deregulation such as has been experienced by the pig, poultry, and even dairy sectors, a decreasing number of farmers, increasing corporate control of the land, and land investments by agribusiness and private equity firms, especially in Eastern Europe. At the same time, consumers' growing interest in organic and local food, combined with events such as Brexit, signal scepticism about industrial agriculture and what is seen as the centralization of power by an arrogant top-down bureaucracy that makes policy without reference to the people it supposedly serves. Rønningen analyses the effects of these trends and developments upon multifunctionality policies and goods delivered by European and Norwegian agriculture.

The following three chapters, by Jacob Muirhead, Siri Granum Carson, and Jennifer Clapp, have been grouped together as they chart change in the international governance of agricultural products. Some of this shift has been from the public sphere, where it sat from the end of the Second World War, overseen by agencies like the FAO, to the public-private or private domains by the early 2000s. This private-sector oversight incorporates regulatory standards for land management and food production. Included in their analyses are initiatives to regulate food and its production with "good intentions" for food safety reasons. However, the case is made that ethical principles fall short because of internal contradictions, asymmetric power relationships, and lack of democratic institutions to govern contracts and interactions.

Muirhead examines what can be conceptualized as land grabbing, but is more closely related to business-to-business private standards applied to agricultural products. Most often the literature attributes land grabbing to a combination of processes that include financial speculation, rising energy prices, and/or food insecurity. However, for-profit, private standards developed cooperatively by an oligopoly of food retailers including Fortune 500 companies like Wal-Mart, McDonald's, and Carrefour are closely associated with land grabbing. Their impact is not addressed, however, in the usual way. Such standards are quickly becoming the global norm and a de facto prerequisite for trade in international produce, livestock, and aquaculture markets, especially if that trade is destined for Western markets. In a sense, supermarkets pay a private sector agent, usually operating in the Global South, to ensure food traceability, security, and safety.

In addition, while some argue that private standards play an important and beneficial role in reshaping global supply chains with structural adjustments forced upon the Global South smallholder, Muirhead shows that such standards are most often exclusionary and favour a particular type of large-scale, capital-intensive, industrial farming. He has studied the pineapple sector in Ghana and uses it to show causal mechanisms often involved in the large-scale transfer of land (or its crop), from smallholders, especially in the Global South, to international investors most often in the Global North. The chapter contributes to the theme of debates over land questions and land management by highlighting the centrality of discourses about science, technical expertise, and objectivity that are tied up with private business to business standards. These standards are imbued with legitimacy, while they also mask the significant ways in which they are implicated in reinforcing the power and agency of influential agrifood actors who in turn alter how agricultural land is being used and managed, and simultaneously enable the possibility for land grabbing of an indirect sort.

Siri Carson's chapter notes that not only do private companies seek economic revenue on their investments, but also that states are major players in the finance market. Such investments often raise ethical considerations that are important to consider for both private and public activities. However, as she points out, state activities in this area are generally more transparent than those of the private sector, and the public is much more aware of the issues that arise with the former and not so much with the latter. That is the case for the Norwegian Government Pension Fund – Global (GPFG), the largest sovereign wealth fund (SWF) in the world.

Carson examines whether large-scale land acquisitions should be a prioritized issue for the GPFG, especially given its ethical investment strategy that sees this sort of activity as a criterion to exclude such pursuits. Underlying this discussion is the question of whether the ethical investment strategy should avoid contributing to unethical business – "to keep our hands clean" – or use the financial power of the fund to influence global business in a more sustainable direction, even at the risk of "getting our hands dirty." In this way, GPFG's investments in large-scale land acquisitions can serve as an example where the basic principles of sustainable investment may be reviewed in the public. She argues that land investments and food security could be prioritized in a fund ownership strategy that entailed ongoing dialogue with relevant companies about how environmental damage and human rights violations can be prevented.

Just as Siri Carson is concerned about the international activities of the GPFG, so Jennifer Clapp is critical of global attempts to develop systems to govern global trade responsibly. She examines the recent rise of initiatives for accountable agricultural investment and provides a preliminary assessment of the likely success in curbing the ecological and social costs associated with the growth of private financial investment in the sector. Her argument is that voluntary responsible investment initiatives for agriculture are likely to face weaknesses similar to those experienced by investment initiatives more generally. These have proved to be vague and often illusory. Further, it has been difficult to enforce guidelines, participation rates are low, and confusion arises about a jumble of competing initiatives. In addition, the diversity of investors and the financially complex investments complicate efforts to discover who is responsible in practice. As a result, it is likely that voluntary governance for open and transparent agricultural investment will only shift the discourse rather than make the needed change in practices.

The following four chapters highlight current issues about land questions in Australia, Canada (as seen through the Canadian province of Saskatchewan), and Norway. These represent the case studies, noted above, of current challenges to agricultural land in countries that depend on natural resources. The examples differ substantially, with Australia and Canada home to vast swaths of productive agricultural land that produces surplus food for export markets, and with food self-sufficiency rates (FSSR), according to the FAO, of 207 and 183 per cent, respectively, among the highest in the world. On the other hand, Norway, with only 3 per cent of its already-small land mass comprising productive agricultural land, has a FSSR of 50 per cent, ranking it among the globe's lowest such ratio and very dependent upon food imports. The three cases, presented in four chapters, provide narratives on how policy, society, and economy negotiate land use questions.

Geoffrey Lawrence, Sarah Ruth Sippel, and Nicolette Larder provide an early history of agricultural development in Australia, before tracing the ways new state-owned and finance-backed entities are investing in Australian farming. They also point out how these new investment mechanisms are challenging local (and rural) cultures and environments.

Since the global financial crisis of 2008 there has been a discernible shift in the sources of foreign investment in Australian agriculture with the emergence of new state-led and finance-backed actors. Finance capital is considering a move from uncertain and volatile markets in urban real estate and other less profitable commodity portfolios to seek longer-term investments in farmland. As well, state-led actors have now come to represent increasingly important investment sources, pursuing objectives such as food cultivation in foreign countries to meet their own caloric requirements.

While politicians and much of the media have interpreted such purchases as beneficial for the nation in that they provide a much-needed injection of funds into a farming sector that has experienced financial difficulties over a number of decades, populations are much less convinced. Food security and food sovereignty issues have been raised and have led to increased scrutiny of foreign investment in agriculture more generally. Significantly, questions are now being raised about the short- and long-term impacts of changes in the citizenship of owners and their subsequent control, especially of land and water, but also other natural resources that feed agriculture.

In chapter 9 Jostein Tapper Brobakk and Bruce Muirhead discuss how financialization is challenging both local and provincial regulation of farmland and how this also affects ownership, succession, and farming practices. Soil quality is considered good, and under the mild climate-warming scenario predicted for the Prairie region, Saskatchewan's agricultural productivity is expected to rise. That output has also been reserved, more or less, for residents of the province. Prior to 2003, it had among the most restrictive rules governing land ownership in North America, limiting foreigners to about 4 hectares of land and Canadians who lived beyond its borders to nearly 130. These restrictions focused on preventing land speculation and limiting the size of farms in order to maintain the ability of Saskatchewanians to acquire farmland for agricultural purposes. Even with a limited open-ing for foreign investment in Saskatchewan's farmland, Saskatchewan land policy appears to represent an explicit rejection of financialization, contrary to what is happening in Australia. Moreover, provincial farms remain overwhelmingly family owned, even if that family has incor-porated. Similarly, almost all farm sales are farmer to farmer, with very few such transactions occurring outside of that matrix.

The next two chapters address Norwegian farmland challenges. In the first, Hilde Bjørkhaug, Katrina Rønningen, and Heidi Vinge explore how farmland is negotiated (literally) in Norway and discuss how a de-termination of what is "in the interest of society" is becoming *the* critical factor in deciding whether or not agricultural land should be protected. On the one hand, pressure on land is exerted by such requirements as the need for infrastructure, and especially roads, and housing for a growing urban population. When this is coupled with an intense focus on climate change, Norwegian debates about land are often protracted. On the other hand, in the Norwegian discourse about food security and food sovereignty, land available for growing food has become a deter-mining measure of such discussions. Many now believe it is imperative to sustain the present land area devoted to growing food or, even better, to increase the amount of agricultural land or at least its productivity. The chapter investigates recent developments in this debate on the pro-tection of arable land and what happens when that impetus collides with others, such as where the next road should be built or the next housing development put up. Agricultural sustainability, concern for future generations, and the moral responsibility of adopting the most climate-friendly outcomes are examined.

The following chapter in this section, by Heidi Vinge and Siri Øyslebø Sørensen, explores the Norwegian case further, focusing on how resource conflicts can build alliances between partners who have divergent opinions. Vinge and Sørensen find that in many con-temporary controversies over natural resources, environmental and youth activists advocate for farmland in cooperation with corporatist agricultural interests. This represents a major shift from the previous agrarian-corporatist discourse, of which farmland in Norway has for a long time been a part (Vinge 2015). Emerging new values and attitudes are central to this change. The chapter tells the story of how new actors are entering agrarian politics and explains why. Finally, the chapter sheds light on the formation of strategic alliances as a means to influence policy itself. While the chapter is situated in a Norwegian empirical context, it compares the Norwegian situation with dominant discourses and trends in other countries.

In chapter 12 Allen Alvarez and May Thorseth review philosophical challenges to the idea that members of the current generation have an obligation to make land use sustainable for the sake of future generations. They address urgent ethical challenges to the governance of natural resources, particularly in view of global justice, asking whether we should limit current use of land so that it will reduce opportunities to increase contemporary welfare in order to benefit future generations.

The chapter examines the governance of agricultural land, offering principled philosophical and ethical arguments in defence of environmental rights. Explicitly, it also links with the Vinge and Sørensen chapter on new, developing alliances between parties in the public debate about arable land who have heretofore chosen to disagree. Those who are increasingly making common cause include proponents of wildlife preservation, agricultural smallholders, and critics who believe that the neoliberal industrialization of farmland is the way to a bounteous future. With a reference to Rawls's (1971) overlapping consensus, Alvarez and Torseth identify a common concern for humanity's collective well-being as well as for the interests of future generations in this land use debate that increasingly animates discussion of this important problem. The chapter challenges readers to do likewise – to reflect on how seemingly intractable issues dividing people can become less so, given good will and a commitment to future generations.

Climate change, environmental degradation, a growing global population, urbanization, poverty, asymmetric power relations, and conflict and war all challenge the ability to produce and distribute sufficient food to feed billions of people daily. Arable land remains the most important asset for food production, and its sustainability and availability is crucial. No alternative source, like hydroponics, vertical gardens, agro-ecology will suffice. In this book's final chapter, Philip McMichael, Hilde Bjørkhaug, and Bruce Muirhead challenge the globalizing culture of economism, the dominant financial and economic ideologies and practices in land use, discussing how culture creates and transforms discourses and farmland use. With this we propose *culturalization* of farmland as a concept that can recognize the cultural valuation and a better situated and democratic socio-ecological commons culture in decisions on land management.

It is our hope that this book will provide new knowledge to policymakers, civil society, economic actors, and researchers on the ethical, moral, and value-based factors that are at play in this empirical field of agricultural land and food production.

NOTES

1 Agricultural land set aside for conservation.
2 Funded by the Norwegian Research Council program Samkul.

REFERENCES

Ball, E.V., R. Fanfani, and L. Guiterrez, eds. 2010. *The Economic Impact of Public Support to Agriculture: An International Perspective*. London: Springer.
Berthelot, J. 2008. "The Food Crisis Explosion: Root Causes and How to Regulate Them." *Kurswechsel* 3:23–31.
Borras, S.M. Jr, J.C. Franco, S. Gómez, C. Kay, and M. Spoor. 2012. "Land Grabbing in Latin America and the Caribbean." *Journal of Peasant Studies* 39 (3–4): 845–72. https://doi.org/10.1080/03066150.2012.679931.
Brobakk, J., and R. Almås. 2011. "Increasing Food and Energy Prices in 2008: What Were the Causes and Who Was to Blame?" *Journal of Sociology of Agriculture and Food* 18 (3): 236–59.
Clarke, A. 2005. *Situational Analysis: Grounded Theory after the Postmodern Turn*. Thousand Oaks, CA: Sage.
ETC. 2009. "Who Will Feed Us?" ETC Group. https://www.etcgroup.org/whowillfeedus.
Food and Agriculture Organization of the United Nations (FAO). 2015. *Status of the World's Soil Resources*. Rome: FAO. http://www.fao.org/documents/card/en/c/c6814873-efc3-41db-b7d3-2081a10ede50/.
Gardner, B. 1996. *European Agriculture: Policies, Production and Trade*. London: Routledge.
Hole, F. 1966. "Investigating the Origins of Mesopotamian Civilization." *Science* 153 (3736): 605–11. https://doi.org/10.1126/science.153.3736.605.
Mazoyer, M., and L. Roudart. 2006. *A History of World Agriculture from the Neolithic Age to the Current Crisis*. New York: Monthly Review.
McMichael, P. 2009. "A Food Regime Genealogy." *Journal of Peasant Studies* 36 (1): 139–69. https://doi.org/10.1080/03066150902820354.
– 2011. "Food System Sustainability: Questions of Environmental Governance in the New World (Dis)Order." *Global Environmental Change* 21 (3): 804–12. https://doi.org/10.1016/j.gloenvcha.2011.03.016.
– 2013. "Land Grabbing as Security Mercantilism in International Relations." *Globalizations* 10 (1): 47–64. https://doi.org/10.1080/14747731.2013.760925.
Ontario Ministry of Agriculture, Food and Rural Affairs. (2017). "Number and Area of Census Farms, Canada and the Provinces, 1996, 2001, 2006, 2011 and 2016." http://www.omafra.gov.on.ca/english/stats/census/number.htm.

Patel, R., and P. McMichael. 2009. "A Political Economy of the Food Riot."
   Review 32 (1): 9–35. https://doi.org/10.1007/978-1-137-30553-4_13.
Polanyi, K. 1957. *The Great Transformation*. Boston: Beacon.
Rawls, J. 1971. *A Theory of Justice*. Cambridge, MA: Belknap Press of Harvard
   University Press.
Smedshaug, C. 2010. *Feeding the World in the 21st Century: A Historical Analysis
   of Agriculture and Society*. London: Anthem.
Vinge, H. 2015. "Food Security, Food Sovereignty, and the Nation-State:
   Historicizing Norwegian Farmland Policy." In *Food Sovereignty in
   International Context: Discourse, Politics and Practice in Place*, edited by Amy
   Trauger, 87–105. New York: Routledge.
Weis, T. 2007. *The Global Food Economy: The Battle for the Future of Farming*.
   London: Zed.

2 The Twenty-First-Century Land Question and Its Politics

PHILIP MCMICHAEL

Introduction

The contemporary land question, colloquially known as the "land grab," includes several different answers. These concern the form and scale of land confiscation or enclosure, as well as how it is accomplished. The latter refers to the impact on small-scale producers who constitute the majority of land users and food producers across the world – many of whom are threatened by displacement and/or resettlement.

Modern "development" has the displacement of peasantries embedded in its DNA, given the tendency to replace labour with scale technologies. So the act of "disappearing" peasants has been a key register of capitalist modernity, as expressed from Marx and Lenin through Rostow (1960) and Barrington Moore (1967) to contemporary World Bank publications. From the 1960s through the 1990s, Green Revolution and structural adjustment programs (SAPs) implicitly fostered de-peasantization in the name of modern-industrial and export agriculture, respectively. Only well-endowed family farmers could afford GR technology, and SAP-driven private investment in export agriculture replaced domestic public supports for small producers (Patel 2013; Ajl 2014). And yet today there is a new focus on providing technical and market support to "smallholders" across the world. As Deborah Bryceson remarks, "In a better-late-than-never attempt to resuscitate the African agricultural advances that SAP's short-circuited in the 1980s, donors are now scrambling to think of ways of boosting smallholder agriculture" (2010, 82). This chapter will review this shift in focus, suggesting that the apparent paradox conceals a new neoliberal solution to the land question.

What Is the Land Question?

The exercise of "land grabbing" is time-bound. It is commonly associated with the extension of the European enclosure movement to colonial territories, including settler colonial regions in the Americas, Australasia, and southern Africa. But its colloquial use today concerns a new spike in land confiscation associated with financialization and the general socio-ecological crisis of the neoliberal "globalization project" (McMichael 2016). One manifestation was the 2007–8 food crisis, which accelerated land grabbing in service of purported global "food security" (McMichael 2012).

Since the food crisis, some land deals have "backfired or failed for different reasons," such as water scarcity, lack of investor farming expertise, civil resistance, volatile financial and currency markets, and unstable governments and legal ambiguities regarding land tenure (GRAIN 2016). Nevertheless, GRAIN reports many new deals are underway "to expand the frontiers of industrial agriculture," and beyond gaining access to food supplies, oil palm expansion beyond Southeast Asia into Africa complements "a broader corporate strategy to profit from carbon markets, mineral resources, water resources, seeds, soil and environmental services" (2016). Oxfam claims more than 1,500 large-scale land deals have been signed since 2000, and that "we're entering a new and even more dangerous stage of the global land rush. The frenzied trade in millions of hectares of forests, coastlines and farmlands has led to murder, eviction and ethnocide. Land contracts are being signed and projects are breaking ground without the full consent of the communities living there" (2016, 5). Furthermore, such deals threaten to uproot rural and indigenous inhabitants, who, if adequately supported, are capable of protecting landscapes and waterways. According to Oxfam, "Half of the world's landmass is home to indigenous peoples and local communities that are its traditional owners. But they have no formally recognized ownership to 80% of this land ... often considered fair game for plunder, typically under the guise of 'economic development.' There is a long list of benefits to securing people's rights to these lands. It would protect more than 5,000 human cultures, and 4,000 different languages, as well as 80 percent of the planet's biodiversity" (2016, 5).

Under neoliberalism, with states beholden to investors and legitimacy tropes such as "green fuels" and "feeding the world," land has become a new "financial asset" (Fairbairn 2014). A report by the Greens/European Free Alliance in the European Parliament notes,

"The rush for land in Europe has a different character than for instance in Africa. Ordinarily, the concentration of land in the EU takes place legally.... [But] land has increasingly become an investment and an object of speculation and is no longer primarily the basis of small-scale farming. At the same time, agriculture is becoming more intensive and farms are getting bigger. This is a threat to biodiversity, the groundwater, our rural social structures, and the quality of food. Soil, grassland, and arable land are not a commodity but the livelihood of farmers" (Heubuch 2015, 3).

According to the Transnational Institute, "Tens of thousands of small farmers are being thrown out of farming every year" (2013). And Julian Cribb suggests that with current trends, by 2050 another 1.3 billion small farmers will be evicted from the land (2010).

Interpretations of the reasons for the land grab spike are many, condensing into a general confluence of conversion of land into a financial asset at a time when financialization faces reduced returns on industrial investment, and public mandates for "green fuel" investment have encouraged biofuel expansion, which – in addition to commandeering land for sugar, oil palm, and jatropha production – forced a substantial food price rise in 2007–8. The spike in hunger on a global scale generated two developments: (1) it legitimized a renewed focus on expanding food supplies: "To meet projected demand, cereal production will have to increase by nearly 50 per cent and meat production 85 per cent from 2000 to 2030" (World Bank 2007, 8); and (2) it also legitimized civil society's voice, via the International Planning Committee for Food Sovereignty (IPC), in the UN's Committee on World Food Security (CFS), which opened a space for a civil society mechanism (CSM) to represent the interests of small-scale producers, agricultural workers, and indigenous peoples across the world.

The alarm about future food supplies provided the impetus and justification for closing the "yield gap" by intensifying industrial agriculture. For example, the World Bank argued, "None of the African countries of most interest to investors is now achieving more than 30 percent of the potential yield on currently cultivated areas" (2011, xiv). In 2008, at the height of the food crisis, FAO Secretary-General Jacques Diouf claimed that "high food prices represent an excellent opportunity for increased investments in agriculture by both the public and private sectors to stimulate production and productivity," adding that "governments, supported by their international partners, must now undertake the necessary public investment and provide a favourable environment for private investments" (quoted in Urquhart 2008, 2).

In a co-authored article with France's International Development Agency, Diouf underlined the need to "bring African agriculture into line with changing conditions worldwide," to prevent "its agricultural trade deficit to deteriorate any further" in the event that food surplus nations reduce exports (Diouf and Severino 2008). These remarks not only advocated full-scale agro-industrialization in Africa and elsewhere, they also presaged the rise of "agro-security mercantilism" in the late 2000s, as East and South Asian states joined Middle Eastern states in direct investment of sovereign wealth funds and by state companies in land acquisition for offshore food and fuel production (McMichael 2013a), complementing the rush of private investment into land acquisition by both foreign and domestic investors. And local governments brokered land grabbing, justifying it as enclosure of "unused" or "unproductive" or "idle" land, evicting local populations who may (especially in Africa and Asia) have an ancestral relation, but no legal title, to the land, now belonging to the state. And state brokering is typically in the name of increased productivity, debt-reduction, export enhancement and rural development, even as officials gain access to largesse. Thus, in Colombia in the first half decade of the twenty-first century, 263,000 peasant families were evicted from 2.6 million hectares by agribusiness and/or paramilitaries interested primarily in oil palm development (Houtart 2010, 107).

Even so, at a time when the enclosure movement, which intensified in the 2000s, has already displaced hundreds of thousands of small producers, there is a counter-trajectory centred on stabilizing "smallholders." This began perhaps with the food price crisis and spike in hunger to one billion. Official discourse surrounding the food crisis saw it as an opportunity to reverse a long period of declining investment in agriculture and to secure world food supplies (FAO 2008). At the same time officials and analysts proposed that smallholders should take advantage of rising food prices by bringing them into, or deepening their connection to, national and global markets. The World Bank's *World Development Report 2008* declared, "It is time to place agriculture afresh at the center of the development agenda" (2007, 1). According to the Bank, the new agriculture would be "led by private entrepreneurs in extensive value chains linking producers to consumers," with the expectation that the private sector would drive "the organization of value chains that bring the market to smallholders and commercial farms" (2007 7). The vision was to improve productivity, farmer incomes, and rural development centred on smallholder farming, with Africa as the principal target of the value-chain-driven "new agriculture," a continent where small-scale producers occupy 80 per cent of land holdings.

At the time, this was a curious policy shift, given the conventional focus on large-scale industrial agriculture. The 2007–8 food price crisis followed two decades of structural adjustment policies that impoverished domestic farm sectors across the world. The Bank itself acknowledged the consequences of the policies:

> Structural adjustment in the 1980s dismantled the elaborate system of public agencies that provided farmers with access to land, credit, insurance inputs, and cooperative organization. The expectation was that removing the state would free the market for private actors to take over these functions. … Too often, that didn't happen. In some places, the state's withdrawal was tentative at best, limiting private entry. Elsewhere, the private sector emerged only slowly and partially – mainly serving commercial farmers but leaving smallholders exposed to extensive market failures, high transaction costs and risks, and service gaps. Incomplete markets and institutional gaps impose huge costs in forgone growth and welfare losses for smallholders, threatening their competitiveness and, in many cases, their survival. (World Bank 2007, 138)

Under the circumstances of a global legitimacy crisis (unfolding since the 1980s in agrarian regions), the development authorities (public and private) saw fit to gesture towards small producers, but via a productivist, industrial method of "value-chaining" them. The public sector was to serve the private sector with infrastructures of encouragement to small producers to convert to contract farming. The World Bank's *World Development Report 2008* expressed this new approach, coinciding with the 2007–8 food crisis. It focused attention on increasing African crop yields via new seed technologies, fertilizers, and other value-chain inputs, supported by private investment. Value-chain agriculture includes production for export and for domestic retailers, in the context of the global "supermarket revolution" (Reardon and Timmer 2005, 35–7).

The Bank argued that, because of competition, "globalization favors larger-scale operations in the quest for increasingly higher trade volumes to counter ever tighter margins" – so that food corporations desire "increasing business concentration on the supply side in value chains." Therefore, "the challenge facing small farmers is how to gain greater access to markets, enhance their value chain position and increase their value-added." And because small farmers are at the "bottom of the value chain," they require specific support to avoid marginalization. The Bank's report goes on to call for public sector support for infrastructure improvements, private market information systems, marketing channels, market contracts, standards compliance entrepreneurial capacity, and so forth (2008, 1). And so the vice-president of the Alliance for a Green Revolution in Africa (AGRA), noted, "Concentrating ODA funds on public goods will free up domestic resources to focus on providing support to smallholder farmers to take advantage of new agricultural technologies to raise agricultural productivity" (Adesina 2009, 10).

Arguably, prosecution of value chains to incorporate small producers is land grabbing by default (by a "control grab"). The necessary debt relations render farmers vulnerable to losing their land over time, and this is also what happens when contract farmers are unable to meet strict retailer standards. In the meantime, conversion of their farms to mono-cropping via technological inputs deskills farmers and removes value to agri-input suppliers and processors (Ploeg 2009; McMichael 2013b). As Jacob Muirhead notes in his chapter of this volume, as private standards become the norm, they tend to legitimize the power of corporate agriculture to shape land use and management, including sanctioning land enclosures. The uneasy juxtaposition of large-scale land grabs and incorporation of smallholders into value chains – in response to anxieties over food supplies, and recognition of small-holder neglect – indicates a modulated response by private and public interests, respectively. While these appear to be two different responses or tracks towards increasing food supplies on international markets, it is even more curious that these tracks do cross. This is the case in two senses. First, the legitimacy issue informs the private sector: "For many agribusiness companies the contract farming solution is a public relations exercise designed to build alliances in the areas where they produce and source their throughput, and to access subsidized credit from agencies buying into the 'smallholder path' to development. In fact, access to subsidized credit seems a significant factor driving agribusiness to engage smallholders" (Oya 2012, 10). And second, it has become clear that land controversies (resource grabbing and resettlement) have propelled some in the investor community towards the value-chain fix. Thus, the most recent assessment of "responsible investment practices in agriculture" by the World Bank acknowledges that "contract farming operations allow farmers to remain in control of their most important asset, their land, thus avoiding disputes over access to resources and community displacement. Outgrower schemes also support far more jobs than estate farms" (2014, 26).

Under these conditions, "smallholders" are understood to be potential entrepreneurs, given appropriate incentives. The "smallholder" desig-nation implicitly situates small-scale producers on a scale spectrum, obscuring any substantive difference in agricultural practice. Thus, the declaration following the FAO's November 2009 World Summit on Food Security stated, "We will pursue policies and strategies that improve the functioning of domestic, regional and international markets and ensure equitable access for all, especially smallholders and women farmers from developing countries. We support WTO-consistent, non-trade distorting special measures aimed at creating incentives for small-holder farmers in developing countries, enabling them to increase their productivity and compete on a more equal footing on world markets" (FAO 2009, 4).

Given the experience of Southern smallholder farmers with highly subsidized cheap imports of foodstuffs from the Global North, driving many out of business (Rosset 2006), "equal footing on world markets" means marketing high-value foodstuffs within established food empires (Ploeg 2009). Under these circumstances, the autonomous small-scale food system producer disappears.

Land Question Politics

The rendering of the small-scale producer as invisible, whether through reclassification of land as "unused," or through absorption into contract relations of value-chain agriculture, lies at the centre of land question politics. As above, the peasant/farmer is considered increasingly obsolete, in the dominant development narrative. One way of confirming this is to redefine the peasant-farmer as a "smallholder," simply lacking the incentives and technologies of productivist agriculture. Here, "Science has made peasant farming invisible. It has created an ideal model of what the agricultural entrepreneur should be and obscured the way in which peasants do operate today in the countryside" (Hilmi 2012, 60). Obscurity depends also on epistemic erasure: "Peasant-like ways of farming often exist as *practices without theoretical representation.* This is especially the case in developed countries. Hence, they cannot be properly understood, which normally fuels the conclusion that they do not exist or that they are, at best, some irrelevant anomaly. And even when their existence is recognized (as in developed countries), such peasant realities are perceived as a hindrance to change (Ploeg 2009, 19; emphasis added). And such redefinition and erasure have provided the principal source of contention in negotiations in the UN's Committee on World Food Security (CFS) in response to the "land grab."

Negotiations in the CFS over the years 2012–14 focused on investment in what the Bank had termed in its 2008 *World Development Report* "new agriculture for development." These negotiations were precipitated by the Bank's initiative in elaborating what it called governing Principles for Responsible Agricultural Investment (PRAI), in the context of food price inflation and intensifying land grabbing in 2010. Sylvia Kay noted, "Yet in failing to challenge the false premise that large-scale, corporate investment is necessary for rural development and instead facilitating this type of investment with minimal regulatory controls – a process that the former UN Special Rapporteur on the Right to Food, Olivier De Schutter, has called 'responsibly destroying the world's peasantry' – the PRAI in fact paved the way for further corporate and state predation over peasant lands" (2015, 3). The fact that the Bank, along with the International Fund for Agricultural Development (IFAD), FAO, and the United Nations Conference on Trade and Development (UNCTAD) crafted the PRAI with no consultation with civil society, and no transparency, raised questions of legitimacy that resulted in rejection of the PRAI in the CFS 36 plenary in October 2010. In this moment of legitimacy crisis, the International Planning Committee for Food Sovereignty led the charge to convince the CFS to reject the PRAI and support a CFS-based process for developing responsible agricultural investment principles (rai). This process would follow the crafting of Voluntary Guidelines on the Responsible Governance of Tenure of Land, Fisheries and Forests in the Context of National Food Security (VGGT) – which involved significant input from the CSM.

Whereas the Bank's PRAI sanctioned investment in the WTO trade regime's agro-export model, thanks in good part to pressure from civil society organizations the Tenure Guidelines offered a different approach – advocating recognition of customary property tenure and gender equity, as well as principled government practices in administering land, fisheries, and forests rights. Nevertheless, Sofia Monsalve-Suárez emphasizes that the guidelines promote transfer of tenure rights to serve large-scale investment (2013). In other words, the Tenure Guidelines are internally contradictory. For example, Section 12.2 of the Tenure Guidelines note, "Considering that smallholder producers and their organizations in developing countries provide a major share of agricultural investments that contribute significantly to food security, nutrition, poverty eradication and environmental resilience, States should support investments by smallholders as well as public and private smallholder-sensitive investments" (CFS 2012, 21). Whereas Section 13.1 states, "Where appropriate, States may consider land consolidation, exchanges or other voluntary approaches for the readjustment of parcels or holdings to assist owners and users to improve the layout and use of their parcels, or holdings, including for the promotion of food security and rural development in a sustainable manner" (23).

When the investment chapter was discussed during negotiations on the Tenure Guidelines, it became clear that the consultation on the rai principles would need to build on this and further clarify this specific issue. Nevertheless, being anchored in the Universal Declaration of Human Rights, and the United Nations Declaration on the Rights of Indigenous Peoples, the Tenure Guidelines enable advocacy in the name of human rights, with legal consequence at national and international levels (Monsalve-Suárez 2012). In other words, soft law, however ambiguous, has the moral (and possibly legal) force of human rights monitoring with which to contend.

The CFS Terms of Reference to develop "rai" principles emerged in the context of food crisis export bans and price volatility, competition for land between food and fuel crops, accelerated land grabbing, and growing awareness of ecosystem degradation (e.g., UN *Millennium Ecosystem Assessment* 2005). At this moment, development authorities acknowledged that after decades of neglect and erosion of small-producer supports, agricultural renewal was a question of legitimacy, framed as critical to rural development, food security, and environmental sustainability.

The CFS recognized the overwhelming role of small-scale producers in feeding the majority world and working the land. As the Tenure Guidelines noted, smallholders were the majority investors in agriculture. This capacity was spelled out by the CFS's High Level Panel of Experts' Report, *Investing in Smallholder Agriculture for Food Security*, which regards smallholder agriculture as "the foundation of food security in many countries and an important part of the social/economic/ecological landscape in all countries" (CFS 2013, 11). Further, the "potential efficiency of smallholder farming relative to larger farms has been widely documented, focusing on the capacity of smallholders to achieve high production levels per unit of land through the use of family labour in diversified production systems" (12). The HLPE report defines smallholder agriculture as "practised by families (including one or more households) using only or mostly family labour and deriving from that work a large but variable share of their income, in kind or in cash ... it includes crop raising, animal husbandry, forestry and artisanal fisheries.... Off-farm activities play an important role in providing smallholders with additional income and as a way of diversifying risk ... smallholders producing only or mainly for subsistence are not uncommon ... smallholders' families are part of social networks within which mutual assistance and reciprocity translate into collective investments (mainly through work exchanges) and into solidarity systems" (10–11).

In spite of such recognition from the CFS experts of the diversity, pluri-activity, and social networks defining small-scale farming, in addition to its key role in food provisioning and stewarding landscapes, debate in the CFS regarding principles of responsible agricultural investment has obfuscated these defining features. One example is a comment by Gregory Myers, participant in the rai debates as division chief for the Land Tenure and Property Rights Division at the USAID. On securing tenure rights, he wrote, "Local people and communities are granted new economic opportunities: they can rent out land to prospective investors or enter into joint ventures with them. In addition, when people believe their land and resource rights are secure, they are more likely to invest in their property" (Myers 2014). The emphasis on *financial* investment is unmistakable here – either locals can cede the use of their land to extra-local commercial operations, or they can mortgage their farms with financial loans to "increase crop yields."

The invisibilization of farmer investment here represents an epistemic subordination of labour to capital in the sense that financial investment in production agriculture favours labour-saving technologies, which necessarily displace farmer knowledge and practice. Small-scale producers, by contrast, invest in sustaining the natural resource base (soil fertility, water cycles, seed exchange, and knowledge-sharing networks), building agro-ecological wealth, valuing land regeneration and reproduction of local and national communities. Ideally this kind of investment is "de-commodified." Ploeg puts it this way: "A non-commoditized exchange with nature allows the building of an important line of defence: the more that farming is grounded on ecological capital the lower the monetary costs of production will be. Ecological capital, if cared for, also allows for patterns of growth that are independent of the main markets for factors of production and non-factor inputs: herds are enlarged and improved through on-farm breeding and selection; fields are well cultivated and made more fertile; new experiences are translated into expanded knowledge" (2010, 4–5).

This description stems from Ploeg's research into a phenomenon of "re-peasantization" that he observes widely across Europe and elsewhere, such as Peru, that involves the enhancement of self-provisioning as ecological-value-adding, as distinct from a conventional value-adding through commercial operations. The latter, when applied to value-chain agriculture, removes value from the farm and relocates it in upstream (agro-input) and downstream industries (processing, retailing). Ploeg's point is that "the more the farm is distanciated from the large upstream markets (and the imperial control rooted in them) the larger the room for maneuvre to construct the new alternatives on the downstream side" (Ploeg 2010, 20).

The essential difference between commercial and "peasant" farming is the centrality of labour – in both material and epistemic terms. For the latter, farmer practices (investments) are guided by knowledge of the landscape and its biophysical properties, seed and livestock varieties, and local weather patterns. Financial investment in agriculture, by contrast, is driven by profitability concerns of non-local agribusiness or financiers, or simply speculative interest.

To summarize, small-scale producers and large investors do not share a single vision and mode of operation. Large-scale investors favour commercial input-output "agriculture without farmers," as La Vía Campesina notes, overriding the natural resource base with alien seeds and agro-chemicals. Industrial agriculture is not sustainable, nor does it have an evident social purpose – it is driven by distant market signals and private wealth and not the cultural needs of local citizens.

The Rai Negotiations

Negotiations in the CFS over the establishment of "principles of responsible agricultural investment" took place from October 2011 through October 2014, with member states supporting "an inclusive consultation process within CFS for the development and the broader ownership of principles for responsible agricultural investment that enhance food security and nutrition" and "ensure consistency and complementarity with the Tenure Guidelines" (quoted in Kay 2015, 3). Civil society organizations, in particular, participated on the grounds that "the CFS is the legitimate platform to consolidate a single set of standards on investment developed through the food security lens and anchored in a human rights framework" (3).

As it happened, the standard of investment "responsibility" that resulted from the negotiations eluded the fundamental rights claims made by the CSM. The difference is evident between the CSM Vision in appendix 1, and the adopted CSF Principles in appendix 2. The CSM Technical Support Group (TSG)[1] argued consistently that "responsible investment" should not be simply a rhetorical phrase or a long-term goal – rather it should define constant practice in respecting and advancing the rights of food producers, workers, and consumers as well as women and indigenous communities. Thus the TSG argued for a benchmark or performance standard to apply to the impact of investment on all these constituencies: "Investment *is only responsible insofar as it* ... contributes to the progressive realization of the right to adequate and nutritious food for all." Draft and final versions of the rai principles eschewed this approach, allowing only passive reference to "responsible investment." Thus, in a "do no harm" clause that civil society fought to include, paragraph 20 states, "Responsible investment should respect and not infringe on the human rights of others and address adverse human rights impacts. It should safeguard against dispossession of legitimate tenure rights and environmental damage."

The problem with this framing is that it expresses an ideal, rather than an implemented practice subject to monitoring. It is a hope at best, a gesture at worst, but certainly not a requirement. Ultimately the human rights foundation insisted on by the CSM is compromised by the insistence by the Private Sector Mechanism (PSM) and free trade governments such as the United States, Canada, and Australia for economic rights as laid down in trade agreements. Thus paragraph 34 proclaims, "States should not apply the Principles in a manner that may create or disguise barriers to trade, or promote protectionist interests, or in a way which imposes their own policies on other nations." In a post–Doha Round world, it is now widely acknowledged that trade rules instituted by the WTO, and extended in bilateral and regional trade agreements, have enabled powerful agro-export states to establish unfair trade practices by artificially lowering the price of food exports at the expense of small producers across the world, thereby undermining their rights to produce and to food security (Rosset 2006). Trade rights trump human rights.

The question then is what this trade override of human rights has to do with "responsible investment." In the first place, the land-grab context involved evidence of irresponsible investment, often by financiers with no agricultural experience, and certainly usually at the expense of inhabitants on the land or downstream (Houtart 2010). As above, this represented a legitimacy crisis in the midst of a food-price inflationary crisis, drawing the development agencies, led by the World Bank, into initiatives to manage the fallout, without denying the rights of financiers and corporations. "Responsible investment," in "sustainable intensification" and "smart agriculture," are preferred/recommended approaches – notably concerned with reducing environmental "externalities" (deforestation, carbon emissions, biodiversity decline) associated with industrial agriculture, rather than protecting *extant* farming systems (ecosystems, seed exchanges, and farmer knowledges) as investment complexes themselves (McMichael 2014, 46).

The drive for "responsible investment" not only grants financial investment a continuing role in agriculture, it also implicitly forecloses recognition of small-scale farming as an investment complex itself, even as farmers themselves do not generally define their activity as "investment." As one commentator puts it, "The investment made by generations of a community who have enriched a particular strain of traditional knowledge pertaining to the cultivation of a food staple is both implicit in the way their lives are led and implicit in their status as members of a community. In such a case (and there are fortunately still numerous such cases to be found), the term 'investment' becomes a vulgar one and is neither used nor translated'" (Goswami 2014).

There are two issues here. In the first place, insofar as land users/ food producers do not conceive of their practical activity as "investment," as they reproduce their farming systems, in the context of the CFS negotiations they have had to adopt and attempt to appropriate "investment" language as a political tactic of representation to protect and distinguish their life-world from a world seen through the eyes of financiers. This is analogous to (but not the same as) Martinez-Alier's notion of the "environmentalism of the poor," by which peasants, forest-dwellers, and pastoralists have learned to represent themselves as "environmentalists" to gain the "modern" world's attention to their vulnerability (2002). The difference here is that conventional understandings of "investment" are *incommensurate* with peasant "investment," which involves an alternative ontology in land and landscape management (see McMichael and Müller 2014; Hart et al. 2015): it is working with, rather than overriding, the biophysical properties of the land (see Weis 2007). That is, small-scale producers invest in sustaining the natural resource base (soil fertility, water cycles, seed exchange, and knowledge-sharing networks), building an agro-ecological wealth that is different from financial wealth, valuing land regeneration and reproduction of local and national communities.

A CFS report emphasized the point that "smallholders are the main investors":

> Alongside labour investments that result in improved soils, buildings, animal breeds, crop varieties, etc., smallholders also invest in and through: (i) the accumulation of experience and knowledge; (ii) collective action; (iii) crafting appropriate governance rules and corresponding enforcements to maintain individual and joint investments over time, as has been empirically and theoretically demonstrated.[2]
>
> In smallholder agriculture, capital formation does not necessarily occur as investment of financial or physical capital, as is the case in corporate agriculture. It is more the exception than the rule. In smallholder units, capital formation basically occurs through labour investments (in which human and ecological capital, instead of financial and physical capital, are central). (2013, 34)

From the CSM point of view, then, investment is responsible only if it centres on supporting small-scale producer models of farming and their contribution to local and national food security. Accomplishing this requires a strong state presence to organize public investment in domestic farming capacity as the alternative to imported food dependency and/or expanding high-value export agriculture. Civil society organizations consistently argued for the public interest, and responsible state practices constitute 40 per cent of CSM's vision for responsible agricultural investment. By contrast, the new forms of "land acquisition" are profit-oriented via speculation in land as a financial asset or growing food/feed/fuel crops for global markets, using chemically managed mono-cultivation. As the Pesticide Action Network notes, "By failing to put emphasis on small food producers, the rai Principles do not provide an outright protection against land and resource grabs that are perpetrated by large corporate investors and often supported by national and local governments" (PANAP 2014).

The focus on state responsibility drives civil society monitoring of implementation of the Tenure Guidelines as well as now monitoring human rights issues in relation to the principles. Grassroots mobilizations include:

- Contestation of the Indian Land Acquisition and Rehabilitation and Resettlement Bill under review in 2013 – successfully reversing the government's decision to sell common grazing lands of forty-four villages;
- A Malian "Convergence against Land Grabbing" involving peasant and other civil society organizations formed to provide legal assistance to communities threatened with land grabs and pressure the government on land laws;
- Local Ugandan fishing communities around Lake Victoria addressing water and land grabs [as Ruth Hall notes, "Securing rights to the land, access to the lake and rights to fish are demands that are interwoven in a society where identities as 'farmers' and 'fishers' are fairly fluid and where the economy is based on the linkages between these activities" (2015)];
- Argentinian and Italian peasant organizations deploy the Guidelines in their struggles for restitution and rights;
- TNI launched a report on the extent of land grabbing in Europe in 2013 to the European Parliament, with a directive regarding how to apply the Guidelines in European contexts. (McKeon 2015, 163)

Arguably, monitoring realizes the original demand for "food sovereignty" made by peasant organizations in Rome in 1996. Use of this term was a form of strategic essentialism, insofar as the peasant coalition politicized neoliberal claims for "food security" via "free trade." The coalition argued that the trade regime was deepening food dependency at the expense of small-scale producers across the world who were unable to compete with "cheap food" dumped in their markets by large grain traders. In this sense, "food sovereignty" appealed to a conventional understanding of national autonomy in food policy, but it also advocated state protection of small farmers and fishers' right to produce food and manage their own food and ecosystem systems (McMichael 2006). In so doing, the food sovereignty movement established claims on the state, now materializing in attempts to enforce the Tenure Guidelines and monitor investment in agriculture. It is noteworthy here that during the reform process of the CFS (2009–10), a sympathetic UN official proposed civil society should be granted a vote, alongside member governments. This invitation to enjoy decision-making status was "firmly rebutted by the civil society participants, who cautioned against any dilution of the principle of ultimate government responsibility for food and agricultural decision-making and hunger elimination" (Brem-Wilson 2015, 83). State sovereignty was the legacy of the food sovereignty movement in demanding a moral global economy on the one hand, and an ethic of civic responsibility on the other, to be monitored by the autonomous civil society organizations within states and their CSM voice in the inter-national CFS.

Assessment

The rai negotiations, while focusing contention upon elaborating principles of responsible agricultural investment, expressed a broader, epistemic issue: the power of discourse in framing and instituting forms of "authoritative knowledge." As mentioned above, the deployment of the term *responsible investment* was always double-edged – in inviting civil society to negotiate about regulating a process that was ostensibly out of control, on the one hand, and on the other limiting the terms of reference to large-scale financial investment.

Economically driven financial "investment" was the discourse of choice in the proceedings, with most governments and the PSM disregarding the alternative ecological investment of small-scale producers. The argument that smallholders were the "main investors" in their own agriculture was reductionist and/or opportunistic insofar as conventional understandings of "investment" are incommensurate with small-scale farming practices. Another argument, from a PSM representative during CFS 40, was that "while there is a consensus that farmers are at the center, farming needs to be understood as a profession, and food security is about economic growth, not just grow-ing food – thus farmers need to break the subsistence cycle and become entrepreneurs, produce more with less land, and stabilize via land ownership, inputs (agro-chemicals), knowledge, and market access" (CFS 2013). In March 2015, at a "rai Kickstart Meeting," the Private Sec-tor Mechanism statement read,

> It is important that as we move to operationalize the guidelines, we should emphasize their role as a means to enhance and attract investment, both foreign and domestic. The private sector is already the biggest engine of poverty reduction and economic growth in the developing world.... To help leverage this potential, governments must prioritize creating stable, predictable and transparent regulatory frameworks and legal systems to attract sustainable investments in agriculture.... To ensure investment in agriculture to support food security and development, all stakeholders need to work together collaboratively. Investments should help foster choices among consumers and producers.

In addition to the discursive preference for the private sector's role in economic growth, and the importance of marketplace "choice" – substituting corporate priority over small-scale producer rights – there is also the reduction of all actors to "stakeholders."

A recurring theme in rai discussions was that rai is for all investors, big and small, as stakeholders sharing an interest in the capitalization of agricultural resources. The PSM and its government allies routinely conflate "smallholders" with "large-holders" as if they practise the same kind of agriculture. The CSM continually insisted on using the term *small-scale producers and workers* to distinguish these constituencies from agro-industrial interests. The CFS dialogue is constructed upon an artificial balancing of very different interests, represented as "stake-holders" with equal voice. But this is clearly artificial, for two main rea-sons: (1) large investors claim more resources and lobbying power, they enter partnerships with governments that are short of funds, and their land grabbing is at the expense of many small-scale producers; (2) the relation between large and small "investors" is not balanced, as their "investments" are neither commensurate nor compatible. Their invest-ment principles apply neither *equally* nor *similarly* across this divide.

In 2015 it was reported that

> the civil society and social movements sought to take distance from this multi-stakeholder language and approach in which the difference between public and private interests are blurred. The fact that the two constituencies

sit at the same table doesn't mean that they have convergent interests and needs. Rather, the committee needs to distinguish between right holders, duty bearers and third parties....

This is not just an ideological position or a philosophical speculation that civil society organizations want to champion. It is rather a substantive question: civil society is basically asking for a governance model where right-holders are at the front, in order to counterbalance the growing weight that the private sector has acquired in the recent years on public policy making, particularly within the UN institutions. (Zarro 2015)

The ultimate question here is that while civil society has gained a voice in the UN's CFS on tenure guidelines and investment principles, has it participated in an entrapment that bestows legitimacy on a private-sector governed set of voluntary/soft-law negotiations, or carved out a space from which to attempt to hold governments accountable to public interest over the longer term?

Clearly the private sector is positioning itself and its market ideology as the solution to challenges such as ecosystem degradation, hunger, poverty, and climate change. With the G7 instituting initiatives such as the New Alliance for Food Security and Nutrition (NAFSN),[3] public authorities are partnering with private interests in alienating common property resources, subsidizing agribusiness in the name of food security and rural development, and deepening commodity relations (including ecosystem services) as market power conditions policymaking and management of the future.

Evidently landed property is not only increasingly privately commandeered, but also its capture for offshore production, speculation or carbon sinks (as offsets) forecloses possibilities for managing landscapes for the common good rather than for private gain. This is a double foreclosure: on democratic access and control, and on land-use practices that work with, rather than against, nature. In this sense, the property regime under construction, through commodification, is not just a bid for profit, but for long-term control, in the (problematic) name of "shared humanity."

At the larger scale, this questionable claim to be "securing" the future for a "shared humanity" resonates with the language adopted in the CFS – a language that reduces quite distinctive interests and rights to a singular language of private interest in economic gain, thereby eliding quite different understandings and capacities for building social and ecological stability and resilience. It is this discursive "levelling" that enables and legitimizes enclosure of people of the land and of democratic engagement in how best to manage the future.

Acknowledgment

This work was supported at different stages by the Research Council of Norway, and the Ministry of Education of the Republic of Korea and the National Research Foundation of Korea (NRF-2016S1A3A2924243).

Appendix 1: CSM's Vision/Principles for "Responsible" Agricultural Investment

1 Investments must contribute to and be consistent with the progressive realization of the right to adequate and nutritious food for all.
2 Investments in food and agriculture must ensure protection of ecosystems and environments.
3 All investments in food and agriculture must ensure decent jobs, respect workers' rights, and adhere to core labour standards and obligations as defined by the ILO.
4 All investments in agriculture and food systems must ensure decent incomes, livelihoods, and equitable development opportunities for local communities, especially for rural youth, women, and indigenous peoples.
5 Investments must respect and uphold the rights of small-scale food producers, indigenous peoples, and local communities to access, use, and have control over land, water, and other natural resources.
6 All investments must respect the rights of indigenous peoples to their territories and ancestral domains, cultural heritage and landscapes, and traditional knowledge and practices.
7 All investments must respect women's rights and prioritize women in benefit sharing.
8 States must mobilize public investments and public policies in support of small-scale food producers and workers. Small-scale food producers, workers, and their organizations must be meaningfully involved in the formulation, implementation, monitoring, and review of these investments and policies.
9 States must protect small-scale producers and workers from market fluctuations and price volatility by regulating local, national, regional, and international food markets, and curbing food price speculation.
10 States must respect and support timely and non-discriminatory access by small-scale producers, workers, indigenous communities, local communities, and the public to justice, grievance mechanisms, fair, effective, and timely mediation, administrative and judicial remedies, and a right to appeal.

11 Trade and investment agreements and treaties must not undermine or compromise the rights of small-scale food producers, workers, and indigenous peoples, and food sovereignty. States must monitor and assess the impacts of such agreements on the realization of the right to food, and take appropriate action where necessary, including through renegotiation or cancellation of the agreements/treaties.

12 States should enact appropriate national laws to regulate and monitor extraterritorial investments and investors. In so doing, they should apply the Maastricht Principles on Extraterritorial Obligations of States in the Areas of Economic, Social, and Cultural Rights as the guiding document.

13 The effective, meaningful, and democratic participation of small-scale producers, workers, and indigenous peoples, particularly women, must be guaranteed in the planning and decision-making around agricultural investments, area development, and land and resource use and management.

Appendix 2: The Ten Official Rai Principles

Principle 1:   Contribute to food security and nutrition
Principle 2:   Contribute to sustainable and inclusive economic development and the eradication of poverty
Principle 3:   Foster gender equality and women's empowerment
Principle 4:   Engage and empower youth
Principle 5:   Respect tenure of land, fisheries, forests and access to water
Principle 6:   Conserve and sustainably manage natural resources, increase resilience, and reduce disaster risks
Principle 7:   Respect cultural heritage and traditional knowledge, and support diversity and innovation
Principle 8:   Promote safe and healthy agriculture and food systems
Principle 9:   Incorporate inclusive and transparent governance structures, processes, and grievance mechanisms
Principle 10: Assess and address impacts and promote accountability

NOTES

1 In which this author participated.
2 By Elinor Ostrom (1990).
3 In question in the European Parliament (Barbière 2016), followed by withdrawal by the French government.

REFERENCES

Adesina, A.A. 2009. "Africa's Food Crisis: Conditioning Trends and Global Development Policy." Keynote speech at the International Association of Agricultural Economists Conference, Beijing, August.

Ajl, M. 2014. "The Hypertrophic City versus the Planet of Fields." In *Implosions/Explosion*, edited by Neil Brenner, 533–50. Berlin: Jovis.

Barbière, C. 2016. "European Parliament Slams G7 Food Project in Africa." *Guardian*, 8 June.

Brem-Wilson, J. 2015. "Towards Food Sovereignty: Interrogating Peasant Voice in the United Nations Committee on World Food Security." *Journal of Peasant Studies* 42 (1): 73–95. https://doi.org/10.1080/03066150.2014.968143.

Bryceson, D. 2010. "Sub-Saharan Africa's Vanishing Peasantries and the Specter of a Global Food Crisis." In *Agriculture and Food in Crisis: Conflict, Resistance and Renewal*, edited by F. Magdoff and B. Tokar, 69–84. New York: Monthly Review.

Committee on World Food Security (CFS). 2012. *Voluntary Guidelines on the Responsible Governance of Tenure of Land, Fisheries and Forests in the Context of National Food Security (VGGT)*. Rome: FAO.

– 2013. *Investing in Smallholder Agriculture for Food Security*. HLPE Report, June. Rome: FAO.

Cribb, J. 2010. *The Coming Famine: The Global Food Crisis and What We Can Do to Avoid It*. Berkeley: University of California Press.

Diouf, J., and J-M. Severino. 2008. "Africa Must Grow to Rely on Its Own Farms." *Guardian Weekly*, 2 May.

Fairbairn, M. 2014. *Farmland Meets Finance: Is Land the New Economic Bubble?* In Land and Sovereignty in the Americas, no. 5. Oakland, CA: Food First.

Food and Agriculture Organization of the United Nations (FAO). 2008. "Initiative on FAO's Soaring Food Prices." Information note, 20 May. http://www.fao.org/fileadmin/templates/worldfood/Reports_and_docs/Food_Prices_web1.pdf.

– 2009. "Declaration of the World Food Summit on Food Security." Rome, 16–18 November. www.fao.org/fileadmin/templates/wsfs/Summit/Docs/Final_Declaration/WSFS09_Declaration.pdf.

Goswami, R. 2014. "Why Agricultural Investment 'Principles' Must Be Buried." *Pambazuka*, 6 February.

GRAIN. 2016. "The Global Farmland Land Grab in 2016: How Big, How Bad?" https://www.grain.org/article/entries/5492-the-global-farmland-grab-in-2016-how-big-how-bad.

Hall, R. 2015. "Can the FAO Tenure Guidelines Stop Land and Water Grabs?" PLAAS, 23 January. http://farmlandgrab.org/post/print/24459.

Hart, A.K., P. McMichael, J.C. Milder, and S.J Scherr. 2015. "Multi-functional Landscapes from the Grassroots? The Role of Rural Producer Movements." *Agriculture and Human Values* 33 (2): 305–22. https://doi.org/10.1007/s10460-015-9611-1.

Heubuch, M. 2015. *Land Rush: The Sellout of Europe's Farmland.* Greens/European Free Alliance. https://www.greens-efa.eu/files/doc/docs/19abd146a6f61773450e58f438b3d287.pdf.

Hilmi, A. 2012. *Agricultural Transition: A Different Logic.* Yaoundé, Cameroon: More and Better Network.

Houtart, F. 2010. *Agrofuels: Big Profits, Ruined Lives and Ecological Destruction.* London: Pluto.

Kay, S. 2015. "Political Brief on the Principles on Responsible Investment in Agriculture and Food Systems." Transnational Institute Briefing, March.

Martinez-Alier, J. 2002. *The Environmentalism of the Poor: A Study of Ecological Conflict and Valuation.* Cheltenham, UK: Edward Elgar.

McKeon, N. 2015. *Food Security Governance: Empowering Communities, Regulating Corporations.* London: Routledge.

McMichael, P. 2006. "Reframing Development: Global Peasant Movements and the New Agrarian Question." *Canadian Journal of Development Studies* 27 (4): 471–83. https://doi.org/10.1080/02255189.2006.9669169.

– 2012. "The 'Land Grab' and Corporate Food Regime Restructuring." *Journal of Peasant Studies* 39 (3/4): 681–701.

– 2013a. "Land Grabbing as Security Mercantilism in International Relations." *Globalizations* 10 (1): 47–64.

– 2013b. "Value-Chain Agriculture and Debt Relations: Contradictory Outcomes." *Third World Quarterly* 34 (4): 671–90.

– 2014. "Rethinking Land Grab Ontology." *Rural Sociology* 79 (1): 34–55. https://doi.org/10.1111/ruso.12021.

– 2016. *Development and Social Change: A Global Perspective.* 6th ed. Thousand Oaks, CA: Sage Publications.

McMichael, P., and B. Müller, 2014. "The Land-Grab Trap: Is There a Will to Govern Global Land-Grabbing." focaal Blog. https://www.focaalblog.com/2014/09/19/philip-mcmichael-birgit-muller-the-land-grab-trap-is-there-a-will-to-govern-global-land-grabbing/.

Monsalve Suárez, S. 2013. "The Human Rights Framework in Contemporary Agrarian Struggles." *Journal of Peasant Studies* 40 (1): 239–90.

Moore, B. Jr. 1967. *Social Origins of Dictatorship and Democracy: Lord and Peasant in the Making of the Modern World.* Boston: Beacon.

Myers, G. 2014. "Food Security and the Need for Responsible Investment Guidelines." Development Channel, Council on Foreign Relations, 15 September. http://blogs.cfr.org/development-channel/2014/09/15/food-security-and-the-need-for-responsible-investment-guidelines/.

Ostrom, E. 1990. *Governing the Commons: The Evolution of Institutions for Collective Action*. New York: Cambridge University Press.

Oxfam. 2016. *Custodians of the Land, Defenders of Our Future: A New Era of the Global Land Rush*. https://www-cdn.oxfam.org/s3fs-public/file_attachments/land_rights_en_final.pdf.

Oya, C. 2012. "Contract Farming in Sub-Saharan Africa: A Survey of Approaches, Debates and Issues." *Journal of Agrarian Change* 12 (1): 1–33. https://doi.org/10.1111/j.1471-0366.2011.00337.x.

Patel, R. 2013. "The Long Green Revolution." *Journal of Peasant Studies* 40 (1): 1–63. DOI: 10.1080/03066150.2012.719224.

Pesticide Action Network Asia and the Pacific (PANAP). 2014. "Three Reasons Why the 'Rai Principles' Undermine the Right to Food, Land and Resources." 6 November. http://farmlandgrab.org/post/print/24227.

Ploeg, van der J.D. 2009. *The "New" Peasantries: Struggles for Autonomy and Sustainability in an Era of Empire and Globalization*. London: Earthscan.

– 2010. "The Peasantries of the Twenty-First Century: The Commoditization Debate Revisited." *Journal of Peasant Studies* 37 (1): 1–30.

Reardon, T., and C. Timmer. 2005. "Transformation of Markets for Agricultural Output in Developing Countries since 1950: How Has Thinking Changed?" In *Handbook of Agricultural Economics – Agricultural Development: Farmers, Farm Production and Farm Markets*, edited by R. Evenson, P. Pingali, and T. Schultz, 2807–55. Oxford: Elsevier.

Rosset, P. 2006. *Food Is Different: Why We Must Get the WTO out of Agriculture*. Halifax: Fernwood.

Rostow, W.W. 1960. *The Stages of Economic Growth: A Non-Communist Manifesto*. Cambridge: Cambridge University Press.

Transnational Institute. 2013. *Land Concentration, Land Grabbing and People's Struggles in Europe*. April. https://www.tni.org/files/download/land_in_europe-jun2013.pdf.

United Nations (UN). 2005. *Millennium Ecosystem Assessment*. New York: United Nations.

Urquhart, S. 2008. "Food Crisis, Which Crisis? Our Crisis or Theirs? The Battle over the World's Food Supply Relocates to Rome." Guerrilla News Network, 2 June. http://gnn.to/articles/3718/food_crisis_which_crisis.

Weis, T. 2007. *The Global Food Economy: The Battle for the Future of Farming*. London: Zed.

World Bank. 2007. *World Development Report 2008: Agriculture for Development*. Washington, DC: World Bank.

– 2008. "Value Chains and Small Farmer Integration." Agriculture for Development. http://documents.worldbank.org/curated/en/489001468270654669/pdf/693840BRI0P1100sed06060201200Agri05.pdf.

– 2011. *Rising Global Interest in Farmland: Can It Yield Sustainable and Equitable Benefits?* Washington, DC: World Bank.

– 2014. "Benchmarking the Business of Agriculture."

Zarro, A. 2015. "Civil Society Deeply Concerned about Multi-Stakeholder Language at the CFS42." SID Forum. Society for International Development. Available at: https://www.sidint.net/content/civil-society-deeply-concerned-about-multi-stakeholder-language-cfs42.

3 Last In, First Out? The Uncertain Future of Agricultural Trade Liberalization

HUGH CAMPBELL AND DAVID REYNOLDS

Introduction

This chapter explores one element of global free trade agreements (FTAs) that indicates the extent to which the underlying logics and pragmatic possibilities of FTAs have shifted significantly over the last three decades. The key element under examination is the place of agriculture in negotiations, as this sector of the global economy has both been one of the most hotly contested elements of FTA negotiations and also holds considerable significance for the future of the planet. The fate of FTAs in agriculture also links to the wider themes of this book, as the liberalization project in agricultural commodities was the first major foray into liberalization of elements of agri-food systems. It was the first political project yet is now increasingly challenged and thwarted just as its sister project – the financialization and marketization of farming land – is starting to pick up momentum.

The argument presented here is, in short, that the "last in" might be about to become the "first out" of global free trade negotiations. This chapter, using New Zealand as its primary case study, will review the way in which agriculture was kept out of FTAs prior to the 1980s and was the very last traditional economic sector to enter such negotiations. The chapter will then review the twists and turns of the subsequent thirty years of negotiations: the high point of the conclusion of the Uruguay Round of the General Agreement on Tariffs and Trade (GATT) in 1995, when agriculture looked set to move steadily towards free trade status; and the current moment with the conclusion of the (Comprehensive and Progressive) Trans-Pacific Partnership negotiations, when it appears increasingly unlikely that agriculture will remain a significant element of future changes to free trade status in the world economy. Rather, the current extent of reduction in sub-sidies in key trading blocs like the United States and European Union has likely reached long-term stasis. The chapter will conclude with a discussion of how the failure of the production and international trade in food products to be successfully liberalized opens up possibilities for how we might reimagine policy futures for food and farming. It also suggests that FTAs have become a cul-de-sac based upon a narrow focus on tariffs and border protections against *food* imports, which don't actually consider the wider realignments in the global transfer of ownership of *farms* themselves. This distinction between agriculture/food and land/farming becomes increasingly important as the liberalization of one stalls while the other gathers pace.

The Disconnected Position of Agriculture and Free Trade

While the narrative about agriculture and FTAs often assumes the tone that there has been a slow and inevitable trend towards liberalization, this misrepresents the exceptional status of agriculture in twentieth century trade negotiations. The reality was that agriculture formed one of the last remnants of older imperial orders of global trading. New Zealand's situation is instructive. European-style farming was established in New Zealand during the second half of the nineteenth century as an essential part of British imperial strategy to create a stable food supply for the burgeoning population of the Industrial Revolution (Le Heron 1993). The colony's role as "Britain's farm in the South Pacific" tied its external trading closely to the demands of the British home market (Campbell 2012). From the 1880s, when refrigerated shipping opened up the opportunity to trade in frozen meat and in dairy products, New Zealand became a key supplier to the food needs of the rapidly growing industrial population of Britain. This relationship was solidified through the Ottawa Agreement of 1932, which reinforced the specialization of the ex-colonies as suppliers of food to the British market. New Zealand's special role as a supplier of meat and dairy products to Britain created highly protected agricultural exporting (Moran, Blunden, and Bradly 1996). Farming wealth in New Zealand rose largely upon this protected relationship, along with the purchasing of wool by governments to produce military uniforms during periods like the Korean War. For both food and fibre, agricultural exports from New Zealand, and the prosperous farming economy that produced them, were highly embedded in government purchasing or highly protected market arrangements (Le Heron 1993). Under these arrangements – which Friedmann and McMichael (1989) term the "First Food

Regime" – the once-forested hillsides and river valleys of New Zealand were transformed into a pastoral facsimile of the English farmed landscape, populated by family farms complete with introduced stock and crops, English grasses, and even insects to act as pollinators in this new landscape (Pawson and Brooking 2002).

While New Zealand's highly protected relationship with the British market for agricultural exports was quite an extreme example of protectionism, it was not out of keeping with the time. From the late 1940s, when the GATT negotiations were commenced to create greater freedom in world trade, the main parties to the original negotiations all agreed that the compelling problems of global food security after the Second World War meant that agriculture and food should be exempted from all GATT negotiations (Muirhead and Almås 2012; Pritchard 2012). Key players like the United States thought it was essential that agricultural trade be retained under the protected control of governments and, in the post-war period, agriculture became one of the most highly protected and subsidized economic sectors in the world economy (Muirhead and Almås 2012). In a policy sense, this was considered to be logical in a world where food security was a highly compelling policy problem. Instead of participating in GATT negotiations in the 1950s–1970s, agriculture was subject to its own agreements that reinforced the protected and subsidized nature of agricultural production in regions like North America and Europe (Pritchard 2012). At the same time, surplus food production – a logical consequence of the highly subsidized character of an increasingly industrialized agricultural sector – was disposed of internationally through the mechanism of food aid, yet another highly subsidized form of international food trading (Friedmann and McMichael 1989).

The 1970s economic downturn began to shake some of the foundations of these arrangements (Lawrence and Campbell 2014). Aid decreased – including many elements of food aid – as the debt crisis began to emerge in the developing world. Britain entered the European Common Market in 1973, with devastating consequences for New Zealand's status as the last ex-colonial protected supplier of agricultural products to Britain (Le Heron 1993; Le Heron and Pawson 1996; MacDermott et al. 2008). The failure of the Soviet grain harvest resulted in a boom, then bust, in world food commodity prices around 1973/4, and the resulting years of crisis in the world food economy fuelled a sense of urgency that new policy and trade frameworks were needed for global food trading (Campbell 2012). The political opportunity had arrived for agriculture to enter free trade discussions.

It was a sign of how powerful the trade liberalization movement became in the 1980s that agriculture was actually included in the Uruguay Round of GATT negotiations that commenced in 1985. The Uruguay Round was the eighth "round" of GATT negotiations and was notable because it included agriculture (and textiles), which were sectors that had previously been held out of negotiations (Muirhead and Almås 2012; Pritchard 2012). It also prefigured future discussions by including negotiations on services, intellectual property, and investment policy for the first time. It was also the trade round that most excited politicians from what was termed the "Cairns Group" of free-trade advocating countries (including New Zealand and Australia) who saw it as the first step in a seemingly inevitable transition to free trade for the world's agricultural exports (Campbell and Coombes 1999).

The Uruguay Round took ten years to conclude (resulting in the Uruguay Round Agricultural Agreement – URAA) and included compromises on agriculture that were necessary in order to reach a signable agreement (Campbell and Coombes 1999). The most important outcome was the formation of the WTO as a permanent institution to replace the periodic GATT negotiations as well as to police new trade regulations (Pritchard 2012). For agriculture, the negotiations took two forms: first, the conversion of all supports to agriculture into the form of tariffs ("tariffication"), and second, the negotiation of a timeline by which all tariffs would be reduced to nil (Campbell and Coombes 1999). The first aim was mostly achieved, but the second was not. The final acceptance of some level of tariffs for farm producers in places like the European Union was coupled with a very long timeline for compliance with de-tariffication, which left many participants sceptical from the outset that the URAA would result in major changes to support for agriculture in places like the European Union or United States. In hindsight, this emphasis on liberalization of food production and cross-border protections was quite narrow. Looking back thirty years later, this focus on the trade in food was happening in complete isolation from nationally specific arrangements for potential trading in farmland. This separation would become increasingly obvious post-2008 as the phenomenon of land-grabbing – happening in a set of processes completely different from the liberalization of food trading – became more evident. In sum, the URAA sought to create a framework for markets in tradable agricultural goods and did not anticipate the emergence of new, and potentially highly contentious, markets in either derivatives or, more specifically for this collection, agricultural land.

The Subsequent Short History of Liberalization
of Agricultural Trade

The subsequent twenty years have been very disappointing for the acolytes of agricultural free trade. Two successive rounds of WTO negotiations (the Millennium Round and the Doha Round) encountered increasing opposition from emerging, empowered negotiators from the developing world who considered that the wealthier countries were somewhat hypocritical in their zealous pursuit of market access into emerging markets while being increasingly tardy in reducing protection for their domestic agricultural sectors (Pritchard 2012). Agriculture was placed front and centre of increasingly rancorous negotiations. Pritchard (2012, 49–51) argues that this was partly because the actual liberalization of agriculture under the URAA was significantly overstated. Actual targets for de-tariffication and overall subsidy reduction were modest and difficult to enforce. He notes that OECD statistics for the total support estimate (TSE) of the contribution of subsidies to the value of sales at the farmgate sat at 49.93 per cent in the European Union at the conclusion of the URAA in 1995 but had fallen to only 38.76 per cent by 2009.

By the middle of the first decade of the 2000s any sincere attempts to reduce subsidies in the United States or European Union seem to have dissipated, with many countries' negotiators pointing to the U.S. Food, Conservation, and Energy Act of 2008 as one of the largest legislative attempts of the last decades to actually subsidize agriculture in the United States. Others highlighted the manoeuvring within the Common Agricultural Policy of the European Union (Muirhead and Almås 2012), which utilized Sanitary and Phytosanitary provisions in the Uruguay Round Agricultural Agreement to legitimize the shifting of subsidies from Blue Box (direct) to Green Box (indirect environmental) subsidies (Campbell and Coombes 1999; Pritchard 2012).

These charges of hypocrisy slowed negotiations in the Doha Round. This was further exacerbated by the global food crisis of 2008–11, which witnessed a dramatic spike in world food prices (Rosin, Stock, and Campbell 2012). Faced with the highest real food prices since the 1940s, many developing world economies began to openly advocate for the right to retain state intervention in domestic markets for staple foods, the return of market interventions, stockpiling, and even tariffs – all of which exacerbated the loss of political impetus for liberalization in agriculture – which had seemed so unstoppable at the end of the Uruguay Round in 1995. To quote Muirhead and Almås (2012, 24–5), this seemed, above all, to be not so much a failure as a return to the status quo: "Indeed, the list of those [countries] protecting agriculture from foreign competition is larger in 2012 than it was in 1945: arguably *no country*, other than New Zealand and Australia (and these only since 1984), can be said to have systematically and consistently rejected agricultural protectionism as a domestic policy tool."

New Zealand's reputation as one country that consistently adhered to the virtues of trade liberalization is supported by its recent success in opening up an important new market in China. In terms of regional politics, Sally (2006) argued that China used a multitude of regional trade agreements to solidify political relationships in East Asia, although he described the character of these agreements as weak in liberalizing effects, calling them "a hub and spoke pattern of dirty FTAs" around China (320). A significant break with this pattern came with the China-NZ FTA that was signed in April 2008 – just a few months before the global food crisis struck. This was the first FTA that China had signed with any Western country and provided significant opportunities for New Zealand food exporters to target the Chinese domestic market. The de-tariffication commenced with the immediate removal of tariffs for 35 per cent of NZ exports to China in 2008 and then a schedule of tariff reduction that will be completed by 2019. The immediate winner was the NZ dairy industry, which was well positioned to provide milk powder/infant formula to a rapidly growing domestic market in China, in which a significant deficit in supply was evident. Dairy export prices escalated to historic highs from 2008 to 2014.

However, while the NZ-China Free Trade Agreement does conform to the legal character of a free trade agreement between the two countries, the reality is that the resulting boom in dairy prices was not a function of free trade, but rather reflected New Zealand's position as the *first* Western country to gain market access to China. The period of the dairy boom coincides with exactly that period in which New Zealand's exports were subject to reducing tariffs, whereas those of its competitors were not. It resembled, above all, New Zealand's privileged position as Britain's exclusive imperial supplier of dairy and sheep meat. It operated as a facilitator of massive expansion of farmed land being devoted to feeding the population of China, just as New Zealand had functioned as Britain's "farm in the South Pacific" in the earlier food regime. Now that the China boom is over – with decreasing demand, and a growing list of competitors like Australia now also gaining market access and/or European countries that are dumping their surplus dairy production into China, no matter what the tariff – those prices are unlikely to ever be seen again. New Zealand's small window of lucrative returns in China represented not so much the benefits of free trade as the first-mover advantage of being the initial invitee into a previously highly protected market. New Zealand's boom was created not by the expansion of global market rule, but by the temporary moment when New Zealand's dairy farms became, by proxy, China's dairy farms.

Culmination or Crunch Time for Free Trade in Agriculture?: The TPPA

While the NZ-China FTA is interesting for its insight into a food supply strategy linking Asia to Oceania, it was assembled in the shadow of a much larger attempt to integrate Pacific Rim economies into a free trade zone – the Trans-Pacific Partnership Agreement (TPPA). Initial hopes were that the TPPA would be a breakthrough moment for free trade, uniting the kinds of economy that had increasingly found WTO progress to be slow and frustrating. These high hopes were expressed in the Trans-Pacific Partnership Leaders Statement by the leaders of Australia, Brunei Darussalam, Chile, Malaysia, New Zealand, Peru, Singapore, the United States, and Vietnam in 2011, asserting a "common vision to establish a comprehensive, next-generation regional agreement that liberalizes trade and investment and addresses new and traditional trade issues and 21st-century challenges" (Office of the Press Secretary 2011).

The TPP is particularly significant for the size of the economies that are involved – "the 12 members of the TPP constitute approximately 36% of world GDP" (MFAT 2016a, 1). The significance of the agreement for New Zealand, in particular, is often described in terms of the economic benefits of free trade. New Zealand negotiators hoped some large political actors would align their national interests with the free trade agenda and create significant new opportunities for agricultural exports. The focus was on big consumer markets like Japan, the United States, and Canada – which all have highly protected agricultural sectors that the WTO never managed to prise open: "Joining TPP would provide immediate economic benefit for New Zealand goods exporters on entry into force of the Agreement, particularly from reduced tariff rates in key markets with which New Zealand does not currently have an FTA" (Currie 2016).

In December 2013 the NZ minister of trade negotiations, Tim Groser, stated, "We will take as long as needed to achieve a deal that eliminates trade barriers for New Zealand exporters and can advance our vision of regional economic integration in the Asia Pacific" (Groser 2013). In the same hopeful tone of significant trade reform, a spokesperson for the NZ Ministry of Foreign Affairs and Trade explained that the TPP "aims to achieve comprehensive tariff elimination" (Edlin 2014).

The reality of the final months of negotiations dashed these high hopes. "During the negotiations it became evident that promise of a 'gold standard' agreement with removal of all tariffs and quotas was not possible" (Coates et al. 2016, 12). MFAT acknowledges that "TPP has not delivered the full elimination of tariffs on our exports that New Zealand sought" (MFAT 2016b, 9). This failure has prompted disappointment in New Zealand – most vocally from the dairy sector, which received surprisingly little from the deal, given its being the country's largest export industry.

Taking the most positive view of the outcomes, one editorial suggested, "New Zealand's primary sector looks to have come out of the Trans-Pacific Partnership (TPP) agreement favourably, with the notable exception of the country's biggest export – dairy" (*New Zealand Herald* 2015). Looking in more detail, there are divergent outcomes for dairy as against beef and for large established commodity sectors versus small niche export products.

For meat exporters there were some gains, with all tariffs and quotas on beef exports to Canada scheduled to be eliminated over five years, to Mexico over ten years, and the tariff on beef exports to Japan reduced from 38.5 per cent down to 9 per cent over fifteen years. Sheep meat also has had some success, with tariffs on exports to Canada, Peru, and Japan scheduled to be eliminated immediately, and to Mexico over eight years (MFAT 2016a, 3–4). The late withdrawal of the United States from the agreement took away one of the key prizes for beef and lamb – access to the lucrative U.S. market.

Schedules of tariff reduction setting immediate, five-, ten-, and fifteen-year targets were set for horticultural exports, wine, forestry, wool, leather, textiles, and miscellaneous other niche export food products like honey, sauces, soups, and even moss (MFAT 2016a).

In contrast, the major hopes of the dairy sector returned only token changes to trading conditions. MFAT's summary document, "Goods Market Access" (MFAT 2016a), puts the best possible spin on the outcomes, explaining that after full implementation (up to thirty years from when the TPPA comes into force [Coates et al., 2016, 12]), tariff eliminations will include (MFAT 2016a, 5):

- A number of protein products having tariffs eliminated in Japan, the United States, and Canada, most at entry into force.
- Tariffs on cheese being eliminated in Japan.
- Tariffs on one of New Zealand's highest-traded U.S. cheese lines will be eliminated.
- Tariffs for milk powders will be eliminated in the United States.
- Tariffs on infant formula will be eliminated in the United States, Canada, and Mexico.

This hopeful analysis predated the disappointment of U.S. with-drawal from the agreement in early 2017. The document notes, however, that "tariffs will not be completely eliminated on all dairy products" (MFAT 2016a, 5). The failure to achieve outcomes for dairy exports is expanded upon in an alternative report produced by prominent academics and business journalists (Coates et al. 2016, 12–13):

- The increased access to Japan over the next five years for butter and milk powder is so slight as to be derided by Dairy NZ Chairman John Luxton as representing the output of only three large NZ dairy farms.
- Canada's supply management system for dairy is still intact with only an increased 3.25% share of imports allowed over the next five years with slightly increased scheduled over a nineteen year period.
- The US tariff on milk powder will be phased out over a 30–35 year period with safeguards for backtracking if market share from imports grows too rapidly.
- Again, these analyses only become more pessimistic with the disappearance of the US as a partner.

It is unsurprising, then, that the final TPPA has not been lauded as a "gold standard" for future trade agreements. Fonterra, the near-monopoly dairy exporter – and largest institution in the New Zealand economy – is "disappointed with the dairy outcome in the Trans-Pacific Partnership deal" (RNZ 2015). As its chairperson, John Wilson, explained, "We're in a better position than before we had TPP, but it's not the elimination of tariffs that had been the undertaking or the expectation some years ago as TPP got underway and built out of the original P4" (RNZ 2015).

What is not so clearly evident in these schedules of tariff reduction is that such schedules have meaning only in the context of trading partners who have engaged sincerely in de-tariffication as started by the URAA in 1995. In the absence of any success in confronting the failed tariffication, "the trade-distorting non-tariff barriers of most relevance to New Zealand – domestic subsidies to American, Japanese and Canadian farmers – have escaped essentially unscathed from the TPP process" (Fallow 2016).

Concessions gained in dairy exports are minuscule compared to the barriers to free trade – tariffs, quotas, and domestic subsidies – that remain. Tariff savings amount to $102 million annually, 2.2 per cent of export value (after full implementation of the TPPA – thirty years after it comes into force) (Coates et al. 2016, 12). A gain perhaps, but certainly not the advent of free trade: "Significant tariffs and quotas will remain on New Zealand's dairy exports to Japan, the US, Canada and Mexico" (12). Beef exports might be considered more of a success for New Zealand, with most tariffs being removed over five years, with the exception of Japan (from 38.5 per cent to 9 per cent over fifteen years) (MFAT 2016a). This amounts to $72 million annually, 3.1 per cent of export value. A small step towards trade liberalization certainly – but for only one product.

Japan's concessions here are interesting and demonstrate the significance of national politics in trade agreements. "Opening Japan to imported beef may be less politically disagreeable than other agricultural commodities. Japanese beef, for instance, is highly differentiated, with unique cattle breeds and production methods. It is the most expensive and sought after beef in the world. Lowering beef tariffs would likely expand the beef market in Japan and lower prices while preserving the dominance of Japanese producers in the high-end market" (Rogowsky and Horlick 2014, 11).

Is This an Incremental Step or the New Normal?

There are two ways of understanding the outcome of what finally became known as the CPTPPA negotiations. For free trade advocates, this is just another incremental step towards the eventual surrender of world markets to the economic wisdom of unsubsidized agricultural production and the cheaper consumer prices that will flow from it. To use the language of liberalizers, eventually major economies like those of the United States and Canada will tire of "holding their [national] dairy consumers to ransom" (Luxton 2015).

There is another way of understanding what has happened: this is the high-water mark for trade liberalization in agriculture. For example, in the words of one report on the outcomes of the TPPA, "New Zealand farmers may receive a small gain in terms of tariff reductions,.... [T]hese are likely to be far outweighed in the future by a lock-in of tariffs, quotas and trade-distorting agricultural subsidies" (Coates et al. 2016, 16).

The prospect of the new levels of trade access being "locked in" is particularly revealing: "The dairy markets for the largest TPPA countries remain heavily protected by tariffs and quotas. Only a small proportion of the markets have been opened up to New Zealand exports. The inability to remove tariffs and quotas in TPPA negotiations may serve to lock in these barriers so they become the *new normal* during an era when tariffs and quotas have been eliminated for all but a very few products, especially amongst the developed countries" (Coates et al. 2016, 14; our emphasis).

The alternative way of understanding what has happened is that the TPPA reflects what every other multilateral free trade negotiation of the last twenty years has also demonstrated: countries are just not particularly enthusiastic about opening up domestic food markets to international competition. Rather than representing a break-through moment in trade liberalization for agriculture, the CPTPPA has sketched out the maximum extent to which major economies are prepared to liberalize their major domestic food sectors, like dairy. The current small concessions to liberalization in sectors like dairy describe what will likely now be the new normal for that sector. Other sectors like beef seem much more likely to be subject to ongoing global integration.

A second observation is that, like the URAA before it, the CPTPPA once again restricted its liberalizing vision to specific issues around trade in agricultural commodities, tariffs, and legal jeopardy for large corporations. It once again failed to build dialogue or a framework to introduce food security – defaulting to the post-1985 consensus that an integrated world market for food represents a full and sufficient solution to food security needs – while neglecting to create a regulatory project for either derivatives trading in food or for the new trade in farmland itself.

If the outcome of the CPTPPA is that a new normal has been established – in limits that negotiators set to the scope and ambition of liberalizing domestic agriculture sectors like dairy – the question remains why the impetus for liberalization that seemed so strong in 1985 has dissipated. We suggest two reasons: a shift of emphasis to new economic sectors, and the ongoing entrenchment of domestic political alliances on agricultural protection.

First, the political and economic game has moved on, and the major players are now much more engaged with the global elaboration of pharmaceutical intellectual property rights, new information and communications technology, and media investment rules, and procedures to resolve disputes. All have significant implications for the wider global economy but they fail to excite agricultural export industries in countries like New Zealand or Australia. One element is the role of the United States as a key negotiator in this agreement. A powerful economic player, the United States entered with a geo-political/economic agenda. President Obama said, "We can't let countries like China write the rules of the global economy. We should write those rules, opening new markets to American products while setting high standards for protecting workers and preserving our environment" (Office of the Press Secretary 2016). Indeed, these geopolitical concerns of the United States are not about agriculture but with intellectual property: "As the

TPPA stands, its rules on IP and trade in services are very US-centric. As a result, US companies will be the greatest beneficiaries" (Coates et al. 2016, 28). Or not, as political events in the United States swept aside this assumption. The clear logic that emerged from final negotiation of the CPTPPA is that agriculture is not interesting or an area that might prompt major growth in the global economy. New technologies and IP, however, are the kind of sector where negotiations might position some nations in a highly advantageous situation.

The second reason is that the thirty years since the conclusion of the GATT Uruguay Round Agriculture Agreement have not seen significant transformation of the domestic political constituencies in many of the major economies. The incomplete tariffication after GATT URAA means that internal subsidy structures, and the political alliances they uphold, still remain in Japan, Europe, and North America. Three kinds of alliance are immediately obvious in the CPTPPA outcomes: those that protect local niches (like Japan), those that subsidize local sectors to enable international expansion (like the United States), and those that protect major domestic food production sectors (like Canada).

In Japan, the niche domestic beef industry is protected through consumer preference and local marketing arrangements (strongly protected by government). The world market for cheaply produced beef is already highly integrated, and in Japan the reduction of tariffs was not anticipated to erode local producer security. This partly explains the highly differentiated outcomes for dairy and beef in Japan market access under CPTPPA. The former is still a highly domestic-oriented industry in all economies, with notable exceptions like New Zealand. The latter is a globally integrated, industrialized sector with highly integrated production, supply, and retailing.

The next kind of domestic alliance appears in countries like the United States where politically powerful agricultural lobbies position themselves to be internationally aggressive while protected by local subsidies. This kind of alliance had already played a major role in bilateral agreements before the CPTPPA that locked in advantage for groups of domestic producers. This was most evident for the United States in its prior negotiations with Japan: "Although the TPPA is often termed a regional trade agreement, access for agricultural products between the US and Japan was negotiated initially on the basis of a bilateral agreement. As a result, the TPPA allowed better access for US exporters to the Japanese market than for exporters of dairy products from other countries, including New Zealand" (Coates et al. 2016, 12). It is this have-it-both-ways advantage that has been partly ceded in the United States and earned President Trump the ire of farm-state politicians.

The final kind of domestic alliance can be seen in Canada, where the supply management system for Canadian dairying (Muirhead and Campbell 2012) emerged almost entirely unscathed from the CPTPPA negotiations. By rescinding any interest in serving international markets, the Canadians demonstrated the quintessentially domestic character of dairying as an economic sector in many major economies.

It is worth emphasizing here that the wider themes of this book collection – the liberalization of markets for farmland itself – seem absent from the concerns of these domestic political alliances. It appears that de-tariffication provokes a much more coordinated and resolute response than the piecemeal sale of farmland to foreign owners. While it is clearly a matter of domestic political concern – as evidenced in other chapters in this collection – it is a more ambiguous concern for farmers, who are threatened by and yet also the beneficiaries of the increasing demand for farmland created by foreign purchasers.

What Becomes Thinkable?: Agriculture and Food Policy without Liberalization

In conclusion, just as agriculture was the last economic sector to enter trade liberalization negotiations in the 1980s, it also appears to be the first to cease to be a major site of aspirations for further liberalization (except in a small minority of countries like New Zealand). The GATT Uruguay Round is the only major multilateral negotiation that even partially shifted agriculture from being a predominantly protected domestic sector of major economies to being an arena subject to global free trade. The creation of a "new normal" of substantially protected agricultural sectors like dairying with only token concessions to liberalization has significant implications for how we understand the global future of food and agricultural policy. If the main policy impetus for liberalization that emerged thirty years ago has now dissipated, many things that were unthinkable for that period start to become thinkable again. Five things come immediately to mind:

1 *Reframing from Trade in Goods to Trade in Land:* In keeping with the wider themes of this book collection, this analysis of the decline of agricultural trade as a focus for FTAs exposes what has become, in hindsight, the narrow and sectoral focus of such negotiations on only the trade in *food*. This was entirely reasonable in the context of a post–Second World War political economy in which *farms* were solidly fixed within domestic political and economic arrangements, and the key site of international trade engagement was the flow of goods between countries. Now, in hindsight, this focus on goods feels

narrow. While FTAs have focused on a diminishing set of potential irresolvable issues in tariffs and domestic supports for production, a wider tide of globalization has brought land markets and farms themselves into the forefront of financialization and international trading. In the wake of the collapse of any WTO-based momentum on trade negotiations on domestic support for agricultural products, a parallel forum is urgently needed to allow for countries to discuss the implications of international trading in farms themselves.

2 *Value-Creation:* Many agricultural export economies have been so focused on acquiring better prices for agricultural exports by reducing tariffs in target markets that there has been little need to ask what foods are being exported, what their qualities are, and how these tangible qualities actually create export value. Stalled agricultural liberalization forces us to think about how we create greater economic value from food exports.

3 *Global vs Local:* The post-1985 economic blueprint was focused entirely on *exports* to drive value-creation in global food production. A more globally integrated agricultural market would drive innovation in producing ever-cheaper food and provide benefits by continuing to reduce the cost of feeding the average labourer. This emphasis on export-driven value creation seemed obvious in a country like New Zealand that exports over 90 per cent of the food it produces. But the final outcome of the CPTPPA negotiations, coupled with the curious nature of other bilateral negotiations in agriculture, is that food exports are not the only place where policy attention should be placed. If the failure of trade liberalization in agriculture is one major trend in the global food economy, another is the move towards local foods in affluent countries.

4 *Food Security:* The market liberalization plan was to address deficits in global food markets when markets were actually awash with cheap, industrial foods. It was the wrong strategy for the wrong problem. Now that the 2008–11 global food crisis has rekindled political concern about the security of food arrangements, a new set of policy responses and governmental strategies is required. In light of the wider discussion in this book collection, such policy and political responses must start to stitch back together the split ontologies of agriculture: the production of *food* as well as the *land* upon which such food is being produced.

5 *Sustainability:* In a country that has intensified its production base with little national policy attention to environmental outcomes, rural economies, or the necessity to support strategies for high-quality food products, the promise of liberalization of agricultural trade sent a message that New Zealand could just stay the course

and liberalization would eventually ensure that the economic challenges of agriculture would resolve themselves. What the twenty years since the conclusion of the Uruguay Round have shown is that global agriculture is subject to unexpected shocks, new concerns, and increasing environmental fragility, and that increasing the efficiencies of agricultural markets at a global scale does not provide a full or sufficient response to such challenges.

The agricultural liberalization agenda since 1985 was based on a future promise that told us to stay the course – that the challenges of agriculture would be resolved once our trade negotiators had prevailed. This will not happen. Countries like New Zealand will celebrate small successes in opening up new markets, but any big "step change" to the structure and direction of global agriculture that has been promised since the Uruguay Round now won't happen. In the space left by the wreckage of this dream, we can now envisage different futures for global agriculture and food. Projects to sketch alternative futures like the IAASTD project in 2006–9 (World Bank 2019) would have seemed utopian ten years ago. Now, on the other side of the global food crisis and the outcomes of the CPTPPA, it begins to look vastly more pragmatic. Above all, it outlined a set of concerns that are now characterized by the political project of food sovereignty. It is increasingly clear that the underwhelming conclusion of the CPTPPA brings us to the point where both food and the land that produces it now need to be brought back into the same political discussion on the challenges we face in the twenty-first century. Attempts to create a free market for global food have foundered on both the contradictions of the liberalization project and the entrenched political power of farm lobbies to stymie removal of economic protections for farmers and their products. Now we need a similar political project to thwart attempts to elaborate a global market for agricultural land itself.

REFERENCES

Campbell, H. 2012. "Let Us Eat Cake?: Historically Reframing the Problem of World Hunger and Its Purported Solutions." In *Food Systems Failure: The Global Food Crisis and the Future of Agriculture*, edited by C. Rosin, P. Stock, and H. Campbell, 30–45. London: Earthscan.
Campbell, H., and B. Coombes. 1999. "'Green Protectionism' and Organic Food Exporting from New Zealand: Crisis Experiments in the Breakdown of Fordist Trade and Agricultural Policies." *Rural Sociology*, 64 (2): 302–19. https://doi.org/10.1111/j.1549-0831.1999.tb00020.x.

Coates, B., R. Oram, G. Bertram, and T. Hazledine. 2016. *The Economics of the TPPA.* https://tpplegal.files.wordpress.com/2015/12/ep5-economics.pdf.

Currie, S. 2016. Editorial: NZ Can Take Pride in TPP Deal on Trade. *New Zealand Herald,* 4 February. http://www.nzherald.co.nz/business/news/article.cfm?c_id=3&objectid=11584220.

Edlin, B. 2014. "Expanding Dairy Export Opportunities." *New Zealand Dairy Exporter,* 1 May. https://farmersweekly.co.nz/article/expanding-dairy-export-opportunities?p=118.

Fallow, B. 2016. "Brian Fallow: TPP Economy Figures Tell Us Nothing." *New Zealand Herald, Business,* 29 January. http://www.nzherald.co.nz/business/news/article.cfm?c_id=3&objectid=11581535.

Friedmann, H., and P. McMichael. 1989. "Agriculture and the State System." *Sociologia Ruralis* 29 (2): 93–117. https://doi.org/10.1111/j.1467-9523.1989.tb00360.x.

Groser, T. 2013. "Minister Welcomes Progress on TPP Negotiations." News release.

Lawrence, G., and H. Campbell. 2014. "Neoliberalism in the Antipodes: Understanding the Influence and Limits of the Neoliberal Political Project." In *The Neoliberal Regime in the Agri-Food Sector: Crisis, Resilience and Restructuring,* edited by S. Wolf and A. Bonnano, 263–83. London: Routledge (Earthscan).

Le Heron, R. 1993. *Globalized Agriculture, Political Choice.* Oxford: Pergamon.

Le Heron, R., and E. Pawson, eds. 1996. *Changing Places: New Zealand in the Nineties.* Auckland, NZ: Longman Paul.

Luxton, J. 2015. "John Luxton: Major TPP Players Holding Their Dairy Consumers to Ransom." *New Zealand Herald, Business,* 20 August. http://www.nzherald.co.nz/business/news/article.cfm?c_id=3&objectid=11499924.

MacDermott, A., C. Saunders, E. Zellman, T. Hope, and A. Fisher. 2008. *Sheep Meat: The Key Elements of Success and Failure in the NZ Sheep Meat Industry from 1980–2007.* Wellington, NZ: Agribusiness Research and Education Network.

Ministry of Foreign Affairs and Trade (MFAT). 2016a. "Trans-Pacific Partnership: Goods Market Access." Ministry of Foreign Affairs and Trade.

– 2016b. "Trans-Pacific Partnership: National Interest Analysis." Ministry of Foreign Affairs and Trade. https://www.tpp.mfat.govt.nz/assets/docs/TPP%20National%20Interest%20Analysis.pdf.

Moran, W., Blunden, G., and A. Bradly. 1996. "Empowering Family Farms through Cooperatives and Producer Marketing Boards." *Economic Geography* 72 (2): 161–77. https://doi.org/10.2307/144264.

Muirhead, B., and R. Almås. 2012. "The Evolution of Western Agricultural Policy since 1945." In *Rethinking Agricultural Policy Regimes: Food Security, Climate Change and the Future Resilience of Global Agriculture,* edited by R. Almas and H. Campbell, 23–49. Bingley, UK: Emerald.

Muirhead, B., and H. Campbell. 2012. "The Worlds of Dairy: Comparing Dairy Frameworks in Canada and New Zealand in Light of Future Shocks to Food Systems." In *Rethinking Agricultural Policy Regimes: Food Security, Climate Change and the Future Resilience of Global Agriculture*, edited by R. Almas and H. Campbell, 23–49. Bingley: UK: Emerald.

New Zealand Herald. 2015. "Who Will Cash In on TPP?" 7 October. http://www.nzherald.co.nz/business/news/article.cfm?c_id=3&objectid=11524799.

Office of the Press Secretary. 2011. "Trans-Pacific Partnership Leaders Statement." 12 November. https://www.whitehouse.gov/the-press-office/2011/11/12/trans-pacific-partnership-leaders-statement.

– 2016. "Statement by the President on the Signing of the Trans-Pacific Partnership." 3 February. https://www.whitehouse.gov/the-press-office/2016/02/03/statement-president-signing-trans-pacific-partnership.

Pawson, E., and T. Brooking, eds. 2002. *Environmental Histories of New Zealand*. Melbourne: Oxford University Press.

Pritchard, B. 2012. "Trading into Hunger? Trading out of Hunger?: International Food Trade and the Debate on Food Security." In *Food Systems Failure: The Global Food Crisis and the Future of Agriculture*, edited by C. Rosin, P. Stock, and H. Campbell, 46–59. London: Earthscan.

RNZ. 2015. "Should Dairy Have a Cow over TPP Deal?" 6 October. http://www.radionz.co.nz/news/national/286178/should-dairy-have-a-cow-over-tpp-deal.

Rogowsky, R.A., and G. Horlick. 2014. "TPP and the Political Economy of U.S.-Japan Trade Negotiations." Washington, DC: Woodrow Wilson International Center for Scholars. https://www.wilsoncenter.org/sites/default/files/TPP%20and%20the%20Political%20Economy%20of%20US-Japan%20Trade%20Negotiations_1.pdf.

Rosin, C., P. Stock, and H. Campbell, eds. 2012. *Food Systems Failure: The Global Food Crisis and the Future of Agriculture*. London: Earthscan.

Sally, R. 2006. "Free Trade Agreements and the Prospects for Regional Integration in East Asia." *Asian Economic Policy Review* 1 (2): 306–21. https://doi.org/10.1111/j.1748-3131.2006.00036.x.

World Bank. 2019. "International Assessment of Agricultural Science & Technology for Development (IAASTD)." http://www.worldbank.org/projects/P090963/international-assessment-agricultural-science-technology-development-iaastd?lang=en.

4 Food Security and the Multifunctionality of Agriculture: Paradoxes in European Land Questions

KATRINA RØNNINGEN

Introduction

Agricultural policies in Europe may be described as multifunctional, although the content and emphasis of the functions of agriculture have shifted. Increasing production and productivity to ensure food sufficiency and security in the aftermath of the hunger and starvation suffered during the Second World War, rural employment, and settlement, as well as balanced monetary policies, have been important elements of the European Union's (EU) Common Agricultural Policy (CAP), as well of non-EU members such as Norway and Switzerland (Potter and Tilzey 2005; Schweizerischer Bundesrat 1984; Blekesaune 1999). Modernization and reform of agriculture and rural areas was to take place within structured mechanisms, thereby avoiding the collapse of rural social structures. Balancing different power interests has been important, including those of the often-strong farmers lobby while simultaneously securing a liveable income level for farmers and reasonable prices for consumers (Rønningen 1999; Almås 2004).

The food security dimension of these policies may be claimed to have been successful as agriculture, especially in the EU, has moved into what seems to be permanent surplus, which necessitates the export, but also the dumping, of that excess production. Support-driven agricultural intensification also led to serious environmental degradation, and the response was the "greening of agricultural subsidies" through agri-environmental payments and even the set-aside of land to reduce over-production during the late 1980s and 1990s. Through a revised emphasis on agricultural and rural diversification, and also attempts to strengthen the role of agriculture as a provider of ecosystem services, multifunctionality has turned into "a new paradigm for European" development in those areas (Durand and van der Huydenbroeck 2003).

Following the 2007/8 food price shock there was a renewed focus on food security (Almås and Campbell 2012). The recent deregulation and repeal of quotas have again led to surplus production, and farmers' indebtedness and often their bankruptcy are making headlines (e.g., *Bondebladet* 2016; DutchNews.nl 2015). These developments relate to land ownership structures and control, and land investments play an increasing role in Europe, yet the land question is in general poorly articulated in the rich literature on agricultural policies and multifunctionality studies.

This chapter addresses several paradoxes contained within, and recent developments of, agricultural policies and land-use development and control in Europe. It is influenced by and reflects the wider international context. It draws on the research literature, public documents, and "grey literature" reports from international organizations.

Food and Double Movements

Food and agriculture have been treated as "exceptional" policy fields (Clapp 2015) as a result of their crucial importance in securing food security, as states need to cater to the basic needs of their people. There are historical examples of grain storage and measures to keep small farmers on the land, as in the Chinese Qing dynasty from the seventeenth century. Even earlier, food protests in 51 CE in the Roman Empire led to state support for securing grain and its transport to disadvantaged areas (McKeon 2018). "Peace! Land! Bread!" was the essence of the Russian October Revolution of 1917 and, as referenced elsewhere in this book, the Arab spring of 2010 and the beginning of the civil war in Syria were triggered by drought and food shortages.

The significance of these developments is often forgotten in the seemingly never-ending debate on agricultural liberalization versus protectionism. Similarly, governments that are wedded to the notion that the corporate sector in agriculture can do it more cheaply and efficiently, largely support the sector on that basis. Food prices are at least partial determinants of personal well-being in that the cheaper they are, the smaller the proportion of household budgets they consume. While it is unlikely that local food brands and urban farming can feed the new billions expected in the decades ahead, it is also unclear that trade liberalization, with its results dominated by corporations, will achieve the benefits so often claimed for it in reducing costs and lowering food prices. For example, four companies have oligopolistic control of more than 70 per cent of the world's grain trade, which hardly seems like a recipe for more robust competition (Murphy, Burch, and Clapp 2012).

Food regimes are characterized by contradictory forces (McMichael 2009) and paradoxical developments – what Polanyi (1944/1957) has termed "double movements": "Building on Polanyi's analysis of liberalism, several scholars writing from a political economy perspective have argued that neoliberalism, like nineteenth-century liberal forms of capitalism, is characterized by a 'double movement' in which accelerating social and environmental degradation produces social resistance to market liberalization" (Dibden, Cocklin, and Potter 2009, 54). This social resistance provides the basis for calls for regulation and restraint, and "apparently oppositional projects such as organics, value-based labels and fair-trade initiatives [which] are seen by some scholars as part of a Polanyian double movement – a means of protecting producers and the environment from the intensification and exploitation resulting from exposure to the global market.... Polanyi's notion of a countermovement is, however, not just about the protection of vulnerable groups or environments but may also be about defending the market itself" (54).

This line of reasoning follows on from Lockie and Higgins (2007), who argue that resistance to the neoliberal political project often results in measures that actually make neoliberalism "workable." Social regulation increasingly takes place by individualization and "responsibilization" through ethical or intentional consumption, such as fair trade, organic food, and local food. In line with Michel Foucault, consumer choice rather than politics and regulatory responsibility are pushed, while the various forms of resistance in the agri-food systems are self-limiting (Bonnano and Wolf 2017).

Troublesome but Needed Multifunctional Agricultural Policies

Guaranteed prices, import levies, and export subsidies have been the basis for the CAP system since its establishment (Muirhead and Almås 2012). By 1985 the CAP absorbed 73 per cent of the EU budget when it comprised ten member states. The high cost level could not be maintained, and with the many new entrants it has decreased to 40 per cent, covering twenty-seven member states. The CAP's success in increasing production and productivity had devastating environmental and landscape effects, along with massive surplus production, resulting in "butter mountains" and "lakes of wine," exported and dumped on the world market. With the WTO negotiations on the liberalization of agricultural trade in the mid-1990s, change was prescribed, and the concept of multifunctionality became strengthened in the Uruguay trade negotiations when the EU, Japan, South Korea, Norway, and Switzerland advocated changing several previously direct production-oriented subsidies (the "blue box") and into indirect, agri-environmental payments (the "green box") (see Campbell and Reynolds, this book). Further, restrictions were placed on the "amber box" that entailed budget support and were thought to distort trade. Those opposed to this move generally constituted the so-called Cairns group, established in 1986, initially comprising fourteen countries, most of them less developed but also including Australia, Canada, and New Zealand (Turpin et al. 2010).

Multifunctionality then came to be associated with the provision of environmental services and rural development. The OECD definition of the term is that beyond its primary function of producing food and fibre, agricultural activity can also shape the landscape, provide environmental benefits such as land conservation, the sustainable management of renewable natural resources and the preservation of biodiversity, and contribute to the socio-economic viability of many rural areas. Agriculture is multifunctional when it has one or several functions in addition to its primary role of producing food and fibre (OECD 2001).

The need to diversify rural incomes, as articulated by the 1996 Cork Declaration of the EU on Rural Development, recognized "the declining economic role of conventional agriculture in marginal rural areas and the need to find other rationales for public subvention" (Potter and Tilzey 2005, 581). These rationales, it later came to be realized, could also be based on capitalizing on agriculture's "ancillary functions," such as the preservation of biodiversity and cultural heritage.

This post-productivist turn did not spell an end to intensification and increasing productivity. What did emerge was a differentiation of agricultural policies into market- and environmentally oriented policies, Since the 1990s, agri-environment schemes have been an integral part of the CAP, currently costing approximately €1.7 billion annually, and are the major source of nature conservation funding within the European Union (Batáry et al. 2015). At the same time, large-scale, industrialized agriculture is often seen as undermining the foundation for continued food production through eradicating ecosystems and insect pollinators (IPBES 2018).

European agri-environmental schemes and payments have been described as "protection in disguise" (Potter and Tilzey 2005) or a "European euphemism for protection" (Swinbank 2001). However, subsidies and protection can take many forms. For example, Fonterra, the largest New Zealand dairy cooperative, which dominates the national market, pays a premium to its dairy farmers that parallels the effects of production subsidies. Within a deregulated agricultural policy sphere with few environmental regulations, this has had huge negative environmental consequences, particularly in polluted waterways

(Muirhead and Campbell 2012; Burton and Wilson 2012). Similarly, former president Barack Obama famously described the U.S. Farm Bill (2014–18) as "a Swiss Army knife," because of its many functions, relating to conservation, safety net, infrastructure, health, nutrition, and much more. The Farm Bill was budgeted over ten years at US$1 trillion, with 80 per cent targeted to keep demand up for American agricultural products through the Supplemental Nutrition Assistance Program, commonly known as food stamps (Hillestad 2016). U.S. agricultural policies are more widely known for subsidizing the corn and sugar industries, one negative externality of which may have been the obesity epidemic, especially among lower income groups (Ng et al. 2014).

The Canadian system of supply management has been described as a success, securing stable prices and avoiding overproduction, given that it is based on production quotas, but not subsidies (Muirhead and Campbell 2012). However, supply management is under pressure by the renewal of the North American Free Trade Agreement (NAFTA). Indeed, as the negotiations continued, the Trump administration threatened to seek its abolition, which would lead to the loss of a large numbers of jobs and serious economic and social impacts for many Canadian regions in the long term (Cision 2018). When the dust cleared and the U.S.-Mexico-Canada Agreement was declared, however, U.S. milk producers were granted an additional 3.6 per cent of market share in Canada, which is not fatal to supply management. It is, however, an irritant.

Multifunctionality of European Agricultural and Rural Areas

Multifunctionality, diversification, and pluri-activity are key strategies through which a large share of small and medium-sized farm holdings in Europe plan their survival and perhaps even future prosperity. In many places pluri-activity has been crucial for farm livelihoods, while it has often been seen as an obstacle to agricultural modernization. Agricultural policies and subsidies have had ambiguous effects on small and medium-sized farms. On the one hand they have driven structural changes and scale enlargement. Yet, at the same time, they have also enabled small and medium farms, and to some extent the landscapes that they farm, to survive through payments for agri-environmental schemes and less-favoured areas (LFAs).

Norway, being outside the EU, has maintained an agricultural model that builds upon a social contract between the state and the two farmers' organizations with annual negotiations that settle price and production levels. Restrictions and levies on imports and regulations to prevent the concentration of agricultural land and farm properties into a few hands have been central to these policies (Almås 2004). Regionally differentiated payments have sustained relatively small and medium-scale farms and are perceived as the main guarantor of farming vitality and as a contribution to a certain level of agricultural self-sufficiency while maintaining cultural landscapes across the country. With only 3 per cent of the country comprising arable land, food security and defence aspects of food production were also part of the post-war legitimacy of agricultural policies (Almås 2004; Rønningen, Burton, and Renwick 2012). At the same time, they have been heavily criticized for being expensive and with the concomitant effect of increasing domestic food prices. Further, by the twenty-first century these policies are now thought by some to be unnecessary, since as a very wealthy country Norway could easily import all the food it needs.

Counterarguments are compelling, however, and these include such considerations as the societal benefits of the value of healthy, Norwegian-grown food, the maintenance of low-antibiotic farming systems, and landscapes with a high environmental value that may attract tourism (see, for example, Olsson et al. 2011). As well, dispersed food production may be seen as food security insurance. Almås (2018) makes this point, referring to the Chernobyl nuclear reactor disaster in 1986 and its effect on grazing resources, and the Krakatoa volcano eruption of 1883, which caused global temperatures to fall with an effect on agricultural productivity. Interestingly for Norway, Edvard Munch's *The Scream*, painted in 1893, with its red sky in the background may reflect the continuing after-effects of that eruption.

These Norwegian initiatives were seen, in the decades following the Second World War, as important consumer protection measures against high and unstable prices. When expensive international prices prevail, the system would ensure stable and reasonable prices for consumers below world market cost (see Almås 2004). However, that period may now be coming to an end as the liberalization of the country's production levels, along with the import of cheap soya feed, have recently led to overproduction, lower prices, and income loss for farmers (see *Trønderavisa* 2018).

Agri-Environmental Payments for Cultural Landscapes Near Collapse?

Agriculture covers about 40 per cent of land within the EU (SOER 2015). About half of that land is under agricultural management and in many places has been so for more than 6,000 years. Clearly, this has had an impact on the "natural" environment, and many species and important ecosystems have grown to depend on low-intensive agricultural management, and a number of these are now experiencing declines. The environmental challenges following the industrialization, specialization, and intensification of European agriculture have been immense. For example, 97 per cent of grasslands in Wales and England were lost between the 1930s and 1984 through the introduction of industrial agriculture and other intensification schemes (Fuller 1987). At the same time in other parts of the EU, many small-scale farming systems in relatively marginal areas, the LFAs, often in mountainous regions (see Soliva et al. 2008), have been able to maintain what are referred to as "high nature value farming systems," although in many places that is now in question as extensification and land abandonment has led to increased forest, woodland, and scrub cover that subtracts from the agricultural inventory (Forest Europe, UNECE, and FAO 2011).

Industrial agriculture has also had spilled over into the environment more widely. The Intergovernmental Science Policy Platform on Biodiversity and Ecosystem Services (IPBES 2018), for example, points to the fact that about one-third of global food produced benefits from animal pollination. Pollinators face numerous threats, including changes in land use and management intensity, climate change, pesticides and genetically modified crops, pollinator management and pathogens, and invasive alien species (Potts et al. 2016). IPBES (2018) states that strengthening diversified farming systems is an important strategic response, because such systems, integrating a mix of crops and/or animals, support a higher diversity and abundance of pollinators.

These trends are not encouraging, nor are others. In spite of the large payments that are channelled through agri-environmental schemes, the results they achieve are not always encouraging. Since 1990, common farmland bird populations have declined by 30 per cent, thought to be linked to increased specialization and intensification in agriculture and habitat loss. Between 1990 and 2011, populations of grassland butterflies declined by almost 50 per cent, a dramatic loss of biodiversity and pollination activity (SOER 2015). A recent, much referenced study found a decline of more than 75 per cent over twenty-seven years in total flying insect biomass within sixty-three protected areas in Germany (Hallmann et al. 2017). These are staggering losses.

The general lesson from the European experience is that agri-environmental schemes can conserve wildlife on farmland, but they are expensive and need to be carefully designed and targeted (see Batáry et al. 2015). Others have pointed to the lack of incentives for *improvement* of landscape values and biodiversity (Burton, Kuczera, and Schwartz 2008; Burton and Schwartz 2013), while some recent work highlights bleak prospects in agriculture, the result of problems surrounding succession plans from one generation to the next – there often is no successor – which means that hitherto successful landscape management schemes may collapse when the owners/land users retire or die. Many ageing farmers are happy to accept landscape management payments, facilitating the success of these agri-environmental schemes, but without successors, these landscapes and biodiversity are potentially on the brink of collapse (Wehn et al. 2018).

Structural changes, farmland ownership, and people and animals on the land are thus crucial factors when designing systems to maintain or enhance landscape, cultural heritage, or ecosystem services. Thus they are also crucial for further rural economic development linked to commodification, including tourism and recreation (Shucksmith and Rønningen 2011; Olsson et al. 2011). Europe's many iconic cultural landscapes, such as England's Lake District or Norwegian fjord areas, are also drawing mass tourism, not only farm tourism. How to fund maintenance of these important landscapes, drawing on the collective goods produced by farmers and their animals, is an unresolved problem where both the general public and the private sector have been unwilling to support through financial means. Further, the future of the Brexit landscapes is uncertain, as Britain will have to design – and fund – new systems for agricultural and environmental support.

Changing Farming

The traditional profile of farmers is rapidly changing, whether from transnational investments in land (or land grabbing), crowd-funding between farmers and consumers in niche markets or community farming and the feminization of farming (Stroink, Nelson, and Davis 2017; Hardman and Larkham 2014; Heggem 2014). Innovative farmers and pastoralists are finding allies among citizen-consumer groups. Some efforts to diversify farm and rural incomes have been successful, notably agri-tourism and green care (Brandth and Haugen 2011, 2014; Leck, Evan, and Upton 2014). As well, with the development of short supply chains for local and regional foods, often trading on regional distinctiveness and a direct link with the producer, and organic produce experiencing enhanced popularity, farmers can be the beneficiaries (Kvam, Magnus, and Stræte 2014). While these are relatively small markets (see the critique above, offered by Bonanno and Wolf 2017), they are growing in both scale and scope. A 2000 survey of seven EU member states (then representing 76 per cent of farm enterprises and

84 per cent of the EU's farmland) found that 40 per cent of farm enterprises were involved in such activities, which added 20 per cent to the net value added from "traditional economic activities" (Ploeg, Long, and Banks 2002, 185). In 2015 Norway, a late adopter of local food diversification, had three times stronger growth within the local food sector than with that of staple foods and goods of supermarkets and shops (Hambro 2015). These developments also link to an increasing trend towards the "feminization of agriculture," with daughters taking over the family farm (Heggem 2014), or newcomers, often women with higher education, buying into agriculture or marrying farmers (see Brandth and Haugen 2011, 2014). Heggem (2014) finds a "significant and positive relationship between the potential recruitment of women, a higher level of education among farm property owners, and farm property owners' involvement in farm diversification associated with farm tourism and Green Care," and "this outcome is of importance for recruitment of women to rural areas and for rural viability" (439). This aligns with Rico and Fuller, who argue that such developments may signal a move towards a new rurality in Europe: "This change may be referred to as a shift from an agro-industrial to an agro-social paradigm and, together with new social and environmental relations in food systems, forms a new rurality in Europe" (Rico and Fuller 2016). In Southern Europe another "double movement" of re-peasantization is taking place, partly as a response to the region's economic crisis and high unemployment, but also for ideological reasons. In many cases, young people from cities move back to take over ancestral land, but also migrants contribute to the re-valuation of un/underutilized farmland (Ploeg 2018; Verinis 2014). Nelson and Stock (2018, 83) point to the U.S. experience, noting that "entrepreneurial farmers demonstrate peasant principle practices and therefore a process of repeasantization is occurring in the USA." Proponents of Scottish land reforms have argued that individual land ownership and cooperation between small-scale landholders as they are found in Scandinavia and especially Norway, are important also for rural entrepreneurship and development (see Bryden, Brox, and Riccoch 2015).

Many of those returnees and newcomers will depend at least partially on diverse income sources from outside farming, and a functioning labour market allowing pluri-activity, but they may also play a crucial role in revitalizing rural areas (see Shucksmith and Rønningen 2011). However, to what extent they can counteract the stronger trends of fewer, larger, and more specialized farms in socially and environmentally deserted landscapes is a moot point.

Entering the Neo-Productivist Phase

Following the 2007/8 "food price spike" (see Bjørkhaug, McMichael, and Muirhead in this book), arguments about national food self-sufficiency and food security have once again gained some prominence. However, the role of biofuel here is crucial; Borras and Franco (2010) estimated that the growth in land dedicated to growing biofuels was responsible for 30 per cent of the 2008 food price spike. As well, Clapp (2015, 9) has observed that the "turmoil on global food markets since 2007 has prompted greater use of trade-relevant policy measures, such as export bans, price controls, and public-stockholding schemes by a number of countries as a means to enhance domestic food security. Many countries in Asia, Africa, and the Gulf region also announced plans to become more self-sufficient in food in order to reduce their reliance on global markets for their food supply. Trade advocates have actively argued against these types of policies, which they see as harming, rather than enhancing, food security. Instead, they argue that more trade, supported by more open trade policies, is required to enhance food security."

An interesting EU reaction to the new focus on food security and on biofuel production was the abolition of the set-aside scheme in 2008 (Jack 2016). Set-aside had been introduced in the EU in 1987 as a way to take agricultural land out of production and to reduce the agricultural surpluses that had largely been created by the subsidy regime. It obliged farmers to take between 5 and 15 per cent of their farmland out of production and provided them with some compensation to do so. Set-aside involved several different sorts of changes in management practice: the establishment of green covers (by natural regeneration, sowing, or sowing non-food crops), reductions in the use of inputs (pesticides, organic and inorganic fertilizers), or changes in cutting and cultivation regimes, that would encourage flora and fauna (Tscharntke, Batáry, and Dormann 2011). The scheme was initially extremely unpopular among farmers, as it represented the negation of everything they understood about being a good farmer – a farmer should produce food, which the world needs, in the best possible way. Farmers found getting paid for not farming (the fields were to be cut, but not used) to be deeply disturbing and wrong (Rønningen 1999). The efficiency of the program was questioned. While the intention was to remove some of the most productive land from farmer inventories, they usually took out the more marginal land – "the rubbish land," as they might have said. However, over the years, many of these areas developed into valuable habitats for plants, birds, and animals and came to be valuable refuges in otherwise intensively farmed areas. Their re-ploughing caused a sudden loss in habitat and biodiversity in agricultural landscapes (Tscharntke, Batáry, and Dormann 2011; Morris et al. 2011).

Almås and Campbell (2012) point out the emergence of neo-productivist arguments about agriculture that seek to re-establish productivism as the central function and policy rationale for agriculture. Midgley and Renwick (2012) analysed how the Scottish agricultural sector responded to this policy move back to a productive focus, allowing farmers to return to focusing on what they prefer doing – "proper food production." Most farmers identify more with being food producers than landscape managers, although many see cultural landscape maintenance as an additional and meaningful contribution (see Daugstad, Rønningen, and Skar, 2006).

Levidow (2015) points out two visible agricultural development trajectories being promoted within Europe. One is based on the "bio-economy," a life sciences–based approach, and the other focuses upon "sustainable intensification," which is essentially neo-productivism but can also encompass increased productivity and efficiency through improved and smarter agronomic and production systems. One important difference is that the bio-economy approach seems to marginalize multifunctional (agro-ecological) practices, while "sustainable intensification" seems to selectively incorporate such practices. Both approaches emphasize a neo-liberal productivist narrative – the need for more resource-effective methods that will increase production to meet increased market demand for food, feed, and fuel. The criticism of these approaches is that business needs and their wish for growth have been turned into an objective truth about "market needs" or demand (Levidow 2015).

The interest in cultural landscapes, heritage, and their management is weakened in policies and rhetoric, partly replaced by a climate focus. Water and flood control and the potential for carbon storage in soil is now attracting attention. Biochar production, for example, represents a complex system that may deliver a number of services and functions, and it can additionally be used for biofuel and heat (Lehmann and Joseph 2015).

During past decades in Western Europe, agricultural policies coupled with large-scale infrastructure, transportation, and urbanization projects have reduced the amount of farmland significantly. In Europe 1,500 hectares of farmland disappear daily, and the Continent imports more food than it produces (IPBES 2018). Nevertheless, surplus production has again become a problem as European quotas and regulations are gradually being removed or loosened as part of market deregulation.

The removal of milk quotas among a number of European countries has followed from deregulation of pig and chicken production. Milk quotas were abolished in EU as of 1 April 2015 as a part of more market orientation. The EU Commission (2015) stated, "Even with quotas, EU dairy exports have increased by 45 per cent in volume and 95 per cent in value in the last five years. Market projections indicate that the prospects for further growth remain strong – in particular for added-value products, such as cheese, but also for ingredients used in nutritional, sports and dietary products." The consequences have varied, but overproduction and sharp fall in prices were immediate consequences that struck many dairy farmers hard and have continued to plague the industry.

Developments in Farm and Land Ownership in Europe

Ploeg, Franco, and Borras Jr (2015) point out a Global North land rush, and that land concentration may be as problematic as land grabbing. They also note that corporate and state interests in land interact. GRAIN (2014) offers an overview on distinct developments in land ownership development. In Western Europe, and especially in Belgium, Finland, France, Germany, and Norway, around 70 per cent of farms no longer exist since the 1970s, and this trend is accelerating in some cases. In Eastern Europe from 2003 to 2010, Bulgaria, Estonia, the Czech Republic, and Slovakia lost over 40 per cent of their farms, while in Poland alone almost one million farms out of more than two million disappeared between 2005 and 2010.

Within the EU as a whole, over six million farms disappeared between 2003 and 2010, bringing the number of farms down to almost the same level as in 2000, before the process began of including twelve new member states, with 8.7 million new farmers. The United States has lost 30 per cent of its farms in the last fifty years. However, developments in the United States differ from those in Europe, as the number of very small farms has almost tripled, while the number of very large farms has grown more than five-fold (GRAIN 2014). While it is arguably not tragic that fewer people gain low income from hard work on often very small farms in agriculture, these changes represent an important shift in control over land as well as crucial social and landscape changes.

The shock of exposure to free markets upon the collapse of the Union of Soviet Socialist Republics was calamitous, resulting in the decline in industrial and agricultural production, and people's incomes being halved (Reinert 2017). Kalugina (2014) has described how this led to increased reliance on subsistence production and a barter economy during the past few decades. Russia apart, land concentration in

Eastern Europe started in earnest after the fall of the Berlin Wall and the enlargement of the European Union. Millions of Eastern European farmers went out of business when their domestic markets were opened up to subsidized farm produce from Western Europe. Large farms now represent less than 1 per cent of all farms in the European Union as a whole, but they control 20 per cent of EU farmland. Farms of 100 hectares or more represent only 3 per cent of farms in the EU but cover 50 per cent of all farmed land (GRAIN 2014).

In Poland land prices have increased by 500 per cent since the country's entry into the EU in 2004 (Havro and Dypvik 2018). Foreign investors as well as local buyers have bought in heavily. Poland has Europe's highest share of farmers and work force in agriculture – 14.5 per cent compared to the EU average of 5.6 per cent, while in Norway the share is approximately 2 per cent. At the same time, Poland is an important supplier of farm labour to Northern European farms. While the fall of communism led to declining food production all over Eastern Europe, Poland was the exception, as many farmers there maintained ownership and control over their land, even during the days of collectivism. While the state formally controlled 22 per cent of farmland, most was farmed by small producers. Polish farmers were against EU membership, fearing being out-competed by subsidies for Western food producers, but the opposite has happened. Poland today is Europe's largest producer of chicken, potatoes, rye, and sunflower seeds.

The International Coalition to Protect the Polish Countryside estimates that 120,000 hectares have been bought up, and that, in addition, 200,000 hectares are rented by foreign companies (Bårdsgård 2018). Polish authorities state that agricultural land ownership is fragmented and inadequate, with an average size of 10 hectares in 2014 (up from 5.8 hectares in 2002), and half of the farms are not producing for the market, partly as the result of food safety and sanitary regulations. While production and exports are increasing, farmers' incomes are declining. Most farmers prefer to rent out their land, rather than sell it, and to keep a small lot for subsistence production. Foreign investors also often prefer to lease land rather than to buy it. While some Poles are outraged at the alienation of Polish land, they are powerless to stop it, especially given that investors are largely EU residents. Warsaw has made it clear that it will follow European Union regulations on this sensitive matter, but it remains problematic.

State-owned companies as well as cooperatives are also investing in Eastern European farmland. An EU report (European Parliament 2015) points to Romania as the favourite target, and foreigners may control 70 per cent of the land, although statistics from 2013 put the figure at

10 per cent foreign ownership, with a further 20–30 per cent leased to foreigners. It must be stressed that the farm-unit size in Romania is very small, with most properties being less than five hectares (Eurostat 2015).

Danish farmers are among the "foreign" investors who intend to buy and lease farmland in Eastern Europe. The Danish experience is interesting. During the past twenty-five years the number of Danish farms halved (to 30,000 units in 2014), while the average size doubled, to close to seventy hectares. There are no price ceilings on agricultural land, and prices increased sharply up until the financial crisis in 2008. The abolition of milk quotas in 2015 and consequent price fall led to a debt crisis, with 191 farm bankruptcies in 2015 (*Bondebladet* 2016), and 160 in 2016 (Undheim 2018). There was also a decline in productivity per hectare. As farm unit sizes increase, it becomes more challenging to optimally manage the farmland and make efficient use of fertilizers and equipment. Facing high levels of indebtedness and a need for capital for further investment, many Danish farmers plan to sell their farms to companies, lease them back, then work directly for the companies or develop various types of co-ownership. With the increasing size of farm units, high levels of debt, and long working hours, recruitment to farming is decreasing, however, and taking over the family farm is becoming less attractive to potential successors (Hageberg 2012).

Klimek and Hansen (2017) offer an insightful comparison between Norwegian agriculture, which is still strongly regulated and protected, and that of Denmark, which is internationally integrated with a high volume of exports and similar exposure to world market competition on its domestic market. Norway's agriculture, by contrast, is characterized by structural barriers to national growth and is only tepidly connected to EU and world markets. Klimek and Hansen point out that Denmark has pursued a continuous path of export dependent agricultural indus-trialization, whereas Norway is still able to sustain food production for its (domestic) market in a relatively protected setting. Needless to say, oil-exporting Norway does *not* rely upon agricultural exports for its national well-being, while Denmark does, at least to some extent.

While a gradual "softening" of regulations following structural change in Norway has continued for decades, the current Norwegian Conservative / Populist Right / Liberal coalition government is eager to further liberalize regulations. In 2017 new easements on concession requirements when buying farm properties, removal of price controls for forest properties, and easements on regulations for people operat-ing agricultural holdings to also dwell on them were introduced. One aim of these moves is to stimulate the sale of agricultural properties (Ministry of Agriculture and Food 2017). This approach is based largely on the belief that Norwegian farms must increase size in order to become more efficient and competitive. Many are not convinced of this necessity, and counterarguments generally focus on the fact that Norwegian topography and geography make large-scale farms untenable. Further, climate discourages this strategy, with the result that focusing upon exports, except for a few niche products, is largely unrealistic.

Concluding Discussion

Development in European agricultural policies and the discourse that animates them can be described as having gone from productivist to post-productivist and more recently to neo-productivist. Food security has gained increased prominence and legitimacy in policy formation. Now deregulation has again led to surplus production, and the evidence suggests that the state needs to play a stronger role in imposing quotas and enforcing environmental regulations. This is necessary to secure long-term, predictable production and thus food security, as well as some socio-economic sustainability and predictability. While Norway used to be at the forefront of promoting pioneering multifunctional agricultural policies, it has recently implemented a number of easements and deregulated certain sectors.

The focus on cultural landscape management and cultural heritage as part of agricultural multifunctionality has weakened, while climate change and climate adaptation strongly influence approaches and perceptions of agricultural policies and practices. Indeed, climate measures are now included as part of the new multifunctionality of farmed areas. While large-scale, industrialized farms are perceived as poor contributors to landscape diversity, biodiversity, and cultural heritage, one may ask whether climate mitigation may be more efficient and cost-effective on larger properties. However, this possibility does contradict another imperative – the necessity to maintain diverse, low-intensively farmed landscapes (high nature value farming) crucial in order to maintain the ecosystem services that pollinating insects give us. This follows on from the marked decline in pollinating insects and the potentially devastating effects on food production that it poses.

The EU invests heavily in rural development and innovation. It is also possible to identify new alliances between farmers, processors, and consumers, and substantial social innovation and entrepreneurship. However, the social basis for driving such developments may be weakened with the concentration of land ownership in fewer hands, often held by external capital. The dominant trends are a growing separation between the classical production factors: land, labour, and capital. It is difficult not to see farmers, and also rural communities as well as the environment, as the losers in the continuing evolution of food systems and the changing concentration of land ownership, although the effect of these changes may vary in different contexts.

It seems inevitable that biofuel and other biomass production will influence land ownership and that this will have a knock-on effect upon the use to which land is put. The processes that are driving land grabbing are based on fundamentally unstable economics. For example, fuel prices are notoriously volatile. This may be seen as a form of market environmentalism, that is, markets being used as a solution to environmental problems and at the same time being fuelled largely by green subsidies, with the social and environmental costs being externalized.

The processes described in this chapter are contradictory and paradoxical. A major argument is that agricultural multifunctionality is needed to maintain economically, environmentally, and socially sustainable rural areas, but also to sustain ecosystem services that the entire society relies upon. In order to do so, we need to strengthen the essential social structures that are linked to agricultural land. If we do not, we will have to rethink the policies and management strategies designed to maintain the key values and services that agriculture still supports.

REFERENCES

Almås, R. 2004. *Norwegian Agricultural History*. Trondheim: Tapir Academic Publishers.
– 2018. *Klimasmart landbruk*. Riga: Snøfugl forlag.
Almås, R., and H. Campbell, eds. 2012. *Rethinking Agricultural Policy Regimes: Food Security, Climate Change and the Future Resilience of Global Agriculture*. Bingley, UK: Emerald.
Bårdsgård, H. 2018. "Familiebruk under press." In *Kven skal eige jorda? Ei bok om mat og makt*, edited by H.L. Havro and A.S. Dypvik, 77–87. Oslo: Res Publica.
Batáry, P., L.V. Dicks, D. Kleijn, and W.J. Sutherland. 2015. "The Role of Agri-Environment Schemes in Conservation and Environmental Management." *Conservation Biology* 29 (4): 1006–16. https://doi.org/10.1111/cobi.12536.
Blekesaune, A. 1999. *Agriculture's Importance for the Viability of Rural Norway*. Report 8/99. Trondheim: Centre for Rural Research.
Bondebladet. 2016. "Konkursras i dansk landbruk. 191 konkurser på ett år – og stigning er ventet," 7 April.
Bonnano, A., and S. Wolf. 2017. *Resistance to the Neoliberal Agri-Food Regime: A Critical Analysis*. London: Earthscan/Routledge.

Borras, S. Jr, and J.C. Franco. 2010. "From Threat to Opportunity? Problems with the Idea of a 'Code of Conduct' for Land-Grabbing." *Yale Human Rights and Development Law Journal* 13 (2): 507–23.

Brandth, B., and M.S. Haugen. 2011. "Farm Diversification into Tourism: Implications for Social Identity?" *Journal of Rural Studies* 27 (1): 35–44. https://doi.org/10.1016/j.jrurstud.2010.09.002.

– 2014. "Embodying the Rural Idyll in Farm Tourist Hosting." *Scandinavian Journal of Hospitality and Tourism* 14 (2): 101–15. https://doi.org/10.1080/150 22250.2014.899136.

Bryden, J., O. Brox, and L. Riddoch. 2015. *Northern Neighbours: Scotland and Norway since 1800*. Edinburgh: Edinburgh University Press.

Burton, R.J.F., C. Kuczera, and G. Schwartz. 2008. "Exploring Farmers' Cultural Resistance to Voluntary Agri-Environmental Schemes." *Sociologia Ruralis* 48 (1): 16–37. https://doi.org/10.1111/j.1467-9523.2008.00452.x.

Burton R.J.F., and G. Schwarz. 2013. "Result-Oriented Agri-Environmental Schemes in Europe and Their Potential for Promoting Behavioural Change." *Land Use Policy* 30 (1): 628–41. https://doi.org/10.1016/j. landusepol.2012.05.002.

Burton, R.J.F., and G.A. Wilson. 2012. "The Rejuvenation of Productivist Agriculture: The Case for "Cooperative Neoproductivism." In Almås and Campbell, *Rethinking Agricultural Policy Regimes*, 51–72.

Cision. 2018. "58,000 to 80,000 Jobs Threatened in Canada in the Event That the Supply Management System Disappears for the Poultry and Egg Sectors Alone." La Coop fédérée, 19 January. https://www.newswire.ca/ news-releases/58000-to-80000-jobs-threatened-in-canada-in-the-event-that-the-supply-management-system-disappears-for-the-poultry-and-egg-sectors-alone-670134113.html.

Clapp, J. 2015. "Food Security and International Trade: Unpacking Disputed Narratives." Background paper prepared for FAO, The State of Agricultural Commodity Markets 2015–16. Food and Agriculture Organization of the United Nations, Rome.

Daugstad, K., K. Rønningen, and B. Skar 2006: "Agriculture as an Upholder of Cultural Heritage? Conceptualisations and Value Judgements – A Norwegian Perspective in International Context. *Journal of Rural Studies* 22 (2006): 67–81.

Dibden, J., C. Cocklin, and C. Potter. 2009. "Contesting the Neoliberal Project for Agriculture: Productivist and Multifunctional Trajectories in the European Union and Australia." *Journal of Rural Studies* 25 (3): 299–308. https://doi.org/10.1016/j.jrurstud.2008.12.003.

DutchNews.nl. 2015. "Dutch Pig Farmers and Farm Minister Make No Progress in Crisis Talks," 26 August. http://www.dutchnews.nl/news/archives/2015/08/ dutch-pig-farmers-and-farm-minister-make-no-progress-in-crisis-talks/.

Durand, G., and G. van der Huylenbroeck, eds. 2003. *Multifunctionality as a New Paradigm for European Agriculture and Rural Development*. Aldershot, UK: Ashgate.

European Commission. 2015. "The End of Milk Quotas." https://ec.europa.eu/agriculture/milk-quota-end_en.

European Parliament. 2015. *Extent of Land Grabbing in the EU*. Directorate General for Internal Policies, Policy Department B: Structural and Cohesion Policies. Brussels.

Eurostat. 2015. *Eurostat Regional Yearbook*. Luxembourg: Eurostat.

Forest Europe, UNECE, and FAO. 2011. *State of Europe's Forests 2011: Status and Trends in Sustainable Forest Management in Europe*. https://www.foresteurope.org/documentos/State_of_Europes_Forests_2011_Report_Revised_November_2011.pdf.

Fuller, R.M. 1987. "The Changing Extent and Conservation Interest of Lowland Grasslands in England and Wales: A Review of Grassland Surveys 1930–1984." *Biological Conservation* 40 (4): 281–300. https://doi.org/10.1016/0006-3207(87)90121-2.

GRAIN. 2014. "Hungry for Land: Small Farmers Feed the World with Less than a Quarter of All Farmland." 7 May. https://www.grain.org/article/entries/4929-hungry-for-land-small-farmers-feed-the-world-with-less-than-a-quarter-of-all-farmland.

Hageberg, E. 2012. *Oslo Slipp bonden fri! Gjeld og jordbruk i Danmark*. Report 5/2012 AgriAnalyse Oslo.

Hallmann, C.A., M. Sorg, E. Jongejans, H. Siepel, N. Hofland, H. Schwan et al. 2017. "More Than 75 Percent Decline over 27 Years in Total Flying Insect Biomass in Protected Areas." *PLoS ONE* 12 (10): e0185809. https://doi.org/10.1371/journal.pone.0185809.

Hambro, S. 2015. "Lokalmat selger som aldri før." 29 October. Dagens Næringsliv. https://www.dn.no/smak/2015/10/29/1508/Mat-og-drikke/lokalmat-selger-som-aldri-fr.

Hardman, M., and P. Larkham. 2014. *Informal Urban Agriculture: The Secret Lives of Guerrilla Gardeners*. Cham: Springer.

Havro, H.L., and A.S. Dypvik, eds. 2018. *Kven skal eige jorda? Ei bok om mat og makt*. Oslo: Res Publica.

Heggem, R. 2014. "Diversification and Re-Feminisation of Norwegian Farm Properties" *Sociologia Ruralis* 54 (4): 439–59. https://doi.org/10.1111/soru.12044.

Hillestad, M.E. 2016. *Den synlige hånd: USAs landbrukspolitikk*. Report 1/2016 AgriAnalyse. Oslo.

IPBES. 2018. *Summary for Policymakers of the Regional Assessment Report on Biodiversity and Ecosystem Services for Europe and Central Asia of the Intergovernmental Science-Policy Platform on Biodiversity and Ecosystem Services*. Edited by M. Fischer, M. Rounsevell, A. Torre-Marin Rando, A. Mader, A. Church, M. Elbakidze, V. Elias et al. Bonn: IPBES Secretariat.

Jack, B. 2016. *Agriculture and EU Environmental Law*. 2nd ed. London: Routledge.

Kalugina, Z.I. 2014. "Agricultural Policy in Russia: Global Challenges and the Viability of Rural Communities." *International Journal of Sociology of Agriculture and Food* 21 (1): 115–31.

Klimek, B., and H.O. Hansen. 2017. "Food Industry Structure in Norway and Denmark since the 1990s: Path Dependency and Institutional Trajectories in Nordic Food Markets." *Food Policy* 69:110–22. https://doi.org/10.1016/j.foodpol.2017.03.009.

Kvam, G.T., T. Magnus, and E.P. Stræte. 2014. "Product Strategies for Growth in Niche Food Firms." *British Food Journal* 116 (4): 723–32. doi.org/10.1108/bfj-06-2011-0168.

Leck, C., D. Evans, and D. Upton. 2014. "Agriculture: Who Cares? An Investigation of 'Care Farming' in the UK." *Journal of Rural Studies* 34: 313–25. https://doi.org/10.1016/j.jrurstud.2014.01.012

Lehmann, J., and S. Joseph. 2015. "Biochar for Environmental Management: An Introduction." In *Biochar for Environmental Management: Science, Technology and Implementation*, 2nd ed., edited by J. Lehmann and S. Joseph, 1–12. London : Routledge.

Levidow, L. 2015. "European Transitions towards a Corporate-Environmental Food Regime: Agroecological Incorporation or Contestation?" *Journal of Rural Studies* 40:76–89.

Lockie, S., and V. Higgins. 2007. "Roll-out Neoliberalism and Hybrid Practices of Regulation in Australian Agri-Environmental Governance." *Journal of Rural Studies* 23 (1): 1–11. https://doi.org/10.1016/j.jrurstud.2006.09.011.

McKeon, N. 2018. "Ein rettferdig og berekraftig matpolitikk." In *Kven skal eige jorda? Ei bok om mat og makt*, edited by H.L. Havro and A.S. Dypvik, 7–14. Oslo: Res Publica.

McMichael, P. 2009. "A Food Regime Genealogy." *Journal of Peasant Studies* 36 (1): 139–69. https://doi.org/10.1080/03066150902820354.

Midgley, A., and A. Renwick. 2012. "The Food Crisis and the Changing Nature of Scottish Agricultural Discourse." In Almås and Campbell, *Rethinking Agricultural Policy Regimes*, 123–46.

Ministry of Agriculture and Food. 2017. "Endringer i konsesjonsloven, jordloven og odelsloven trer i kraft" [Changes in Concession Act, Farmland Act and alludial law enforced]. 21 June. https://www.regjeringen.no/no/aktuelt/endringer-i-konsesjonsloven-jordloven-og-odelsloven-trer-i-kraft/id2558386/.

Morris, A.J., J. Hegarty, A. Báldi, and T. Robijns. 2011. "Setting Aside Farmland in Europe: The Wider Context." *Agriculture Ecosystems & Environment* 143 (1): 1–2. https://doi.org/10.1016/j.agee.2011.07.013.

Muirhead, B., and R. Almås. 2012. "The Evolution of Western Agricultural Policy since 1945." In Almås and Campbell, 23–49.

Muirhead, B., and H. Campbell. 2012. "The Worlds of Dairy: Comparing Dairy Frameworks in Canada and New Zealand in Light of Future Shocks to Food Systems." In Almås and Campbell, 147–68.

Murphy, S., D. Burch, and J. Clapp. 2012. *Cereal Secrets: The World's Largest Grain Traders and Global Agriculture*. Oxfam Research Reports. www.oxfam.org.

Nelson, J., and P. Stock. 2018. "Repeasantisation in the United States." *Sociologia Ruralis* 58 (1): 83–103. https://doi.org/10.1111/soru.12132.

Ng, M., T. Fleming, M. Robinson, B. Thomson, N. Graetz, C. Margono, E.C. Mullany, S. Biryukov, C. Abbafati, and S.F. Abera. 2014. "2013." *Lancet* 384 (9945): 766–81.

OECD. 2001. *Multifunctionality: Towards an Analytical Framework*. Paris: OECD.

Olsson, G.A., K. Rønningen, S.K. Hanssen, and S. Wehn. 2011: "The Interrelationship of Biodiversity and Rural Viability: Sustainability Assessment, Land Use Scenarios and Norwegian Mountains in a European Context." *Journal of Environmental Assessment Policy and Management* 13 (2): 251–84. https://doi.org/10.1142/s1464333211003870.

Ploeg, J.D. van der. 2018. *The New Peasantries*. 2nd ed. London. Routledge.

Ploeg, J.D. van der, J.C. Franco, and L.S.M. Borras Jr. 2015. "Land Concentration and Land Grabbing in Europe: A Preliminary Analysis." *Canadian Journal of Development Studies / Revue canadienne d'études du développement* 36 (2): 147–62. https://doi.org/10.1080/02255189.2015.1027673.

Ploeg, J.D. van der, A. Long, and J. Banks. 2002. *Living Countrysides: Rural Development Processes in Europe, the State of the Art*. Doetinchem: Elsevier.

Polanyi, K. (1944) 1957. *The Great Transformation: Political and Economic Origins of Our Time*. Boston: Beacon.

Potter, C., and M. Tilzey. 2005. "Agricultural Policy Discourses in the European Post-Fordist Transition: Neoliberalism, Neomercantilism and Multifunctionality." *Progress in Human Geography* 29 (5): 581–600. https://doi.org/10.1191/0309132505ph569oa.

Potts, S.G., V.L. Imperatriz-Fonseca, H.T. Ngo, M.A. Aizen, J.C. Biesmeijer, T.D. Breeze, L.V. Dicks et al. 2016. "Safeguarding Pollinators and Their Values to Human Well-Being." *Nature* 540:220–9. https://doi.org/10.1038/nature20588.

Reinert, E.S. 2017. *Global økonomi*. Oslo: Spartacus.

Rico, N.M., and A.M. Fuller. 2016. "Newcomers to Farming: Towards a New Rurality in Europe." *Documents d'Analisi Geografica* 62 (3): 531–51. https://doi.org/10.5565/rev/dag.376.

Rønningen, K. 1999. *Agricultural Policies and Countryside Management: A Comparative European Study*. Report 18/1999. Trondheim: Centre for Rural Research.

Rønningen, K., R. Burton, and A. Renwick. 2012." Approaches to and Interpretations of Multifunctional Agriculture – and Some Implications of a Possible Neo-Productivist Turn." In Almås and Campbell, 73–97.

Schweizerischer Bundesrat. 1984. *Sechster Landwirtschaftsbericht. 6. Bericht über die Lage der Schweizerischen Landwirtschaft und die Agrarpolitik des Bundes.* Bern.

Shucksmith, M., and K. Rønningen. 2011. "The Uplands after Neoliberalism? The Role of the Small Farm in Rural Sustainability." *Journal of Rural Studies* 27 (3): 275–87. https://doi.org/10.1016/j.jrurstud.2011.03.003.

SOER. 2015. *The European Environment: State and Outlook.* Copenhagen: European Environment Agency.

Soliva, R., K. Rønningen, I. Bella, P. Bezak, B.E. Flø, P. Marty, and C. Potter. 2008. "Envisioning Upland Futures: Stakeholder Responses to Scenarios for Europe's Mountain Landscapes." *Journal of Rural Studies* 24 (1): 56–71. https://doi.org/10.1016/j.jrurstud.2007.04.001.

Stroink, M., C.H. Nelson, and A.C. Davis. 2017. "Using a Complexity Lens to Address Local Food Dilemmas in Northern Ontario: The Viability of Crowdsourcing and Crowdfunding." In *Nourishing Communities,* edited by I. Knezevic, A. Blay-Palmer, C. Levkoe, P. Mount, and E. Nelson. Cham: Springer.

Swinbank, A. 2001. "Multifunctionality: A European Euphemism for Protection?" AG Conference Multifunctional Agriculture: A European Model. National Agricultural Centre, Stoneleigh, 29 November.

Trønderavisa. 2018." Prioriterer de små – men det kan straffe de store," 27 April.

Tscharntke, T., P. Batáry, and C.F. Dormann. 2011. "Set-Aside Management: How Do Succession, Sowing Patterns and Landscape Context Affect Biodiversity?" In "Set-Aside: Conservation Value in a Changing Agricultural Landscape," special issue, *Agriculture, Ecosystems & Environment* 143 (1): 37–44. https://doi.org/10.1016/j.agee.2010.11.025.

Turpin, N., L. Stapleton, E. Perret, C.M. van der Heide, G. Garrod, F. Brouwer, and D. Cairol. 2010. "Assessment of Multifunctionality and Jointness of Production." In *Environmental and Agricultural Modelling: Integrated Approaches for Policy Impact Assessment,* edited by F.M. Brouwer and M. van Ittersum, 11–35. Dordrecht: Springer.

Undheim, E.A. 2018. "Den leigde jords logikk." In *Kven skal eige jorda? Ei bok om mat og makt,* edited by H.L. Havro and A.S. Dypvik, 45–51. Oslo: Res Publica.

Verinis, J. 2014. The Black Swans of Greece's Global Countrysides. *Studia Universitatis Babes-Bolyai, Sociologia* 59 (2): 9–34.

Wehn, S., R.J.F. Burton, M. Riley, L. Johansen, K.A. Hovstad, and K. Rønningen. 2018. "Adaptive Biodiversity Management of Semi-Natural Hay Meadows: The Case of West-Norway." *Land Use Policy* 72:259–69. https://doi.org/10.1016/j.landusepol.2017.12.063.

5 "Indirect" Land Grabbing, Private Certification, and GlobalGAP

JACOB MUIRHEAD

Introduction

In the intervening years since the publication of the non-governmental organization (NGO) GRAIN's 2008 headline-grabbing report on land grabbing, land grabbing has become an umbrella term or catch-all phrase[1] for an explosion of literature on large-scale commercial land acquisitions and transactions as well as land speculation occurring primarily in the Global South. This massive growth has been for good reason. Estimates of the scope of this phenomenon suggest that land grabbing is happening on a very large scale. For example, data from the Land-Matrix project, a joint initiative run by a variety of civil society and intergovernmental organizations as well as the University of Bern estimate that since 2000, over 38 million hectares of land have switched hands through transnational land deals, with the majority of these deals occurring after 2006–7 (D. Hall 2011; Land Matrix 2015). Similarly, a 2010 report from the World Bank put the number at 45 million hectares grabbed (World Bank 2010). As a point of reference, 45 million hectares of land is roughly equivalent to the total land area of Spain and larger than Portugal, Greece, and the United Kingdom combined. As shocking as these estimates are, they should be taken only as a loose benchmark. As a number of authors have noted, it is exceptionally difficult, for example, to obtain credible, up-to-date information on land transfers, given the opacity of transactions, the number of exchanges that never materialize, or fail in short order, and the definitional conundrums associated with the determination of definitions of ownership (leasing, licensing, joint-domestic/ international investment, etc.), as well as what constitutes a fair exchange of land, and what constitutes land grabbing (Borras and Franco 2012, 36; D. Hall 2011, 837; D. Hall 2013, 1584–5; Locher and Sulle 2014; Scoones et al. 2013, 473; White et al. 2012, 620).

Initial academic and media attention on land grabs scrambled largely to quantify the scale of the phenomenon and to take stock broadly of the rationalities underlying it in what Edelman, Oya, and Borras Jr (2013, 1520) have described as the "making sense period." More recent research, however, has stressed the qualitative dimensions of land grabbing to emphasize, for example, the social, economic, and environmental impacts of the phenomenon in local contexts, but also in order to explore and understand the unique ways in which land grabs unfold and are resisted in different locations to affect people in different ways, depending on the institutions, structures, and actors involved (Millar 2015, 2). In addition, research has started to grapple with land grabbing within an analytical historical framework, which is attempting to situate the phenomenon within a broader political economy framework with deep historical roots (White et al. 2012).

This chapter seeks to contribute to both the qualitative and local impacts of land grabbing as well as contribute to the development of a historical analytical framework of land grabbing. It seeks to do this by closely tracing the interrelationship between the emergence of private business-to-business (B2B)[2] standards over the past two decades within an increasingly neoliberal global political economy and their impact on Ghana's export pineapple industry. As the global trading system has been opened up and the global agri-food system has become concentrated in a handful of powerful transnational corporations (TNCs), and food retailers in particular, these TNCs have developed and implemented B2B standards such as GlobalGAP in order to exert substantial governance power over agricultural supply chains that transcend borders and span the globe.

The organizational forms of B2B standards are distinct from other private standards in a couple of ways. First, B2B standards are industry-led initiatives with very strict membership requirements. In the case of GlobalGAP, the world's largest agricultural B2B standard, for example, only food retailers and producers are able to apply as members and participate directly in the development and alteration of standards. In this respect, such standard-setting bodies do not include the state or civil society stakeholders such as consumers, financial actors, or other NGOs as members. This differentiates these types of standard-setting bodies from other well-known private standard setters such as the Marine or Forest Stewardship Councils or the Roundtable on Sustainable Palm Oil, which are known as multi-stakeholder initiatives because of their more diverse and inclusive membership (Djama, Fouilleux, and Vagneron 2011, 185).

Second, in order to enhance the perceived legitimacy of B2B standards, these organizations often separate standard-setting and enforcement from standard monitoring. GlobalGAP sets the standards and determines the penalties for non-compliance but hires independent professional auditors trained on the GlobalGAP standard in order to monitor and ensure member compliance. This division of power between auditors and standard-setter is designed to increase the transparency and accountability of private governance.[3] It is through these B2B governance mechanisms that food retailers have used their privileged positions within the agricultural supply chain to set agricultural process standards that are voluntary in theory, but de facto mandatory, given monopsonist retailer control over access to lucrative international markets. Consequently, food retailers have become key governance actors within the supply chain involved in the regulation of global public goods such as food safety, proper working conditions, and environmental sustainability.

Based on these developments, this chapter will argue that the relatively recent introduction of a market requirement to meet private B2B standards in Ghana has played an essential role in restructuring the export pineapple market there, subsequently leading to the widespread failure of local Ghanaian smallholder producers and their replacement by large-scale, foreign-owned plantations such as Golden Exotics, a joint subsidiary of Compagnie Fruitière and, up until 2015, Dole Food Company. Very few academics have directly acknowledged the role of private B2B standards in the land grabs literature in any great detail, despite the influential role that standards have played over the past few decades in restructuring the global agri-food system, especially in the Global South.[4] Particularly relevant is how standards have promoted and privileged a very specific type of farming – large-scale, capital-intensive, Western industrial farming (Loconto and Dankers 2014; Maertens, Minten, and Swinnen 2012; Santacaloma and Casey 2011). I hope to show, in this respect, how the nature of dispossession, expulsion, and displacement need not necessarily occur through anything other than the "dull compulsion of economic relations" influenced and shaped to a large degree by the proliferation of private B2B agricultural standards (Edelman, Oya, and Borras Jr 2013, 1522–3).

In order to make this argument, the remainder of this chapter is divided into five sections. The first very briefly outlines GlobalGAP, which is the primary B2B standard analysed here. The second section develops a critical theoretical framework by weaving together literature from science, technology, and society studies, Foucauldian governmentality, and neocolonial studies. The purpose of this theoretical section is to deconstruct the perceived legitimacy and appeal of private B2B standards in order to politicize them as instruments or technologies of power. I argue that this appeal helps to institutionalize a particular Western mode of agricultural production in Africa and other parts of the world. I further argue that this mode of production disproportionately serves the interests of powerful transnational corporations, Western states, and consumer interests and indirectly helps to create the conditions for large-scale land acquisitions. The third section briefly delves into empirical studies illustrating the impact of private standards on smallholders in the Global South. Finally, following this broad theoretical and empirical overview of private B2B standards, the fourth section links the use of B2B standards with land grabbing by using Ghana as a case study to investigate more closely how GlobalGAP standards affected the Ghanaian pineapple industry. The fifth section concludes by suggesting future areas of research based on the analysis presented.

GlobalGAP: The World's Largest B2B Agricultural Standard-Setting Body

GlobalGAP was founded in 1997 by eleven British and Dutch food retailers as a non-profit organization and released its first set of industry standards for widespread industry adoption in 2001 (Bain 2010). As of July 2014, GlobalGAP boasted over 140,000 certified producers in 118 countries and had greatly expanded its retailer membership to forty-nine members. This expanded membership comprises some of the largest European and North American food retailers, including Carrefour, Wal-Mart, McDonalds, Metro, Sainsbury's, and Wegmans (GlobalGAP 2015b). Consequently, the GlobalGAP-regulated food market amounts to literally billions and billions of dollars and it is not uncommon for GlobalGAP certified retailers in conjunction to make up in excess of 80 per cent of total food sales volume in their countries of origin (Dannenberg and Nduru 2013, 49). Furthermore, in the intervening years since its founding, GlobalGAP has broadened its membership to include agricultural producers as well. These producer members can also be quite large and include producing giants such as Dole, Del Monte, McCain, and Driscolls (GlobalGAP 2018).

The organization is a retailer-led private standard-setting body that is process-oriented. This is in contrast to B2B standards focused on product standards that are interested in ensuring visible, standardized characteristics such as the size, weight, shape, or colour of the product at the point of sale. Process standards such as GlobalGAP are much more onerous, as they require producers to conform to specified standards throughout the entire process of production from farm to plate. The GlobalGAP standard itself is a "best practices" standard that includes

218 "control" points specifying best practice production standards in either labour conditions, worker or animal welfare, environmental sustainability, traceability and documentation, or food safety (GlobalGAP 2015a). Furthermore, these control points are divided into three separate categories: "major must" (87), "minor must" (113), and "recommendation" (18). In order to become certified, producers must meet all 87 major musts as well as 95 per cent of the 113 minor musts and must demonstrate action towards the eighteen recommendations. Generally the recommendations and minor musts apply to labour standards or environmental regulations, whereas the majority of major and minor musts deal with food safety, traceability, and documentation control points (GlobalGAP 2015a). In fact, together traceability, documentation, and food safety standards make up 163 of the total of 218, or 75 per cent of control points.

Towards a Critical Theoretical Framework of Private B2B Standards

The continuing growth and widespread adoption of B2B standards like GlobalGAP suggest they are broadly accepted as legitimate. But on what basis do private B2B standards secure legitimacy? Following this discussion, we can explore the ways in which B2B standards advance neocolonial and corporate interests in the Global South. Legitimacy is a central concept in global governance. It is closely associated with concepts such as effectiveness, authority, and power, and it is widely recognized as having critical importance to achieving governance stability and objectives (Cashore 2002; Fuchs and Kalfagianni 2010; Hachez and Wouters 2011). Indeed, there is a clear difference between the authoritative imposition of rules through the use of state violence or market power and the voluntary perception that the actions of an entity are appropriate, desirable, or proper within a socially constructed community (Bain, Higgins, and Ransom 2010, 163). Of course, the possession of structural or material power likely makes achieving and maintaining legitimacy easier, given that these resources often also confer on actors the ability to frame discourses, control information, and set agendas (Clapp and Fuchs 2009).

Typically, our conceptions of political authority and legitimacy are tied up in the democratic process and imagery of the state. At the domestic level, accountability and legitimacy are most often achieved in government through democratic representation, elections, and the consent of the people. Clear hierarchies of power within a sovereign territory clarify, discipline, and order the responsibilities and powers of various actors and work well alongside a system of checks and balances. In this respect, democracy has become the hallmark of what is considered to be legitimate government (Pierre and Peters 2005). A complicating factor in moving from the government of public goods to the private governance of public goods, as is the case with transnational agricultural B2B standards, is that private actors do not achieve their legitimate authority through the democratic process. In this respect, the international sphere is anarchical. There is no parallel to the territorially confined democratic legitimacy of most nation states at the global level (Abbott and Snidal 2010; Johansson 2013).

While there are various different strategies to pursue governance legitimacy outside the confines of the nation state, a common way in which private actors seek to achieve legitimacy is through a discourse of complexity, expert knowledge, and practices that appeal to techno-scientific norms and values (Bain, Ransom, and Worosz 2010; Hatanaka 2010). B2B standards usefully advance such a discourse, through the design of the governance process as well as the substantive rules outlined in standards themselves. For example, in the case of GlobalGAP, the regulatory system is separated between a private standard-setting body (GlobalGAP) and independent third-party "expert" auditors who audit farms, and certify their compliance with GlobalGAP control points outlined in their standard guidelines. Arguably, from a governance perspective, the effectiveness of the audit in ensuring compliance with the standard is not necessarily what confers governance legitimacy onto GlobalGAP. Rather, the performativity of the inspection is much more important in conferring organizational legitimacy by creating an environment of professionalism, transparency, and accountability whereby an "expert" auditor with specialized knowledge develops relationships with those being audited. Indeed, in many cases the formal criteria for education, training, and experience required to become an "expert" auditor for a standard-setting body like GlobalGAP are relatively low, and their ability to permanently alter production patterns of agriculture in the Global South are somewhat ambiguous (Bain, Ransom, and Worosz 2010, 163; Dannenberg and Nduru 2013; Hatanaka 2014; GlobalGAP 2015).

Equally important is the substantive content of standards themselves, which also appeal to techno-scientific values, such as objectivity, value-freedom, and neutrality. By and large, standards are developed by a community of experts to improve the efficiency of a system or enhance the quality of a product. In order to accomplish these objectives, standards rely on rules of measurement and grades, which are quantifiable, scientific, testable, and objective. By incorporating very clear and specific measurement elements into their design tied to objective, scientific testing, standards also clearly distinguish between what is best or optimal ,and everything else. In this respect, they construct a division between proper use of pesticides and improper use, proper documentation systems and improper systems, good growing techniques and bad, and so on.

Finally, a point unrelated to the techno-scientific aspects of standards, but rather their mobility as governance tools, is that private standards are perceived to have a comparative advantage in filling a regulatory gap that has developed alongside a proliferation of transnational interactions and relationships that transcend the borders of multiple nation states simultaneously. These new realities have led to a regulatory tension between transnational market relationships and state-based regulation that is territorially bounded and qualitatively different from place to place. Indeed, the underlying position (explicitly acknowledged or not) is that states have become over-burdened by the degree of integration within markets and are generally ill-suited to regulating the emerging transnational arena (Henson and Reardon 2005; Jahn, Schramm, and Spiller 2005, 56; Reardon and Farina 2002; Ruggie 2004). By contrast, private standard-setting bodies and B2B standards are not territorially limited, are capable of monitoring the entire supply chain, and can guarantee enforcement and inspections at any point in the production process, as well as anywhere in the world (Jahn, Schramm, and Spiller 2005, 56). In this respect, private standards gain legitimacy through the perception that they fill a regulatory space that has emerged in tandem with economic globalization that states cannot regulate as efficiently (or at all). An important point to highlight thus far is that when standards are presented from these techno-scientific or market-oriented perspectives, they are often viewed as apolitical governance tools created only to advance, optimize, and improve. They are the outcome of the work of politically disinterested experts who come together to create technically optimal solutions to recurring problems in the name of progress. As Higgins and Hallström note, "Standards apply scientific knowledge to the real world of getting things done and making things work." Standards are functional necessities, and this perception of value-free functionality affords them a type of legitimacy that is not tied to democratic principles such as participation, transparency, or accountability (Higgins and Hallström 2007, 688). Indeed, the elitist monopoly that experts have over access to determining standards resultant from their specialized knowledge, combined with the similar credibility that auditors possess in determining conformity, are both highly exclusionary and undemocratic.

The legitimacy of B2B standards can be further conceptualized by using Michel Foucault's concept of governmentality or political rationality. There have been several political rationalities over the past few centuries. These rationalities refer somewhat abstractly to political discourses that speak to an idealized schema for representing reality, analysing it and rectifying it in that image. In this respect, a political rationality usually takes a moral form and provides some account of the objects and people to be governed (Higgins and Hallström 2007, 689). Although Foucault is unclear exactly on how each political rationality comes into being, each rationality nevertheless comes with an intellectual paradigm attached that renders reality thinkable in specific ways and consequently depends on different technologies of government in order to operationalize concrete programs of action. In this respect, technologies of government can be thought of as the governmental levers through which subjects are disciplined and political rationalities are enacted into reality. Neoliberalism is the political rationality of the current era, and it is no secret that its guiding intellectual principles revolve around efficiencies of the market, the reduction of all social phenomena and choices to market-economic ones, and a rejection of state intervention and involvement.

Consequently, in an era where direct state regulation and intervention is eschewed and individual autonomy and freedom have been valorized, private standards are ideally situated as legitimate technologies of government capable of disciplining actors and regulating their behaviour. Indeed, as Higgins and Hallström (2007, 700) explain, "Their pretensions to autonomy, disinterested rationality and scientifically established truth-claims endear them to private and public interests simultaneously as legitimate forms of governance" in an era where neoliberalism as political rationality usually governs indirectly at a distance, or from the shadows of hierarchy rather than through direct intervention (Overdevest and Zeitlin 2014).

I have focused to this point on explaining how private B2B standards secure their legitimacy based on epistemic expertise on one hand, and the suitability of private standards as technologies of government in a neoliberal world on the other. Based on the analytic framework developed to this point, we can proceed to critically analyse private B2B standards. Specifically I will now advance a primary contention of this chapter: private agricultural B2B agricultural standards in their current form are insidious governance mechanisms rather than politically neutral, objective, or universally desirable. Private agricultural B2B standards have played an exceptionally important role in delegitimizing local agricultural practices across the Global South while directly exporting or transplanting the preferred farming practices of multinational retailers and Western states around the world through B2B standards. All the while, standards have been rolled out with little regard for fit, cultural resonance, local impact, or consequences, subsequently reshaping supply chains and creating the conditions for land grabbing (Campbell 2005, 16).

Given that B2B standards are private arrangements developed, maintained, and controlled by private actors and do not include the state as members, one might ask how these standards can be described as neocolonial. The governmentality framework presented above is helpful in articulating an answer. A key insight taken from Foucault is that political rationalities shape reality in specific ways and consequently enable or preclude specific ways of being based on the idealized or normative vision of reality projected. In the neoliberal era, certain technologies of government will be considered more legitimate than others. As already mentioned, neoliberal political rationality rejects the imposition of direct rule on objects of government, but rather operates by indirectly moulding subjectivities through more appropriate and decentralized means, which encourages self-regulation (as standards do). While this has, in many respects, led to a "hollowing out" of the state, as Nikolas Rose notes, "The perennial liberal rhetoric of small government by no means betokens governing less or abandonment of the will to govern" (Rose 1996, 53).

Indeed, instead of governing directly, governments have increasingly begun to govern through standards, where they can relay and translate their priorities and directives into action more effectively. In other words, private standards adapt well to the neoliberal way of doing business and consequently have increasingly been used as vessels of governance by governments themselves. Indeed, this is why we are increasingly seeing the emergence of private standards that have, in recent years, moved beyond the esoteric minutiae of standardizing the dimensions of elevator cars or seatbelt buckles, to standards regulating global public goods such as worker welfare, food safety, and the environment. In fact, private standards are increasingly replicating, mimicking, and benchmarking their own standards on important public international conventions and agreements already in place, such as the International Labour Organizations' Fundamental Principles and Rights at Work.

It is noteworthy within the context of agricultural governance that this extension of public government interests through private standards is extremely visible in the global regulation of agriculture and the emergence of private agricultural B2B standards. Indeed, a "market" for private B2B standards did not emerge organically and in isolation within the retailer industry, but rather was a closely coordinated response to the introduction of new British (in 1990) and European Union (in 2002) legislation enacted following numerous food scares throughout the 1990s (Van der Meulen 2013). These new laws were a political response to EU citizens' concern over food safety. As a result, regional EU and national member-state legislators greatly enhanced the liability of the private sector. They did so by downloading legal responsibility for food safety onto food retailers through the introduction of a legal concept known as "due diligence" (Van der Meulen 2013). This process ensured that food retailers had an obligation to perform their due diligence in ensuring that the food being sold in their stores was safe and traceable to its origin. In addition, it became illegal to bring food that was "unsafe" into the European Union.

Following this legislation, which has recently been mirrored by the United States to a large extent as well, in its updated 2011 Food Safety Modernization Act, retailers and producers began to take proactive steps to more closely monitor their supply chains and ensure the food they were being supplied was produced safely. In particular, retailers pursued this requirement primarily by developing the private B2B process standards that we have focused on in this chapter, including GlobalGAP, which articulated very specific ways for growing, processing, documenting, and transporting a variety of fresh food products to European and North American markets. As Aasprong (2013, 92) notes in relation to the development of B2B standards in the UK specifically, a key factor in the rapid growth of retailer-led private standards from the early 1990s was the threat that if retailers did not do more to protect the integrity and safety of their supply chains, then governments would force them to do so. The UK Food Safety Act of 1990, for example, established financial and custodial penalties for a variety of acts, including those that render food injurious to health or that mislead consumers. Indeed, legislators in the Global North have begun to legally recognize the legitimacy of private standards and standard-setting bodies in legislation and reference them as important transnational regulators. In tandem, an increasingly specific set of processes outlined in B2B standards and based primarily on Western farming practices have been institutionalized as the dominant representation of safe food within global agricultural markets (Van der Meulen 2013).

A final indication of the close relationship many Global North states have with private B2B standards can be seen in their defence of these institutions at the World Trade Organization (WTO). Private B2B standards are an important trade issue for many countries in the Global South who argue that meeting the certification requirements of B2B standards are so expensive that they act like a non-tariff trade barrier to their agricultural products (Wouters and Hachez 2012, 259). Consequently, states in the Global South, such as St Vincent and the Grenadines, have threatened to bring a case against private agricultural B2B bodies to the WTO's arbitration panel based on their violation of the Agreement on the Application of the Sanitary and Phytosanitary Measures (SPS Agreement) of the WTO. The SPS Agreement was created in 1994 to strike a balance between a county's right to protect human, animal, and plant life, while simultaneously ensuring that states did not use these measures as technical barriers to trade in order to protect their own agricultural industries (Huige 2011, 177).

In order to accomplish this objective, the SPS lays out a specific and limited number of cases where signatories are allowed to impose restrictions on international trade for animal, human, or plant safety. Specifically, parties to the SPS Agreement must ensure that the requirement to limit trade is justified on the basis of scientific evidence of potential health risks and must also demonstrate that their proposed solution is the least trade-restrictive option available to them (Stanton 2012, 236). Signatories of the SPS Agreement also collectively agree to recognize public intergovernmental standards found in the United Nations Codex Alimentarius standards as the baseline for scientifically justified food safety standards. Nearly every country in the world is a signatory to this agreement. It is obvious from the wording of the SPS Agreement that its intent has been to harmonize food safety standards across countries and specifically to remove the ability for states to protect their agricultural industries through technical manipulations. What parties likely did not anticipate in 1994 during the initial creation of the agreement was the concentration that would develop in the market among retailers, and the subsequent importance of private standards as regulatory mechanisms for agricultural governance. If the *private* standards of today were adopted nationally as *public* standards, they would be illegal according to the SPS Agreement.

Regardless, the issue of regulating private standards has been on the SPS Agreement agenda of the WTO since 2005, although with virtually no progress (Committee on Sanitary and Phytosanitary Measures 2014). In this respect, a major reason so little progress has been made is the clear interests of powerful European and North American countries who have been vocal defenders of private B2B standard-setting bodies. Over the years, they have been consistent in maintaining their support for B2B standards, have forestalled committee discussions on private standards within international organizations, including the WTO,

Food and Agriculture Organization, the United Nations Conference on Trade and Development, and the UN's Codex Alimentarius, and have argued against any kind of regulation of B2B standards by states or international organizations (Committee on Sanitary and Phytosanitary Measures 2014).

The shared history and close relationship at the national and regional level between private retailer–led B2B standards and public legislators in the EU and North America certainly blur the common distinctions many make between public and private regulation. Indeed, private agricultural B2B standards should be understood as closely shaped by and associated with the EU and increasingly the preferences of other Global North countries as well as transnational retailers concerned with market reputation and legal liability, rather than in isolation as industry initiatives (Campbell 2005, 3).

Under the guise of objectivity, functional necessity, and good agricultural practice, certification with B2B standards of all kinds, but especially GlobalGAP, has become a ubiquitous requirement for agricultural exports beyond local markets. Yet arguably B2B standards are better understood as a *political response* to food safety concerns and the collapse of confidence of European citizens in their public food safety institutions. Indeed, in many respects, the emergence of private B2B standards was an exceptionally political process. As many have noted, despite broad claims to ensuring agricultural sustainability through commitment to strong social and environmental protection and food safety, GlobalGAP standards are largely effective in ensuring food safety in very rigid terms and demonstrate less concern for sustainability in a more holistic sense (Bain, Higgins, and Ransom 2013; Busch 2007; Campbell 2005).

It is important to emphasize that none of this is to say that the science behind agricultural B2B standards outlining best practices for food safety does not lead to the production of safer food when the prescriptions are followed. However, what is most troublesome about B2B standards such as GlobalGAP is the self-interested and selective manner in which they choose to apply their standards. For example, Bain (2010) makes this point forcefully through a study of the Chilean grape industry and GlobalGAP standards. Specifically, in the case of pesticides, the GlobalGAP standard demands that producers test their food for minimum residue levels (MRL) and comply with a rigorous set of pesticide standards, including documenting what type of pesticides have been used, on what dates, in what quantities, who applied them, what their expertise was, how they were applied, for what reason, whether there was a chance of cross-contamination with other crops, and so forth. All food safety requirements related to pesticides are labelled as "major musts" as laid out in the agricultural control points, meaning they must be followed if producers are to obtain GlobalGAP certification. In stark contrast with these rigorous food safety standards for pesticide use on crops, there is very little content within the standard that requires producers to demonstrate specific measures to ensure worker health, safety, and welfare in the application of pesticides. In fact, it has been argued that the very business strategies of retailers, such as just-in-time delivery and exceptionally slim profit margins, serve to create and sustain labour conditions that are precarious and unsafe As Bain explains, "One of the central health and safety issues facing farm workers everywhere is their acute and chronic exposure to pesticides. While GLOBALGAP *requires* the testing of pesticide residue levels on plants it only *recommends* that workers who apply pesticides undergo an annual health check. Furthermore, whether the results of these health checks demonstrate worker exposure to pesticides or not is irrelevant to meeting the standard. Most notably absent here is any requirement that auditors should interview workers to verify that the standards are being met" (Bain 2010, 180; emphasis added).

When looking past the "performativity" of standards as purely objective instruments of scientific progress, and into the actual substance and enactment of these standards in practice, the political dynamics and power asymmetries these standards help to legitimize come into focus. Indeed, standards are shaped by the political and strategic considerations of the standard-makers themselves (food retailers, Global North states, and consumer interests) often at the expense of Global South stakeholders who must comply and be governed by these standards, yet hold no power or control over their development. The work of Latour (1999) has been central in problematizing such appeals to techno-science by powerful actors. As he explains, the use of science as objective, neutral, and value-free is often tied up in modern sentiments (sometimes with good reason) towards objective truth. Yet often it is used as a weapon to disguise what are essentially political and moral questions – including, in this case, who should be involved in the decision-making process of standard setting, how the costs of certification should be shared, what goals should be prioritized, what is valued, what definition of "sustainable" should be accepted as normative, and conversely, what is bad agricultural practice and who should be excluded from the decision-making process.

The GlobalGAP case demonstrates that under the guise of scientific standards, major food retailers, supported and influenced by powerful northern states, pursue their strategic interests with limited concern for these moral questions (Bain, Higgins, and Ransom 2013, 4–5). This is not to say that their priority on enhancing food safety is sinister or misplaced. This is a laudable goal. What is problematic, however, is the exclusionary and self-interested manner in which B2B standards, backed by powerful state actors, pursue this goal. Subsequently, these standards then contribute to the constitution of legitimate, yet highly unequal institutions which perpetuate a Eurocentric ideal of sustainable farming that is exceptionally expensive, and requires high levels of technological sophistication and know-how such as access to computers, the internet, knowledge of Microsoft Suite, and so forth (Campbell 2005, 15). In this respect, there are parallels between the colonial and mercantilist agricultural relationships of the past and the emerging structure of agricultural relationships in the present.

Indeed, these standards increasingly preclude the possibility of local smallholders in the Global South from gaining access to privileged Global North markets, and production is consequently becoming increasingly concentrated in large-scale, mechanized, and sophisticated Western-owned farms in the Global South. The structure of this system is not dissimilar to the colonial legacies and dependencies of old. Perhaps somewhat of a stretch, given the despicable violence and brutality of Europe's colonial history in Africa, Peluso and Lund (2011, 672) nevertheless argue that the primary novelty of land grabs today, as opposed to in the past, are "the new mechanisms of land control, their justifications and alliances for 'taking back' the land, as well as the political economic context of neoliberalism that dominates this particular stage of the capitalist world system." I would argue that indirectly, private B2B agricultural standards are exactly the "new mechanisms of land control" of which Peluso and Lund speak. By establishing institutional fences around the production of agricultural products that restrict smallholder access to massive agricultural export markets, private B2B standards help to secure access for the actors in control (672). Presented in this manner, the rhetoric associated with B2B standards as sustainable and objective loses much of its credibility (675).

GlobalGAP: Its Empirical Impact

A primary issue with GlobalGAP standards from a smallholder perspective is that the standards are too technically complex and too expensive to meet (Brown 2005, 143; Graffham, Karehu, and Macgregor 2007; Ouma 2010, 199). The costs of B2B standards compliance can be divided into fixed non-recurring costs and recurring costs. Non-recurring costs include investments in farm infrastructure, training, and certification to be able to achieve compliance. Recurrent costs include recertification, monitoring, training, labour, equipment, and MRL analysis, alongside soil and water quality analysis. Moreover, while not technically required, technological investment in computers, printers, and the Internet make the onerous documentation and traceability requirements easier to comply with, but also represent significant costs.

Although few empirical studies have estimated the exact costs for smallholder farmers in a variety of different export industries in the Global South, data do exist. For example, the International Institute for the Environment and Development (IIED) conducted an empirical case study on the costs of GlobalGAP certification on smallholders in the primary agricultural export industries of Kenya, Zambia, and Uganda following the introduction of GlobalGAP standards to many African markets in the early 2000s. Although the recurrent and non-recurrent costs varied from country to country, nowhere could the average smallholder afford to acquire and maintain GlobalGAP certification without the vast majority of those costs being paid by donors (whether NGOs, FDA, local government, or private sector) (IIED 2008, 11).

Indeed, because GlobalGAP offers no price premium on goods and promises only access to the slim profit margins found in global markets, the average maintenance costs of certification exceeded half of a smallholder's yearly income in all three countries (IIED 2008, 11). As a point of empirical reference, in Zambia, where compliance was most expensive, the average initial start-up costs of certification for a smallholder was over $6,500 in 2006, and recurring costs totalled over $1,400 per year. In Kenya and Uganda, both the recurrent and non-recurrent costs were lower, but still unaffordable (11). As a result of these certification requirements, the IIED estimates following the introduction of GlobalGAP standards between 2000 and 2006, that approximately 97 per cent of smallholders in Zambia exited the export business for baby corn, 60 per cent of smallholders in Kenya left the production of green beans, and 40 per cent of Ugandan small-scale farmers exited from the production of chili beans (11). Explained differently, this meant that over 5,500 smallholders left the high-value green bean export industry in Kenya following the introduction of GlobalGAP standards. Graffham, Karehu, and Macgregor estimate that at its height, this industry would have provided a livelihood for approximately 70,000 smallholders and their dependents (Graffham, Karehu, and Macgregor 2007, 27–8). Similarly, they note that in Kenya, the "threshold" size of a farm had to be two to ten hectares in order to be able to entertain the possibility of affording compliance with GlobalGAP certification. The average smallholder farm in Kenya is approximately 0.5 hectares (12). Another GlobalGAP impact case study put out by the Food and Agriculture Organization in 2011 noted similarly inaccessible costs for smallholders in South Africa, Malaysia, and Chile as those presented by the 2008 IIED study of Kenya, Zambia and Uganda (IIED 2008; Santacaloma and Casey 2011).

This evidence suggests the exclusionary impacts of private B2B standards on smallholders, who make up the majority of farms in the Global South. As Swinnen, Colen, and Maertens (2013) recognize that, increasingly, large exporters engage in fully vertically integrated estate production in which wage labourers are hired to work at large-scale plantations. The primary reason for this shift, according to their research, was because the largest companies wanted to change their procurement systems as part of a strategy to become GlobalGAP certified (303).

Land Grabbing by Other Means: The Introduction of GlobalGAP Standards and Dispossession in Ghana's Pineapple Export Industry

Throughout the mid-1980s to the early 2000s, Ghana's export industry for fresh whole pineapple was viewed as an exceptional success story, and pineapple was Ghana's major horticulture export product (Whitfield 2011). The increases in production coincide with the adoption of structural adjustment programs and a series of policy changes towards economic liberalization since 1983 in Ghana, as well as the broadly market liberalizing impacts of the WTO following 1995 (Takane 2004, 30). This latter development in particular opened up access to large and lucrative European markets where there is a demand for fresh fruit and vegetables all year round. For Ghana, pineapple emerged as the product of choice for producers, and it continued to dominate fresh fruit and vegetable exports into the twenty-first century (Whitfield 2011, 12). Growth rates within the industry were impressive. Between 1995 and 2004, the export tonnage of pineapples increased by over 500 per cent, with the vast proportion destined for Europe. At its peak in 2004, Ghana exported over 70,000 tonnes of fresh pineapple, which equates to 10 per cent of European market share (Gatune et al. 2013, 12). With over 70 per cent of Ghana's population employed in the agricultural sector, this growth was exceptionally important for Ghanaian development (Ouma, Boeckler, and Lindner 2013, 230).

Indeed, part of what was so impressive about this emerging market for pineapple exports, from a development perspective, was how accessible the industry was for smallholders (Amanor 2012, 743; Fold and Gough 2008, 1692; GRAIN 2010; Takane 2004). This partly had to do with the low start-up costs associated with pineapple production in Ghana, which in turn led to a competitive price point for smallholders selling to exporters and eventually European retailers (Danielou and Ravry 2005). Moreover, the production methods required for pineapples were relatively simple and created low barriers to entry. Finally, B2B private standard-setting bodies still under development at the time had yet to gain de facto control over access to European markets. This would not occur until 2003–5, when GlobalGAP standards became mandatory for fresh fruit and vegetable exports destined for European markets (Fold and Gough 2008, 1688).

A brief look at the composition of the export industry for pineapples in Ghana indicates the diversity of the sector. Near the end of the 1990s and into the early 2000s, smallholders contributed approximately 50 per cent of export volumes to exporters (Gatune et al. 2013, 12). In this respect, Whitfield (2012, 309) estimates that pineapple production for export was split between approximately twelve large farms (300–700 ha), about forty medium farms (20–150 ha), and possibly as many as 10,000 smallholders (0.2–10 ha). Similarly, there were about sixty-five active domestic and transnational exporters selling to European markets, and only two of these companies exported more than 2,000 tonnes (Amanor 2012, 743; Gatune et al. 2013, 12).

In 2003–5 crisis hit the Ghanaian pineapple industry. There has been a great deal written on this crisis already, and so it will be mentioned here only briefly (Amanor 2012; Fold 2008; Fold and Gough 2008; Gatune et al. 2013; Whitfield 2012). Important for the purposes of this chapter, however, are two interrelated points. The first point is that in 2003, a Del Monte intellectual property patent became void, and a new pineapple variety known as the MD2 was picked up by a number of major transnational pineapple producers. From a marketing perspective, this variety had some advantages, including golden colour, long shelf life, sweet taste, and uniform size that allowed for closer storage on retailer shelves and slices of uniform size. Del Monte had developed this variety in Costa Rica during the previous decade, and it quickly became the most popular pineapple variety in North American supermarkets. Unfortunately, Ghana grew a different variety of pineapple known as the Sweet Cayenne, which sold less well following the defeat of Del Monte's patent in 2003. In the aftermath of this patent defeat, the world's largest fruit producers, including Dole, Chiquita, and Fyffe, in addition to Fresh del Monte, all backed the MD2 variety in 2003–4, and shelf space for Sweet Cayenne evaporated almost completely by 2005 (Fold 2008, 106). The shift in consumer preference towards the MD2 variety was devastating to the Ghanaian pineapple industry and has been discussed in detail within the literature (Fould and Gough 2008; Ouma 2010; Whitfield 2012). What has received less attention, however, was the introduction of de facto mandatory requirements to meet GlobalGAP standards for pineapple producers in Ghana in 2003.

Indeed, at the same time that the world's major retailers switched to the MD2 variety, they also began to require all fresh fruits and vegetables from Ghana be GlobalGAP certified (Amanor 2012; Whitfield 2012). In this respect, these two separate events were pro-cyclical. With very limited finite resources and next to no access to financial actors or loans, smallholders could come nowhere close to making the switch from one pineapple variety to another while at the same time meeting costly GlobalGAP requirements. Each requirement on its own required large amounts of financial investment and technical sophistication, and together they served to close off the market to smallholders completely (Whitfield 2012). The restructuring of pineapple production in Ghana in the intervening years has been remarkable. The most recent data available put out by the FAO in 2013 reveal that although Ghana is beginning to recover export volume (46,000 tonnes in 2011, down from a peak of 71,000 tonnes in 2004), the way in which this tonnage is produced is quite different (FAO 2018). It is estimated that currently thirty large farms and fewer than 200 smallholders are now engaged in commercial MD2 pineapple production for export in Ghana (Gatune et al. 2013). In this respect, Gatune et al. (2013, 16) estimate that smallholders now supply for less than 10 per cent of the export market, down from 50 per cent in 2004.

A key point in this narrative of pineapple restructuring is that many of the large farms that are producing in Ghana today are foreign-owned or joint-local/foreign ventures that arrived in Ghana either during or after the 2003–5 pineapple crisis. Golden Exotics is the largest of these new plantations and is a subsidiary of the French transnational Compagnie Fruitière, and up until 2015 was also a subsidiary of American giant Dole, the world's largest fresh produce company. Golden Exotics arrived in Ghana in August 2003 by acquiring a locally owned but failing operation known as Paradise Farms, just as the pineapple crisis was reaching its peak (Danilou and Ravry 2005, 21–2). Golden Exotics also arranged to lease parts of the surrounding territory for expansion. Because the majority of small-scale farmers inhabiting this land had lived on the basis of a customary system of land tenure that operated outside "official" legal discourses around the right to the land, the chief and elders have legally approved private fifty-year lease-holds on thousands of hectares of local land to Golden Exotics as if it were uninhabited

Table 5.1. Change in Ghana's Pineapple Exportation 2004–2013

2004	2013
Approximately 40–50 per cent smallholder production for export market	Approximately 5–10 per cent smallholder production for export
Average size of plantation of 150 hectares	Average size of plantation of 600 hectares
71,000 tonnes produced	46,000 tonnes produced (2011)
65 pineapple exporters	14 pineapple exporters
Smallholder cooperative Farmapine is largest pineapple producer, accounting for 25 per cent of all pineapples exports (went out of business in 2006)	Golden Exotics produces nearly 25 per cent of all fresh pineapples for export
50 per cent of producers and exporters EurepGAP/Global GAP certified	100 per cent of producers and exporters GlobalGAP certified
60,000 people directly employed in pineapple production	Approximately 15,000 people directly employed in pineapple production

(Fold and Gough 2008, 1693; Suzuki, Jarvis, and Sexton 2011, 1615). Also important to note is that the land leased to Golden Exotics was some of the most ideally situated in Ghana. It is quite close to Ghana's capital of Accra, as well as the country's only modern port with refrigerated storing. This refrigeration is essential to modern supply chains if they wish to ship fresh produce to European markets (Fold and Gough 2008, 1693).

A summary of the primary changes that have taken place in the pineapple industry can be seen in table 5.1.

The transformation of the pineapple sector is remarkable. Where it was once a relatively diverse sector, it is now highly concentrated and vertically integrated among less than a dozen large-scale producer/ exporters. Unsurprisingly, these producers grow the MD2 variety, and sector compliance against GlobalGAP certification has gone from 50 per cent in 2004 to 100 per cent in 2012 (Jaeger 2008, 6; Whitfield 2012, 317). In order to present some of these changes more coherently, table 5.2 indicates the date of incorporation, ownership, and size of Ghana's twelve largest pineapple producers.

As the table indicates, many of the largest pineapple plantations in Ghana emerged after the 2003 crisis. In addition, although a number of locally owned plantations still exist (running contrary to the arguments presented in this chapter), table 5.2 is slightly misleading. In production capacity, the two largest plantations by far in terms of exports

Table 5.2. Incorporation Date, Ownership, Staff Strength, and Size of Ghana's Largest Pineapple Producers

Company Name	Date of incorporation	Ownership	Staff strength	Size (ha)
*Golden Exotics	2003	French/American	2,403	3,500
*HPW	2006	Swiss/Ghanaian	1,335	8,400
Koranco Farms	1980s	Ghanaian	230	2,500
Prudent Exports	1990s	Ghanaian	160	2,000
Chartered Impex	2001	Ghanaian	150	2,000
*Unifruit Ltd	2007	German/Ghanaian	150	1,800
*Gold Coast Fruits	2005	Ghanaian/German	306	1,230
*Volta River Estate Ltd	1988	Ghanaian/Dutch	100	1,000
*Bio Exotica Ltd	2003	Dutch/Ghanaian	80	1,000
Greenspan Farms	?	Ghanaian	75	750
Mashaco Farms	1990s	Ghanaian	45	483
Pioneer Quality Farms	?	?	50	400
TOTAL			4,934	25,063

* Foreign involvement.

are Golden Exotics and HPW. These companies are both GlobalGAP certified, are owned wholly or extensively by foreign investors, and arrived in Ghana following the 2003 pineapple crisis. Together these two producers account for over 50 per cent of fresh pineapple exports from Ghana. Moreover, these two ventures together occupy over 10,000 hectares of some of the best agricultural land in Ghana.

How has the implantation of transnational companies like Golden Exotics been perceived by local smallholders whose land has been given away? A study by Fold and Gough (2008) investigating the impact of Golden Exotics's arrival on local communities indicates smallholders have been devastated. Smallholders have lost their rights to the land they and their families have farmed for generations. Moreover, because these farmers worked the land without ever obtaining an official deed to delineate and enclose the land as theirs, they have not even received compensation, as they hold no "formal" legal claim over the land. As Fold and Gough (2008, 1694) note, "Not only are they losing their livelihoods, but in some cases are also losing their homes where small settlements located in the middle of new plantations are removed. Although some can find employment as labourers on the pineapple farms, many of those interviewed considered this to be the last option as the work is hard and the hours long. Consequently, some inhabitants are moving away in search of land to farm elsewhere and others are struggling to find alternative sources of income, hampered by the lack of electricity."

The Ghanaian pineapple case study provides an empirical reference point for the theoretical framework outlined above. In this respect, it is worthwhile to look more closely at the Ghanaian town of Pokrom. Pokrom was a town built around the pineapple export industry. Since the early 1980s, smallholders there had grown pineapples for export, and the area had flourished as a result. Pineapple production was so central to this community that inhabitants' identities eventually formed in large part around farming and pineapple production. As the chief of Pokrom was quoted as saying cited in Fold and Gough (2008, 1691), "If you were born in Pokrom, you will be a pineapple farmer." At the time the village's chief made this statement, Pokrom was still an exceptionally vibrant, affluent, and busy community. Following the introduction of standards and the switch in pineapple variety to the MD2 in 2003–5, however, the community has declined significantly. The streets in Pokrom are no longer vibrant. Indeed, as GlobalGAP standards were introduced as a requirement for access to most European markets, the community's way of life, practised for over twenty-five years was extinguished almost overnight. Very few smallholders remain in Pokrom. Instead, many of these workers have abandoned their land, migrated to the cities, or moved to work on the nearby plantations of Golden Exotics.

The analysis as presented to this point is all to argue that the recent concern with land grabbing by new players in agricultural markets detracts from relatively well-established and coercive practices articulated clearly in private B2B standards. These standards are resulting in a complex, unrelentingly gradual process of ruin of family farms and dispossession from below.

Conclusion

The objective of this chapter was to present an alternative conception of land grabbing through private B2B standards. Private B2B agricultural standards have proliferated enormously over the past few decades. Their appeal as governance mechanisms in a neoliberal era, combined with their ability to appeal to techno-scientific language, has conferred substantial governmental legitimacy and authority on them. Consequently, they now act as key governance mechanisms regulating agriculture in meaningful ways by controlling access to the largest and most valuable global agricultural markets. Yet if we move beyond the thin veneer of appeals to scientism, we can see private B2B standards for what they are – effective, yet also highly political tools of governance. These mechanisms serve to advance neocolonial and corporate interests through their ability to draw agricultural producers in the Global South into a particularly rigid, technically complex, and expensive form of agricultural production. Often the cost and technical complexity of B2B agricultural standards like GlobalGAP force smallholders out of export markets and create the conditions necessary for land grabbing and agricultural dispossession. I argue that this is what occurred in Ghana's export pineapple sector. As recently as 2003, this sector was characterized by smallholder access and participation. Following the introduction of GlobalGAP standards to Ghana and a global switch in pineapple variety, however, smallholders were ejected from the market for lack of finance and technical know-how. These smallholders have subsequently been replaced by a number of multinational producers and exporters exemplified by the arrival of Golden Exotics to Ghana in 2003. The indirect role of private B2B standards in facilitating land grabbing can be seen most clearly through the arrival of this transnational corporation in particular.

Through this chapter, I hope I have contributed broadly to the land grabbing literature and land grabbing as a phenomenon. In terms of future research, the type of land grabbing described here has very specific implications for labour, gender, and social relationships more broadly. For example, what happens to those smallholders who are dispossessed? Are most employed on plantations? How might gender relationships and family dynamics be redefined through such processes? If smallholders are the most significantly affected by private standards, how do standards and land dispossession affect inequality within communities?

From a different perspective, does the agricultural product matter to land grabbing? Do the product properties of certain agricultural products lend themselves to land grabbing while others do not? On the basis of the analysis presented above, these areas of future research are necessary for a more complete understanding of land grabbing through private B2B standards.

NOTES

1 The use of the term somewhat freely by a variety of actors, including activists, academics, and media, although provocative and attention-grabbing, has resulted in definitional muddiness about the clarity, precision, and

significance of the term. See, for example, Edelman (2013); Edelman, Oya, and Borras Jr (2013); D. Hall (2013); R. Hall (2011).

2   Standards as governance mechanisms have proliferated within the agri-food system, as well as within global governance systems more broadly in the past few decades. There are numerous different kinds of private standards that incorporate a variety of different actors with diverse governance objectives. The arguments made within this chapter apply uniquely to B2B private standards, although some of the arguments may apply to other types of private standards as well.

3   Although the neutrality of independent auditing organizations in relation to standard setters has been questioned within the literature, based in particular on the conflict of interest of auditors in maximizing a client base for increased profit vs their professional duty to audit rigorously. See, for example, Lytton and McAllister (2014).

4   For exceptions, however, see Amanor (2012); De Schutter (2011); D. Hall (2011); and Ouma (2010).

REFERENCES

Aasprong, H. 2013. "Recreating the Banana Grower: The Role of Private Certification Systems in the Windward Islands Banana Industry." *Culture Unbound: Journal of Current Cultural Research* 4 (4): 721–45. https://doi.org/10.3384/cu.2000.1525.124721.

Abbott, K.W., and D. Snidal. 2010. "International Regulation without International Government: Improving IO Performance through Orchestration." *Review of International Organizations* 5 (3): 315–44. https://doi.org/10.1007/s11558-010-9092-3.

Amanor, K.S. 2012. "Global Resource Grabs, Agribusiness Concentration and the Smallholder: Two West African Case Studies." *Journal of Peasant Studies* 39 (3–4): 731–49. https://doi.org/10.1080/03066150.2012.676543.

Bain, C. 2010. "Governing the Global Value Chain: GlobalGAP and the Chilean Fruit Industry." *International Journal of Sociology of Agriculture and Food* 17 (1): 1–23.

Bain, C., V. Higgins, and E. Ransom. 2013. "Private Agri-Food Standards: Contestation, Hybridity and the Politics of Standards." *International Journal of Sociology of Agriculture and Food* 20 (1): 1–10.

Bain, C., E. Ransom, and M.R. Worosz. 2010. "Constructing Credibility: Using Technoscience to Legitimate Strategies in Agrifood Governance." *Journal of Rural Social Sciences* 25 (3): 160–92.

Borras, S., and J. Franco. 2012. "Global Land Grabbing and Trajectories of Agrarian Change: A Preliminary Analysis." *Journal of Agrarian Change* 12 (1): 34–59. https://doi.org/10.1111/j.1471-0366.2011.00339.x.

Brown, O. 2005. "Supermarket Buying Power, Global Commodity Chains and Smallholder Farmers in the Developing World." In *Human Development Report 2005*, edited by H.D.R. Office, 1–32. New York: United Nations Development Programme.

Busch, L. 2007. "Performing the Economy, Performing Science: From Neoclassical to Supply Chain Models in the Agrifood Sector." *Economy and Society* 36 (3): 437–66. https://doi.org/10.1080/03085140701428399.

Campbell, H. 2005. "The Rise and Rise of EurepGAP: European (Re)Invention of Colonial Food Relations." *International Journal of Sociology of Agriculture and Food* 13 (2): 6–19.

CanadaGAP. 2015. "Overview." April. http://www.canadagap.ca/uploads/file/English/Publications/Overview%20Presentation/CanadaGAP%20Overview%20April%202015%20ENG.pdf.

Cashore, B. 2002. "Legitimacy and the Privatization of Environmental Governance: How Non-State-Market-Driven (NSMD) Governance Systems Gain Rule-Making Authority." *Governance* 15 (4): 503–29. https://doi.org/10.1111/1468-0491.00199.

Clapp, J., and D. Fuchs. 2009. *Corporate Power in Global Agri-Food Governance.* New York: MIT Press.

Committee on Sanitary and Phytosanitary Measures. 2014. *Report of the Co-Stewards of the Private Standards E-Working Group on Action.* Committee on Sanitary and Phytosanitary Measures/SPS/55.

Danielou, M., and C. Ravry. 2005. "The Rise of Ghana's Pineapple Industry: From Successful Takeoff to Sustainable Expansion." World Bank Africa Region Working Paper Series no. 93.

Dannenberg, P., and G.M. Nduru. 2013. "Practices in International Value Chains: The Case of the Kenyan Fruit and Vegetable Chain beyond the Exclusion Debate." *Tijdschrift voor economische en sociale geografie* 104 (1): 41–56. https://doi.org/10.1111/j.1467-9663.2012.00719.x.

De Schutter, O. 2011. "How Not to Think of Land-Grabbing: Three Critiques of Large-Scale Investment in Farmland." *Journal of Peasant Studies* 38 (2): 249–79. https://doi.org/10.1080/03066150.2011.559008.

Djama, M., E. Fouilleux, and I. Vagneron. 2011. "Certifying and Benchmarking: A Governmentality Approach to Sustainability Standards in the Agro-Food Sector." In *Governing through Standards: Origins, Drivers and Limitations*, ed. S. Ponte, P. Gibbon, and J. Vestergaard, 184–209. New York: Palgrave Macmillan.

Edelman, M. 2013. "Messy Hectares: Questions about the Epistemology of Land Grabbing Data." *Journal of Peasant Studies* 40 (3): 485–501. https://doi.org/10.1080/03066150.2013.801340.

Edelman, M., C. Oya, and S. Borras Jr. 2013. "Global Land Grabs: Historical Processes, Theoretical and Methodological Implications and Current Trajectories." *Third World Quarterly* 34 (9): 1517–31. https://doi.org/10.1080/01436597.2013.850190.

Food and Agriculture Organization (FAO). 2018. "FAOSTAT: Ghana: Country Profile." http://www.fao.org/faostat/en/#country/81.

Fold, N. 2008. "Transnational Sourcing Practices in Ghana's Perennial Crop Sectors." *Journal of Agrarian Change* 8 (1): 94–122. https://doi.org/10.1111/j.1471-0366.2007.00164.x.

Fold, N., and K.V. Gough. 2008. "From Smallholders to Transnationals: The Impact of Changing Consumer Preferences in the EU on Ghana's Pineapple Sector." *Geoforum* 39 (5): 1687–97. https://doi.org/10.1016/j.geoforum.2008.06.004.

Fuchs, D., and A. Kalfagianni. 2010. "The Causes and Consequences of Private Food Governance." *Business and Politics* 12 (3): 1–34. https://doi.org/10.2202/1469-3569.1319.

Gatune, J., M. Chapman-Kodam, K. Korboe, F. Mulangu, and M.A. Rakotoarisoa. 2013. "An Analysis of Trade Impacts on the Fresh Pineapple Sector in Ghana." FAO Commodity and Trade Policy Research Working Paper 41.

GlobalGAP. 2015a. "GlobalGAP Control Points and Compliance Criteria in IFAVersion 5 Fruits and Vegetables: Summary of Changes." https://www.globalgap.org/export/sites/default/.content/.galleries/documents/150630_Summary_Changes_V5-0_CPCC_AF_CB_FV_en.pdf.

– 2015b. "GlobalGAP General Regulations Part II: Quality Management System Rules." http://www.bioagricert.org/images/doc-en/globalgap/150630_gg_gr_part-ii_v5-0_en.pdf.

– 2018. "Producer and Supplier Members." https://www.globalgap.org/uk_en/who-we-are/members/supplier/.

Graffham, A., E. Karehu, and J. Macgregor. 2007. *Impact of EurepGAP on Small-scale Vegetable Growers in Kenya: Fresh Insights*. London: International Institute for Environment and Development.

GRAIN. 2008. "Seized! The 2008 Land Grab for Food and Financial Security." Grain Briefing, October 2008.

– 2010. "Turning Africa's Farmland Over to Big Business: The US Millennium Challenge Corporation." *Seedling*, April, 2–11.

Hachez, N., and J. Wouters. 2011. "A Glimpse at the Democratic Legitimacy of Private Standards Assessing the Public Accountability of GLOBALG.A.P." *Journal of International Economic Law* 14 (3): 677–710. https://doi.org/10.2139/ssrn.1809674.

Hall, D. 2011. "Land Grabs, Land Control, and Southeast Asian Crop Booms." *Journal of Peasant Studies* 38 (4): 837–57. https://doi.org/10.1080/03066150.2011.607706.

– 2013. "Primitive Accumulation, Accumulation by Dispossession and the Global Land Grab." *Third World Quarterly* 34 (9): 1582–1604. https://doi.org/10.1080/01436597.2013.843854.

Hall, R. 2011. "Land Grabbing in Southern Africa: The Many Faces of the Investor Rush." *Review of African Political Economy* 38 (128): 193–214. https://doi.org/10.1080/03056244.2011.582753.

Hatanaka, M.A.K.I. 2010. "Assessing Rule-Based Governance Mechanisms in an Era of Scientism." *Journal of Rural Social Sciences* 25 (3): 141–59.

– 2014. "Standardized Food Governance? Reflections on the Potential and Limitations of Chemical-Free Shrimp." *Food Policy* 45:138–45. https://doi.org/10.1016/j.foodpol.2013.04.013.

Henson, S., and T. Reardon. 2005. "Private Agri-Food Standards: Implications for Food Policy and the Agri-Food System." *Food Policy* 30 (3): 241–53. https://doi.org/10.1016/j.foodpol.2005.05.002.

Higgins, W., and K.T. Hallström. 2007. "Standardization, Globalization and Rationalities of Government." *Organization* 14 (5): 685–704. https://doi.org/10.1177/1350508407080309.

Huige, M. 2011. "Private Retail Standards and the Law of the World Trade Organization." In *Private Food Law: Governing Food Chains through Contract Law, Self-Regulation, Private Standards, Audits and Certification Schemes*, edited by Bernd van der Meulen, 175–86. Wageningen: Wageningen Academic Publishers.

International Institute for Environment and Development (IIED). 2008. "Costs and Benefits of EurepGAP Compliance for African Smallholders: A Synthesis of Surveys in Three Countries." *Fresh Insights* 13:1–21.

Jaeger, P. 2008. *Ghana Export Horticulture Cluster Strategic Profile Study. Part I: Scoping Review*. Report prepared for World Bank Sustainable Development Network, Africa Region, Agriculture and Rural Development, Republic of Ghana Ministry of Food and Agriculture and European Union All ACP Agricultural Commodities Programme.

Jahn, G., M. Schramm, and A. Spiller. 2005. "The Reliability of Certification: Quality Labels as a Consumer Policy Tool." *Journal of Consumer Policy* 28 (1): 53–73. https://doi.org/10.1007/s10603-004-7298-6.

Johansson, J. 2013. "Constructing and Contesting the Legitimacy of Private Forest Governance: The Case of Forest Certification in Sweden." PhD diss., Umea University, Sweden.

Land Matrix. 2015. "The Online Public Database on Land Deals." https://landmatrix.org/.

Latour, B. 1999. *Pandora's Hope: Essays on the Reality of Science Studies*. Cambridge, MA: Harvard University Press.

Locher, M., and E. Sulle. 2014. "Challenges and Methodological Flaws in Reporting the Global Land Rush: Observations from Tanzania." *Journal of Peasant Studies* 41 (4): 562–92. https://doi.org/10.1080/03066150.2014.919263.

Loconto, A., and C. Dankers. 2014. "Impact of International Voluntary Standards on Smallholder Market Participation in Developing Countries: A Review of the Literature." *Food And Agriculture Agribusiness and Food Industries Series* 3:1–104.

Lytton, T.D., and L.K. McAllister. 2014. "Oversight in Private Food Safety Auditing: Addressing Auditor Conflict of Interest." *Wisconsin Law Review* 2:289–335.

Maertens, M., B. Minten, and J. Swinnen. 2012. "Modern Food Supply Chains and Development: Evidence from Horticulture Export Sectors in Sub-Saharan Africa." *Development Policy Review* 30 (4): 473–97. https://doi.org/10.1111/j.1467-7679.2012.00585.x.

Millar, G. 2015. "Knowledge and Control in the Contemporary Land Rush: Making Local Land Legible and Corporate Power Applicable in Rural Sierra Leone." *Journal of Agrarian Change* 16 (2): 206–24.

Ouma, S. 2010. "Global Standards, Local Realities: Private Agrifood Governance and the Restructuring of the Kenyan Horticultural Industry." *Economic Geography* 86 (2): 197–222. https://doi.org/10.1111/j.1944-8287.2009.01065.x.

– 2014. "Situating Global Finance in the Land Rush Debate: A Critical Review." *Geoforum* 57:162–6. https://doi.org/10.1016/j.geoforum.2014.09.006.

Ouma, S., M. Boeckler, and P. Lindner. 2013. "Extending the Margins of Marketization: Frontier Regions and the Making of Agro-Export Markets in Northern Ghana." *Geoforum* 48:225–35. https://doi.org/10.1016/j.geoforum.2012.01.011.

Overdevest, C., and J. Zeitlin. 2014. "Assembling an Experimentalist Regime: Transnational Governance Interactions in the Forest Sector." *Regulation & Governance* 8 (1): 22–48. https://doi.org/10.1111/j.1748-5991.2012.01133.x.

Peluso, N.L., and C. Lund. 2011. "New Frontiers of Land Control: Introduction." *Journal of Peasant Studies* 38 (4): 667–81. https://doi.org/10.1080/03066150.2011.607692.

Pierre, J., and B.G. Peters. 2005. *Governing Complex Societies: Trajectories and Scenarios*. Basingstoke, UK: Palgrave Macmillan.

Reardon, T., and E. Farina. 2002. "The Rise of Private Food Quality and Safety Standards: Illustrations from Brazil." *International Food and Agribusiness Management Review* 4 (4): 413–21. https://doi.org/10.1016/s1096-7508(02)00067-8.

Rose, N. 1996. "Governing 'Advanced' Liberal Democracies." In *Anthropology of the State: A Reader*, edited by Aradhana Sharrma and Anil Gupta, 144–62. Oxford: Blackwell Publishing.

Ruggie, G.J. 2004. "Reconstituting the Global Public Domain: Issues, Actors, and Practices." *European Journal of International Relations* 10 (4): 499–531. https://doi.org/10.1177/1354066104047847.

Santacoloma, P., and S. Casey. 2011. "Investment and Capacity Building for GAB Standards: Case Information from Kenya, Chile, Malaysia and South

Africa." Agricultural Management, Marketing and Finance Occasional Paper (FAO).

Scoones, I., R. Hall, S. Borras, B. White, and W. Wolford. 2013. "The Politics of Evidence: Methodologies for Understanding the Global Land Rush." *Journal of Peasant Studies* 40 (3): 469–83. https://doi.org/10.1080/03066150.2013.80 1341.

Stanton, G.H. 2012. "Food Safety–Related Private Standards: The WTO Perspective." In *Private Standards and Global Governance: Economic Legal and Political Perspectives,* edited by A. Mrax, M. Maertens, J. Swinnen, and J. Wouters, 235–54. Cheltenham, UK: Edward Elgar.

Suzuki, A., L.S. Jarvis, and R.J. Sexton. 2011. "Partial Vertical Integration, Risk Shifting, and Product Rejection in the High-Value Export Supply Chain: The Ghana Pineapple Sector." *World Development* 39 (9): 1611–23. https://doi.org/10.1016/j.worlddev.2011.02.007.

Swinnen, J., L. Colen, and M. Maertens. 2013. "Constraints to Smallholder Participation in High-Value Agriculture in West Africa." In *Rebuilding West Africa's Food Potential,* edited by A. Elbehri, 289–311. Rome: FAO/IFAD.

Takane, T. 2004. "Smallholders and Non-Traditional Exports under Economic Liberalization: The Case of Pineapples in Ghana." *African Study Monographs* 25 (1): 29–43.

Van der Meulen, B.M. 2013. "The Structure of European Food Law." *Laws* 2 (2): 69–98. https://doi.org/10.3390/laws2020069.

White, B., S. Borras, R. Hall, I. Scoones, and W. Wolford. 2012. "The New Enclosures: Critical Perspectives on Corporate Land Deals." *Journal of Peasant Studies* 39 (3–4): 617–47.

Whitfield, L. 2011. "Political Challenges to Developing Non-Traditional Exports in Ghana: The Case of Horticulture Exports." Danish Institute for International Studies Working Paper 2011 (29): 1–50.

– 2012. "Developing Technological Capabilities in Agro-Industry: Ghana's Experience with Fresh Pineapple Exports." *Journal of Development Studies* 48 (3): 308–21. https://doi.org/10.1080/00220388.2011.635198.

World Bank. 2010. *Rising Global Interest in Farmland: Can It Yield Sustainable and Equitable Benefits?* Washington, DC: World Bank.

Wouters, A., Marx, A., and N. Hachez. 2012. "Private Standards, Global Governance and International Trade: The Case of Global Food Safety Governance." In *Private Standards and Global Governance: Economic Legal and Political Perspectives,* edited by A. Mrax, M. Maertens, J. Swinnen, and J. Wouters, 255–92. Cheltenham, UK: Edward Elgar.

6 Dirty Hands, Clean Conscience? Large-Scale Land Acquisitions and the Ethical Investment Strategy of the Government Pension Fund – Global

SIRI GRANUM CARSON

Introduction

The Norwegian Government Pension Fund – Global (GPFG) is the largest sovereign wealth fund (SWF) in the world (Sovereign Wealth Fund Institute 2017). What kind of ethical commitments follow from this fact? Is it sufficient to refrain from clearly unethical investments, or should SWFs use their considerable financial influence more proactively? Through its investments in companies renting or buying agricultural land, often in vulnerable areas, GPFG is arguably profiting from so-called land grabbing. The ethical investment practices of GPFG have attracted international attention for several reasons – not least due to the sheer size of the fund. During the decade following the implementation of the ethical guidelines in 2005, the public debate has continued, concerning their financial soundness, their moral justification, the extent of constraints, and the "ethical tools" put into use (e.g., exclusion of vs dialogue with companies). This chapter concentrates on a small section of this debate, the part concerning investments in companies accused of land grabbing,[1] in order to identify and discuss to what extent the ethical investment strategy of the GPFG may be useful for addressing the complex challenges of large-scale land acquisition and sustainable food production.

The question under exploration in this chapter is whether large-scale land acquisitions should be a prioritized issue for the ethical investment strategy of GPFG – that is, as a criterion for exclusion from the portfolio and/or as a priority for active ownership initiatives. Underlying this discussion is the more principled question of whether the point of an ethical investment strategy should be to avoid contributing to unethical business – to "keep our hands clean" – or rather to use the financial power of the fund to influence global business in a more sustainable direction[2] – even at the risk of "getting our hands dirty." Via the global food regime (McMichael 2009), agricultural land becomes an increasingly attractive object for investment. This chapter addresses the ethical responsibilities of large investors in this market, focusing on the case of GPFG's investments in large-scale land acquisitions. Section 1 presents the ethical investment strategy of GPFG, while section 2 discusses the normative foundations for this strategy. Section 3 gives a short introduction to the issue of large-scale land acquisitions, as well as to GPFG's investments in companies involved. Section 4 discusses if and how large-scale land acquisitions as a threat to sustainable food production should be a prioritized topic for the ethical investment strategy of GPFG, and in section 5 some concluding remarks are made.

The Ethical Investment Strategy of the GPFG

The Norwegian oil fund was established in 1990, partly to avoid over-heating the Norwegian economy through the potential investment of billions of kroner in a small economy. By investing the oil revenues abroad, it avoided this complication. As well, the state did so in order to secure the Norwegian state's future ability to carry the economic burdens of an increasingly aging population into the post-fossil-fuels era. A central argument was that future generations of Norwegians have a right to a part of the value generated by the extraction of non-renewable resources from the Norwegian continental shelf. Following on from the success of the fund, by the end of the 1990s, a public debate arose concerning the feasibility of implementing ethical guidelines for the GPFG. The argument was that the ethical obligations associated with managing the petroleum fortune extended beyond the considerations of inter-generational justice. Considerations should also be made concerning how people today are affected by the investments, that is, whether the company invested in areas that respected basic human rights.[3] In 2004 the guidelines were implemented, on the basis of recommendations by the Graver Committee (cf. Graver et al. 2003).

The Ministry of Finance (2010) summed up the ethical commitments of GPFG in two main points:

I. Fiduciary duties towards the beneficiaries of the Fund; in other words that the petroleum fund should benefit future as well as current genera-tions of Norwegians: "This ethical commitment is met through the contin-uous effort to secure high return given a moderate risk, including active ownership in order to take care of the financial interests of the fund" (Min-istry of Finance 2010, 10, my translation). According to modern portfolio theory, investments should not be evaluated in isolation, but according to how they contribute to the larger portfolio. It is important to note that for a large, institutional owner such as GPFG, this means that issues such as climate change and other long-term risks should be considered, not simply for the sake of the profitability of specific companies or even branches, but for the sake of a general interest in a healthy and stable global finance market. This point is often referred to as the "universal owner hypothesis," defined in the following way by the Ministry of Finance (2009, 9): "The [universal owner] hypothesis suggests that one portfolio company's externalization of costs (which will, when taken in isolation, increase returns on that company) will, for a universal owner, have a negative effect on other companies in the portfolio, with the outcome being a negative impact on the overall return on the portfolio. A universal owner will therefore have a good reason for seeking to reduce the incidence of negative externalities (for example pollution and corruption) and to increase the incidence of positive externalities (for example those resulting from good corporate management).

II. A commitment to avoid investments involving an "unacceptable risk that the fund contributes to severely unethical deeds" (Ministry of Finance 2010, 10). This ethical commitment is maintained both through active ownership and by excluding certain companies from the investment universe of the fund.

Consequently, the set purpose for Norges Bank Investment Management (NBIM), which manages GPFG, is to secure the highest possible returns within the limits set by the Ministry of Finance. Two main mechanisms are at NBIM's disposal, by which it can keep the investments in line with this purpose. The first is to engage with companies as *active owners* in order to influence them in the direction of economically sound, yet socially and environmentally responsible business operations. Engaging with these entities in terms of active ownership is the responsibility of NBIM.

The second mechanism is the exclusion of companies violating the principles of ethical investment. In this, NBIM is advised by a Council of Ethics.[4] The council consists of five people, whose main task is to advise NBIM (earlier the Ministry of Finance) on divestments from specific companies, and a secretariat that performs investigations of companies as well as conducting reviews of current topics in socially responsible investing. Decisions to exclude companies from the GPFG portfolio are made on the basis of *either* that the products made or traded by the company are considered ethically unacceptable (tobacco, certain kinds of weapons such as cluster bombs and anti-personnel mines and – since

February 2016 – coal or coal-based energy production), *or* that the conduct of the company is considered to be ethically unacceptable. Serious or systematic violation of human rights, gross corruption, and serious environmental damages are among the criteria on which companies may be excluded from the GPFG investment universe.

Where there is doubt whether the criteria of exclusion are met, the companies put under observation are contacted and allowed to comment before the final decisions on divestment are made. Based on its investigations and potential input from the company, the Council of Ethics concludes and sends its recommendation to NBIM, which finally decides whether to follow the recommendation. The whole process can take several months. Once a decision is reached, it is made public on the council's webpage,[5] even in cases where the recommendations are not followed. This process is, in other words, quite transparent, as opposed to the active ownership initiatives of NBIM, which normally does not comment on ethical (or any other) considerations made in relation to individual companies.

Since the beginning the amount of exclusions on the basis of the ethical guidelines has gone from very few to a relatively high number. In 2002, only 1 company was excluded, whereas by March 2017, over 130 companies were on the excluded list (Norges Bank Investment Management 2018). In relation to a portfolio of almost 9,000 companies, it is debatable whether this is a very significant number, but there has clearly been a remarkable development in volume, that is, the number of exclusions, and in the rationale for taking that step, that is, the basis on which the exclusions are made. In 2001 only clear violations of international law informed decision-making in this area, while by 2017 a multitude of reasons resulted in exclusion.

From "Clean Hands" Strategy to Role Model

What kind of moral responsibility does a big financial actor such as GPFG have for the investments it makes? As mentioned, the Ministry of Finance distinguishes between Ethical Commitment I – to secure a high return on investments for the benefit of coming generations, and Ethical Commitment II – to secure the rights of those who are affected by the business operations in which investments have been made. Both commitments are difficult to specify and delimit. Commitment I can be viewed as a matter of balancing the profitability of companies with their effects on society and the environment, and may be conceptualized as a consequentialist principle of how to achieve the best overall results (Graver et al. 2003, 11). Commitment II may be conceptualized as a deontological (duty ethical) principle stating a duty to reduce the risk that the investment directly or indirectly harms people or the environment. However, it is problematic to define under which circumstances companies are responsible for such harm, and even more so to delimit the responsibility of a financial investor. In a letter to the Ministry of Finance, the Council of Ethics mentioned a few examples of such challenging grey zones: "The Council of Ethics acknowledges that evaluations of companies' purchase of products from "unethical origin" can give rise to difficult demarcations.... If, for example, companies in GPFG buy tropical timber from states with export bans, the Council of Ethics could evaluate if the buyer commits a severe violation of norms. Another current topic is related to illegal or unregulated fishing. For example, it could be considered whether it would constitute a severe breach of norms if companies in the GPFG buy fish caught without concession in a state's economic zone" (Ethics Council 2011; my translation).

The explicit normative justification behind introducing ethical screening as a tool in the management of the GPFG was to *avoid complicity*. In other words, it was to prevent GPFG from assuming any responsibility through its investments for the wrongdoings of companies.[6] In the report from the Graver Committee, it is established that "owning shares or bonds in a company that can be expected to commit grossly unethical actions may be regarded as complicity in these actions" (Graver et al., 2003, 9).

However, the report concedes that the issue of complicity raises difficult questions. It has been argued that the language of complicity is both problematic, in the sense that an investor's complicity in the wrongdoings of a company (of which it owns but a tiny share and over which it thus has little or no direct influence) is hard to define and delimit (Ministry of Finance 2014, 9; Nagell 2011, s 82), and at the same time that it is too limited to capture the full extent of the moral responsibility involved in the managing of a gigantic sovereign wealth fund such as the GPFG. Therefore, in addition to being responsible for taking steps to reduce the risk that their investment directly or indirectly contributes to harm, investors should also take into consideration the symbolic and signalling effects of an investment decision (Ministry of Finance 2014, 90). The GPFG is the world's largest SWF and by far the world's largest investor applying ethical assessments, which contributes to considerable international attention regarding its investment policy. In addition, the policy and profile of the GPFG is far more open and transparent than comparable funds based in less democratic countries (Chambers, Dimson, and Ilmanen, 2012, ss 67–81). Consequently, signals from the fund in the form of divestments, and even considered divestments, potentially have a significant influence on the decisions of both companies and other investors.

Ingierd and Syse (2011) distinguish between *causal responsibility*, of which complicity is a subcategory, and *role responsibility*, focusing on what they term "attitude responsibility," defined as "the responsibility one has for the forming of attitudes, characters and culture" (178). The latter is identified as a kind of obligation particularly relevant for large institutional investors such as GPFG, since both the investment community and the general public typically will pay more attention to the movements of these investors. In one sense, it seems that the argument from complicity could run counter to the argument from signalling effect. The first argument seems to rest on a deontological premise that we ought to avoid contributing to wrongdoings, while the other appears to be a more consequentialist argument about how to achieve the overall best outcome.

Consider the following example: In 2006, the Council of Ethics recommended exclusion of Monsanto, based on serious violations of human rights in relation to the worst forms of child labour. The Ministry of Finance decided against divestment, on the basis of the argument that engaging with the company (as well as with other companies in the same line of production) would be a better alternative under the circumstances. An important reason was that NBIM had recently put child labour on top of their agenda as a prioritized issue for their active ownership strategy. After three years, the minister of finance concluded that the strategy had been a success, when not only Monsanto, but also several other companies signed an industry standard with the aim to abolish child labour from the seed industry. "This is an important agreement. Our savings are used to improve the situation for thousands of poor children. In addition, we change the conduct of several multinational companies," declared Kristin Halvorsen, then minister of finance (e24, 2009). If the only normative justification for the ethical investment strategy of the GPFG had been to avoid complicity, this would have been an uncertain or even irresponsible strategy. However, if the justification is that the GPFG should use its significant influence in the global market in the most effective way possible, it could arguably achieve better results though active ownership than by exclusion in situations like this.

The emphasis by the Graver Committee and the ethical guidelines on avoiding complicity has been criticized as a "clean hands" strategy serving self-righteousness rather than actually contributing to improving corporate conduct (e.g., Føllesdal 2007; Nagell 2011). As we have seen, however, in practical policy this argument is complemented by the argument from role responsibility. The two justifications do not necessarily run counter to each other, but will, on the contrary, often re-inforce each other. Divesting from companies avoids complicity, but is also often justifiable from the perspective of signalling effect, since the divestments and the reasons behind them are public acts and thus serve as "naming and shaming" of the companies in question. A broad con-cept of moral responsibility, with a keen eye for how to influence com-panies and other investors, is arguably present from the outset in the ethical guidelines of GPFG in the sense that they are forward-looking, emphasizing how divesting or active ownership strategies should be used to prevent *future* norm violations. Past norm violations are relevant only to the degree that they make future norm violations more probable; see Ministry of Finance (2014, section 3, § 4): "In assessing whether a company shall be excluded in accordance with Paragraph 3, the Ministry may among other things consider the probability of future norm violations."

In the following section, I turn to large-scale land acquisitions, in order to ask whether the ethical investment strategy of GPFG is capable of handling this complex issue.

Large-scale Land Acquisitions: The Involvement and Ethical Responsibility of GPFG

Fluctuating food prices, anticipated food shortages resulting from pop-ulation growth, and the global demand for biofuels are all important factors behind what has been called a global hunt for food soil (e.g., McMichael 2009). After the world food price crisis of 2007–8, large-scale land investments (also termed land grabbing) were put on top of the global agenda. Affluent countries and multinational corporations (MNCs) are investing heavily in food soil in developing countries, with problematic effects for the local communities, such as displacement and decreasing food security. This highly controversial phenomenon has been labelled as neocolonialism. Arguably such investments may in certain cases have positive effects for the local communities by, for example, increasing productivity. However, it is vital to protect the interests of poor and vulnerable farmers, and to counteract any forced movement of people. A focus on obtaining free and informed consent from local farmers is central to secure a just process. However, many would argue that this is not sufficient to avoid unjust outcomes.

In an attempt to mitigate harmful results of large-scale land acqui-sitions, the World Bank, in cooperation with United Nations Food and Agricultural Organization (FAO) and the International Food Policy Research Institute (IFPRI) developed RAI, a global code of conduct emphasizing consultation and participation (World Bank 2010). The code aims to regulate land acquisitions within the current scheme of a global market and has been criticized for legitimizing the underlying unfair political and economic structures leading to the global food soil hunt in the first place (e.g., De Schutter 2011). The debate concerning RAI highlights the complex nature of the issue of land grabbing, suggesting that it is less than likely that it could be regulated simply through a set of ethical guidelines.

As one of the world's biggest investors in African land projects,[7] Norway is a major actor on the global land market, and the GPFG has significant ownership in companies accused of land grabbing. But even though more and more issues over the years have come up as grounds for exclusion or exertion of active ownership, a company's involvement in land grabbing has yet to be used as an explicit reason for divestment, observation, or shareholder engagement by the GPFG. For a few years now, the active ownership strategy has been focused on the issue of climate change and extraction from environmentally damaging lines of business. In 2013 the fund created waves in international finance by pulling out of twenty-three palm oil companies on the grounds that their business model was "not sustainable." The withdrawal from coal companies for the same reason was also duly noted internationally. It is worth noticing, however, that the explicit argumentation backing these decisions points to the fiduciary duty to avoid the financial risk of investing in unsustainable lines of business rather than the moral duty to avoid harm – that is to Ethical Commitment I (future generations) rather than II (rights of those affected). Similarly, while the fund's investments previously were made almost exclusively in industrialized countries, the strategy has shifted towards significant investments in emerging economies, prominently in Asia and Latin America. This shift has been prompted by NGOs and activist groups for a number of years, arguing that the GPFG has a duty to mitigate injustices caused by the global finance market. The stated aim of the shift of strategy is, however, again, the first rather than the second commitment: new evaluations of economic risk and sustainability rather than avoiding complicity in harm. Given that the basic ethical justification for establishing the GPFG in the first place was the consideration of future generations of Norwegians, the emphasis on the first commitment is perhaps not unreasonable. A practical reason for the priority of the first rather than the second commitment in these cases is that they are initiated by NBIM directly, as part of their active ownership strategy for sustainable, long-term investment. The Council of

Ethics, on the other hand, is responsible for advising NBIM on cases involving the possible withdrawal from individual companies based on "gross or serious ethical violations."

In 2013 the youth organization Spire campaigned against "Norwegian land grabbing," arguing among other things that this issue should be addressed expeditiously by the GPFG (Spire 2013). They presented two case studies on GPFG's investment objects: Malaysian MNC Sime Darby and French MNC Bolloré, both companies involved in palm oil production. With regards to Sime Darby, they described the conflict over the establishment of palm oil plantations in Liberia. In 2009 Sime Darby signed a rental agreement with the Liberian government, securing the rights to about 768,500 acres of land for sixty-three years with the possibility to extend the agreement. The document included the possibility of Sime Darby asking the authorities to resettle inhabitants who, according to the company, hindered development in certain of the areas over which it had staked a claim. An independent report prepared by the University of Reading concluded that there was a high risk that the agreement would lead to decreasing food security and biological diversity, and result in further deforestation and increasing conflict and gender inequality (Evans and Griffith 2013).

While the Rainforest Foundation Norway acclaimed the divestments from some of the world's most controversial palm oil companies, they pointed out that GPFG's total investment in palm oil actually continued to rise in 2013 and 2014. It is also noteworthy that while NBIM had a focus on palm oil companies – among other things, as a result of a campaign by the Rainforest Foundation Norway – and withdrew from many of the "worst" companies,[8] at the same time they increased by a factor of four GPFG investments in Sime Darby. The reason for this increase is not easy to establish, since NBIM does not comment on single investments,[9] and the process leading up to active ownership decisions is far less transparent than the one leading up to exclusion based on the recommendations of the Council of Ethics. In general, however, NBIM has framed the divestment from palm oil companies primarily as an environmental issue, while social and ethical sides of large-scale land acquisitions have been less prominent in the debate. This could be a reason for the continued and even increasing investments in Sime Darby, as the negative attention surrounding this company has been more in relation to forced resettlement and other human rights violation than with environmental hazard. As I argue below, this reveals a too limited approach to the concept of sustainability.

This last point will be pursued in the following and last section, where the concept of sustainability is suggested as a point of departure for handling the complex issue of investments in large-scale land acquisitions.

Sustainability and Food Security: A Case for a New Priority for GPFG?

Growing populations and consumption implies that the global demand for food will increase for at least another forty years (Godfray et al. 2010). Consequently, food security and the need for sustainable growth in food production are high on the global agenda but have so far not been singled out as a prioritized issue for GPFG's investment strategy, whether by the Council of Ethics or by NBIM. According to a 2011 series of reports by the Oakland Institute, GPFG substantially contributes to a worldwide weakening of food security through its investments in large-scale land acquisitions (Oakland Institute 2011a, 2011b). The series builds on field research of seven African countries, and uncovered skyrocketing investments in sub-Saharan Africa, as well as how these investments pose significant threats to livelihood, local food security, and human rights. Norway is highlighted as one of the major investors, mainly through the investments of GPFG. That elicited a response from NBIM: "We cannot think about everything all of the time" (Dvergedal 2011). NBIM noted that large-scale land acquisitions and food security are not prioritized issues for GPFG; adding that the focus is on other areas, specifically child labour, climate, and water management.

Seen in isolation, this statement is in line with the rationale of the ethical guidelines of GPFG. According to the report from the Graver Committee, which laid the basis for the guidelines, the fund is not a suitable vehicle for attending to all of Norway's ethical obligations (Graver et al. 2003, pt 3.2). The efficiency of the guidelines depends on a certain focus, and this is the reason for choosing some key areas of commitment in NBIM's exercise of active ownership. In NBIM's annual report to the Storting for 2007, three focus areas were singled out: good corporate management (transparency), children's rights and health, and environmental problems with a particular emphasis on climate change (NBIM 2007, 89). The reasons stated for selecting these particular issues is that this is in line with NBIM's long-term perspective as an investor, since they "obviously are ethically and socially important in themselves, whilst being at the same time of key importance to the future functionality, legitimacy and profitability of global markets" (89).

This quote points to the "universal owner hypothesis," mentioned above, applying to large institutional owners such as GPFG, for whom the interest in a stable and healthy global finance market trumps any narrow concern for the profitability of investing in selected industries or companies. According to this hypothesis, for a universal and long-term investor such as GPFG, there is no disconnect between sustainable development and the prospect of profit. In the 2007 report it was argued that the reason for focusing on child labour and climate change was the connection between sustainable markets and long-term financial performance. As the Ministry of Finance pointed out in its evaluation of the Ethical Guidelines in 2009, "Negative externalities from climate change and social effects from child labour will in the long run be detrimental to the portfolio, given Norges Bank's role as a universal investor" (Ministry of Finance 2009). In other words, by considering issues such as climate change and child labour, in accordance with the "role responsibility" of a large, universal investor, GPFG is at the same time managing its portfolio according to the long-term, low-risk profile of a universal owner.

In 2014 there was a newspaper debate in Norway concerning whether GPFG should divest from petroleum stocks. Paal Bjørnestad, then secretary of state at the Ministry of Finance, used the opportunity to reiterate the first and basic ethical commitment associated with the investments of GPFG: "The purpose of the investments in GPFG is to achieve the highest possible profit within a moderate risk level. The fund is not an instrument to solve foreign or climate political challenges" (Bjørnestad 2014). With reference to the "universal owner hypothesis," however, this is a truth with modifications. Although the obligation to ensure favourable long-term returns for the fund's beneficiaries (current and future generations of Norwegians) remains the basic ethical commitment of GPFG, these favourable returns depend in the long run on sustainable development in economic, ecological, and social terms (Ministry of Finance 2009, 11).

On this basis, it is not unreasonable that civil society actors as well as politicians frequently refer to the obligation to use the unique position of GPFG to influence the global finance market. In 2015 the Storting instructed NBIM to withdraw completely from the coal sector.[10] In this matter, a broad consensus was achieved at the Storting, but the arguments stated by representatives from the different parties were diverse. Here is a sample:

A   "It will reduce climate-related, financial risks."[11]
B   "It gives a clear signal for those who deal in coal that they should look for other forms of energy."[12]

C "It will be noticed internationally, and will contribute to changed behaviour by companies."[13]

D "The Storting now sends an important signal into the negotiations for a global climate agreement in Paris this autumn, that Norway will not invest our savings in the destruction of the world's climate."[14]

As we can see from these quotes, politicians point towards different commitments in the management of GPFG's investments. Quote A points towards Ethical Commitment I, to achieve the highest possible return within a moderate risk for the benefit of present and future generations of Norwegians. Quotes B and C both seem to point towards the "role responsibility" of GPFG, that is the commitment to consider the signalling effect of investment and divestment decisions. Quote D points towards Ethical Commitment II, to avoid complicity in unethical business conduct, but at the same time it points to the signalling effect this might have. There is no disconnect here between a "deontological" argument to avoid harm and a more "consequentialist" argument to optimize the best result – rather, it is argued that by adhering to the duty not to contribute to harm, the Norwegian fund *at the same time* utilizes its influence in order to improve the overall outcomes in the world. For a universal owner, this ought to be part of a long-term, moderate risk investment strategy.

The question remains then, of why the issue of large-scale land acquisition is not singled out as a part of this investment strategy. Given the challenges addressed throughout this book – the vital importance of securing agricultural land for future food security and the vulnerability of a fluctuating global market and the recent food price crisis – this topic arguably deserves the attention of a universal owner. Large-scale land acquisitions constitute an environmental hazard, a social threat, and an economic risk; thus, the issue illustrates how the three elements of the Brundtland Commission's definition of sustainable development are intertwined and should not be evaluated in isolation from each other. This was emphasized in the report by the Graver Committee as well, stating on this basis that "combating poverty is the greatest single challenge the global community will be facing in the decades ahead" (Graver et al. 2003, 11).

This quote might, however, supply us with a clue to understand why large-scale land acquisitions are not visible in the ethical investment strategy of GPFG. The relationships between land investment, poverty, and food security are complex and controversial, and the suggested solution to the global challenge of food security differs wildly between different actors. Notably, the World Bank Group (WBG) promotes and supports large-scale land investments in developing countries as the road towards economic development, improved agricultural infrastructure, and rising employment for the host countries, while a number of civil society actors argue the opposite case, that such investments undermine the livelihoods and basic rights of a large number of people in these countries. The issue is complex from the overall perspective of how to promote global food security, and even single investments may appear ambiguous. Even for projects where there are no obvious violations of human rights, it may be argued that while the acquisition of farmland by a large, foreign investor is economically beneficial for the local community, it undermines the long-term food security of that same community.

Concluding Remarks

Given the challenges to global food security shown among other things in the recent food price crisis, it would seem that the topic of large-scale land acquisitions deserves the attention of a universal owner like GPFG. Large-scale land acquisitions pose an environmental hazard, social threat, and economic risk, and thus demonstrate how the three elements of sustainable development are linked. The complexity of unethical conduct in relation to large-scale land acquisition might help to explain why it has not yet been stated as a reason for divestment from any company in the portfolio of GPFG. According to the ethical guidelines, "Serious or systematic violation of human rights" is a criterion for withdrawal, but the human rights issues concerned in these cases are often complex and hard to measure. Thus screening or exclusion based on violation of norms might be a less than fitting instrument to deal with the environmental and social problems that follow from large-scale land acquisitions.

Arguably, a better option would be for NBIM to launch responsible land investments and food security as a priority for their active ownership strategy. This would entail entering into dialogue with the relevant companies and branches over how environmental damage and human rights violations can be prevented. This way GPFG's influence as a universal owner and role model for ethical investment could be used to pressure companies in the direction of more responsible conduct in land acquisitions. The advantage of this strategy is that it is more flexible and result-oriented than an ethical screening strategy. The problem of such a strategy is the lack of transparency as well as the difficulty in measuring the results of the strategy, given the mentioned complexities and ambiguities of large-scale land acquisitions. Attending to these challenges should be the topic for further research.

NOTES

1 This debate was initiated by Spire, the youth organization of the Norwegian Development Fund, through their 2010 campaign Stopp Norsk Landran [Stop Norwegian land grabbing], and the following 2013 report *Solgt* [Sold].
2 Sustainability is defined in accordance with the report of the Brundtland Commission from 1987, as a matter of balancing environmental, economic, and social considerations (Brundtland 1987).
3 This argument seems to specify that the ethical commitments of GPFG consist of fiduciary duties to current and future Norwegians, and ethical duties to those currently affected by the investments of the fund. A further question, in light of the final chapter of this book, is whether the argument (and the commitments, as specified later by the Graver Committee) encompasses the rights of future generations globally and/or environmental rights.
4 Until 2014, the Council of Ethics gave their recommendations to the Ministry of Finance, who in turn sent the recommendation on political hearing in relevant ministries, before concluding on whether or not to follow the recommendations – a process that could take several months. In the spring of 2014, the minister of finance, Siv Jensen, suggested closing down the Council of Ethics and let NBIM take over its tasks. This was voted down in the Storting, but the council was instructed to give its recommendations on observation and exclusion directly to the NBIM rather than to the Ministry of Finance.
5 www.etikkradet.no.
6 See section 3 in "Guidelines for Observation and Exclusion from the Government Pension Fund: Global's Investment Universe 2010": "The Ministry of Finance may, on the advice of the Council of Ethics, exclude companies from the investment universe of the Fund if there is an unacceptable risk that the company contributes to ... serious violation of ethical norms" (Ministry of Finance 2014).
7 The fourth largest, according to Schoneveld (2011).
8 Among the companies divested from was Wilmar, which *Newsweek* named "the worst company in the world" in 2013; see Ronenberg and Barstad (2013).
9 One conclusion in Spire's report (2013, 26) is that this process needs more transparency.
10 The new regulations were implemented from January 2016 and include companies where more than 30 per cent of the income comes from coal, as well as where more than 30 per cent of the activity is coal-based. In March 2019, the Norwegian government announced that GPFG was to disinvest from petroleum as well.
11 Terje Breivik (V), (Aarø 2015).
12 Hans Olav Syversen (KrF), (Krekling, Norum, and Kolberg, 2015).
13 Geir Pollestad (Sp), (Aarø 2015).
14 Rasmus Hansson (dG), (Aarø 2015).

REFERENCES

Aarø, J.T. 2015. "Oljefondet ut av kull." E24, 25 July. https://e24.no/boers-og-finans/oljefondet-ut-av-kull/23459941.
Bjørnestad, P. 2014. "Oljeaksjer i oljefondet." Dagens Næringsliv, 10 August. https://www.dn.no/paal-bjornestad/oljefondet/spu/oljeaksjer-i-oljefondet/1-1-5167071.
Brundtland, G.H. 1987. *Our Common Future*. Report for the World Commission on Environment and Development, United Nations.
Chambers, D., E. Dimson, and A. Ilmanen. 2012. "The Norway Model." *Journal of Portfolio Management* 38 (2): 67–81. https://doi.org/10.3905/jpm.2012.38.2.067.
De Schutter, O. 2011. "How Not to Think of Land-Grabbing: Three Critiques of Large-Scale Investments in Farmland." *Journal of Peasant Studies* 38 (2): 249–79. https://doi.org/10.1080/03066150.2011.559008.
Dvergedal, P. 2011. "Ny rapport: Norge svekker matsikkerheten." VG, 21 June. http://www.vg.no/nyheter/innenriks/ny-rapport-norge-svekker-matsikkerheten/a/10087355/.
E24. 2009. "Oljefondet overtaler selskap til å kutte ut barnearbeid" [The Oil Fund persuades company to cut out child labour], 19 August. https://e24.no/nyheter/oljefondet-overtaler-selskap-til-aa-kutte-ut-barnearbeid/3222833.
Ethics Council. 2011. "Vedrørende tilrådning om utelukkelse av selskaper som kjøper fosfat fra Vest-Sahara." https://www.regjeringen.no/contentassets/a9879245f0f141ac934f17a9609e1941/fosfat_brev_til_fin_mars_2011.pdf.
Evans, R., and G. Griffiths. 2013. "Palm Oil, Land Rights and Ecosystems Services in Gbarpolu County, Liberia." Research Note 3. Reading: Walker Institute for Climate System Research, University of Reading. http://centaur.reading.ac.uk/33817/.
Follesdal, A. 2007. "Ethical Investment and Human Rights: A Norwegian Case." *Nordic Journal on Human Rights* 25 (4): 420–33.
Godfray, H.C.J., J.R. Beddington, I.R. Crute, L. Haddad, D. Lawrence, J.F. Muir, ... and C. Toulmin. 2010. "Food Security: The Challenge of Feeding 9 Billion People." *Science* 327 (5967): 812–18.
Graver, H.P. et al. 2003. *Forvaltning for fremtiden* [Managing for the future]. Ministry of Finance. https://www.regjeringen.no/contentassets/d8124659de12416dbe2a942b5461be93/no/pdfs/nou200320030022000dddpdfs.pdf.
Ingierd, H., and H. Syse. 2011. "The Moral Responsibilities of Shareholders: A Conceptual Map." In *Human Rights, Corporate Complicity and Disinvestment*, edited by G. Nystuen, A. Follesdal, and O. Mestad, 156–82. Cambridge: Cambridge University Press. doi: 10.1017/CBO9781139003292.009.
Krekling, D.V., H. Norum, and M. Kolberg. 2015. "Enighet om å trekke oljefondet ut av kull." NRK, 27 May. https://www.nrk.no/norge/enighet-om-a-trekke-oljefondet-ut-av-kull-1.12381238.

McMichael, P.2009. "A Food Regime Analysis of the 'World Food Crisis.'" *Agriculture and Human Values* 26 (4): 281–95. https://doi.org/10.1007/s10460-009-9218-5.

Ministry of Finance. 2009. "Consultation Paper: Evaluation of the Ethical Guidelines for the Government Pension Fund – Global."

– 2010. *SPU: Ansvarlige investeringer* [GPFG: Responsible investments]. https://www.regjeringen.no/globalassets/upload/FIN/brosjyre/2010/spu/SPU.pdf.

– 2014. "Guidelines for Observation and Exclusion from the Government Pension Fund Global." /fin/statens-pensjonsfond/guidelines-for-observation-and-exclusion-14-april-2015_new.pdf.

Nagell, H.W. 2011. "Investor Responsibility and Norway's Government Pension Fund: Global." *Etikk i praksis / Nordic Journal of Applied Ethics* 5 (1): 79–96. https://doi.org/10.5324/eip.v5i1.1734.

Norges Bank Investment Management (NBIM). 2007. *Annual Report 2007.* http://www.nbim.no/globalassets/reports/2007/nbim_07_eng.pdf.

– 2018. "Observasjon og utelukkelse av selskaper." https://www.nbim.no/no/oljefondet/ansvarlig-forvaltning/utelukkelse-av-selskaper/.

Norges Bank Investment Management. 2017. "Observasjon og utelukkelse av selskaper [Observation and exclusion of companies]." https://www.nbim.no/no/oljefondet/ansvarlig-forvaltning/utelukkelse-av-selskaper/.

Oakland Institute. 2011a. *Understanding Land Investment Deals in Africa: Country Report, Ethiopia.* https://www.oaklandinstitute.org/sites/oaklandinstitute.org/files/OI_Ethiopa_Land_Investment_report.pdf.

– 2011b. *Understanding Land Investment Deals in Africa: Country Report, Sierra Leone.* https://www.oaklandinstitute.org/sites/oaklandinstitute.org/files/OI_SierraLeone_Land_Investment_report_0.pdf.

Ronenberg, K., and S. Barstad. 2013. "Oljefondet kvittet seg med "verdens verste selskap." *Aftenposten,* 8 March. https://www.aftenposten.no/okonomi/i/zG7G9/Oljefondet-kvittet-seg-med-verdens-verste-selskap.

Schoneveld, G. 2011. *The Anatomy of Large-Scale Farmland Acquisitions in Sub-Saharan Africa.* http://www.cifor.org/publications/pdf_files/WPapers/WP85Schoneveld.pdf.

Sovereign Wealth Fund Institute. 2017. "Top 81 Largest Sovereign Wealth Fund Rankings by Total Assets." http://www.swfinstitute.org/sovereign-wealth-fund-rankings/.

Spire. 2013. *SOLGT: Finansierer offentlige norske midler landran?* http://www.spireorg.no/files/spire/documents/LANDRAN_RAPPORT_ENDELIG.pdf.

World Bank. 2010. "Principles for Responsible Agricultural Investment That Respects Rights, Livelihoods and Resources."

7 Responsibility to the Rescue? Governing Private Financial Investment in Global Agriculture

JENNIFER CLAPP

Introduction

In the past decade there has been massive growth in private financial investment in agricultural commodity futures contracts, shares in agricultural firms, farmland funds, and commodity index funds. These agricultural investment products enable financial investors to capitalize on gains in food, farm, and farmland assets without taking on the risk of actually owning those assets outright (Fuchs, Meyer-Eppler, and Hamenstädt 2013; Fairbairn 2014). The large increase in financial investment in commodity and farmland investments has been highly controversial because of the potential social and ecological externalities – i.e. external costs – associated with these types of investments. On one hand, those promoting these investments point out that private financial resources can provide an important source of much-needed capital for the agricultural sector in developing countries (Hallam 2011). On the other hand, critics have countered that in a number of cases any positive benefits have been outstripped by the costs of this investment, such as more volatile food prices, environmental degradation, and human rights violations (Ghosh 2010; White et al. 2012; McMichael 2010). Although the exercise of weighing the costs and benefits of these investments is highly charged, the potential for negative outcomes associated with these investments is not in question (Deininger and Byerlee 2011; UNCTAD 2011a; World Bank and UNCTAD 2014). What is unclear is how to prevent negative outcomes from occurring, while enabling the positive features of investment in the sector.

In this context, voluntary international governance initiatives to promote "responsible" private financial investment in agriculture have begun to emerge. In 2010 the World Bank, the Food and Agriculture Organization (FAO), and the United Nations Conference on Trade and Development (UNCTAD) sponsored the Principles for Responsible Agricultural Investment (PRAI). In 2011 a number of investment funds associated with the UN Principles for Responsible Investment (PRI) unveiled the Principles for Responsible Investment in Farmland. Around the same time, the FAO shepherded the adoption of the Voluntary Guidelines on the Responsible Governance of Tenure of Land, Fisheries and Forests in the Context of National Food Security by the Committee on World Food Security (CFS) in 2012. In 2014, the CFS adopted the Principles for Responsible Investment in Agriculture and Food Systems (PRIAFS).

As newly adopted initiatives, it is too early to provide a full assessment of their performance and impact. Instead, this chapter draws on lessons from the literature on voluntary initiatives and responsible finance more broadly and makes a preliminary assessment of their likely ability to rein in the potential social and environmental costs of agricultural investment. I argue that in their current form, the responsible agricultural investment governance efforts are unlikely to bring substantial changes in practice, for several reasons. First, the responsible investment initiatives for agriculture are likely to suffer from the weaknesses associated with responsible investment initiatives more generally, which include guidelines that are vague and difficult to enforce, low participation rates, a weak business case, and a confusing array of competing initiatives. Second, financial investment in agriculture introduces additional complexity with the large diversity of investors and financial investment products involved, which obscures their impact. This complexity makes it extremely difficult to discern precisely who should be held responsible in practice, which further compounds the problems of accountability within voluntary initiatives, and within agricultural systems more broadly. In this highly ambiguous context, voluntary initiatives for responsible agricultural investment are likely to be weak and ineffective.

The Changing Landscape of Food, Finance, and Farmland

Financial actors have historically had a close relationship with the food system. Financial speculators have been engaged in commodity futures markets dating back several centuries since the rise of commodity exchanges in the United Kingdom and the United States (Cronon 1991). In the United States, home to the Chicago Mercantile Exchange, the largest agricultural commodity exchange in the world, these markets were tightly regulated for much of the twentieth century in a bid to avert excessive financial speculation that could result in market manipulation and price volatility. These regulations included reporting requirements and position limits (limits on the number of contracts any single trader can hold at one time) by non-commercial (i.e., financial) players involved in these markets (see Berkovitz 2009). Recent decades have seen intensification of the role of financial actors within the agri-food system, from commodity exchanges, to agri-food value chain functioning, to land markets (Burch and Lawrence 2009; Fuchs, Meyer-Eppler, and Hamenstädt 2013; Isakson 2014). This "financialization" of the food system, whereby financial actors, financial markets, and financial motives have taken on greater importance in the organization, structure, and trends in food, land, and agricultural relations, has occurred alongside financialization in the broader global economy (see Epstein 2005).

The involvement of financial actors across a range of agricultural value chains intensified following the adoption of neoliberal economic policies in a number of countries in the 1980s. The decades that followed saw progressive deregulation of financial markets, including regulations that governed commodity exchanges and banks. In the United States, for example, banks and other financial institutions pressured regulators and won exemptions from position limits in commodity markets in the 1980s and 1990s (Clapp and Helleiner 2012). This relaxation of financial rules governing commodity futures markets was further solidified with the passage of the Commodity Futures Modernization Act of 2000, which exempted over-the-counter trades (that is, trades outside of formal exchanges) from regulatory oversight (Ghosh 2010). These regulatory changes enabled the development of a new breed of financial investment products linked to food and agriculture, based not only on agricultural commodities, but also on farmland and agri-food company shares.

After 2000 there was a sharp rise in investment in what are referred to as commodity index funds (CIFs), which bundle different commodities together and track their prices (IATP 2008). CIFs typically include some combination of agricultural commodity, mineral, and energy futures, with agricultural commodities often making up a third of the index. Other kinds of index funds have also emerged, such as general agricultural index funds that combine and then track prices of agricultural farmland, agricultural input and equipment firm shares, and agricultural commodities (Daniel 2012). Many governments around the world have also relaxed regulations on foreign direct investment more broadly since the 1980s. This general deregulation in investment regimes took place as part of the broader neoliberal agenda, which advocated a reduced role for state regulation in markets, including for investment. Over the course of the 1990s, approximately 95 per cent of changes to foreign investment rules resulted in a more favourable environment for foreign investment (UNCTAD 2001). This trend continued in the following decade, although the 2008 financial crisis led to a marginal increase in stricter rules, while the overwhelming majority of changes were more liberalizing (UNCTAD 2012).

This more open foreign investment regime across a number of countries opened the door for wealthy financial investors to tap into foreign direct investment, including in food, land, and agriculture operations across the globe in ways, and at scales, that were not possible just a few decades earlier when governments took a more active role in setting boundaries on foreign investment. A range of investors stepped into this new investment space: hedge funds serving large-scale wealthy investors, pension funds managing massive amounts of money, private equity funds investing directly into private companies, mutual funds providing investment vehicles to retail investors, commodity trading firms hedging on their own accord as well as selling investment products for third parties, investment banks selling investment products and hedging their risks, sovereign wealth funds investing on behalf of governments, and insurance companies hedging risks, among others (see McNellis 2009). These investors interact with one another in complex ways – some investing in other investors, some selling products, some buying as investments.

Since the early 2000s agricultural commodity and land investments have risen sharply. Investment in CIFs, which typically include an agricultural component as noted above, grew markedly between 2003 and 2008, increasing from US$13 billion to US$317 billion (De Schutter 2010). Between 2006 and 2011 speculative investment in agricultural commodities almost doubled, from US$65 billion to $US126 billion (Worthy 2011). And since 2000, over 900 land deals covering more than 35 million hectares have been concluded, with deals covering some 14 million more hectares still under negotiation (Land Matrix 2019; see also Kugelman and Levenstein 2012). This increase in food and agriculture investments has been fuelled by two key discourses within financial circles. First, many financial institutions market their products on the premise that agriculture is the "last big industrialization." This discourse posits that the sector will only see increased profit as the demand for commodities increases alongside a rising world population undergoing demographic shifts that result in greater incomes in emerging countries, accompanied by diets higher in grain-rich proteins such as meat and dairy (see HighQuest Partners 2010). Financial institutions offer their customers a chance to capitalize on these changes. Second,

investment funds market land and agricultural commodity investments on the grounds that they act as a good hedge against inflation
because their performance is not correlated to other more traditional
asset classes such as equities and bonds.

As money has flowed into this sector, a complex set of trends has
emerged where energy, food, and land markets are increasingly
interwoven with and affected by changes in financial markets (Isakson
2014). Stakes in agricultural commodities, food production, and farmland are increasingly being sliced up and repackaged as financial
derivatives that are very attractive to investors because of their expected
high returns and the hedging properties that they hold.

As these investments have increased, so has a growing chorus of
concern over the social and ecological consequences of these investments. To be sure, the balance sheet has been deeply contested. Some
make the case that these investments provide much-needed capital
for the sector, and that they provide liquidity for commodity markets,
assisting in price discovery and calming market volatility (Sanders
and Irwin 2010). Others have pointed out the potential for commodity
speculation to drive food price volatility, with direct implications for
hunger in the world's poorest countries (Ghosh 2010). Critics have also
connected financial actors to large-scale land acquisitions for biofuel
crop production, which has the potential to displace smallholders and
drive ecological damage due to land clearing for industrial agricultural operations (McMichael 2010; White et al. 2012; Wise 2012).

Civil society organizations jumped fully into the debate after 2010,
arguing for regulatory efforts to curb speculative financial investments
in the food system, which they linked to food price volatility, hunger,
and environmental degradation (WDM 2011; Foodwatch 2011; Oxfam
France 2013; FOE 2012; GRAIN 2012). At roughly the same time, a
number of international organizations, including the Bank for International Settlements (BIS) and UNCTAD, noted that financial investment in commodities has the potential to influence prices for those
commodities, especially in the short term (BIS 2011; UNCTAD 2011a).
Similarly, the World Bank has acknowledged that there is widespread
neglect of environmental and social norms in international farmland
investments (Deininger and Byerlee 2011, xxxii). Concerned that "race
to the bottom" practices may contribute to conflict and instability,
which ultimately reduce investment incentives, a number of governments and international organizations have promoted precautions in
order to ensure that these investments are not undertaken in ways that
can cause social and environmental harm (Deininger and Byerlee 2011;
World Bank and UNCTAD 2014).

The Rise of Responsible Investment Initiatives
for Agriculture and Land

The idea of establishing voluntary principles and codes of conduct to govern agricultural investments emerged within a broader context of voluntary measures for responsible investment, which have been promoted by both governments and business in recent decades. The rise of neoliberal, market-oriented economic policies in the 1980s provided the backdrop for the growing popularity of voluntary initiatives that encourage private companies and investors to operate sustainably. These initiatives became a prominent governance approach following the Rio Earth Summit in 1992 (see Auld, Bernstein, and Cashore 2008; Utting and Clapp 2008) and were based on the idea that voluntary responsible behaviour was in the financial interest of firms because sustainability affects their bottom line over the long term (Schmidheiny 1992). Firms also had an interest in supporting these initiatives because they might pre-empt or weaken future regulation (Lyon and Maxwell 1999).

Some voluntary initiatives were spearheaded by industry, while others have been helped along by international organizations such as the United Nations and Organization for Economic Cooperation and Development (OECD) (Clapp 2005). They include general voluntary principles on corporate practice such as the UN Global Compact, the OECD's Guidelines on Multinational Enterprises, and the International Organization for Standardization's environmental management guidelines ISO 14000 (Fritsch 2008). They also encompass industry-specific certification programs, such as Responsible Care for the chemical industry and the Mining Minerals and Sustainable Development initiative to promote sustainable mining. The Global Reporting Initiative (GRI) establishes standardized templates that firms can voluntarily follow for their corporate social responsibility (CSR) reporting. Disclosure schemes such as the Carbon Disclosure Project and the Extractive Industry Transparency Initiative rely on transparent reporting and release of information to encourage firms to act responsibly (Clapp and Meckling 2013). Voluntary certification programs have also emerged to govern global commodity chains for products ranging from timber, to fisheries, to agricultural goods (Auld 2014).

Among the suite of voluntary initiatives that have emerged in recent years are measures designed specifically to promote responsible private sector financial investment. These finance-specific initiatives in theory encompass all financial investments, including those linked to agriculture and land. The United Nations Environment Program launched its

Finance Initiative (UNEP FI) in 1992 to provide a general set of guidelines on sustainable finance with a series of statements that banks and other private financial institutions are asked to sign onto (Clapp and Dauvergne 2011). Other initiatives include the Equator Principles, launched in 2003, which establish social and environmental benchmarks to be used by private financial institutions for assessing project finance in developing countries. The Equator Principles encourage private banks to provide financing only for socially and environmentally sustainable projects in developing countries (Wright 2012). In 2006 the Principles for Responsible Investment were established on the initiative of UNEP FI and the UN Global Compact. These principles are aimed at institutional investors and encourage them to incorporate environmental, social, and governance (ESG) concerns into their investment analysis and decision-making (Gond and Piani 2012; Sievanen et al. 2013).

Voluntary initiatives aim to convince firms and investors that it is in their own best interest to act responsibly on environmental and social issues. They stress that ESG issues should be incorporated into the business models of firms because they have "material" significance. That is, at the end of the day these issues affect a firm's financial bottom line. Thus, firms are encouraged to sign onto these initiatives not just to "do the right thing" ethically, but also because it matters for their own profitability and returns (Schmidheiny 1992; Carroll and Shabana 2010).

Financial investors have the potential to act as a lever to encourage more sustainable behaviour from firms seeking to raise capital in financial markets by pressuring them to incorporate ESG issues into their business models, which in turn should result in higher returns from their investments (Kell 2009). Because they manage massive sums of money, institutional investors can have a significant influence on the practices of the firms in which they invest. Large institutional investors, pension funds in particular, have a strong interest in participating in voluntary measures for responsible investment because their members are concerned about how their retirement contributions are managed (Gond and Piani 2012). If there is both ethical and material reason to shift investments towards responsible firms, institutional investors are more likely to come on board (Kell 2009, 8). The promotional materials of these initiatives make direct links between social and environmental sustainability and the material performance of the investments. The UN PRI website, for example, stresses: "Mounting evidence of the financial materiality of ESG issues, alongside growing demands from regulators, clients, and beneficiaries for more sustainable approaches to investment, are among the key drivers behind the adoption of responsible investment practices worldwide" (UNPRI 2015).

In the agricultural sector, the prevalent discourse for responsibility is characterized by an appeal to institutional investors' long-term outlooks to ensure the ecological and social sustainability of their agricultural investments and the benefits that flow from them. Pension funds, for example, are typically characterized as having longer-time horizons than other investors, with more passive investment strategies that seek investment vehicles that require little active maintenance. Advocates of responsible investment stress the importance of these investors in ensuring that farmland investments, for example, are sustainably managed over the long term, particularly because land is an illiquid asset that institutional investors will likely hold for some time (Scott 2013). A range of initiatives promoting responsible agricultural investment emerged following the 2007–8 food crisis, when the potential for negative impacts from both commodity and land investments became increasingly evident. Although the precise impact of these investments is contested, support has grown for measures to ensure that the benefits of foreign investment in agriculture outweigh any potential costs (Hallam 2011).

As public concern grew over land grabbing in the wake of the food price spikes, the Group of Eight (G8) noted in the communiqué from its L'Aquila Summit that it was committed to establishing a set of principles and best practices to guide agricultural investment (G8 2009; Stephens 2013; Margulis and Porter 2013). The financial industry also endorsed the idea of voluntary measures, which emerged not surprisingly just as the United States and European Union began to work on strengthening financial regulatory measures to curb problems associated with speculation on commodity derivatives markets (Clapp and Helleiner 2012).

One of the first responses to the G8 call was an international round-table meeting co-hosted by Japan, the World Bank, FAO, the International Fund for Agricultural Development (IFAD), and UNCTAD in September 2009, which brought together thirteen organizations and representatives from thirty-one governments (Japan et al. 2009). This meeting sought to spearhead development of principles to guide agricultural investment that would "create a 'win-win-win' situation" to promote responsible investment in agriculture that would benefit countries, local communities, and investors (Japan et al. 2009, 2). Participants expressed general support for ongoing work by the World Bank, FAO, IFAD, and UNCTAD to further develop these areas into a set of non-legally binding principles. In practice, the World Bank took the lead in this process (Margulis and Porter 2013, 74).

The resulting document, *The Principles for Responsible Agricultural Investment That Respects Rights, Livelihoods and Resources* (PRAI), was unveiled in early 2010 (FAO et al. 2010). The PRAI outlines seven key areas to guide investment: (1) recognition and respect for existing rights over land and natural resources; (2) ensuring that investments support food security; (3) requiring transparency and good governance in land acquisitions; (4) consultation with and participation of those affected by agricultural investments; (5) ensuring economic viability; (6) promotion of positive social impacts of investments; and (7) encourage environmental sustainability. The G8 and G20 subsequently endorsed the PRAI, and it is acknowledged in the G8's New Alliance for Food Security and Nutrition (Stephens 2013; G8 2012). The PRAI are broad in their application, geared towards guiding any and all investment – public, private, foreign, and domestic – including investments from private equity firms, agri-food companies, biofuel firms, financial institutions, sovereign wealth funds, and individual entrepreneurs (FAO et al. 2010). The PRAI are now being field tested for feasibility in some forty-five to fifty investments that were already in place across Africa and Southeast Asia (GRAIN 2012; World Bank and UNCTAD 2014).

Separately, another initiative to ensure responsible investment with a specific focus on land was negotiated at roughly the same time, although discussions on this initiative predate the PRAI. The final declaration of an FAO-sponsored International Conference on Agrarian Reform and Rural Development held in 2006 highlighted the importance of establishing guidelines on land tenure. The process of establishing formal guidelines was launched by the FAO in 2009 (Seufert 2013). The result was the *Voluntary Guidelines on the Responsible Governance of Tenure of Land, Fisheries and Forests in the Context of National Food Security* (FAO 2012). The Voluntary Guidelines are specifically geared towards protecting land and resource tenure rights in cases of investment in land, fisheries, and forests, and call for the protection of customary land rights for indigenous peoples and smallholders, as well as safeguards to protect the environment. They are focused on ensuring that national governments protect those tenure rights and that all stakeholders, including private investors, respect those rights (FAO 2012). The Voluntary Guidelines were developed in a broadly consultative and inclusive process, coordinated by the FAO and involving regional consultations and negotiations at the Committee on World Food Security (CFS), including private sector and civil society participation (McKeon 2013). As such, the guidelines are widely seen to carry more legitimacy than the PRAI (Margulis and Porter 2013).

As the PRAI and Voluntary Guidelines were being discussed in tandem, including at the Committee on World Food Security in 2009–12 period, tensions emerged over the two very different processes behind them (McKeon 2013, 110). Many civil society participants at the CFS refused to formally endorse the PRAI for its lack of a consultative process and instead preferred to focus efforts on the Voluntary Guidelines (McKeon 2013). Recognizing the need for guidelines that went beyond land tenure and encompassed broader aspects of agricultural investment, and unhappy with the PRAI to serve this purpose, the CFS agreed to develop yet another set of responsible agricultural investment guidelines under a more inclusive process (Stephens 2013, 190). Consultations on the new initiative, which came to be known as *The Principles for Responsible Investment in Agriculture and Food Systems*, began in 2012, once the Voluntary Guidelines were finalized and formally adopted by the CFS. The PRIAFS goes beyond the PRAI in that it does more to recognize the role of small farmers as investors alongside corporate and financial investors, it places more emphasis on food security and the right to food, and it seeks to bring in more explicit accountability measures for investors (FAO 2014).

At the same time that the UN and other international organizations were seeking to develop guidelines and principles for responsible agricultural investment, initiatives also came forward from other quarters, including private investors themselves. In 2011 a group of signatories to the PRI launched their own voluntary measure, the Principles for Responsible Investment in Farmland (also referred to as the Farmland Principles) that list five key principles (PRI 2015). The Farmland Principles guide large-scale institutional investors, such as pension funds, on how to invest responsibly in farmland, including respect for environmental sustainability, human and labour rights, land and resource rights, ethical business standards, and transparency. These principles did not come formally out of the PRI, but rather were independently agreed to by several institutional investors themselves. A group of eight investment funds including TIAA-CREF (a U.S. teachers' pension fund), AP2 (a Swedish government pension scheme), and APB (a Dutch government pension scheme), among other investment funds, were the initial signatories. Together, these funds held US$1.3 trillion in assets at the time that they established these principles. As of 2015, some nineteen large institutional investors had signed onto the Farmland Principles. TIAA-CREF is among the largest institutional owners of farmland (with US$2.5 billion in farmland assets) and has led in promoting the Farmland Principles, advertising them prominently through its website and in separate reports on its own investments in farmland (TIAA-CREF 2012).

Additional guides provide advice to investors on how to responsibly invest in commodities and farmland. *The Responsible Investor's Guide to Commodities* is a joint initiative of the Global Compact, the PRI, the Swiss government, and OnValues – a private consulting firm (Knoepfel and Imbert 2011b). The guide maps out best practices for institutional investors seeking returns from investments in commodity derivatives, physical commodities, and farmland, as well as debt and equity in agricultural commodity producing firms. Its recommendations feature transparency and the establishment and maintenance of ESG standards along commodity chains. It acknowledges that negative social and environmental externalities – i.e., external costs – associated with financial investment are possible and warns that the lack of responsible investment to avoid those costs could "'ultimately harm investors' 'license to invest' in those markets" (6). Taking a harder line on the issue, the Interfaith Center on Corporate Responsibility published *Guidelines for Responsible Investing in Food Commodities* in 2012 (ICCR 2012). Its recommendations for institutional investors are summarized on one page. Institutional investors that are not already investing in commodities are advised not to enter into investments in this asset class, and are advised especially to avoid direct investment in commodities and commodity derivatives, commodity index funds, and exchange-traded funds. For those already in this asset class, recommendations further emphasize transparency, the promotion of ESG standards, advocacy for improved global regulation of commodity trading, and seeking out investments that explicitly provide support for smallholders and that have environmental benefits (ICCR 2012).

Familiar Pitfalls of Voluntary Initiatives: Prospects for Agricultural Investment

The broad array of responsible investment initiatives for agricultural commodities and farmland is remarkable in that it represents a major effort from a number of quarters to encourage more responsible agricultural investment from private financial and other investors. Despite the attractiveness of the material rationale for investing responsibly, the academic literature on voluntary measures finds significant weaknesses that compromise their ability to change the environmental and social behaviour of firms in practice (Vogel 2010; Clapp and Thistlethwaite 2012). Voluntary corporate sustainability measures tend to share some common pitfalls, many of which reinforce one another, and which must be considered when assessing the likely success or failure of responsible investment initiatives for agriculture. Four key shortcomings stand out in particular: generally weak requirements, low participation rates, uneven application of the business case, and the proliferation of competing initiatives. Each of these is discussed below in relation to agricultural investments.

Weak Requirements

The requirements of voluntary initiatives vary in their level of stringency, depending on the type of initiative under consideration (Auld, Bernstein, and Cashore 2008). Broad sets of voluntary principles, such as the PRI and the Global Compact, are very vague and weak in terms of what they ask for, as well in implementation and enforcement (Fritsch 2008). As a result, they are largely symbolic, aspirational goals, not legally binding in any way. The terms of engagement are also ambiguous. The UN PRI, for example, asks members to commit to its principles "where consistent with" their fiduciary responsibilities. In other words, investors need only follow the guidance when it does not harm their bottom line.

The responsible agricultural investment initiatives thus far have been broad in scope, without concrete requirements for those that endorse them. The PRAI consists of seven general principles and has no reporting requirements or enforcement mechanisms. A World Bank–UNCTAD report on the application of the PRAI in thirty-nine investments noted, for example, that transparency and disclosure were particularly weak (World Bank and UNCTAD 2014, 11). Similarly, the Farmland Principles are also simply a list of five principles with no real enforcement mechanism for signatories, although the fifth principle does call for public reporting on their implementation. The PRIAFS, while more detailed than the PRAI in its outline of what constitutes responsibility, does not incorporate its own mechanism for ensuring accountability. Rather, it calls for stakeholders to conduct assessments of potential impact and to take remedial action in cases of negative impacts or non-compliance with national laws (FAO 2014).

Low Participation Rates

The vagueness of general sets of principles can help to attract signatories, especially if there are potential gains such as the weakening of future regulation and a boost in firms' reputation for joining. In relative terms, however, voluntary responsibility initiatives tend to have low rates of participation. The PRI, for example, claims to cover 15 per cent of the institutional investment market, amounting to some $34 trillion in assets, but in practice, less than 5 per cent of that money is invested in firms with good ESG ratings (Krosinsky 2013). One recent estimate indicates that sustainably invested funds represent only 1 per cent of all assets managed globally, a very tiny slice (Krosinsky 2013). Similarly, although the Global Compact has some 12,000 members, which sounds impressive, it is only a small portion of global firms, considering that in 2010 there were over 100,000 parent firms of TNCs and nearly 900,000 foreign affiliates (UNCTAD 2011b, tab 34). The firms that do sign on to these broad initiatives may be leaders in their sectors, but many more firms are simply not participants. The Equator Principles appear to enjoy somewhat higher participation rates, although with some caveats. Ninety-six international private lending institutions have signed on to the principles, and the initiative claims that this accounts for the majority of project financing debt in emerging countries (Equator Principles 2019). According to one estimate, however, 90 per cent of the lending of the signatory banks falls outside of the scope of the Equator Principles (Wright 2012).

The responsible agricultural investment initiatives are also likely to have weak participation rates. The PRAI, the Voluntary Guidelines, and the PRIAFS are guidance frameworks for stakeholders, and because they are not collecting signatories among private sector investors, it is difficult to be certain how many investors are following them. The PRI Farmland has nineteen signatories, which are made up primarily of pension funds – a small slice of the 1,200 investment funds that are PRI members. Recent private sector stakeholder meetings on responsible investment in agriculture indicate that most big players in agricultural investment are not yet at the table (Knoepfel and Imbert 2011a, 19).

Uneven Application of the "Business Case"

The "business case" for implementing voluntary corporate responsibility initiatives is weak in many cases and thus helps to explain the low rates of participation. The effort to sign onto a voluntary initiative has to be worth it to the firm (Lydenberg 2013). Usually this is the case when a firm seeks to protect its brand reputation or bottom line (Vogel 2005). Although these factors may apply to some firms that make environmental and social responsibility a key feature of their business model and products, or in cases of high-profile firms whose brand reputations are at risk if they do not take on corporate responsibility activities, these are only a small subset of all firms (Vogel 2005). Firms may undertake cost-saving measures in any case and consider these CSR initiatives, but going further than that has proven to be a challenge for many firms. This constraint has been apparent in the case of climate change initiatives, where energy efficiency and waste minimization are typically undertaken by

firms because they result in immediate cost savings, whereas more difficult and costly measures, such as biodiversity conservation, are typically
left unaddressed (Clapp and Thistlethwaite 2012).

Further, there is only mixed evidence on whether incorporation of
ESG issues into firm management and financial investment actually
results in superior financial performance of either firms or their investors. Most studies indicate that it is a wash: no clear trend either way.
As Vogel notes, "For virtually all firms, their CSR performance and reputations remain largely irrelevant to their financial performance: they
neither improve it nor detract from it" (Vogel 2010, 82). Indeed, only
9 per cent of investments of PRI signatories actually perform well on
ESG indicators, indicating that there is little financial benefit for doing
so (Sullivan 2012).

The weak business case for signing on to voluntary initiatives already
seems to be the case with agricultural investments. In cases where adherence to an initiative is important for "brand reputation," there has
been more involvement. Large transnational agri-food processing companies with widespread name brand recognition, such as Nestlé and
Unilever, for example, have taken the lead in the certification initiatives for sustainable palm oil, which is a key ingredient in many of their
products (WWF 2012). But for less visible firms and financial actors that
are not as concerned about their brand reputation, there is less incentive to pledge responsibility via voluntary initiatives, as is discussed
more fully below.

Confusing Array of Competing Initiatives

There is a proliferation of initiatives servicing the same or similar needs
that could lead to complexity and confusion. Multiple voluntary measures seeking similar outcomes allow firms and investors to pick and
choose which set of guidelines they wish to follow (Utting and Clapp
2008). In the case of forestry, for example, after the Forest Stewardship
Council brought forward its certification initiative, which was based on
multiple stakeholder input and strict certification requirements, other
forest certification schemes emerged that were industry-led and had
less stringent requirements (Cashore 2003). Consumers looking for
sustainably harvested timber products may not realize that there are
important differences in what the different certification logos actually
require of producers, enabling those following lesser standards to still
protect their brand reputation. This crowded landscape, in effect, puts
further pressure on the various responsibility initiatives to not be too
rigorous in their requirements for fear of driving away participants.

There has also been a proliferation of initiatives in the agricultural investment space. The guidelines and principles that have emerged cover overlapping themes, and proponents claim that each applies to multiple stakeholders. But the landscape of these initiatives is already confusing. In farmland investments, for example, confusion over the differences between the PRAI, Voluntary Guidelines on Tenure, the PRIAFS, and PRI Farmland Principles has already led to questions regarding the target, coverage, and scope of each set of principles (Margulis and Porter 2013).

In sum, there are strong parallels between the more general environmental and social responsibility initiatives geared to firms, and those emerging in the realm of agricultural investment aimed at investors. Despite their best intentions, responsible investment initiatives have suffered from weaknesses that limit their transformative potential. In many ways these weaknesses appear to be applicable already to the new responsible investment initiatives in agriculture, indicating that reliance on such initiatives alone is likely to be insufficient to transform the nature of financial investments in the sector.

Private Financial Investment Complicates Responsibility Efforts

Beyond these general pitfalls of voluntary sustainability initiatives for business, there are several unique features of financial investments in agricultural commodities and farmland that make them difficult to govern effectively with voluntary mechanisms. Because the markets are highly complex and the actors are so diverse, it is especially difficult to draw the lines of cause and effect, linking investors to responsibility for specific outcomes. If responsibility cannot be attributed to specific investors or even groups of investors, then those investors are unlikely to be convinced to change their investment practices voluntarily.

Voluntary responsibility efforts have focused on changing the behaviour of firms – either directly through corporate social responsibility, or indirectly via investor or bank pressure. The Global Compact targets firms directly; the PRI targets investors' engagement with firms; and the Equator Principles target banks' financing of firms' projects. Financial investment in agriculture does not always fall into the category of straightforward investment in firms, but also includes investment in agricultural-based derivatives products, which themselves can have an impact on market fluctuations, in turn affecting food prices and access to food. In other words, ensuring investment in agriculture is responsible is not just about altering the behaviour of firms engaged in agriculture, but also the behaviour of financial investors and financial institutions that trade derivatives products. Looking more closely at the role of financial actors in international agricultural investment reveals several interrelated features of agricultural finance and investment that make the effort to ensure responsibility especially challenging.

Complexity of Agriculture-Based Financial Investments

First, the role played by financial investors in agriculture complicates the picture enormously because money is fungible – meaning that because money is mutually interchangeable with other money, it is difficult to determine whose money is responsible for which activities. Further, the agricultural derivatives that financial investors buy into are highly complex, as are the linkages between various financial investors. Bulk commodities that are traded on futures markets are also fungible – that is, a bushel of corn is a bushel of corn, and separating out sustainably produced corn from other corn in these markets is nearly impossible. These features make tracing financial investment in abstract derivatives to certain actors, and to real world outcomes, extremely difficult.

A large portion of the investment in the agricultural sector is in financial derivatives products, including index funds that track prices of a bundle containing different types of investments (Knoepfel and Imbert 2011b). As noted above, some commodity index funds bundle agricultural commodities with non-agricultural commodities, while others focus on a range of agricultural investments, including commodity futures, firm shares, and farmland. Index investments are purely financial and, as such, it becomes much less clear whose money is responsible for which outcomes. Financial institutions that offer agricultural index products to investors often make direct investment in commodity futures markets, another form of financial derivative, in order to hedge their risks associated with selling index products. Both kinds of investments can influence overall commodity price trends, which in turn influence further investment, both financial and in physical commodities and land. Holding financial investors responsible for outcomes in this context is challenging, to say the least.

The complexity of financial derivatives is compounded by the myriad relations different investor groups have to one another, which also makes it difficult to point at any one investor group as being responsible for a particular investment trend. As noted above, a range of actors, including sovereign wealth funds, pension funds, hedge funds, private equity funds, investment banks, and agri-business firms are all involved in financial investment in various types of agricultural-linked investment products. Tracking the activity of institutional investors, as noted in an FAO working paper on private foreign investment in agriculture, is difficult, even for industry analysts. Hedge funds, for example, are not required to publicly disclose their investments (McNellis 2009, 3). Further, these investor groups are often cross-investing in one another. As McNellis notes, "For example, a sovereign wealth fund could be investing in a private equity fund which in turn invests in a specialized hedge fund that is buying agricultural land while at the same time investing in the various commodity markets" (2). This complexity makes it extremely difficult to tease out which investors are driving investments, and which should be held responsible for outcomes.

Not only are the instruments and investors difficult to disentangle from one another, their connection to outcomes is also fuzzy. Consider a case where investors are putting large sums of money into commodity futures and index funds, and these investments in turn contribute to volatility of food prices, which in turn drives investment by unrelated firms in large-scale agricultural and land investments that have social and ecological consequences, such as forest clearing and smallholder displacement from land. Should the financial investors who put their money in index funds be held responsible, when their own investments are not tied to concrete investments in any specific location? The lack of a direct tangible link between the financial investments and the outcomes on the ground complicates the issue. I have referred elsewhere to this problem as one of financial "distancing" in the agri-food value chain (Clapp 2014). The complexity and abstraction of financial investment derivatives in the agricultural sector only compound this distance and make it extremely challenging to draw clear lines of responsibility from investor to outcomes.

The lack of clear lines regarding the responsibility of financial actors also reduces their incentives to participate in voluntary measures. A consultant for the Swiss government, the UN PRI, and the Global Compact interviewed investors about their role in commodities investments and noted that although most investors agreed that growing investments in commodities could lead to greater price volatility, "they do not see themselves as being primary actors in futures markets and question the notion of responsibility for those markets" (Knoepfel 2011, 25). Investors view investment by pension funds in commodity futures, for example, as unproblematic. Instead, investors saw responsibility for environmental, social, and corporate governance issues as being more closely tied to "investments in physical commodities, real assets and equity of extractive/resource intensive companies" (25).

Short-Term / Long-Term Mismatch

Second, the mismatch between long-term needs of sustainable agriculture and the short-term nature of global finance tends to weaken the business case for responsibility even further. Financial markets have been seen as a problem for the environment because they prioritize returns in the short term, which often goes against longer-term environmental aims (Helleiner 2011). Some have argued because institutional investors, in particular pension funds, have a longer-term outlook, they have a stronger chance of seeing benefits in sustainable investments (e.g., MacLeod and Park 2011). Large prominent public pension funds, for example, have been leading signatories of the PRI Farmland, which may be linked to their high visibility among their members. Harmes (2011), however, argues that the business case for environmentally sustainable financial investment, even among institutional investors such as pension funds, is weak at best. He argues that most pension funds hire external managers who are evaluated on short-term performance criteria, which in practice results in decisions that prioritize immediate returns over longer-term stewardship. Moreover, the passive nature of institutional investors makes it difficult for them to switch investments once they are made.

Lack of Branding for Certain Financial Actors

Third, many financial actors lack a public brand image and as such are not necessarily swayed by arguments that investing sustainably is good for their bottom line. As de Man (2013) points out, only a few investor types have a clear business case for responsible agricultural investment. In the case of farmland investors, those that may have some incentive to invest responsibly are those with a high-profile public face, such as development finance institutions, agri-food companies that have strong brands and high visibility, publicly held pension funds, and biofuel firms that are seeking to enter publicly regulated markets (17). For these investors, there is a case for ensuring that their investments, particularly in farmland and commodity production, are responsible, largely because external scrutiny may result in a loss of business or reputation. But for other investors, including large agricultural commodity traders and processors of raw materials, sovereign wealth funds, and private equity funds, there is likely no business case, because these firms do not have the branding or public profiles of the others. These firms are often operating in ways that are not transparent to the public in any case. As de Man notes, wealthy individuals and pure financial speculators actually have a "business case for opacity" rather than transparency (19).

With financial investments in derivatives such as commodity futures and index products, the business case becomes even less clear, because there is only an indirect link to land or production, and thus connections to outcomes, as noted above, are less easily discernible. Yet futures and over-the-counter derivative products are the most common way that investors gain exposure to the commodities sector, which is a large component of agricultural investment overall (Knoepfel and Imbert 2011a, 15). Moreover, fund managers often see greater payoffs when following the herd, which is often driven by high-frequency, algorithmic trading (Skypala 2013). Institutional investors seldom understand commodity markets particularly well, further hampering their ability to demand responsibility measures (Knoepfel and Imbert 2011a, 18). As Skypala (2013) notes, expecting institutional investors to lead the way on responsibility issues is "probably naïve."

Conclusion

Increased financial investment in agriculture has changed the agricultural landscape significantly in recent years. Financial actors are increasingly investing in a range of agricultural investment products, including agricultural commodity futures, commodity index funds, agricultural funds, farmland, and commodity production firms. As concerns have mounted over whether this new financial investment is prone to result in negative externalities, voluntary initiatives for responsible agricultural investment have begun to emerge from a number of quarters, led both by international organizations and investors themselves. This chapter has made the case that voluntary initiatives for responsible agricultural investment are likely to mirror the weaknesses exhibited by more general responsible investment initiatives. Vague guidance on the specifics, combined with a lack of concrete enforcement mechanisms, make it easy to claim adherence to these initiatives, but difficult to verify that claim. Weak rates of participation, a flimsy business case for most firms and investors, as well as confusion due to multiple initiatives are likely to result in little change in investment behaviour in practice.

In addition to these general lessons from the voluntary initiatives literature, there are further features of financial investment in agriculture that pose additional challenges for voluntary agricultural investment initiatives. The highly complex nature of these derivatives markets makes drawing the lines of cause and effect extremely difficult. But even if such linkages could be drawn clearly, the business case for responsible financial investment is far from clear, as fund managers and large institutional investors typically operate on short-term performance criteria rather than longer-term sustainability goals, and they often lack a brand image that would encourage them to ensure that their investments are responsible.

The various agricultural investment initiatives outlined in this chapter do not provide any level of detail that outlines measures to ensure responsibility with respect to financial investment in agricultural derivatives investments, a major category of financial investment in the sector. And because these initiatives are not generally monitored or enforced by governments, there is a risk that the new spate of responsible investment initiatives for agriculture will not shift the practice of financial investment in agriculture, although they may pre-empt or weaken future regulation of this type of investment. If more effective solutions are to be found, it is important that we learn from the past failures of voluntary initiatives and consider the unique features of private finance more centrally in their design.

REFERENCES

Auld, G. 2014. *Constructing Private Governance: The Rise and Evolution of Forest, Coffee, and Fisheries Certification*. New Haven, CT: Yale University Press.
Auld, G., S. Bernstein, and B. Cashore. 2008. "The New Corporate Social Responsibility." *Annual Review of Environment and Resources* 33 (1): 413–35. https://doi.org/10.1146/annurev.energy.32.053006.141106.
Bank for International Settlements (BIS). 2011. *81st Annual Report*. Basel: Bank for International Settlements. https://www.bis.org/publ/arpdf/ar2011e.pdf.
Berkovitz, D. 2009. *Position Limits and the Hedge Exemption, Brief Legislative History*. Testimony of General Counsel D.M. Berkovitz, Commodity Futures Trading Commission, 28 July. U.S. Commodity Futures Trading Commission. http://www.cftc.gov/PressRoom/SpeechesTestimony/berkovitzstatement072809.
Burch, D., and G. Lawrence. 2009. "Towards a Third Food Regime: Behind the Transformation." *Agriculture and Human Values* 26 (4): 267–79. https://doi.org/10.1007/s10460-009-9219-4.
Carroll, A.B., and K.M. Shabana. 2010. "The Business Case for Corporate Social Responsibility: A Review of Concepts, Research and Practice." *International Journal of Management Reviews* 12 (1): 85–105. https://doi.org/10.1111/j.1468-2370.2009.00275.x.
Cashore, B. 2003. "Legitimacy and the Privatization of Environmental Governance: How Non-State Market-Driven (NDSM) Governance Systems

Gain Rule-Making Authority." *Governance* 15 (4): 503–29. https://doi.org/10.1111/1468-0491.00199.

Clapp, J. 2005. "Global Environmental Governance for Corporate Responsibility and Accountability." *Global Environmental Politics* 5 (3): 23–34. https://doi.org/10.1162/1526380054794916.

– 2014. "Financialization, Distance and Global Food Politics." *Journal of Peasant Studies* 41 (5): 797–814. https://doi.org/10.1080/03066150.2013.875536.

Clapp, J., and P. Dauvergne. 2011. *Paths to a Green World: The Political Economy of the Global Environment*. Cambridge, MA: MIT Press.

Clapp, J., and E. Helleiner. 2012. "Troubled Futures? The Global Food Crisis and the Politics of Agricultural Derivatives Regulation." *Review of International Political Economy* 19 (2): 181–207. https://doi.org/10.1080/09692290.2010.514528.

Clapp, J., and J. Meckling. 2013. "Business as a Global Actor." In *The Handbook of Global Climate and Environment Policy*, edited by R. Falkner, 286–303. Chichester, UK: Wiley-Blackwell.

Clapp, J., and J. Thistlethwaite. 2012. "Private Voluntary Programs in Environmental Governance: Climate Change and the Financial Sector." In *Business and Climate Policy: Potentials and Pitfalls of Voluntary Programs*, edited by K. Ronit, 43–76. New York: UN University Press.

Cronon, W. 1991. *Nature's Metropolis: Chicago and the Great West*. New York: W.W. Norton.

Daniel, S. 2012. "Situating Private Equity Capital in the Land Grab Debate." *Journal of Peasant Studies* 39 (3–4): 703–29. https://doi.org/10.1080/03066150.2012.674941.

Deininger, K.W., and D. Byerlee. 2011. *Rising Global Interest in Farmland: Can It Yield Sustainable and Equitable Benefits?* Washington, DC: World Bank Publications.

De Man, R. 2013. "The Business Case for Transparent Land Deals." Paper presented at the Annual World Bank Conference on Land and Poverty, Washington, DC.

De Schutter, O. 2010. *Food Commodities Speculation and Food Price Crises*. UN Special Rapporteur on the Right to Food Briefing Note 2 – September. https://www2.ohchr.org/english/issues/food/docs/Briefing_Note_02_September_2010_EN.pdf.

Epstein, G.A. 2005. "Introduction: Financialization and the World Economy." In *Financialization and the World Economy*, edited by G.A. Epstein, 3–16. Cheltenham, UK: Edward Elgar.

Equator Principles. 2019. "Equator Principles." https://equator-principles.com./about/.

Fairbairn, M. 2014. "'Like Gold with Yield': Evolving Intersections between Farmland and Finance." *Journal of Peasant Studies* 41 (5): 777–95. https://doi.org/10.1080/03066150.2013.873977.

Food and Agriculture Organization (FAO). 2012. *Voluntary Guidelines on the Responsible Governance of Tenure of Land, Fisheries and Forests in the Context of National Food Security*. Rome: FAO. http://www.fao.org/docrep/016/i2801e/i2801e.pdf.

– 2014. *Principles for Responsible Investment in Agriculture and Food Systems*. Adopted by the Committee on World Food Security. http://www.fao.org/3/a-au866e.pdf.

Food and Agriculture Organization (FAO), International Fund for Agricultural Development (IFAD) United National Conference on Trade and Development (UNCTAD), and World Bank. 2010. *Principles for Responsible Agricultural Investment That Respects Rights, Livelihoods and Resources*. Discussion Note. http://siteresources.worldbank.org/INTARD/214574111138388661/22453321/Principles_Extended.pdf.

Foodwatch. 2011. *The Hunger-Makers: How Deutsche Bank, Goldman Sachs and Other Financial Institutions Are Speculating with Food at the Expense of the Poorest*. Berlin: Foodwatch.

Friends of the Earth (FOE). 2012. *Farming Money: How European Banks and Private Finance Profit from Speculation and Land Grabs*. https://www.foeeurope.org/farming-money-Jan2012.

Fritsch, S. 2008. "The UN Global Compact and the Global Governance of Corporate Social Responsibility: Complex Multilateralism for a More Human Globalisation?" *Global Society* 22 (1): 1–26. https://doi.org/10.1080/13600820701740704.

Fuchs, D., R. Meyer-Eppler, and U. Hamenstädt. 2013. "Food for Thought: The Politics of Financialization in the Agrifood System." *Competition & Change* 17 (3): 219–33. https://doi.org/10.1179/1024529413z.00000000034.

Ghosh, J. 2010. "The Unnatural Coupling: Food and Global Finance." *Journal of Agrarian Change* 10 (1): 72–86. https://doi.org/10.1111/j.1471-0366.2009.00249.x.

Gond, J-P., and V. Piani. 2013. "Enabling Institutional Investors' Collective Action: The Role of the Principles for Responsible Investment Initiative." *Business & Society* 52 (1): 64–104. https://doi.org/10.1177/0007650312460012.

GRAIN. 2012. "Responsible Farmland Investing? Current Efforts to Regulate Land Grabs Will Make Things Worse." https://www.grain.org/article/entries/4564-responsible-farmland-investingcurrent-efforts-to-regulate-land-grabs-will-make-things-worse.

Group of Eight (G8). 2009. *Responsible Leadership for a Sustainable Future*. https://www.mofa.go.jp/policy/economy/summit/2009/declaration.pdf.

– 2012. "Fact Sheet: G8 Action on Food Security and Nutrition." http://sedici.unlp.edu.ar/bitstream/handle/10915/44291/Fact_Sheet__G8_Action_on_Food_Security_and_Nutrition_U.S._Bureau_of_Economic_and_Business_Affairs__May_18__2012__5_p._.pdf?sequence=13&isAllowed=y.

Hallam, D. 2011. "International Investment in Developing Country Agriculture: Issues and Challenges." *Food Security* 3 (S1): S91–8. https://doi.org/10.1007/s12571-010-0104-1.

Harmes, A. 2011. "The Limits of Carbon Disclosure: Theorizing the usiness Case for Investor Environmentalism." *Global Environmental Politics* 11 (2): 98–119. https://doi.org/10.1162/glep_a_00057.

Helleiner, E. 2011. "Introduction: The Greening of Global Financial Markets?" *Global Environmental Politics* 11 (2): 51–3. https://doi.org/10.1162/glep_a_00053.

HighQuest Partners, United States. 2010. "Private Financial Sector Investment in Farmland and Agricultural Infrastructure." OECD Food, Agriculture and Fisheries Papers, no. 33. OECD Publishing. https://www.oecd-ilibrary.org/agriculture-and-food/private-financial-sector-investment-in-farmland-and-agricultural-infrastructure_5km7nzpjlr8v-en.

Institute for Agriculture and Trade Policy (IATP). 2008. *Commodities Market Speculation: The Risk to Food Security and Agriculture*. Minneapolis, MN: Institute for Agriculture and Trade Policy. https://www.iatp.org/files/451_2_104414.pdf.

Interfaith Center on Corporate Responsibility (ICCR). 2012. "Guidelines for Responsible Investment in Food Commodities." https://www.iccr.org/sites/default/files/resources_attachments/2012ICCRGuidelinesForInvestingInFoodCommoditiesFINAL.pdf.

Isakson, S.R. 2014. "Food and Finance: The Financial Transformation of Agro-Food Supply Chains." *Journal of Peasant Studies* 41 (5): 749–75. https://doi.org/10.1080/03066150.2013.874340.

Japan, United Nations Conference on Trade and Development (UNCTAD), Food and Agriculture Organization (FAO), World Bank, and International Food for Agricultural Development (IFAD). 2009. *Promoting Responsible International Investment in Agriculture*. https://www.mofa.go.jp/policy/economy/fishery/agriculture/summary0909.pdf.

Kell, G. 2009. "Responsible Investment: Why Should Private Equity Care?" *International Trade Forum* 4 (December): 7–9.

Knoepfel, I. 2011. *Responsible Investment in Commodities: The Issues at Stake and a Potential Role for Institutional Investors*. OnValues, Swiss Federal Department of Foreign Affairs, UN Global Compact, and UN PRI. https://www.onvalues.ch/images/publications/11-01_RI_commodities_Jan2011_v02.pdf.

Knoepfel I., and D. Imbert. 2011a. *Agri-Investing for the Long Term: The Investment Case for Responsible Investments in Agriculture*. Conference Report. Geneva: OnValues. http://www.onvalues.ch/images/publications/agri-investing_meeting_report_2011.pdf.

Knoepfel, I., and D. Imbert. 2011b. *The Responsible Investor's Guide to Commodities*. OnValues, Swiss Federal Department of Foreign Affairs, UN Global Compact, and UN PRI.

Krosinsky, C. 2013. "The State of Ownership." Network for Sustainable Financial Markets White Paper Series, March.

Kugelman, M., and S. Levenstein. 2012. *The Global Farms Race: Land Grabs, Agricultural Investment and the Scramble for Global Food Security*. Washington, DC: Island.

Land Matrix. 2019. Home page. https://landmatrix.org.

Lydenberg, S. 2013. "Responsible Investors: Who They Are, What They Want." *Journal of Applied Corporate Finance* 25 (3): 44–9.

Lyon, T.P., and J.W. Maxwell. 1999. "Corporate Environmental Strategies as Tools to Influence Regulation." *Business Strategy and the Environment* 8 (3): 189–96.

MacLeod, M., and J. Park. 2011. "Financial Activism and Global Climate Change: The Rise of Investor-Driven Governance Networks." *Global Environmental Politics* 11 (2): 54–74. https://doi.org/10.1162/GLEP_a_00055.

Margulis, M.E., and T. Porter. 2013. "Governing the Global Land Grab: Multipolarity, Ideas, and Complexity in Transnational Governance." *Globalizations* 10 (1): 65–86. https://doi.org/10.1080/14747731.2013.760930.

McKeon, N. 2013. "'One Does Not Sell the Land Upon Which the People Walk': Land Grabbing, Transnational Rural Social Movements, and Global Governance." *Globalizations* 10 (1): 105–22. https://doi.org/10.1080/14747731.2013.760911.

McMichael, P. 2010. "Agrofuels in the Food Regime." *Journal of Peasant Studies* 37 (4): 609–29. https://doi.org/10.1080/03066150.2010.512450.

McNellis, P.E. 2009. "Foreign Investment in Developing Country Agriculture: The Emerging Role of Private Sector Finance." FAO Commodity and Trade Policy Research Working Paper (28). http://www.fao.org/fileadmin/templates/est/INTERNATIONAL-TRADE/FDIs/mcnellis.pdf.

Oxfam France. 2013. "Réforme bancaire: Ces banques françaises qui spéculent sur la faim." https://www.oxfamfrance.org/communiques-de-presse/reforme-bancaire-ces-banques-francaises-qui-speculent-sur-la-faim/.

PRI. 2015. "Responsible Investment in Farmland." https://www.unpri.org/download?ac=4001.

Sanders, D.R., and S.H. Irwin. 2010. "A Speculative Bubble in Commodity Futures Prices? Cross Sectional Evidence." *Agricultural Economics* 41 (1): 25–32. https://doi.org/10.1111/j.1574-0862.2009.00422.x.

Schmidheiny, S. 1992. *Changing Course*. Cambridge, MA: MIT Press.

Scott, M. 2013. "Investors Take an Interest in Farmland." *Financial Times*, 22 January.

Seufert, P. 2013. "The FAO Voluntary Guidelines on the Responsible Governance of Tenure of Land, Fisheries and Forests." *Globalizations* 10 (1): 181–6. https://doi.org/10.1080/14747731.2013.764157.

Sievanen, R., J. Sumelius, K.M. Zahidul Islam, and M. Sell. 2013. "From Struggle in Responsible Investment to Potential to Improve Global Environmental Governance through UN PRI." *International Environmental*

Agreements: Politics Law and Economics 13 (2): 197–217. https://doi.org/
10.1007/s10784-012-9188-8.

Skypala, P. 2013. "Investors Must Use Their Powers for Good." *Financial Times*,
9 June.

Stephens, P. 2013. "The Principles of Responsible Agricultural Investment."
Globalizations 10 (1): 187–92. https://doi.org/10.1080/14747731.2013.760952.

Sullivan, R. 2012. "Managers 'Talk More Than Walk' on SRI." *Financial Times*,
1 April.

TIAA-CREF. 2012. *Responsible Investment in Farmland: Ethical Conduct and
Responsible Stewardship of the Environment.*

United Nations Conference on Trade and Development (UNCTAD). 2001.
World Investment Report. Geneva: UNCTAD.

– 2011a. *Price Formation in Financialized Commodity Markets: The Role of
Information.* http://unctad.org/en/Docs/gds20111_en.pdf.

– 2011b. "Web Table 34: Number of Parent Corporations and Foreign Affiliates,
by Region and Economy, 2010." Geneva: UNCTAD. http://unctad.org/
Sections/dite_dir/docs/WIR11_web%20tab%2034.pdf.

– 2012. *World Investment Report.* Geneva: UNCTAD.

United Nations Principles for Responsible Investment (UNPRI). 2015.
"Introducing Responsible Investment."

Utting, P., and J. Clapp, eds. 2008. *Corporate Accountability and Sustainable
Development.* Delhi: Oxford University Press.

Vogel, D.J. 2005. "Is There a Market for Virtue? The Business Case for
Corporate Social Responsibility." *California Management Review* 47 (4): 19–45.
https://doi.org/10.1177%2F000812560504700401.

– 2010. "The Private Regulation of Global Corporate Conduct: Achievements
and Limitations." *Business & Society* 49 (1): 68–87. https://doi.
org/10.1177/0007650309343407.

White, B., S.M. Borras Jr, R. Hall, I. Scoones, and W. Wolford. 2012. "The New
Enclosures: Critical Perspectives on Corporate Land Deals." *Journal of Peasant
Studies* 39 (3–4): 619–47. https://doi.org/10.1080/03066150.2012.691879.

Wise, T. 2012. "The Cost to Developing Countries of US Corn Ethanol Expansion."
Global Development and Environment Institute Working Paper no. 12-2.
http://www.ase.tufts.edu/gdae/Pubs/wp/12-02WiseGlobalBiofuels.pdf.

World Bank and United Nations Conference on Agriculture and Development
(UNCTAD). 2014. *The Practice of Responsible Investment Principles in Larger-
scale Agricultural Investments: Implications for Corporate Performance and Impact*
2011. http://documents.worldbank.org/curated/en/135321468158370655/
pdf/861750RAI0P1253560Box385174B00PUBLIC0.pdf.

World Development Movement (WDM). 2011. "Stop Gambling on Food &
Hunger." https://www.globaljustice.org.uk/sites/default/files/files/
resources/food_spec_statement_02.2011_0.pdf.

Worthy, M. 2011. *Broken Markets: How Financial Market Regulation Can Help Prevent Another Global Food Crisis*. World Development Movement. http://www.globaljustice.org.uk/sites/default/files/files/resources/broken-markets.pdf.

Wright, C. 2012. "Global Banks, the Environment, and Human Rights: The Impact of the Equator Principles on Lending Policies and Practices." *Global Environmental Politics* 12 (1): 56–77. https://doi.org/10.1162/glep_a_00097.

WWF. 2012. *The 2050 Criteria: Guide to Responsible Investment in Agricultural, Forest and Seafood Commodities*. http://awsassets.panda.org/downloads/the_2050_critera_report.pdf.

8 State-Led and Finance-Backed Farming Endeavours: Changing Contours of Investment in Australian Agriculture

GEOFFREY LAWRENCE, SARAH RUTH SIPPEL, AND NICOLETTE LARDER

Introduction

Since the conjunction of food, energy, and financial crises of 2007/8 there has been a discernible shift in the sources of foreign capital inflows in Australian agriculture with the emergence of new state-led and finance-backed actors. While finance capital has been looking to move away from uncertain markets in urban real estate, and other less-profitable commodity portfolios, to seek longer-term stable returns from farmland investment, state-led actors have come to represent increasingly important investment sources, pursuing objectives such as food security. The changing contours of investment reveal how projections about the development of global food (in)security are closely linked to the involvement of new financial players such as pension funds, as well as the intensified engagement of "traditional" actors, such as states, which, at the same time, increasingly turn to financial vehicles for their investment. The new kinds and origins of capital channelled into agriculture and food reverse patterns of capital flows in the global food system while underlining the persisting strategic importance of food.

Questions about agricultural investments have been discussed intensively in the Australian context in recent years, with a certain bias towards, and sustained interest in, investment by state-led actors from China and the Middle East. While politicians and much of the media have interpreted farmland acquisitions on behalf of financial actors such as pension funds as beneficial for the nation – providing a much-needed injection of funds into a farming sector that has experienced financial difficulties over a number of decades – investment motives such as food security have received much more ambivalent responses, leading to an increased scrutiny of foreign investments. Questions have been raised about the short- and long-term impacts of the associated changes in ownership and control of land, water, and other natural resources. Concerns have included the lack of transparency in transactions, the appropriateness of the foreign investment rules for agricultural land, and the involvement of foreign sovereign entities.

In this chapter we provide an early history of agricultural development in Australia, before tracing the ways new state-owned and finance-backed entities have invested in Australian farming and food industries. We then outline examples of investment by actors from three regional contexts – North America, the Middle East, and China – and the different ways these actors have been perceived. The chapter concludes with a discussion of the way new investments in farmland investments have been renegotiated in Australia, with a special focus on the ambiguous role the state has played in facilitating capital inflows, on the one hand, while appeasing public concern, on the other.

From British Colonization to the Neoliberal Turn: Patterns of Past Investment in Australian Agriculture

After at least some 65,000 years of Aboriginal occupation of the Australian continent, the British colonized the lands from 1788. The successive appropriation of land and resources that allowed for European-style agriculture to be developed in the settler colony was grounded essentially on the doctrine of Australia being *terra nullius* (unowned land), which served to legitimize the dispossession of indigenous peoples of their land (Banner 2005; Moran 2002). Britain desired a distant location for the disposal of convicts – often people displaced during the enclosure movement and who had subsequently turned to petty crime to survive. Also among those on the first fleet were the political activists who opposed Britain's colonization of Ireland. Self-sufficiency in food production in the new colonies of Australia was a strong priority of the British government; the convicts were not to be an economic burden on the British nation.

Early attempts at utilizing European farming methods for food production were hampered by a combination of infertile and nutrient-leached soils, limited water availability, and the difficulties of clearing lands of native eucalypts (Henzel 2007). After initial failures, movement of grain production to the fertile river flats and newly discovered deeper soils outside the colonial capitals of Sydney, Hobart, Adelaide, and Melbourne resulted in steadily increasing output. The colonizers established the same architecture of governance and the same norms of social demeanour as in Britain – importing familiar laws, bureaucratic structures, political organizations, and cultural institutions (Horne 1976). Australia was economically and socially tethered to Britain. With British industrialization proceeding at a rapid rate and textile manufacturing being a mainstay of

British industry in the late eighteenth century and throughout the nineteenth century, Australia was able to secure an expanding market for wool. Wool became the colony's most valuable export within fifty years of settlement (Henzel 2007, 47). Extensive pastoral activities on supposedly "vacant" lands in the continent's interior provided growing income to the colonial administrations and fuelled the development of both rural and urban settlements. Gold discoveries in the 1850s brought renewed economic prosperity, but it was wool that dominated exports from the 1870s to the 1960s. Australia was said to be "riding on the sheep's back" (47; Horne 1976). The 1800s was a period of nation-building capitalism (Dovers 1992) – or "statist developmentalism" – with white Australians having the highest standard of living in the world in the second half of the nineteenth century. Much of this was due to overseas investment, which was close to 35 per cent of all new capital investment in the mid-1800s, rising to 50 per cent in the 1880s (Business Council of Australia 2014, 7).

Investment in the nineteenth and much of the twentieth century was largely British-based. The opening up of inland Australia encouraged entrepreneurs like Lord Vestey to acquire vast pastoral estates (cattle ranches and sheep stations), using credit from British banks to fund development. Colonial governments – always eager to secure income from trade – also encouraged the settlement and development of farmlands, with many immigrants from England, Scotland, Wales, and Ireland venturing to Australia with small amounts of capital (often family-based loans) hoping to profit from the growing and export of crops like wheat. Another significant export crop, sugar, was produced in Australia's north, initially by the British, using cheap convict and indentured labour (Henzell 2007).

While wealth was generated from the farm sector, there were many business failures associated with drought. Following federation of the various states and territories in 1901, the Commonwealth government sought to stimulate capital accumulation in agriculture via public investment in irrigation, roads, rail, ports, and research and development (Lawrence 1987). Such infrastructure, and the pro-foreign investment stance of most federal Australian governments during the twentieth century, helped to attract U.S. money into Australia for cotton production during the 1960s, Japanese investment in feedlot operations in the 1980s, and further Asian investment in the sugar industry in the first decade of this century (Keogh and Tomlinson 2014). Countries to which Australian farm goods have been exported have typically been the ones seeking to invest in Australian supply chains, affording them a degree of control over Australian-based food production and distribution operations (Keogh and Tomlinson 2014). Up until the mid-1970s, the combination of domestic and foreign investment, along with government underwriting of agriculture via direct subsidies, bounties, tax write-offs, and tariffs, helped to build and protect the "family farm" sector of the economy (Lawrence 1987). However, following a series of oil price shocks, the demise of the Bretton-Wood agreement, and Britain's entry into the European Union during the 1970s, Australian governments developed a number of measures to expose farming to global forces, with the desire of generating greater industry efficiencies (Gray and Lawrence 2001; Gray, Oss-Emer, and Sheng 2014). Various rural reconstruction schemes encouraged farm amalgamations, tariff levels were reduced, subsidies to farming were removed, and governments continued to look for overseas capital to stimulate investment in agriculture. The neoliberal "turn," apparent in Australia as early as the mid-1970s (with neoliberalism becoming hegemonic at the beginning of the twenty-first century; see Lawrence and Campbell 2014), provided a justification for the removal of virtually all government support for agriculture. The level of support for rural producers is estimated to be some 3 per cent of the value of agricultural production – the second-lowest in the OECD after New Zealand at 1 per cent (Gray, Oss-Emer, and Sheng 2014).

According to the logic of neoliberalism, rural producers will become more cost-efficient, and consumers will benefit from lower commodity prices through enhanced competition. This will be achieved via removal of government subsidization to farming, increased exposure of the farm sector to global market forces, deregulation (including the elimination of statutory marketing arrangements that previously provided growers with power in the marketplace), and the removal of foreign exchange controls (Lawrence and Campbell 2014; and see Gray, Oss-Emer, and Sheng 2014). The future progress of such a free and open agricultural economy is viewed as requiring large capital investment from abroad. Foreign investors in Australian agriculture face fewer restrictions than the OECD average, and they are viewed by government and industry as "vital" for the development of the sector. Over the past two decades, the most viable agricultural establishments have provided a consistent 10–12 per cent annual return on investment, with half of that being increases in land value (Sanyal 2014, 17). This makes the larger, more productive Australian farms very attractive to foreign financial capital.

New Finance-Backed and State-Led Actors: Drivers of Recent Investment

Global economic and social integration has been taking place for hundreds of years. But it is in the past twenty years that information technologies have allowed for the instantaneous transfer of both knowledge and capital across the world. Those involved in financial capital investment have the responsibility of managing "impatient capital," which is often "exceedingly volatile" and desirous of quick gains (Newman and Kliot 2000). This, together with neoliberalism as an ideology justifying and promoting free markets and government deregulation (along with business-friendly re-regulation), has helped to foster globalization and, in more recent times, financialization (Lawrence 2015; Visser 2015; Lawrence and Smith 2018). Neoliberal ideologies have been translated into policy settings that have a basis in "economic rationalism." To achieve freer markets, and to promote globalization, economic rationalist measures such as deregulation/re-regulation, privatization, fiscal discipline, tax reform (to support capital), structural adjustment (to purportedly remove inefficiencies), and trade liberalization, among others, have been implemented by right-leaning governments throughout the world. Another measure – that of freeing up capital markets – has contributed to what writers have described as "financialization."

Although a somewhat slippery term (Christophers 2015; and see Ouma 2014), *financialization* is generally understood to be the increasing importance of financial institutions – such as merchant banks, private equity firms, hedge funds, and sovereign wealth funds – in shaping the operation of the global economy and national economies (Epstein 2005). The new investors employ a host of financial instruments such as derivatives, high-yield bonds, sub-prime mortgages, index funds, and credit default swaps, among others, to transform commodities into financial assets that can be traded, in the hope of increased profit, on financial markets (Tricarico 2012; Clapp, Isakson, and Visser 2016; Ducastel and Anseeuw 2016). For Krippner (2005, 174; and also 2011) this is part of a growing tendency within capitalism for "profits [to] accrue primarily through financial channels rather than through trade and commodity production."

The increased interest of financial actors in agriculture and food (Burch and Lawrence 2009; Clapp 2014; Isakson 2014; Bjørkhaug, Magnan, and Lawrence 2018) has been one key driver of the recent capital inflows to farmland. Farm commodity price increases from around 2006 were interpreted by finance capital as a signal that profits could be made from speculation on food, while other signals were seen as indicating that investment in farmlands could yield strong returns in the medium term (Fairbairn 2014). These signals included the growing scarcity of farmland on a global basis (the availability of arable land is declining and land values are rising accordingly) combined with increasing need for food (with regard to population growth); concerns about the future availability of natural resources like water and phosphate; opportunities to profit from biofuel production, particularly where governments have legislated for a blend of biofuels and fossil fuels in motor vehicles; and the growing demand of the middle classes in countries like China, India, and Indonesia for meat products and value-added processed foods (Cribb 2010; Lawrence, Sippel, and Burch 2015; Plunkett 2015; Weis 2013). The prospect of future food insecurity following a neo-Malthusian logic has thus been a crucial narrative and incentive to stimulate capital inflows into agricultural investment funds (Larder, Sippel, and Lawrence 2015).

A second driver of capital flows in to agriculture and food has been the move of some states such as the Gulf States and China to ensure food supplies for growing populations by seeking direct access to farmland and resources abroad. Likewise emerging against the backdrop of the conjunction of crises in 2007/8, this development has been described as "agro-security mercantilism" (McMichael 2013) or "neomercantilism" (Belesky and Lawrence 2018). The direct acquisition of land and natural resources for food security involves a circumvention of market mechanisms, thereby defying the neoliberal WTO architecture of the Agreement on Agriculture. At the same time, as these investments often come from contexts that had been predominantly beneficiaries of investment, established geographies of "North-South" directions in regard to capital origins and targeted contexts are being reshaped. To make the picture even more complex, some of the state-backed investments are closely interlinked with sovereign wealth funds established by various nations in recent years. In this way, food security interests are further coupled with commercial rationales and financial motives in terms of speculating on returns from farmland investment (Sippel, Böhme, and Gharios 2018). As Keulertz and Woertz (2015) point out, the agricultural investment policy choices made by the Gulf States and China underline the continued strategically important role of food for state power in the twenty-first century.

A Changing Picture of Investments?

There is no detailed information on the scale of foreign ownership of Australian agricultural land. Since the foreign ownership debate emerged in 2008, three surveys have been undertaken by the Australian Bureau of Statistics (in 2010, 2013, and 2016), which, however, received widespread criticism for the methodology applied. Similarly, the long-expected release of the data collected for the Foreign Land Ownership register as part of the revision of the foreign investment regime (see below) were regarded as largely disappointing (ATO 2016, 2017). The ongoing lack of "hard facts" on foreign land ownership is due to a skewed process of knowledge production reflecting practical obstacles as well as vested interests involved. Major issues are the different ways data are collected (depending on the state or territory), the protection of the confidentiality of private businesses, and controversies about the appropriate collection and interpretation of those data. In addition, there is the challenge of defining and tracing "foreign" ownership in a highly integrated global economy marked by fluid and territorially detached flows of capital. Hence, data need to be carefully interpreted.

Figures on foreign investment as collected by the Foreign Investment Review Board (FIRB) indicate that in the five years up until June 2012 – corresponding to the period of intensified interests in farmland following the conjunction of crises in 2007/8 – some A$12.6 billion investment in agriculture had been approved by the FIRB. This is the equivalent of 1.5 per cent of the A$844.8 of foreign investment entering Australia over that period (Sanyal 2014, 3). To interpret these numbers, two aspects are important. First, FIRB approval is needed for all proposals by foreign *government* entities; moreover, during that period, approval was required for those foreign private entities seeking to acquire an interest of 15 per cent or more in an Australian business or corporation valued above a certain annually indexed threshold (A$252 million in 2015) (see Hay and Girdler 2015). Second, as the numbers refer to the *intended* investment, they do not indicate the realized investment (although refusals have been relatively rare, as discussed below). FIRB data further show that the main sources of approved investment were Canada (24.8 per cent), the United Kingdom (21.6 per cent), the United States (11.8 per cent), the United Arab Emirates (4.9 per cent), New Zealand (4.3 per cent), and China (0.2 per cent) (Sanyal 2014, 3).

This picture of origin countries of foreign investment largely corresponds with the data published from the Register of Foreign Ownership of Agricultural Land which, in 2017, indicated that the United Kingdom, the United States, and Canada were among the top five largest foreign landowners in Australia.[1] Land under ownership structures that involved Chinese interest reached 14,422,000 hectares (corresponding to a "Chinese-only" owned portion of 9,112,000 hectares) mainly due to the participation of a Chinese investor in the sale of the Kidman cattle empire to Australian Outback Beef, realized in 2016 (discussed in more detail below) (ATO 2017, 8).

It is worth noting that in terms of foreign ownership of Australian agribusinesses, levels are likely to be much higher than land ownership, per se, which is also due to the much higher level of ownership concentration in agribusiness. For instance, according to data collected by ABARES in 2011 (Moir 2011), more than 50 per cent of the milk produced in Australia was processed by foreign-owned firms (with New Zealand–owned Fonterra and Japanese-owned Lion as major players), around 60 per cent of Australia's raw sugar production was undertaken by three foreign-owned milling groups (Singapore-Malaysian joint-venture Wilmar, Belgian-owned Finasucre, and Chinese-owned Top Glory/COFCO), Brazil's JBS alone accounted for around 24 per cent of Australia's red meat processing, and only twelve of twenty-three licensed wheat exporters operating in Australia were Australian-owned. Foreign ownership levels for most of these industries grew as a consequence of the (neo)liberalization of the economy from the mid-1980s and, for dairying, from early 2000 when the industry was deregulated (Keogh 2012, 2014).

In finance-backed investment, there is even less official information available, given that "finance capital" is not a category that appears in official Australian farm(land) ownership statistics (as provided by the Australian Bureau of Statistics). Furthermore, information is often treated confidentially by companies and government institutions alike. Available data rely mostly on media sources and the information provided by companies themselves. Magnan (2015, 6) estimates that some A$3 billion of investments have been made by farmland investment firms and finance-backed companies in recent years, suggesting that financial actors have emerged as important players in Australian agriculture. Major actors include pension funds such as the U.S.-based Teachers Insurance and Annuity Association – College Retirement Equities Fund (TIAA-CREF) and the agricultural funds that have been set up by the Australian-based Macquarie Group.

Below, a number of case studies from different actors and regional contexts illustrate the diverse picture of recent state-led and finance-backed capital inflows in to Australian farmland and food industries. We point to the different motives associated with investments and, where possible, outline public perceptions and local responses to those investments.

North America

As outlined above, firms from North America have had a history of investment in Australia. In what follows, investments by the Hancock Agricultural Investment Group and Westchester Agriculture Asset Management from North America will be presented. Both were established asset managers investing in agriculture in the United States before expanding to Australia in the early 2000s. The Boston-based Hancock Agricultural Investment Group (HAIG) is one of the world's

most prominent farmland managers, with some US$3 billion commit-
ted to agriculture on behalf of institutional investors (HAIG 2018). The
company manages some 335,000 hectares of prime agricultural land
in the United States, Australia, and Canada (HAIG 2016). HAIG con-
siders high-quality farmland to be "among the world's most valuable
assets" and has pointed to globalization and the free-trade regime of
neoliberalism as fuelling investment: "As globalization in the agricultural industry continues amid falling trade barriers, major agricultural
producing regions stand to benefit. With an increasing global population and finite amounts of quality property, farmland is likely to remain
a valuable asset class with attractive attributes for institutional investors" (HAIG 2018, 3).

These "attributes" include "attractive returns, excellent capital preservation, portfolio diversification and low to moderate risk" (HAIG
2016). For a minimum investment of some US$5 million, pension funds
and other public and private investors can use HAIG's services. Separate accounts, individually managed by HAIG, require a minimum
commitment of US$100 million. Income is maximized via the purchase
of permanent croplands, but the company also leases permanent crop-
land for customers who want lower-risk (albeit lower-return) investments. Australian farmland investments, which started in 2000, have
now reached some 4,000 hectares. These are in row crops (such as corn
and wheat) and in permanent crops (like macadamia nuts and wine
grapes), with most production concentrated in the states of New South
Wales and Queensland. HAIG's activities in Australia are operated by
the Hancock Farm Company (HFC).

Westchester Agriculture Asset Management is a global agricultural
asset manager and has some US$8 billion of assets and commitments un-
der management (WAAM 2016a). Since 2010 it has been a subsidiary of
TIAA-CREF, one of the largest non-profit retirement services company
in the United States, and serves as its affiliated asset manager. By 2014
TIAA-CREF's farmland portfolio comprised some 570,000 hectares of
farmland in the United States, Australia, and Brazil (TIAA-CREF 2015,
10), with plans to also expand into Eastern Europe (WAAM 2014). Since
2007 Westchester has invested in Australian farmlands and, to facilitate
this expansion, has established its headquarters in the wheat/sheep
farming area of Wagga Wagga, New South Wales (WAAM 2011). The
group has acquired some 200,000 hectares of land in New South Wales,
Western Australia, Queensland, and Victoria, which is being leased
out to farmers on an "own lease-out" model (Magnan 2015). Similar to
the one for HAIG, the rationale for farmland investment is tied to the
projected need for increased global food supply. Under the headline of

"Leveraging the Global Food Demand" Westchester states, "Investing in agricultural land is the most basic way to benefit from the growing worldwide demand for food.... Westchester has deep understanding of worldwide agricultural trends, and assists investors in leveraging this global demand into investment returns" (WAAM 2016b).

There are a number of reasons advanced for investments in Australia. HAIG refers to the continent's Mediterranean climate, which is considered advantageous for the production of crops not able to be grown in North America. Crop yields in Australia are viewed as high by international standards. The role of government in Australian agriculture is "limited," which means there are "few[er] regulatory constraints on production." Proximity to growing Asian markets and the "scale and efficiency" of farms are also highlighted on the company's website (HAIG 2016d). Westchester's investment is motivated by the "goal of owning farmland in all the major grain exporting countries around the world" (WAAM 2011, 3). Australia's strong export orientation is considered as a "fundamental driver for growth," while, similar to HAIG, the "proximity to Asia and the world's fastest growing countries of China and India" is emphasized: "Agricultur[al] production in Australia is well located and well positioned as these Asian economies become hungry for more and better quality food that Australia can export. Within a 24-hour period Australia can move a cargo ship of grain to Asia!" (WAAM 2011, 3).

A further consideration for investment is the ageing of the Australian farm population. Many farmers will retire without successors, and that development "open[s] the door for opportunities to purchase quality properties that haven't been on the market for generations" (WAAM 2011, 3). Moreover, Westchester sees itself in the position to develop the tenant-farmer market in Australia (younger operators who cannot afford to purchase properties evince interest in entering lease-based contracts with the company).

Field research conducted in two locations of New South Wales where Hancock and Westchester had purchased land indicated that – contrary to the food security motive of Gulf State investments (see below) – rural residents did not primarily object to the financial rationales of investors (Sippel, Larder, and Lawrence 2017; Sippel, Lawrence, and Burch 2017). Investors did, however, face backlash when they failed to engage or consult with – let alone contribute to – rural communities. This response became particularly apparent when, in 2010, rural residents felt that their rights to have their health protected and their environment unpolluted were being compromised by the Hancock Farm Company's macadamia nut operations in one of the largest areas for macadamia nut production in Australia. Nut processing sits within a "lifestyle" region of natural beauty. When the company hired helicopters to spray its crops, chemical drift affected other farms and residential housing in the district. The company failed to deal with concerns about the types of chemical sprays used and the inappropriate application of chemicals, and, when interaction with the community occurred, the company's strategy was to protect its interests.

This was not the only example of the company's apparent lack of concern. In June 2013 a court ruled that a farm worker employed on one of Hancock's Queensland-based farms was required to drive a tractor in an unsafe manner. The worker suffered neck injuries and was awarded over A$260,000 (WorkCover 2015). Then, in July 2013, Hancock cleared a stand of tallowwood trees on one of its Dunoon macadamia properties. Tallowwoods provide a habitat for koalas, and removal of the trees placed the animals' lives in jeopardy. There were no legal sanctions that could have been imposed – "boundary" clearing can occur without the need for council approval. When asked to explain the actions of the company, the manager of the property replied, "No comment" (Parks 2013). Hancock was one of the first companies to venture into agricultural land investment and, as the above examples indicate, has demonstrated a low level of corporate social responsibility. Arguably the increasing distance between the actors involved supports this low level of social responsibility, as it helps to abstract from the social contexts. Financial investment can thus work as a further distancing mechanism in the agri-food system (Clapp 2014). More field research is needed to find out if other financial actors might be operating in the same vein and put returns to shareholders above local community concerns.

The Arab Gulf States

Established in Australia in 2009, Hassad Australia is a subsidiary of the Hassad Food Company, which is itself owned by the Qatar Investment Authority, the sovereign wealth fund of the Qatari government founded in 2008. Hassad Australia owns fourteen aggregated pastoral and cropping properties – mostly located in the states of New South Wales, Victoria, and Western Australia – comprising some 300,000 hectares (Hassad Australia 2016). Established at a time of global price volatility in food, when food imports to Qatar had become increasingly expensive as well as uncertain (as the result of a number of export bans), Hassad Australia was part of the wider strategy of the Qatar National Food Security Programme to establish a worldwide food network. Investments were originally driven by the company's aim to obtain reliable food supplies for the people of Qatar – that is, to re-patriate food to Qatar in case of food shortages (RRATRC 2013, 56). This was criticized by the Australian Senate's Rural and Regional Affairs and Transport References Committee (RRATRC 2012, 11), which argued foreign nations and companies should invest on a commercial basis, "not for food security purposes." It also criticized the possibility, in non-commercial ventures, of "tax revenue leakage" from Australia, indicating this could undermine Australia's sovereignty while depriving the federal government of revenue needed to provide infrastructure and public services (11). Hassad Australia's position is that its investments in farming should provide a commercially based dividend to the Hassad Food Company: it is looking to maximize shareholder value. Nevertheless, its "backup" function in case of future food shortages in Qatar remains, as Hassad Food is to be able to make the first offer on food, albeit at world market prices (see Sippel 2015, 991).

On its website, Hassad Australia emphasizes the "Australianness" of the company by pointing out that while the company chair, Nasser Mohamed Al Hajri, is Qatari, four of its six board members are Australian, and its Sydney head office is "fully managed and staffed by Australians" (Hassad Australia 2016). It also is keen to display its commitment to Australia's governance regimes: "As an Australian company, we are bound by all Australian Legislation and Regulations, Foreign Investment Review Board requirements and operate according to international best practice corporate governance standards" (Hassad Australia 2016).

The company produces livestock (mainly sheep) and grain for the Australian and export markets and seeks to reduce production risk via geographic diversification. It prides itself on "supporting local communities" and "emphasising local buying in each region" (Hassad Australia 2016). Interviews conducted in one location where Hassad properties are located have revealed mixed feelings about Hassad's presence. Some interviewees saw the inevitability of foreign capital entering local farming and recognized it has been part of a continuing pattern. The issue was, rather, whether foreign owners would become "good corporate citizens" and engage with the community. For others, foreign ownership was deemed to be less preferable to family-farm agriculture, with some seeing it eventually undermining the family-farm sector altogether – with negative consequences for rural society (Sippel 2015, 993–6). Other local responses reflected the national discourse around the nexus between foreign ownership and food security, identifying the company as a vehicle for agro-security mercantilism exploiting Australian resources in order to feed another nation's population.

More recently, Hassad started to reorganize its farming portfolio in Australia and divested some of its major holdings to instead invest in downstream operations such as food marketing and processing. This can be interpreted as a response to the backlash the land acquisitions received, as well as a more general shift away from food security to "overall returns for investors" (CEO John McKillop, quoted in Cranston 2017). This change of strategy is in line with the more general observation that sovereign wealth funds have moved away from the focus on primary production to become more active investors further up the value chain of agri-businesses (Sippel, Böhme, and Gharios 2018).

China

Self-sufficiency in food production was, until the turn of this century, a key strategy in China's food security policy (Zhang 2014). In 2001, when China joined the World Trade Organization, barriers to food (and other) imports to China were lowered, and international trade to and from China burgeoned. In 2012–13 the United States supplied some US$26 billion, or 24 per cent, of total agricultural imports to China, with oilseeds (particularly soybean), cotton, and meat being the main imports, followed (from other countries) by products such as dairy, wine, coffee, and tea (Gale, Hansen, and Jewison 2015, 2). A combination of escalating demand for meat and processed foods from an increasingly wealthy middle class, together with water shortages, farm soil degradation, and the removal of rural labour via urbanization policies, has placed considerable pressure on the Chinese to increase their food import (Department of Foreign Affairs and Trade 2012; Zhang 2014). The apparent over-reliance upon the United States for food supplies was perceived to be a problem (Zhang 2014). In an effort to overcome possible dependence, and in line with a continuing "deep seated Sino-US distrust" (1) the Chinese government developed a number of policy initiatives in an effort to diversify the sources of its food imports.

In contrast to the move east by the U.S. government in search of new markets, China has begun "marching west," identifying soil resource–rich areas in locations like Russia, Central Asia, and Europe for food production and export (Zhang 2014, 1). The "one belt, one road" – introduced in 2013 by President Xi Jinping – will open up new farming areas in Eurasia to Chinese investment, potentially reducing reliance upon the United States for food supply (EY 2015). But the Chinese search for new and reliable food sources has not been contained to Eurasia. By 2012 Chinese investment in Australia reached US$50 billion. Nearly all of this investment was in the mining and gas sectors, but there has been considerable and growing interest in renewable energy, real estate, and farming and food industries (KPMG 2013, 1; Felton-Taylor 2016). Major motives for investment in Australian food and farming industries are profit-seeking and stable returns over the long term (Felton-Taylor 2016). Moreover, Chinese investors have viewed Australia as a producer of quality "clean and green" food products, as a nation that welcomes and facilitates foreign investment, and as an economic partner via the China-Australia Free Trade Agreement, which came into effect in October 2015 (Ge 2015; Vidot 2015; Felton-Taylor 2016).

Agricultural investments have been made by both privately owned companies, whose ownership is often concentrated in the hands of their founders and close family members, and by the state – via state-owned enterprises (SOEs). The information in the adjacent box provides a snapshot of some of the recent investments in Australian food and farming industries.

Private Company Investments

2012: Shandong Ruyi bought Queensland's Cubbie Cotton Group for A$277 million

2013: New Hope Investment Fund bought Queensland's Kilcoy Pastoral abattoir for A$60 million

2015: Dashang purchased the beef grazing property, Glenrock Station, central NSW, for A$45 million

2016: Lu Xianfeng, owner of Ningbo Xianfeng New Materials, bought Tasmanian Van Diemen's Land dairy company through dedicated investment vehicle Moon Lake Investments, for A$280 million

2016: Australian Outback Beef, a joint venture between Hancock Prospecting (67 per cent owned by Australian billionaire Gina Rinehart), and Shanghai CRED (33 per cent, a private real estate developer owned by Chinese billionaire Gui Guojie) purchased S Kidman for A$386.5 million.

State-Owned Investments

2011: Shanghai Bright Food Group purchased Manassen Food in NSW for A$530 million

2011: COFCO bought Tully Sugar in north Queensland for A$145 million

2014: COFCO/Hasting Fund Management bought the port of Newcastle, to export ore and grain, for A$1.7 billion

Sources: Locke (2014); Rowley (2015); Beavis (2016); Johanson (2016)

The China National Cereals, Oils and Foodstuffs Corporation (COFCO) provides an example of the activities of a Chinese SOE. Formed in 1949, it has a monopoly on importing and exporting foodstuffs, including fats and oils. It is a diversified conglomerate whose operations include farming, food processing, warehousing, transportation, port operations, hotels, real estate, and financial services (GRAIN 2016, 177). Following its acquisition of controlling shares in grain-trading firms Nidera and Noble in 2014, it has become one of the world's largest grain traders. It is a representative of the "dragon head enterprises," which seek vertical integration of global food supply chains as part of the Chinese state's deliberate move from peasant-based food production to national and global agribusiness (179). COFCO is a member of the Australia-Sino 100-Year Agricultural and Food Safety Partnership, which was launched in 2014 by Australian billionaire miner Andrew Forrest (Kitney 2015a). Its largest farm deal was the purchase, for $145 million, of Tully Sugar, supplying 10 per cent of Australia's yearly sugar crush. It is seeking investments in the Australian grain, beef, and dairy industries (Kitney 2015a), looking for vertical integration in supply chains for enhanced business opportunities. Its president, Patrick Yu, informed a business meeting in Melbourne, "For us, it is very important to build a supply chain by working together with our partners. We are becoming a global citizen. We are not just a Chinese company any more" (quoted in Kitney 2015b).

If the company is "going global," as is its mandate, and is seeking to work closely with its partners, should Australians have any concerns? According to Nick Xenophon, a former independent federal senator from the state of South Australia, SOEs such as COFCO are "effectively arms of foreign governments.... We should be selling the food, not the farm" (quoted in Cowie 2011). KPMG, in contrast, points out that Chinese investors have purchased less than 1 per cent of Australian farmland and are not interested in owning "vast tracts of land," preferring, instead, to target processing industries and ensuring the export, from Australia, of "high quality, semi-processed foods" that can be purchased by the Chinese (KPMG 2014, 38). While debates ensue about China's potential neocolonial strategy of "outsourcing the farm," there is counter-evidence of a "genuine commitment" by the Chinese to build strong partnerships that will generate food production increases globally, as well as improve global food trade (Morton 2012). Accordingly, "SOEs are not only attracted to [agri-food assets] as financial opportunities, but also as a means to secure their food supply.... Post-GFC, Australian agricultural assets and agribusinesses are particularly valued in their tangibility, as opposed to abstract financial derivatives.

These alternative assets appeal as long-term and low-risk investments" (Nunzio 2014, 6).

A separate concern is that the SOEs have considerable advantage over fully commercially based entities in receiving preferential interest rates from the Chinese government. Such "privileges" can provide economic advantage to the SOEs, reducing the competitive nature of investment and trade (Ramasamy 2016).

Discussion and Conclusion: The Ambivalent Role of the State in Navigating Investments

This chapter has argued that there has been a shift in capital inflows into Australian farmland and agri-food industries with state-led and finance-backed investors emerging as new actors. As the introduction affirmed, foreign investment has been key to Australian nation building, in general, and the expansion and prosperity of Australian agriculture, in particular. Since 2008, however, the assumed "sell-out" of Australian farmland to foreign investors has been a topic heatedly debated by the Australian public. It figured prominently in two election campaigns, prompted the introduction of a foreign landownership register, and led to a fundamental revision of Australia's foreign investment regime. Below, we outline some of the concerns about foreign investment in Australian farmlands – the lack of transparency in transactions and the appropriateness of foreign investment rules along with the "national interest" – and delineate how the government has responded to these concerns. We conclude by pointing to the ambivalent role of the state in channelling capital in to agriculture, more generally.

In terms of lack of transparency, the foreign investment debate notably revealed that Australia had no reliable data on the ownership of farms and irrigation water, while foreign ownership of firms in the agri-food supply chain was "largely anecdotal" (Keogh and Tomlinson 2014, 6). The government acknowledged that there has been "poor information on the extent, location and origin of foreign investment in Australian agriculture" (quoted in Australian Treasury 2015, 11) with "no definitive data source" available, having a negative impact on the public perception of Australia's investment regime: "The absence of available information on what foreign investors have purchased and how much of Australian land is actually held by foreign investors is further undermining the integrity and public confidence of the foreign investment framework" (14).

In response to this situation and continuing community concerns, the federal government established the Register of Foreign Ownership of

Agricultural Land on 1 July 2015 and launched a "stocktake" of current ownership, requiring foreign persons and companies to notify the government of existing acquisitions. As mentioned above, however, although the publication of data from the register gives a certain understanding about the national origins of foreign landowners in Australia, the aggregate nature of the data has been received with disappointment. Data provided essentially protects business interests involved and does not disclose further information on ownership structures such as private ownership versus institutional ownership. At the same time, the debate has moved from placing the emphasis on the sheer number of "hectares" owned by "foreigners" to questions such as the productive capacity or value associated with the land.

The debate furthermore raised critical questions regarding the appropriateness of the foreign investment rules more generally. As a consequence, the government has substantially reviewed Australia's foreign investment regime, and the rules regarding investments in agricultural land, in particular. Since 2015 a new regime has been in place, which, among other things, includes a special threshold mechanism applied for foreign investments in agricultural land (Jepps 2015). The new threshold for investments in land is now fixed at A$15 million[2] and refers to the cumulative value of farmland owned by a foreign investor (that is, accounts for all investments of that person or company, not just the proposed investments). If investment proposals fall into the respective category, they require approval by the federal treasurer, which includes a "national interest" test whereby the treasurer is assisted by the Foreign Investment Review Board (FIRB). The FIRB is a non-statutory body advising the Australian treasurer on whether the national interest will be served by a particular investment. However, it is not as simple as this. Australia has signed free trade agreements with many governments, and investment levels determined in those agreements are different from (and take precedence over) the new FIRB guidelines. For example, the A$15 million threshold will not apply to the United States, New Zealand, Chile, Singapore, and Thailand (although it will with others in free trade agreements – Japan, Korea, and China) (Australian Treasury 2015, 23). What is more, it should be noted that the treatment of foreign government investors (such as Hassad Australia and COFCO) has remained the same: any government investor has to obtain prior approval before acquiring a financial interest in land, irrespective of the value of that investment (that is, the threshold starts at A$0).

The FIRB is expected to apply the "national interest" test to farmland purchase – ensuring purchases that are contrary to the national interest are rejected (Australian Treasury 2015, 2). As one newspaper reported, the FIRB "rarely, if ever has come across a foreign takeover it did not like" (*News Weekly* 2015). The FIRB is a panel composed largely of business people (Uren 2015), so it is not surprising that they support money flowing into Australia: this is in line with the views of the Business Council of Australia (2015), a strong supporter of neoliberalism. Thus, reducing the threshold at which land purchase will be scrutinized is unlikely to translate into a significant reduction in approvals. At the same time, however, some rejections occurred in the past, demonstrating the thin lines along which Australian governments have steered their position between the neoliberal mantra of "being open for business" and the need to appease heightened public concerns about national control over key resources. One example is the attempted takeover of Australia's largest grain handler and exporter, GrainCorp, by the U.S.-based Archer, Daniels Midland in 2013. The acquisition was rejected on the grounds that it was not in Australia's interests to allow key infrastructure such as silos and ports to be owned by a foreign company.

Another example is the sale of the Kidman company, which is probably the most spectacular land transaction Australia has seen over the past decade. The Kidman company is Australia's largest agricultural business in terms of the size of its property of over 10 million hectares when it came on the market in 2014. During the sale, which took twenty months to be completed, the treasurer twice blocked the intended sale of the majority parts of the company to the Chinese consortium Dakang Australia over concerns regarding national security and the national interest. In the second refusal the treasurer explicitly stated his concern about a limited Australian participation in the bidding process: "The form in which the Kidman portfolio has been offered as a single aggregated asset, has rendered it difficult for Australian bidders to be able to make a competitive bid" (Treasurer 2016). He added that there was significant domestic interest in Kidman while suggesting that the approval of the deal would affect the "broader Australian support for foreign investment in Australian agriculture" (Treasurer 2016). Commentators thus saw the Kidman case as a substantial reinterpretation of the national interest test and observed a new policy objective that allowed Australian firms to have a substantial stake in the bidding process, representing an "inherently protectionist" turn and "de facto introduction of a local ownership policy for agricultural land" (Kazakevitch and Wilson 2016). Eventually, the bid by Australian Outback Beef received FIRB approval, a joint venture between Chinese-owned Shanghai CRED as minority and Australian-owned Hancock Prospecting as majority stakeholder. The Kidman sale can be considered as a unique case that reflects the specific constellation of bad timing of the attempted deal shortly before the federal elections in July 2016, given the contested nature of Chinese investment, on the one hand, and the particular significance of the Kidman company as Australia's largest landowner and "national icon," on the other (Sippel 2018). Nevertheless it demonstrates that investment from China has become highly politicized.

That investments were refused points to the ambivalent character of the term *national interest*. The FIRB would normally consider whether a foreign investment in farming compromised national security, reduced competition, or allowed a company to avoid tax. It would also assess whether it built capacity in agriculture, enhanced that nation's ability to supply farm products, raised farm productivity, conformed with environmental laws, and had positive impacts on regional employment (see Australian Treasury 2015, 4). However, apart from these guidelines there is no definition of what the "national interest" means in concrete terms. This leads to a situation where, as Uren (2015, 193–4) has stated, "It is left entirely up to the treasurer to determine and the decision cannot be appealed through the courts.... For the most part, transactions get waved through.... By the standards set down by the OECD, it is a travesty. Australia's investment policy lacks transparency, predictability and accountability." Given that there had been attempts to define the "national interest" during the revision process, which were unsuccessful, this situation is not random but reflects a deliberate political decision: the non-definition of the national interest allows the treasurer to have greater flexibility in assessing investment proposals.

Importantly, the state has not retreated from involvement in the economy. Instead, it has itself become "neoliberalized," ensuring its economic rationalist policies conform to corporate capital's agenda of exploring all options for enhanced capital accumulation. The deregulated and "hollowed out" state lacks the capacity to provide the infrastructure and investment that might once have occurred, increasing the need for private capital inflows. In the case of Australia this translates specifically into an assumed need of foreign capital: "Australia continues to have considerable need for investment in infrastructure and in our export sectors that cannot be met from domestic savings alone. Significant amounts of capital will be required in sectors where Australia enjoys a comparative advantage in order to improve our productivity and efficiency and enable us to succeed in global markets – for example ... agriculture.... As we have done in the past, we will need access to foreign capital" (Business Council of Australia 2015, 7). Hence, states have not only reshaped investment options around agriculture to make it attractive to private capital investment (Martin and Clapp 2015; Larder, Sippel, and Argent 2018); there is also a need to legitimize capital inflows, often by referring to market logics and the claim that foreign capital is needed to make underutilized land productive (Li 2015, 563). Given the continued adherence to productivism (see Argent 2002) relying on ever more capital inflows, foreign investment is likely to remain a key feature of Australia's agri-food industries in the future, be it in the form of private capital, financial capital, or capital invested by foreign governments. As this chapter has demonstrated, a certain tension has emerged between the asserted need for foreign capital, on the one hand, and the contestation around origins and associated motives and character of capital, on the other, which can be interpreted as a substantial renegotiation of the legitimate grounds upon which investment should occur (Sippel 2018).

In particular, foreign investment has received a backlash when the "real" motives for investment appeared dubious. Here, investment by SWFs and SOEs is being viewed as representing government interests such as food security rather than strict commercial dealings, and are particularly contested in the cases of China or the Gulf States. These concerns are further compounded by a lack of transparency around investments, along with the unclear nature of foreign sovereign interests involvement. Finance-backed investments from North America have not been perceived in a similarly critical manner. When contestation occurred it was less directed to the geographical origin or motives of the companies but directed towards their interaction with local communities. Issues concerned the ability to "fit" with the needs and aspirations of local communities, the capacity to communicate with locals, and ensuring integrity of the environment. Friction occurred when financial actors ignored community concerns and placed their profit-making activities ahead of perceived local and national desires.

Hence, perceptions of recent investments are drawn along an array of complex and multi-layered understandings and connotations of land and food and associated concerns regarding the control over natural resources. The above discussion has shown that while the state is at the forefront of efforts to secure ever-increasing amounts of foreign capital for agriculture, it also has to handle the various interests and concerns involved with care. While the register of transactions can be seen as an attempt to depoliticize investment and help to allay fears, it might just as likely have the opposite effect and fuel further discussion as it reveals that "foreign capital" is becoming an increasingly unsatisfactory term to assess and debate the implications of investments.

Acknowledgments

The research presented in this chapter was part-funded by the Australian Research Council (project nos DP 110102299 and DP 160101318). The fieldwork was part-funded by an LDPI small grant that Dr Sarah Ruth Sippel received from the International Institute of Social Studies, Erasmus University, Rotterdam. Emeritus Professor Lawrence was part-funded by the Ministry of Education of the Republic of Korea and the National Research Foundation of Korea (NRF-2016S1A3A2924243) and the Norwegian Research Council (FORFOOD project no. 220691).

NOTES

1 Detailed numbers provided were as follows: 16,445,000 hectares of land were under ownership structures including UK interest, 2,693,000 hectares of land were under ownership structures including U.S. interest, and 2,130,000 hectares of land were under ownership structures including Canadian interest; this corresponded to a foreign-owned "portion" of 9,752,000 hectares (UK), 2,550,000 hectares (U.S.), and 2,034,0000 hectares (Canada) (ATO 2017, 8). The total area of land that involved some foreign ownership given was 50,515,000 hectares (or a "portion" of 36,573,000 hectares), which is the equivalent of 13.6 per cent of the total area of agricultural land as calculated by the Australian Bureau of Statistics (4).

2 Previously, the threshold for agricultural land was the same as for other areas of investment. FIRB approval was needed for attempted acquisitions of an interest of 15 per cent or more in an Australian business or corporation valued above a certain annually indexed threshold. In 2015, the threshold was A$252 million for most foreign investors.

REFERENCES

Argent, N. 2002. "From Pillar to Post? In Search of the Post-Productivist Countryside in Australia." *Australian Geographer* 33 (1): 97–114. https://doi.org/10.1080/00049180220125033.

Australian Taxation Office (ATO). 2016. *Register of Foreign Ownership of Agricultural Land*. Report of registrations as at 30 June 2016.

– 2017. *Register of Foreign Ownership of Agricultural Land*. Report of registrations as at 30 June 2017.

Australian Treasury. 2015 "Regulation Impact Statement: Implementing Foreign Investment Reforms." https://www.google.com/url?sa=t&rct=

j&q=&esrc=s&source=web&cd=1&cad=rja&uact=8&ved=
2ahUKEwjQq7OAyvvhAhVMXn0KHaMbA_gQFjAAegQIAhAC&url=
https%3A%2F%2Fris.pmc.gov.au%2Fsites%2Fdefault%2Ffiles%2Fposts%
2F2015%2F09%2FForeign-investment-reforms-RIS-web-accessible.
pdf&usg=AOvVaw0JrYza_KOIZE9TbIXJ_fC9.

Banner, S. 2005. "Why *Terra Nullius*? Anthropology and Property Law in Early
Australia." *Law and History Review* 23 (1): 95–131. https://doi.org/10.1017/
S0738248000000067.

Beavis, L. 2016) "Australia's Largest Dairy Firm Van Diemen's Land Company
Sold to Chinese Buyer." ABC, 31 March. http://www.abc.net.
au/news/2016-04-01/chinese-buyer-celebrates-sale-completion-vdl-dairy-
company/7290442.

Belesky, P., and G. Lawrence. 2018. "Chinese State Capitalism and Neomercantilism in the Contemporary Food Regime: Contradictions, Continuity
and Change." *Journal of Peasant Studies* (online 2 May): 1–23. https://doi.org
/10.1080/03066150.2018.1450242.

Bjørkhaug, H., A. Magnan, and G. Lawrence, eds. 2018. *The Financialization of
Agri-food Systems: Contested Transformations*. London: Routledge.

Burch, D., and G. Lawrence. 2009. "Towards a Third Food Regime: Behind the
Transformation." *Agriculture and Human Values* 26 (4): 267–79. https://doi.
org/10.1007/s10460-009-9219-4.

Business Council of Australia. 2014. "Discussion Paper on Foreign Investment
and State-Owned Enterprises: Managing the Risks to Maximise the
Benefits." Melbourne: BCA.

– 2015. *Building Australia's Comparative Advantages: A 21st-Century Agrifood
Sector*. Melbourne: BCA.

Christophers, B. 2015. "The Limits to Financialization." *Dialogues
in Human Geography* 5 (2): 183–200. https://doi.org/10.1177/
2043820615588153.

Clapp, J. 2014. "Financialization, Distance and Global Food Politics." *Journal
of Peasant Studies* 41 (5): 797–814. https://doi.org/10.1080/03066150.
2013.875536.

Clapp, J., R. Isakson, and O. Visser. 2016. "The Complex Dynamics of Agriculture as a Financial Asset: Introduction to Symposium." *Agriculture and
Human Values* 34 (1): 179–83. https://doi.org/10.1007/s10460-016-9682-7.

Cowie, T. 2011. "Foreign Ownership of Aussie Land: The Peril of Selling
the Farm." Crikey, 16 June. http://www.crikey.com.au/2011/06/16/
foreign-ownership-of-aussie-land-the-peril-of-selling-the-farm/.

Cranston, M. 2017. "Qatar's Sovereign Wealth Fund Offloads Australian
Farm." *Australian Financial Review*, 24 July.

Cribb, J. 2010. *The Coming Famine: The Global Food Crisis and What We Can Do to
Avoid It*. Berkeley: University of California Press.

Department of Foreign Affairs and Trade. 2012. *Feeding the Future: A Joint Australia-China Report on Strengthening Investment and Technological Cooperation in Agriculture to Enhance Food Security.* Canberra: FAT.

Dovers, S. 1992. "The History of Natural Resource Use in Rural Australia: Practicalities and Ideologies." In *Agriculture, Environment and Society: Contemporary Issues for Australia,* edited by G. Lawrence, F. Vanclay, and B. Furze, 1–18. Melbourne: Macmillan.

Ducastel, A., and W. Anseeuw. 2016. "Agriculture as an Asset Class: Reshaping the South African Farming Sector." *Agriculture and Human Values* 34 (1): 199–209. https://doi.org/10.1007/s10460-016-9683-6.

Epstein, G.A. 2005. "Introduction: Financialisation and the World Economy." In *Financialisation and the World Economy,* edited by G.A. Epstein, 3–16. Cheltenham, UK: Edward Elgar.

EY. 2015. *Riding the Silk Road: China Sees Outbound Investment Boom.* http://www.ey.com/Publication/vwLUAssets/ey-china-outbound-investment-report-en/$FILE/ey-china-outbound-investment-report-en.pdf.

Fairbairn, M. 2014. "'Like Gold with Yield': Evolving Intersections between Farmland and Finance." *Journal of Peasant Studies* 41 (5): 777–95. https://doi.org/10.1080/03066150.2013.873977.

Felton-Taylor, A. 2016. "New Foreign Investment Figures Show China's Appetite for Aussie Farms." ABC, 10 April. http://www.abc.net.au/news/2016-04-11/dist-firb-figures-show-china-appetite-australian-farms/7315988.

Gale, F., J. Hansen, and M. Jewison. 2015. *China's Growing Demand for Agricultural Exports.* USDA Economic Information Bulletin No. 136. Washington, DC: USDA.

Ge, J. 2015. "What Else Is China Buying in Australia?" bluenotes, 15 December. https://bluenotes.anz.com/posts/2015/12/what-else-is-china-buying-in-australia/.

GRAIN. 2016. *The Great Climate Robbery.* North Geelong, Australia: Spinifex.

Gray, I., and G. Lawrence. 2001. *A Future for Regional Australia: Escaping Global Misfortune.* Cambridge: Cambridge University Press.

Gray, E., M. Oss-Emer, and Y. Sheng. 2014. *Australian Agricultural Productivity Growth: Past Reforms and Future Opportunities.* ABARES Research Report 14.2, Canberra: ABARES.

Hancock Agricultural Investment Group (HAIG). 2016. "About Us." http://hancockagriculture.com/about/.

Hassad Australia. 2016. "About Us." https://www.hassad.com/English/AboutUs/Pages/default.aspx.

Hay, A., and S. Girdler. 2015. "Red Tape to Be Applied to Foreign Acquisition of Foreign Land." Clayton UTZ. http://www.claytonutz.com/publications/

edition/19_february_2015/20150219/red_tape_to_be_applied_to_
foreign_acquisitions_of_agricultural_land.page.

Henzell, T. 2007. *Australian Agriculture: Its History and Challenges*. Victoria:
CSIRO Publishing.

Horne, D. 1976. *Money Made Us*. Victoria: Penguin Books.

Isakson, S. 2014. "Food and Finance: The Financial Transformation of Agro-
Food Supply Chains." *Journal of Peasant Studies* 41 (5): 749–75. https://doi.org/
10.1080/03066150.2013.874340.

Jepps, L. 2015. "Revision to the Foreign Investment Regime in Australia."
Atanaskovic Hartnell. www.ah.com.au/_uploads/documents/Revision%20
to%20the%20Foreign%20Investment%20Regime%20in%20Australia.pdf.

Johanson, S. 2016. "Government Approves Kidman Cattle Empire Sale to Gina
Rinehart." *Sydney Morning Herald*, 9 December. https://www.smh.com.au/
business/government-approves-kidman-cattle-empire-sale-to-gina-rinehart-
20161209-gt7kgf.html.

Kazakevitch, G., and J. Wilson. 2016. "Morrison's Ruling on Kidman & Co
Sale Redefines the National Interest Test." *Conversation*, 29 April.

Keulertz, M., and E. Woertz. 2015. "States as Actors in International Agro-In-
vestments." *International Development Policy / Revue internationale de politique
de développement* 6. https://doi.org/10.4000/poldev.2023.

Keogh, M. 2012. "An Overview of the Challenges and Opportunities Associated with Foreign Ownership of Australian Agricultural Land and
Agri-Businesses." University of Western Australia. http://www.ioa.uwa.
edu.au/__data/assets/pdf_file/0006/2151690/1Mick-Keogh-Keynote-ad-
dress-speech.pdf.

Keogh, M., and A. Tomlinson. 2014. "Australia Has an Open Door for Foreign
Investment, but Voters Hold the Keys." Australian Farm Institute, February.
http://www.farminstitute.org.au/newsletter/2014/February_2014/
February_2014_featurearticle.html.

Keulertz, M., and E. Woertz. 2015. "States as Actors in International Agro-In-
vestments." *International Development Policy / Revue internationale de politique
de développement* 6. https://doi.org/10.4000/poldev.2023.

Kitney, D. 2015a. "China Giant Cofco Looking at Beef, Dairy Sectors." *Australian*, 27 October. http://www.theaustralian.com.au/business/in-depth/
global-food-forum/china-giant-cofco-looking-at-beef-dairy-sectors/
news-story/afc66e6b147fe5200798567b7dd53946.

Kitney, D. 2015b. "China Giant Cofco Tucks into Food Deal." *Australian*, 2 July.
http://www.theaustralian.com.au/business/china-giant-tucks-in-to-
food-deal/news-story/b7179aec7f0e065223f40456a1e9328a.

KPMG. 2013. *Demystifying Chinese Investment in Australia*. Sydney: KPMG.

– 2014. *Demystifying SOE Investment in Australia*. Sydney: KPMG.

Krippner, G. 2005. "The Financialization of the American Economy." *Socio-Economic Review* 3 (2): 173–208. https://doi.org/10.1093/SER/mwi008.

– 2011. *Capitalizing on Crisis*. Cambridge, MA: Harvard University Press.

Larder, N., S.R. Sippel, and N. Argent. 2018. "The Redefined Role of Finance in Australian Agriculture." *Australian Geographer*, 49 (3): 397–418.

Larder, N., S.R. Sippel, and G. Lawrence. 2015. "Finance Capital, Food Security Narratives and Australian Agricultural Land." *Journal of Agrarian Change* 15 (4): 592–603. https://doi.org/10.1111/joac.12108.

Lawrence, G. 1987. *Capitalism and the Countryside: The Rural Crisis in Australia*. Sydney: Pluto.

– 2015. "Defending Financialization." *Dialogues in Human Geography* 5 (2): 201–5. https://doi.org/10.1177/2043820615588155.

Lawrence, G., and H. Campbell. 2014. "Neoliberalism in the Antipodes: Understanding the Influence and Limits of the Neoliberal Political Project." In *The Neoliberal Regime in the Agri-food Sector: Crisis, Resilience and Restructuring*, edited by S. Wolf and A. Bonanno, 263–83. New York: Routledge.

Lawrence, G., and K. Smith. 2018. "The Concept of 'Financialization': Criticisms and Insights." In *The Financialization of Agri-food Systems: Contested Transformations*, edited by H. Bjørkhaug, A. Magnan, and G. Lawrence, 23–41. London: Routledge.

Lawrence, G., S.R. Sippel, and D. Burch. 2015. "The Financialisation of Food and Farming." In *Handbook on the Globalisation of Agriculture*, edited by G. Robinson and D. Carson, 309–27. Cheltenham, UK: Edward Elgar.

Li, T. 2015. "Transnational Farmland Investment: A Risky Business." *Journal of Agrarian Change* 15 (4): 560–68. https://doi.org/10.1111/joac.12109.

Locke, S. 2014. "Chinese Interest in Australian Farms Is High but Action Is Slow as China Calls for Reduced Scrutiny from the Foreign Investment Review Board." ABC News, 30 October. http://www.abc.net.au/news/2014-10-28/monday-hold-nrn-chinese-investment/5839882.

Magnan, A. 2015. "The Financialization of Agri-Food in Canada and Australia: Corporate Farmland and Farm Ownership in the Grains and Oilseed Sector." *Journal of Rural Studies* 41:1–12. https://doi.org/10.1016/j.jrurstud.2015.06.007.

Martin, S., and J. Clapp. 2015. "Finance for Agriculture or Agriculture for Finance?" *Journal of Agrarian Change* 15 (4): 549–59. https://doi.org/10.1111/joac.12110.

McMichael, P. 2013. "Land Grabbing as Security Merchantilism in International Relations." *Globalizations* 10 (1): 47–64.

Moir, B. 2011. *Foreign Investment and Australian Agriculture*. Canberra: Rural Industries Research and Development Corporation / Australian Bureau of Agricultural and Resource Economics and Science. https://www.agrifutures.com.au/wp-content/uploads/publications/11-173.pdf.

Moran, A. 2002. "As Australia Decolonizes: Indigenizing Settler Nationalism and the Challenges of Settler/Indigenous Relations." *Ethnic and Racial Studies* 25 (6): 1013–42. https://doi.org/10.1080/0141987022000009412.

Morton, K. 2012." Learning by Doing: China's Role in the Global Governance of Food Security." Research Centre for Chinese Politics and Business Working Paper 30. Bloomington, IN: Research Center for Chinese Politics and Business.

Newman, D., and N. Kliot. 2000. "Introduction: Globalisation and the Changing World Political Map." In *Geopolitics at the End of the Twentieth Century: The Changing World Political Map*, edited by N. Kliot and D. Newman, 1–17. London: Frank Cass.

News Weekly. 2015. "Investing Must Be More Than Just Buying Assets." 18 July. http://newsweekly.com.au/article.php?id=56999.

Nunzio, J. 2014. *Unlocking Our Potential: The Need for Foreign Investment in Australian Agriculture*. Nedlands, WA: Future Directions International.

Ouma, S. 2014. "Situating Global Finance in the Land Rush Debate: A Critical Review." *Geoforum* 57:162–6. https://doi.org/10.1016/j.geoforum.2014.09.006.

Parks, A. 2013. "Furore after Koala Trees Torn Down at Dunoon Farm." *Northern Star*, 1 July. http://www.northernstar.com.au/news/furore-after-koala-trees-torn-down-at-dunoon-farm/1927786/.

Plunkett, B. 2015. "PrimeAg Australia 2007–13: A Suitable Structure for Long-term Investment in Agriculture?" *Australasian Agribusiness Review* 23 (3): 26–35.

Ramasamy, B. 2016. "Why China Could Never Sign On to the Trans-Pacific Partnership." Conversation, 13 April. https://theconversation.com/why-china-could-never-sign-on-to-the-trans-pacific-partnership-56361?utm_medium=email&utm_campaign=Latest%20from%20The%20Conversation%20for%20April%2014%202016%20-%204668&utm_content=Latest%20from%20The%20Conversation%20for%20April%2014%202016%20-%204668+CID_6eab49e5302928e6d1acb3d5b961c746&utm_source=campaign_monitor&utm_term=Why%20China%20could%20never%20sign%20on%20to%20the%20Trans-Pacific%20Partnership.

Rowley, L. 2015. "Chinese Investment in Australian Beef: Is It as Big as It Sounds?" Property Central, 28 October. http://www.beefcentral.com/property/weekly-property-review-chinese-investment-in-australian-beef-is-it-as-big-as-it-sounds/.

Rural and Regional Affairs and Transport References Committee (RRATRC). 2012. *Examination of the Foreign Investment Review Board National Interest Test*, 28 November. http://www.aph.gov.au/Parliamentary_Business/Committees/Senate/Rural_and_Regional_Affairs_and_Transport/Completed_inquiries/2012-13/firb2011/interimreport/index.

– 2013. *Foreign Investment and the National Interest.* www.aph.gov.au/~/media/wopapub/senate/committee/rrat_ctte/completed_inquiries/2010-13/firb_2011/report/report.ashx.

Sanyal, K. 2014. *Foreign Investment in Australian Agriculture.* Canberra: Department of Parliamentary Services.

Sippel, S.R. 2015. "Food Security or Commercial Business? Gulf State Investments in Australian Agriculture." *Journal of Peasant Studies* 42 (5): 981–1001. https://doi.org/10.1080/03066150.2014.990448.

– 2018. "Financialising Farming as a Moral Imperative? Renegotiating the Legitimacy of Land Investments in Australia." *Environment and Planning A* 50 (3): 549–68. https://doi.org/10.1177/0308518X17741317.

Sippel, S.R., N. Larder, and G. Lawrence. 2017. "Grounding the Financialization of Farmland: Perspectives on Financial Actors as New Land Owners in Rural Australia." *Agriculture and Human Values* 34 (2): 251–65. https://doi.org/10.1007/s10460-016-9707-2.

Sippel, S.R., G. Lawrence, and D. Burch. 2017. "The Financialisation of Farming: The Hancock Company of Canada and Its Embedding in Rural Australia." In *Transforming the Rural: Global Processes and Local Futures*, edited by M. Miele, V. Higgins, H. Bjørkhaug, and M. Truninger, 3–23. Bingley: Emerald Books.

Sippel, S.R., M. Böhme, and C. Gharios. 2018. "Strategic Financialization? The Emergence of Sovereign Wealth Funds in the Global Food System." In *Financialisation, Food Systems and Rural Transformation*, edited by H. Bjørkhaug, A. Magnan, and G. Lawrence, G., 62–84. London: Routledge.

TIAA-CREF. 2015. "Responsible Investment in Farmland. 2014 Report on Ethical Conduct and Responsible Stewardship of the Environment." https://www.tiaa.org/public/pdf/2014-Farmland-Sustainability-Report.pdf.

Treasurer. 2016. "Preliminary Decision of Foreign Investment Application for Purchase of S. Kidman & Co. Limited." News release, Treasurer of the Commonwealth of Australia, 29 April 2016.

Tricarico, A. 2012. "The Financial Enclosure of the Commons." Red Pepper, 1 September. http://www.redpepper.org.uk/the-financial-enclosure-of-the-commons/.

Uren, D. 2015. *Takeover: Foreign Investment and the Australian Psyche.* Victoria: Black.

Vidot, A. 2015) "Australian Farmers Prepare to Reap the Benefits as China Trade Deal Takes Effect." ABC News, 18 December. http://www.abc.net.au/news/2015-12-18/agricultural-exporters-look-to-benefits-as-chafta-takes-effect/7039772.

Visser, O. 2015. "Finance and the Global Land Rush: Understanding the Growing Role of Investment Funds in Land Deals and Large-Scale Farming." *Canadian Food Studies* 2 (2): 278–86. https://doi.org/10.15353/cfs-rcea.v2i2.122.

Weis, T. 2013. *The Ecological Hoofprint: The Global Burden of Industrial Livestock.* London: Zed Books.

Westchester Agriculture Asset Management (WAAM). 2011. "Taking Australian Operations to the Next Level." *Global Thoughts* 1 (2): 3.

– 2014. "The Black and the Red: What's the Gambit?" *Global Thoughts* 4 (2): 1–2.

– 2016a. "Company Profile." http://www.wgimglobal.com/company-profile.

– 2016b. "Home." http://www.wgimglobal.com/home.

WorkCover. 2015. "Injury of an Employee Due to an Unsafe System of Work." https://www.worksafe.qld.gov.au/forms-and-resources/case-studies/common-law-claim-case-studies/130614-russell-v-hancock-farm-company.

Zhang, H. 2014."China Is Marching West for Food." *Fair Observer,* 12 March. http://www.fairobserver.com/region/north_america/china-marching-west-for-food-72431/.

9 "Plus Ça Change ...": Saskatchewan Farmland Restructuring and Its Effects on Farm Families

JOSTEIN TAPPER BROBAKK AND BRUCE MUIRHEAD

As farmers have retired or changed occupations their land has not gone to another small farmer so that his operation might become more economical. But because the large operator has had the money to purchase the land, he's purchased the land for sale and in so doing his farm has become that much bigger. As that bigger farmer becomes older and wants to retire he is forced to sell to another farmer and it becomes the same old cycle again. Many farmers who want to retire have sons who would like to farm but have no money to buy from father. The father would like the son to have the land but needs to sell his farm so he can retire in some comfort and security. This problem has been facing governments for years and they have done little or nothing to solve [it].

– Frank Meakes,
Saskatchewan NDP MLA for Touchwood and
former minister of cooperation and cooperative development,
Legislative Assembly, 25 April 1972

Introduction

The province of Saskatchewan has nearly 62 million acres of farmland, close to 40 per cent of the total amount in Canada (Ontario Ministry of Agriculture, Food and Rural Affairs 2017). Soil quality is considered good, and under the mild climate-warming scenario predicted for the Prairie region, Saskatchewan's agricultural productivity is expected to rise. That output was also reserved, more or less, for residents of the province before 2003; it had among the most restrictive rules governing land ownership in North America, limiting foreigners to only 10 acres[1] of land and Canadians who lived beyond its borders to 320. These restrictions focused on preventing land speculation and limiting the size of farms in order to maintain the ability of Saskatchewanians to acquire farmland for agricultural purposes. It was also hoped that the policy would support the development of strong rural communities. As of 1 January 2003, however, these restrictions were lifted for Canadians, but maintained for non-nationals. In the years since, land prices have more than doubled, although it may not be a cause-and-effect relationship – other factors have figured in, some of which we will explore. Even so, Saskatchewan farmland is still considered cheap compared to land in neighbouring provinces and cross-border states – a fact that has made it increasingly attractive for financial investment and speculation.

In this chapter we set out to study the effects of the most recent investment trends in the province, the content and effect of successive farmland acts, as well as providing the contextual history. We examine financialization and farm sector restructuring and discuss the relationship between the two trends. In part, as the result of the expanding capital requirements of contemporary farming, traditional family farmers tend to rent larger acreages than in the past, or enter investor-induced leaseback deals in order to grow without reaching unsustainable debt levels (Sommerville and Magnan 2015). We ask, despite the restrictive land-owning rules, whether this represents a paradigm shift, weakening the fabric of rural communities and giving birth to a new class of corporate family farmers, paradoxically removing capital from regional Canada despite a huge inflow of investment. Or is this development merely more of what has been happening in the province for the past century, albeit at a faster pace and with more intensity, caused by the entry of finance capital and the demands of modern agriculture?

Financialization of Farmland

Although there is little consensus on the meaning of *financialization*, we use Palley's (2007) definition as a basis for our theoretical approach. According to Palley the principal impact of financialization:

1 elevates the significance of the financial sector relative to the real sector;
2 transfers income from the real sector to the financial sector; and
3 contributes to increased income inequality and wage stagnation (Palley 2007, 3).

An additional feature, according to Lapavitsas (2011), is that households have increasingly become involved in the operation of finance. For our analysis this notion is particularly important, since a majority of the investments we are investigating are made by family farm operations, drawing farm households closer into the web of financial transactions through new vehicles of capital accumulation (Fairbairn 2014). To the degree that financialization increases the importance of investment capital and adds volatility in agricultural markets (Clapp 2014), small-scale farmers are usually hit hard. As Isakson (2013) observes, this is due to price variations affecting the livelihood of farm families, and because ordinary farmers often lack the financial muscle to compete with corporate finance and institutional investors.

Ouma (2015) argues that there are limits to the effects of financialization within agriculture due to the specific features of farmland. Because of its weather-dependency, socio-ecological embeddedness, moral entanglements, and political and strategic importance, farmland is more difficult to trade financially than other assets and cannot easily be turned into "just another asset class." He goes on to argue that these "bio-geophysical limits" make farmland a peculiar case of economization, somehow protecting it from the most aggressive form of speculation. Fairbairn (2014) makes a distinction between the "productive" and "financial" logics in farm sector investments, arguing that farmland is a "quasi-financial" asset producing short-to-medium term speculative gains as well as long-term production based value creation. In the following, we will analyse farmland legislation, investor opinions, NGO concerns, and family farm perceptions against the wider dominating trends of financialization and farm sector restructuring.

Early Legislation

Generally, Saskatchewan followed its Prairie neighbours, with land ownership initially being covered by federal legislation, An Act Respecting the Public Lands of the Dominion (1872). Its purpose was to encourage settlement of the Canadian West, which had been transferred from the Hudson's Bay Company to the new Dominion of Canada in 1870. Saskatchewan became a province in 1905, whose economy was based on the sale of wheat overseas. That remained the pattern, almost without deviation, until the later 1960s. In search of greater competitiveness and efficiency, farms during the decade became larger, with their number dropping by 16 per cent. That raised red flags in Regina, as an April 1972 debate in the provincial legislature highlighted. It resulted in An Act to Regulate the Ownership and Control of Agricultural Land in Saskatchewan (1974), the first of the pieces of restrictive land legislation. Primary among the issues raised was that corporate ownership would inevitably take the place of the sturdy yeoman farmer, so critical to the "establishment of the West" homily.

That fear was given impetus by crop price rises as the first oil shock of 1973 destabilized Western economies. Wheat, generally, increased in value from $1.75 per bushel to $5.75, while durum wheat had soared to $8.00. Flax prices had increased five-fold, and rapeseed (now called canola) and some pulses had gone up proportionately. In introducing the second reading debate in the legislature in 1974, the minister of agriculture, John Messner, had talked about the "extreme optimism in Saskatchewan ... about the prospects for grain markets in the next few years."[2] That trend had led to interest by foreigners and non-Saskatchewan-based Canadians "to invest in assets tied to primary agricultural production." That would not deter large corporations, or so the provincial government believed, given record profits in 1973 with a surfeit of investment dollars looking for a good, productive home. Land now seemed to be an asset like any other, and it was confidently expected that prices would continue to rise and Saskatchewan would become a target (Ferguson, Furtan, and Carlberg 2006, 60). That was a marked change from the pre-1970s era where, as a government document was later to note, the province did not need restrictions on ownership, "as traditionally there was little interest in Saskatchewan farmland by non-residents" (Government of Saskatchewan 2015, 3). Indeed, people from the province's neighbours, Alberta to the west and Manitoba to the east, had derogatively called it "the gap ... a bit of space to leap over to reach more palatable parts of the country" (anonymous interview, 14 December 2015).

Messner offered a number of reasons for the need to put land ownership protections in place, and these have some resonance forty-five years later. First, there was real benefit in keeping the family farm structure, as this could produce food most economically, and second, the government was very concerned about large corporate interests controlling such a crucial area as food production. "We can be sure," he noted, "that if control of agricultural industry ever fell into the hands of a few powerful corporations, the industry would not be operated and developed in a manner that would benefit the people who live and work in this province producing our primary products." Moreover, farmers were "entitled to protection from competition and capital resources accumulated in other industries and in other countries." Finally, the minister noted that to develop a sound rural economy, it was essential that agricultural assets be owned and controlled by the people who spent a major part of their time in the area where production took place. Critically, those people would also "be spending the major portion of the income generated from that agricultural production in the towns and cities of this province."

The act, according to one member of the Legislative Assembly, was "more important than any ... that has come before this Legislature in the last 20 years" (Legislative Assembly of Saskatchewan, 25 April 1972, 1946). What would happen if legislation prohibiting foreigners and non-Saskatchewan residents from owning vast swaths of land was not passed? The answer was to be found in the adjacent United States, where Tony Deshant, president of the American Farmers Union (AFU), talked about changing land ownership patterns in the U.S. Midwest. Deshant had forecast that unless things dramatically shifted, the corporate sector would own significant amounts of U.S. farmland, reducing farmers to peasants. Later analyses riffed off the AFU president's remarks and most saw disaster just over the horizon as corporate farming seemed to gain a foothold in anticipation of taking over from hard-working American farmers.

Undoubtedly the Saskatchewan government was influenced by these emanations from the United States as those debates spilled over a very porous border. Similar trends were taking place in the province as the number of farms had dropped between 1951 and 1971 from about 112,000 to approximately 77,000. As well, the average size of those farms increased from 550 acres to 845. Indeed, the number of farms in the province, as well as the farm population, had peaked in 1936, ironically one of the worst years of the Great Depression. It was this fear of the corporatization of farms that led in the first instance to the 1974 act. Following its passage, the proscription against non-resident ownership remained until 2002. The act's provisions were changed five times, in 1977, 1980, 1988, 2002 and 2015; each altered the nature of the proscription, but not the proscription itself (Ferguson, Furtan, and Carlberg 2006, 60). In all cases, amendments to the 1974 legislation tightened it further, although the 2002 legislation removed the stipulation against Canadians owning up to 320 acres of Saskatchewan farmland. Further, the 1988 Farm Security Act was passed by a Conservative government "to afford protection to farmers against loss of their farm land" (Saskatchewan Farm Security Act 1988).

That legislation responded to a stark deterioration in worldwide agricultural conditions that had adversely affected Saskatchewan farmers. Farm income had risen dramatically throughout the 1960s and the earlier 1970s, peaking in 1973. The later 1960s and early 1970s was also a period of rising inflation, and the combination of rising farm income and higher inflation had caused the value of farmland to escalate throughout the 1970s. In the first years of the 1970s, the cost of a Saskatchewan acre was about $325 – by 1980, it had peaked at $1,000. But indications were evident by the later 1970s that agriculture was in for a "correction," as "[the farmland price boom] began to show signs of vulnerability" (Barnett 2000, 366).

The collapse, when it came, was dramatic in land values and farm income. Market net income for Saskatchewan farmers fell into negative territory by the mid-1980s, and it would take almost two decades before it became more sustainable (FDIC 1998). The downturn clearly hit Saskatchewan hard. By the end of 1990, Agriculture and Agri-Food Canada projected real net income for Saskatchewan farmers at $96 million, which, when divided by the province's number of farms, worked out to $1,783 per farm, a number last seen in 1938, the year that Canada began the climb out of the effects of the Great Depression (Qualman 2001, 6). Land prices mirrored income. From the $1,000 per acre high of the early 1980s, they reached a low point of $253 by 1993, far less than the cost of land in both Alberta and Manitoba (Statistics Canada 2011). As well, farming was so unprofitable during the twenty years following 1980 that a foreclosure a week was the norm until the Saskatchewan government put a stop to the practice in 1985 (Hammond 2014). Even so, "the exodus of farmers from Saskatchewan exceeded that from both Alberta and Manitoba [and] ... farm numbers declined at a faster rate" (Carlberg and Furtan 2003, 405). The drop was stark. Over the thirty years from the 1966 census, Alberta had experienced a 22 per cent *growth* in rural population, Manitoba's had dropped by 1 per cent, and Saskatchewan's had plunged by 25 (Docksteader 2001). Nor did it stop then. Saskatchewan led Canada with a decline of 12.4 per cent over the decade until 2006, representing the elimination of 6,269 farmers (Statistics Canada 2014). The situation was so distressing that the primary theme of the 2003 provincial election focused on youth out-migration and how to stop it. That responded to bumper stickers in the later 1990s that had asked "the last person in Saskatchewan to turn off the lights."

Perhaps one way was to shift the discourse was the very restrictive land ownership legislation. This was done in 2002 as the government repealed the section on Canadian purchases of Saskatchewan farmland. This was done to stimulate economic activity, or so the provincial minister of agriculture, Clay Serby, told the Canadian Broadcasting Corporation. It also followed on the heels of the establishment by the government of the Action Committee on the Rural Economy. Something had to be done to stimulate demand and economic activity in rural areas.

While the amendment was partially responsible for creating additional demand for land in the province, prices did not respond as some farmers who wanted to sell had hoped. The cost per acre did rise, but only after 2007; an average Saskatchewan acre cost $345 in 2002, rising to $523 eight years later, and within a range of $2,000 to $2,600 by 2017.[3]

Between 2006 and 2015 the combined percentage change in farmland values for Saskatchewan led all of Canada, rising almost 140 per cent over that period (FCC 2016), partly the result of dynamism in the agricultural sector, low interest rates, and healthy crop receipts for harvests of canola, wheat, and pulses. By 2014 "farm cash income reached an all-time record high ... of $13.85 billion, or $67 thousand per farm" (FCC 2015, 5) As Lyle Stewart, the minister of Agriculture, noted, "Farmland appreciates at a reasonable rate in good times in the industry, and that's normal, but what we were seeing with 28.5 per cent [2013], 18.7 per cent [2012] and 22.9 [2011] per cent appreciation over single years was not normal" (Senate of Canada 2016). Saskatchewan farmland had clearly come of age, or so it seemed.

This trend set the stage for the provincial consultation with Saskatchewan residents on land restrictions that was launched during the late spring 2015 and would eventually result in slightly amended and tightened legislation governing ownership in December 2015. Sixty-two per cent of the respondents were farmers, and the surprising statistic remained that a majority of those retiring did not want foreigners to be able to purchase Saskatchewan farmland (Saskatchewan Farmland Ownership 2015). Farmers, it seemed, had taken to heart the notion that "if the ownership law was opened to the rest of the world, then we could sell Saskatchewan four times over before five o'clock this afternoon."[4] And they did not want that, being all too aware that "land is a limited resource. It is estimated that only one to four per cent of [it] exchanges hands each year ... [meaning that] a piece of farmland only becomes available every 40 years on average" (FCC 2015, 1).

Saskatchewan in the Twenty-First Century

As this more salubrious economic environment was taking hold in the province, a perception that some deep-pocketed institutions were on a buying spree in response to these conditions became more pronounced. One of our respondents asked the question on the minds of many: "Could this be the future of agriculture? That people with access to capital own it and others farm it?" (anonymous interview, Elrose, SK). Former National Farmers' Union president, Terry Boehm, called it "the new feudalism" (Waldie and Leeder 2010). With rates of return in the United States from farmland investments running at about 14 per cent per year from 2000 to 2010 (and under-priced Saskatchewan surely on the cusp of following suit), investment funds were anxious to buy in. Pressure on land was such that in 2013 the FCC calculated that the cost of an average acre of farmland in Canada had gone up by 22 per cent, the highest annual percentage increase recorded in two decades, with the Saskatchewan increase reaching into the 30s.

Even given restrictive (but slightly amended) ownership rules, land costs rose rapidly, implicitly working against the expansion of the so-called family farm. In Saskatchewan that remains the predominant model, but it might be changing with the pressure to get ever bigger, raising the question of when an operation ceases to be a family farm, even when it is operated by "a family." While the average size of a Canadian farm is 820 acres (Statistics Canada 2017a), that in Saskatchewan is a league-leading 1,784, according to the 2016 Farm Census. It also represents the largest growth in farm size over the past decade (Statistics Canada 2017b). Critically, a plurality of farmers who responded to the government's April 2015 consultation request farmed at least 3,500 acres (Saskatchewan Farmland Ownership 2015), which put them among the leaders in Canada, at least in farm size.[5] And perhaps that size reflects a more modern paradigm. As one informed critic has noted, the fact "that often gets lost, regardless of what side of the family farm fence you are standing on, is ... that we are trying to fit 21st century farming into a 20th century or even 19th century 'idea' of farming. This romantic notion must give way to a business-like approach or we will see the end of farming altogether" (Hunt 2016).

While the tightening of land ownership regulations in Saskatchewan might be anomalous in 2017 in a world dominated by neoliberalism and globalization, what is happening to Saskatchewan farms is not. As has been seen, they are growing bigger, triggering angst in some quarters about the loss of the family farm. As one of our respondents noted about farming and the ongoing restructuring in the Global North,[6] "As soon as you separate family from farm, it just becomes a business" (anonymous interview, Parkbeg, SK). "Romantic" notions die hard.

But what does *family farm* mean? As has been pointed out, there is no universally agreed upon definition of the term (Garner and O Campos 2014). For example, Elizabeth Garner and Ana Paula de la O Campos reviewed thirty-six definitions and uses of the term. What they found was that the majority "recognize the role of family labour and the role of the family in managing the farm operation. However, the notion of family farming seems to go beyond farming capacity, size and orientation. It is sometimes also used to capture ecological, social, cultural and environmental objectives and therefore has close ties to the local culture and the rural community" (1). They proposed a concept of family farming that emphasizes a recurring aspect of the term – the reliance on family labour – that we will use to inform our discussion of the perceived financialization of farmland and rural restructuring in the province.

Farms in Saskatchewan are getting larger at the same time that they are becoming fewer. As Lyle Stewart, then aged sixty-six, told the federal Senate Standing Committee on Agriculture and Forestry, "In order to stay viable, farms have to continue to expand. The average commercial farm is probably 4,000 acres in this province now, where it would have been 300 acres when I was a child a number of years ago" (Senate of Canada 2016).

As well, the amount of rented land is increasing. In Canada, every census from 1976 to the present shows that the amount of farmer-owned land has decreased, and that rented land has done the opposite (Statistics Canada 2015b). Statistics Canada offers the dry observation that "there were several factors contributing to this shift, such as rising land prices and an aging farm population." Further, the government agency notes that "land rental is a less capital-intensive means of expanding an operation to take advantage of rising commodity prices." The first part of that sentence is certainly true, and our interviews highlighted this fact across Saskatchewan. Farmers reported that they find it increasingly difficult to access land and raise funds to purchase additional farmland, given its cost, resulting in their growing acceptance of the necessity of renting land. Further, private (and public) sector equity firms have become increasingly active in Saskatchewan, buying up hundreds of thousands of acres of farmland, which they then lease back to farmers (Desmarais et al. 2015). Will this trend result in a fundamental reconfiguration of provincial land ownership patterns over time, or will some variant of family farm ownership continue to be the dominant pattern? Does this suggest that financial elites, markets, and institutions will gain greater influence over economic policy and outcomes in the province than before? Crucially, if this happens, will the financialization of farmland result in the unacceptable transfer of income from agriculture to finance?

That does not seem to be happening in the province. Mark Folk, general manager of the Saskatchewan Farmland Security Board (FSB), maintains that his group of five full-time staff review every land transaction in the province. His data show that about 85 per cent of these are farmer to farmer (Folk 2016).[7] New tools in recent legislation allow them to look at the origins of the funding for the purchase, and all of it must be from Canadian sources. Further, the onus is now on owners to prove that they are compliant, a key difference from the old law. If they are not, the FSB can force a sale. The revised and more restrictive legislation was necessary, according to Minister of Agriculture Lyle Stewart, because Saskatchewan land has lately been under pressure. His province "was the discount place," as land values in Alberta and

Manitoba have traditionally been significantly higher, making acquisitions in those provinces more expensive and therefore less desirable (Stewart 2015).[8]

However, the FSB was powerless to take action in 2013 following the announcement by the Canada Pension Plan Investment Board (CPPIB) that it intended to purchase from Assiniboia Farmland Fund (AFF) its holdings in the province totalling about 128,000 acres. AFF, a private equity firm based in the provincial capital, has been active in the province for some years launching a new venture to invest in Saskatchewan farmland in 2006. The announcement seven years later by the CPPIB greatly irritated Saskatchewan's rural residents, although urban residents generally thought it to be an appropriate use of their tax dollars in providing a decent return for their future pensions.

Assiniboia had anticipated trends stemming from the 2002 revisions to land policy. It knew that farmland was undervalued by comparison with the province's neighbours and, being a Saskatchewan company, also understood how critical good land in the province was to a world that was projected to demand calories in ever-rising number. Further, increasing amounts of land were being rented by the fewer farmers still in the game, as larger acreages were now a given, and amassing the required size and farm technology was simply beyond the financial capability of the average farmer. As a result, AFF entered the market at a fortuitous time – before the significant increase in land values. Farmers approached with deals for their land probably saw this as a golden opportunity to make something from property with a price that seemed stuck in neutral, then at about $350 per acre. As well, farmers were often hard-pressed to access capital to increase their productivity and, for those who might have been at the limit of what the banks and Farm Credit would lend to them, the Assiniboia overture would have been most welcome. If the deal also included a guarantee that the farmer would be able to rent the land back on a longer-term lease, so much the better.

And the imperatives of grain farming were becoming more demanding and unforgiving. Underlining this development is the requirement for investment capital in order to expand. This is common in the Global North, where farmers in many jurisdictions have taken on heavy debt in order to increase farm size, believing large acreages are the only way to compete in a global market. At the turn of the century, a good-sized wheat farm would have totalled about 3,000 acres. By 2005 the number had doubled, while in 2015, it was in the 7–10,000 acre range (anonymous interview 2014). Some farms are close to 60,000 acres, but this is, according to one respondent, "arrogance." Vast acreages, he thought, "don't work. Twenty thousand acres was the limit if one wanted to have a personal stake in it" (anonymous interview, Zehner, SK). An-other noted, "Ninety-six quarters [15,360 acres] had been purchased by someone in the oil equipment business – he had lasted four years before selling," an example of pure hubris (anonymous interview, Elrose, SK). Another perspective on size: "At what point do you lose the hands-on management approach? Farming is more risky and involved than peo-ple think. It is not a factory. Quality control is sometimes out the win-dow" (anonymous interview, Grenfell, SK). Finally, some thought that it is simply not possible for the average farm family to accumulate these large acreages. Chris Selness of Saskworks Venture Fund, for example, noted, "The problem for farmers is that the reality of the economically efficient farm size [makes it] impossible to buy more land and finance it to achieve this economy of scale. The natural by-product of this is a substantive component of farmland to rent"[9] (interview, Chris Selness, Saskworks Venture Fund). So rent Saskatchewan farmers now do, at rates greater than at any time in their past; about 40 per cent of farm-land in the province is leased, most often from other farmers who have quit the industry or who have retired but kept their land.[10]

There is also great difficulty in hiring appropriate people for these mega-operations, as One Earth Farms and others have discovered,[11] while equipment breakdowns, which happen regularly, play havoc with seeding and ongoing and harvesting operations. These changing realities – the need for multiple thousands of acres of grain land to be competitive, labour requirements, and equipment costs are very diffi-cult ones for farmers to appropriately address, especially as land costs have increased in Saskatchewan, reliable workers are difficult to find and keep, and the scale of machinery must match the scale of the farm.[12]

Further, the investment associated with putting seeds in the ground is becoming eye-watering. On a 5,000 acre farm, the cost of sowing a crop of durum wheat is about $1.3 million of upfront money (Raine 2015).[13] Equipment prices have also shot up, with ever-larger tractors, ploughs, combines, and seed drills needed to get the crop in and then harvested. It is not unusual for a large tractor to cost $700,000. As profits are not rising at the same rate as input factors, restructuring is not eco-nomically sustainable in the long run and will only increase the overall debt level in Saskatchewan farming. This development represents a sig-nificant burden, especially for young farmers attempting to gain entry.

Machinery is also one of the criteria by which potential renters are evaluated by certain owners on their ability to farm. As was pointed out, farmers can improve the quality of the land they are renting through such mechanisms as proper equipment: "If you seed with a disc seeder, you are not going to generate yields. If you are a laggard here, you will probably be a laggard in all aspects of farm management," or so a senior member of one private equity firm that rents land believes (anonymous interview, Assiniboia). While state-of-the-art machinery can improve crop yield through productivity increases, it is also expensive, costing more than, in the case of that seeder, $300,000, putting it out of the range of all but a small number of farmers. Assiniboia asks for 100 per cent compliance with this demand when considering requests to rent its land (anonymous interview, Assiniboia).

Community Pastures

While these factors are influencing Saskatchewan farmers, and many would claim not to their advantage, another element remains germane to this examination – the fate of community pastures and which entity will ultimately control them. Perhaps that will be a harbinger of the future for Saskatchewan farmers. As described below, this is an example of policy deregulation that could make it more difficult for ordinary farmers (particularly younger ones) to access land in a reasonable way.

Controlled by both the federal and provincial levels of government, the Community Pastures Program had been established during the 1930s to restore land badly eroded by drought, turning large regions of Saskatchewan to a productive state (Grey 1967). Community pastures were established in the three western provinces of Manitoba, Saskatchewan, and Alberta and remained an innovative response to the question posed by adequate access to land for smaller farmers. As AAFC points out, they were "designed to help producers strengthen their operations by providing pastures and a breeding service. Allocation of grazing space is based on a number of factors, the most important being an assessment of need."[14] The formula allotted land to small producers "in inverse proportion to land owned, leased or rented by clients." Ottawa decided to cease its involvement in Saskatchewan by March 2015, ceding federal pastures to the province. Regina, for its part, announced that it would sell all sixty-two pastures totalling 1.77 million acres to those who could afford the land. That elicited a collective groan from rural residents who saw themselves as being left out as corporate interests would swoop in. The resulting public pressure forced the province instead to agree to lease the land to pasture patron groups that were very concerned about corporate money invested in this non-renewable resource.

The idea was to "transition this land to pasture patrons" or others over a five-year period from 2014 through 2018, either through lease or sale.[15] The Saskatchewan Party government saw this as "a once-in-a-lifetime opportunity for producers to take over full ownership and operation of this land" (Government of Saskatchewan 2018). However, the government also emphasized its intent to sell approximately 33 per cent, or 600,000 acres, of this Crown land to those farmers who now rented it (Holtslander 2015, 24). Lyle Stewart, the provincial minister of agriculture, said that the government would offer the land for sale at a 15 per cent discount from its appraised value for those who bought before 31 March 2016. That would drop to 10 per cent on 1 April and 5 per cent on 1 January 2017 (CBC News 2015). Moreover, rental rates for the land, should it not be sold, would rise by 15 per cent in 2016 and 30 per cent in 2017. Stewart pointed out, "The incentive is the carrot, but I'm not going to put a happy face on rental increases. They're also designed to motivate producers to buy this land" (Stewart 2015).

Clearly, the obligations to be placed on these pasture patrons will increase the cost of renting these pastures. Responsibility for them will be passed on to these groups, which will then require these new patron-run businesses "to pay higher fees for grazing on these public lands and provide for the stewardship of public goods and services that were previously managed by professional federal government employees" (Phillips 2015, 2). This scenario is an example of how deregulation of agricultural policy is increasing the cost for farmers to access land.

Farmland Reality

Have these changing circumstances in the province resulted in fundamental adverse change of the Saskatchewan countryside? Some would argue that this change is not detrimental, or that it is inevitable. Others might grieve the loss of what they consider the Saskatchewan of their parents and grandparents, and put it down to the financialization of land with attendant costs now putting it out of the range of all but the very big farmer or the wealthy investment fund. However, we believe that it is happening of its own momentum and still relies basically on the family farm idea to undertake seeding and harvests. Indeed, those who remember a bucolic past, golden age, or good old days of Saskatchewan farming and the vitality of rural communities are most likely misremembering. The province became urban in 1966, that is, more people lived in its urban areas than in the countryside (Statistics Canada 2011). Indeed, in every census since 1901 (except for that of 1951), the rural population has fallen as people voted with their feet.[16] Even in the later 1980s and into the next decade, when land was very cheap, this rural depopulation continued, although certainly the economic climate for farming was disastrous by then. Over the fifteen years from the 1986 census to that of 2001, the rural sector lost 3 per cent of the province's population, or almost 40,000 people, a significant number. In 2011, the date of the last census, approximately 343,000 people, or only 33 per cent of the provincial population, lived in rural areas, albeit a significantly number larger than in either Alberta (17 per cent) or Manitoba (28 per cent).

Some of this change is organic in that it seems to have developed naturally. Living in remote areas in the province is not desirable, especially for women, several of our informants told us. One suggested that had she and her husband moved to any other location than where they now lived, "we wouldn't still be married." Moving to Saskatchewan from British Columbia a number of years ago, they live close to Regina and have multiple thousands of acres. The farmwife likes the fact that their son's school is ten minutes away and that it is easy to buy groceries, travel to see a doctor, or go for a night out (anonymous interview, Dalmeny, SK). Another farmwife told us, "Younger women in particular did not want to live in rural areas where there were too few services." She had to drive thirty minutes for groceries and about forty-five minutes to Moose Jaw for banking, which even she, in her later fifties and used to rural living, found onerous (anonymous interview, Parkbeg, SK). Finally, a dairy farmer mentioned that his wife would not live anywhere other than where they did, which was very close to Saskatoon, mentioning how much of "a mess" she had been when he had bought a farm in Saskatchewan. According to the farmer, his wife's only criterion was that it had to be close to Saskatoon (anonymous interview, Osler, SK).

A development towards fewer and larger farms, with a shrinking rural population, will only make these intra-family tensions more prominent and affect the social sustainability of farming communities in the long run. Small towns that had once serviced larger areas shut down, with the local school and post office shuttered, as people left. When that happened, "the town was dead" (anonymous interview, Dalmeny, SK). The local grain elevators also began to go, as they were battered by the cost of keeping small ones open. As well, the railways began to balk at picking grain up as often as they had in the past. Lashburn, for example, had six elevators in the early 1970s. Now it has none, as collection has moved to a central point serviced by much bigger facilities. In 1950, 3,030 primary grain elevators dotted the Saskatchewan countryside, dropping to a still-robust 2,750 by 1970. As of 1 February 2015, there were 126 grain stations and 189 primary elevators with a total capacity of almost 139 million bushels, as compared with a capacity of 283 million bushels in 1950 (Grains Canada 2015).

This is a classic economics case, Minister Stewart maintains. Farming is generally a high-volume, low-margin business that demands efficiencies and economies of scale – hence the push for the larger. Farm machinery is also much bigger now than it was, necessitating bigger fields in which to operate and more capital with which to buy it (Stewart 2015). However, the factor that affected rural restructuring up to about 2006 more than any other was the migration of young people from rural areas. They voted with their feet, leaving rural areas to struggle along as best they could. While that trend is now beginning to reverse, these newer and younger farmers do not want to farm as their parents and grandparents did. They insist on a life outside of agriculture, as well, which sometimes puts additional strains on farm living.

Many ask if it is possible to have a decent life if the nearest town is 100 kilometres away, and increasingly the answer is no. Certainly the depopulation of rural Saskatchewan has been a theme of this chapter, as it was during many of our interviews. As one explained, he had grown up in the 1940s and earlier 1950s surrounded by twenty-five family members living in the immediate area; now there is only one cousin remaining. Many of those relations left the community for a formal education in Regina, Saskatoon, or points farther away. Dairy farmer Jim Ross in Grenfell stated, "Education makes 'people more mobile' allowing them to consider other, less onerous, options." The scenario outlined above – local schools and hospitals closed, health regions became bigger, and the local grain elevators shuttered – made us ask this farmer, "Why put up with this sort of isolation and marginal existence?" The answer? "It is a way of life, not a job."

Statistics Canada data show that the demographic composition of Canadian agriculture is undergoing significant changes, as many farm operators approach an age when they may retire. The 2011 Census of Agriculture found that farms "where the oldest operator was 55 years or older represented more than half of all farms, compared to 37.7% in 1991. In addition, less than ten per cent of farms had the oldest operator under 40 years old in 2011, whereas two decades earlier it was about 25 per cent. These two trends were found in farms of different types and sizes in all provinces" (Statistics Canada 2015b). About 55 per cent of Saskatchewan farmers were older than fifty-five, whereas only about 12 per cent were younger than forty. This fact, the report notes, "shows no signs of reversing" and may point to more consolidation and significant turnover in farm assets in the future. Indeed, some projections suggest that given no change in the present trajectory, the average age of a

Saskatchewan farmer in 2026 could be an untenable (Statistics Canada 2016). Agriculture and Agri-Food Canada is even less optimistic about the future. A 2007 report noted that by 2017, "50 percent of our farm assets will be transferred and 75 percent of retiring farmers do not have successors" (Canadian Perspective).

This rather startling forecast has opened land sales to the private equity market, albeit slightly. Desmarais et al. (2016) found that between 2002 and 2014, the amount of land owned by investors increased sixteen-fold, from 52,000 acres (0.09 per cent of Saskatchewan farmland) to 837,000 acres or 1.44 per cent of total acres. Statistics from the Farm Land Security Board show that around 20 million acres of farmland was bought and sold in this twelve-year period, and of this about 3.8 per cent was purchased by investors (Desmarais et al. 2016). Despite the relatively small percentage of land being investor-controlled, the trend seems persistent and is of concern among farmers and their organizations (National Farmers Union 2015).

Nevertheless, Saskatchewan land policy does appear to represent an explicit rejection of financialization. At least one critic called the passage of the tightened 2015 legislation "a puzzler" (Cosh 2015). The province, he insisted, "is intentionally diminishing the market value of ... itself. Lowering the value of what Saskatchewan's farmers own is the whole point.... Support for restrictions on land sales must have run at least 20 to one." Cosh continued, "Are there no notorious stereotypes of rural people, no negative habits of mind associated with farming? The Saskatchewan bill would seem to demonstrate some. Farmers are happily holding themselves hostage in order to preserve an antique social order: they would rather see their own net worth slashed by the state than face change, as long as the loss is shared broadly. The few dissenters who like the crazy notion of more valuable farmland will be castigated as greedy strivers, itching to whore their patrimony out to sinister Asians."

Former University of Victoria PhD student Peter Bell supports Cosh's analysis, calculating that in 2012, the price of farmland was 73 per cent lower in the province than it would have been had foreigners also been able to purchase it (Pilger 2015). If this estimate is correct and is a result of Saskatchewan farm land ownership restrictions, farmers and the government have a shared interest in keeping the regulations. Investors looking for a short-term gain from speculation, on the other hand, will not benefit. Nor will farmers seeking to maximize their profit by selling the land as part of their retirement process. Deflated land prices might also reduce the amount of farmland being put on the market. Instead, landowners might hold on to their property longer, counting on land value increases in the future, forcing farmers looking to expand to increase their share of rented land.

Conclusion

Certainly things are changing in the province, but they have been doing that since 1905. Nor does this change seem to be picking up pace over most of the province. Indeed, Saskatchewan family farmers are merely following tried and true paths, primarily the one that leads to bigness. Dan Patterson, former general manager of the province's Farm Land Security Board, wrote about his misgivings about pension funds and other investment concerns in the *Western Producer* in November 2014. He laid out an alarmist scenario with investors having hundreds of billions of dollars and agitating to put their money into "the Last Best West": "Foremost in young farmers' minds is how these acquisition agendas will diminish their own modest aspirations to expand ... Saskatchewan's rural economic and social structure would be radically and irrevocably degraded.... The deterioration of rural communities will accelerate" (Patterson 2014). That is probably true insofar as *farming* communities will continue to disappear. But that had begun at least a half century ago, as small farmers had continuously been bought out by larger ones. Indeed, Frank Meakes had spoken to this issue in the early 1970s, and he had dated it to the 1940s. Nearly a half century later, Patterson could almost be paraphrasing Meakes. The result, Meakes had suggested, would be "less people on the farm and less people in the rural communities" (Legislative Assembly of Saskatchewan 1972).

As shown by Statistics Canada and pointed out by others in recent studies (Desmarais et al. 2015, 2016), farm size *has* increased and farmer numbers *have* decreased, farm debt outstanding is historically high (National Farmers Union 2015) and the amount of rented land has reached 40 per cent of the total farmed area (Saskatchewan Farmland Ownership 2015). The farmers interviewed for this study expressed concern over these trends. With stagnating profits in nominal terms and increasing costs in input factors and equipment, expanding production and productivity through size is the strategy of choice for many. Since expansion most often means taking on more debt, farmers increasingly seek alternatives, either through leasing land, signing co-investment deals, or lease-back deals with private investors. These trends also make it harder for young farmers to enter.

How the government approaches these issues has also been changing. The 1974 act focused on ownership and rural settlement, while the 2002

Farm Security Act shifted towards attracting investment under a more neoliberal and partially deregulated system. With the 2015 tightening, the government responded to the demands of its electorate. Our Saskatchewan farmer interviews show that in order to survive, "the family" goes corporate, perhaps more in line with what Lapavitsas (2011) believes is one of the characteristics of financialization, namely that households have increasingly become involved in finance operations in order to address the rural restructuring that is occurring around them.

NOTES

1 1 hectare equals 2.47 acres.
2 The next two paragraphs are based on second reading of bill no. 79 – *An Act to Regulate the Ownership and Control of Agricultural Land in Saskatchewan*, 3 April 1974, pp. 2029–30. http://docs.legassembly.sk.ca/legdocs/ Legislative%20Assembly/Hansard/17L4S/740403Hansard.pdf.
3 However, land can and does sell for more. HCI Ventures is offering eight quarters quite close to Regina in Lajord for $3.560 million, or $2,850 per acre, and another eleven quarters east of Saskatoon for almost $4 million, or $2,729 per acre. See HCI Ventures Ltd, accessed 1 July 2016, http://www.hciventures.ca.
4 Bob Lane, president of Lane Realty Corp., as quoted in Pratt (2015).
5 Response to the question, "What is the size of your farm?" Response:

< 1,100 acres	22.7%
1,101–2,200 acres	27.2%
2,201–3,500 acres	22.1%
> 3,500 acres	28.0%

Farmers comprised about 65 per cent of 3,200 respondents, while residents of Saskatchewan made up 94.5 per cent of those.

See Government of Saskatchewan, "Farmland Ownership Consultation Results: Completed Surveys," 20 May–10 August 2015.
6 See Lowder, Skoet, and Raney (2016). As they point out, and contrary to the Saskatchewan experience, "Data shows that average farm size decreased in most low- and lower-middle-income countries for which data are available from 1960 to 2000, whereas average farm sizes increased from 1960 to 2000 in some upper-middle-income countries and in nearly all high-income countries for which we have information."
7 For a more detailed description of Saskatchewan farmland transactions, see Desmarais et al. (2016).
8 According to StatsCan (2011), in 2011 an acre of Alberta farmland cost $1,506 on average, in Manitoba it was $896, while in Saskatchewan it was

$523. In 2006 the numbers were, respectively, $1,095, $664 and $391, while in 2000 they were $721, $518 and $336.

9 Land rental is also a competitive exercise, however. A farmer in Grenfell told us that in his area, a lot of land was leased. People around his age of seventy live on their farms but rent it to big operators: "Young guys can't compete against these [big] guys who want to lease" (anonymous interview, family farmer Grenfell). Another interviewee told us that renting land to big famers might be "sometimes more lucrative than farming" (anonymous interview, family farmer Caronport).

10 But renting poses its own risks. When commodity prices fall, as they inevitably do, rent costs often lag behind. Craig Klemmer, FCC's senior agricultural economist, has noted that "rental rates are notoriously sticky," which means that landlords resist entreaties to reduce rents. Further, many producers would have signed onto multi-year rental agreements, which would greatly reduce their ability to react to declining commodity prices. See Yates (2014).

11 For an account of the One Earth Farms debacle, see Cross (2014).

12 Several of our respondents told us how they had gone to Mexico during the off-season to hire workers for the season. Canadians, they insisted, did not do this work or, if they signed on, were basically unreliable. See also Friesen (2012).

13 There are a number of other factors that subtract from the potential amount a farmer might realize. As Agriculture Canada notes when calculating costs, "Costs of production are based on average fertilizer rates and pesticide applications for Western Canada. Land costs are set at $50 per acre. No labour, machinery investment or depreciation or storage costs are included. Those expenses typically run from $50 to $100 per acre" (*Western Producer* 2015).

14 A farm couple interviewed explained how the community pasture concept traditionally worked: A farmer applies to put a number of cows in the pasture for the summer. It might cost, say, $200 per cow for the season, which includes the cost of a person to look after the animals. Getting in is a competitive process, given demand, but the pasture board does favour younger farmers. A meeting is held in January during which all is determined. The community pasture managers and patrons vote and the result is binding. Often those voting already have cattle on the pasture, so new entrants are distinctly limited (anonymous interview, Parkbeg, SK).

15 The wording in a government announcement was ambiguous: "The Saskatchewan Government will not sell pastures *only* to the highest bidder. Patrons are the priority and we are committed to working with them through every step of this process to lease or purchase their pastures and balancing that by using market values to make sure the interests

of all taxpayers are taken into account." Government of Saskatchewan (n.d.; emphasis added).

16 Which brings to mind an old saying about farming. Arthur Fields, a singer/songwriter from the early part of the twentieth century, wrote the song "How You Gonna Keep Them Down on the Farm (after They've Seen Paree)?" It referred to U.S. soldiers returning home from the First World War. Groucho Marx, in his inestimable style, changed it: "How you gonna keep them down on the farm (after they've seen the farm)?"

REFERENCES

Barnett, B.J. 2000. "The US Farm Financial Crisis of the 1980s." *Agricultural History* 74 (2): 366–80.

"A Canadian Perspective on Intergenerational Farm Transfers and Succession Planning." Quoted in "Understanding Sustainable Farmland Investment Strategies Progress and Possibilities within Canada," n.d.

Carlberg, J., and H. Furtan. 2003. "Effects of Government Restrictions on Land Ownership: The Saskatchewan Case." In *Government Policy and Farmland Markets: The Maintenance of Farmer Wealth,* edited by C.B. Moss and A. Schmitz, 391–406. Ames, IA: Iowa State Press.

CBC News. 2015. "Saskatchewan Government Offering Farmland for Sale at a Discount," 4 November. http://www.cbc.ca/news/canada/saskatchewan/sask-farmland-sale-discount-1.3304035.

Clapp, J. 2014. "Financialization, Distance and Global Food Politics." *Journal of Peasant Studies* 41 (5): 797–814. https://doi.org/10.1080/03066150.2013.875536.

Cosh, C. 2015. "Saskatchewan Farmers Are Holding Themselves Hostage in Order to Preserve an Antique Social Order." *National Post,* 23 October. https://news.nationalpost.com/full-comment/colby-cosh-saskatchewan-farmers-are-holding-themselves-hostage-in-order-to-preserve-an-antique-social-order.

Cross, B. 2014. "One Earth Farms Restructures." *Western Producer,* 15 May. http://www.producer.com/2014/05/one-earth-farms-restructures/.

Desmarais, A.A., D. Qualman, A. Magnan, and N. Wiebe. 2015. "Land Grabbing and Land Concentration: Mapping Changing Patterns of Farmland Ownership in Three Rural Municipalities in Saskatchewan, Canada." *Canadian Food Studies* 2 (1): 16–47. https://doi.org/10.15353/cfs-rcea.v2i1.52.

– 2016. "Investor Ownership or Social Investment? Changing Farmland Ownership in Saskatchewan, Canada." *Agriculture and Human Values* 34 (1): 149–66. https://doi.org/10.1007/s10460-016-9704-5.

Docksteader, C. 2001. "Planning to Fail." Farmers for Economic Freedom, Centre for Prairie Agriculture, Regina, SK, 24 December. http://www.enterstageright.com/archive/articles/1201/1201cfen.htm.

Fairbairn, M. 2014. "'Like 'Gold with Yield': Evolving Intersections between Farmland and Finance." *Journal of Peasant Studies* 41 (5): 777–95. https://doi.org/10.1080/03066150.2013.873977.

Farm Credit Canada (FCC). 2015. "Farmland Values Explained." Accessed 20 May 2016 at https://www.fcc-fac.ca/fcc/about-fcc/corporate-profile/reports/ag-economist/ag-economics-farmland-values-explained-summer-2015.pdf.

– 2016. "2015 Farmland Values Report." 11 April. Accessed on 1 July 2016 at https://www.fcc-fac.ca/fcc/about-fcc/corporate-profile/reports/farmland-values/farmland-values-report-2015.pdf.

Farm Ownership Act. 1973–4. c 98, s 7; RSS 1978, c S-17, s 7.

Federal Deposit Insurance Corporation (FDIC). 1998. *An Examination of the Banking Crises of the 1980s and Early 1990s*. https://www.fdic.gov/bank/historical/history/vol1.html.

Ferguson, S., H. Furtan, and J. Carlberg. 2006. "The Political Economy of Farmland Ownership Regulations and Land Prices." *Agricultural Economics* 35 (1): 59–65. https://doi.org/10.1111/j.1574-0862.2006.00139.x.

Friesen, R. 2012. "Farm Labour: Trends to Full-Time Work." *Agri-Success*, July/August, 19. Accessed on 1 July 2016 at https://webcache.googleusercontent.com/search?q=cache:Ecm8GzBIjecJ:https://www.fac-fcc.ca/fcc/agKnowledge/publications/agrisuccess/pdfs/agrisuccess-jul-aug-2012.pdf+&cd=8&hl=nl&ct=clnk&gl=be&client=safari.

Garner, E., and A.P. de la O Campos. 2014. "Identifying the 'Family Farm': An Informal Discussion of the Concepts and Definitions." ESA Working Paper No. 14-10. Rome: FAO.

Government of Saskatchewan. 2018. "Transferring Federal Pastures." https://www.saskatchewan.ca/business/agriculture-natural-resources-and-industry/agribusiness-farmers-and-ranchers/crown-lands/agricultural-crown-land/transferring-federal-pastures.

Grains Canada. 2015. "Grain Elevators in Canada, Crop Year 2014–2015," 1 February 2015. https://www.grainscanada.gc.ca/en/grain-research/statistics/grain-elevators/reports/2014-08-01.pdf.

Grey, J.H. 1967. "Men against the Desert." In *Western Producer Prairie Book*. Saskatoon, SK: Modern.

Holtslander, C. 2015. *Losing Our Grip: How Corporate Farm Buy-Up, Corporate Farm Debt, and Agri-Business Financing of Inputs Threaten Family Farms*. Saskatoon, SK: National Farmers Union.

Hunt, K. 2016. "Is It 'Family Farm' or 'Family Firm?' Which One Matters the Most?" *Bullvine*, 3 July. http://www.thebullvine.com/management/is-it-family-farm-or-family-firm-which-one-matters-the-most/#.

Isakson, S.R. 2014. "Food and Finance: The Financial Transformation of Agro-Food Supply Chains." *Journal of Peasant Studies* 41 (5): 749–55. https://doi.org/10.1080/03066150.2013.874340.

Lapavitsas, C. 2011. "Theorizing Financialization." *Work, Employment and Society* 25 (4): 611–26. https://doi.org/10.1177/0950017011419708.

Lauck, Jon. 1998. "The Corporate Farming Debate in the Post–World War II Midwest." *Great Plains Quarterly* 18 (2): 140.

Lowder, S., J. Skoet, and T. Raney. 2016. "The Number, Size and Distribution of Farms, Smallholder Farms, and Family Farms Worldwide." *World Development* 87:16–29.

Legislative Assembly of Saskatchewan. 1972. "Second reading of the Bill No. 110 – An Act to Facilitate the Acquisition and Disposition of Farm Land in Saskatchewan." Hansard: 25 April, p. 1947. http://docs.legassembly.sk.ca/legdocs/Legislative%20Assembly/Hansard/17L2S/720425Hansard.pdf.

National Farmers Union. (2015). *Losing Our Grip – 2015 Update: How Corporate Farmland Buy-Ups, Rising Farm Debt, and Agribusiness Financing of Inputs Threaten Family Farms*. Saskatoon, SK: National Farmers Union.

Northwest Territories Ordinances, 1894, 2nd Leg., 5th Sess, "Exemption for Seizure and Sale," 1894. Accessed on 19 May 2016 at http://www.ourroots.ca/e/page.aspx?id=3485681.

Ontario Ministry of Agriculture, Food and Rural Affairs. 2017. "Number and Area of Census Farms, Canada and the Provinces, 1996, 2001, 2006, 2011 and 2016." http://www.omafra.gov.on.ca/english/stats/census/number.htm.

Ouma, S. 2015. "Getting in between M and M' or: How Farmland Further Debunks Financialization." *Dialogues in Human Geography* 5 (2): 225–8. https://doi.org/10.1177/2043820615588160.

Palley, T.I. 2007. "Financialization: What It Is and Why It Matters." Paper presented at "Finance-Led Capitalism? Macroeconomic Effects of Changes in the Financial Sector," Berlin, 26–7 October. http://www.levyinstitute.org/pubs/wp_525.pdf.

Patterson, D. 2014. "Gov't Must Address Land Investment Deals." *Western Producer*, 20 November. http://www.producer.com/2014/11/govt-must-address-land-investment-deals/.

Phillips, D. 2015. "PFRA Pastures Transition Study." Frogworks Consultants, 7 January. http://www.naturesask.ca/rsu_docs/pfra-final-report.pdf.

Pilger, G. 2015. "Who's Buying Up Canadian Farmland?" *Country Guide*, 10 February. http://www.country-guide.ca/2015/02/10/whos-buying-up-canadian-farmland/45783/.

Qualman, D. 2001. "The Farm Crisis and Corporate Power." Canadian Centre for Policy Alternatives. https://www.policyalternatives.ca/sites/default/files/uploads/publications/National_Office_Pubs/farm_crisis.pdf.

Raine, M. 2015. "Cost of Production Matters for 2015." *Western Producer*, 7 January. http://www.producer.com/2015/01/cost-of-production-matters-for-2015/.

Saskatchewan Farmland Ownership. 2015. "Summary of Results from Public Consultations." Government of Saskatchewan, 7 October.

Senate of Canada. 2016. "Proceedings of the Standing Senate Committee on Agriculture and Forestry." Issue no. 21 – Evidence – Meeting of December 6, 2016. https://sencanada.ca/en/Content/Sen/Committee/421/AGFO/21ev-52979-e.

Sommerville, M., and A. Magnan. 2015. "'Pinstripes on the Prairies': Examining the Financialization of Farming Systems in the Canadian Prairie Provinces." *Journal of Peasant Studies* 42 (1): 119–44. https://doi.org/10.1080/03066150.2014.990894.

Statistics Canada. 2011. "Value per Acre of Farm Land and Buildings, at July 1: Agriculture Economic Statistics," November. http://www.statcan.gc.ca/pub/21-013-x/2011002/t002-eng.htm.

– 2014. "Snapshot of Canadian Agriculture," 24 March. http://www.statcan.gc.ca/ca-ra2006/articles/snapshot-portrait-eng.htm.

– 2015a. "Demographic Changes in Canadian Agriculture," 30 November. http://www.statcan.gc.ca/pub/96-325-x/2014001/article/11905-eng.htm.

– 2015b. "Land Tenure as a Proportion of Total Farm Area, Canada, 1976 to 2011," 25 January. Accessed on 20 September 2016 at http://www.statcan.gc.ca/pub/95-640x/2011001/p1/figs/figure11-eng.htm.

– 2016. "Agriculture Is Growing and Evolving," 16 January. http://www.statcan.gc.ca/pub/95-640-x/2011001/p1/p1-01-eng.htm.

– 2017a. "2016 Census of Agriculture." https://www150.statcan.gc.ca/n1/daily-quotidien/170510/dq170510a-eng.htm.

– 2017b. "Saskatchewan Remains the Breadbasket of Canada." https://www150.statcan.gc.ca/n1/pub/95-640-x/2016001/article/14807-eng.htm.

Western Producer. 2015. "Cost of Production Matters for 2015," 7 January. https://www.producer.com/2015/01/cost-of-production-matters-for-2015/.

Yates, D. (2014). "Farmland Rental Rates Slow to Respond to Commodity Prices." *Western Producer*, 16 October. http://www.producer.com/2014/10/farmland-rental-rates-slow-to-respond-to-commodity-prices/.

INTERVIEWS CITED

Retired farmer, Lasburn, SK, 17 December 2015.
Family farmer, Kronau, SK, 19 December 2015.
Mark Folk, Regina, general manager of Farm Land Security Board, 15 December 2016.
Tim Hammond, Biggar, SK, real estate agent, 13 July 2014.
Farm couple, family farm, Dalmeny, SK, 17 December 2015.
Family farmer, Zehner, SK, 19 December 2016.
Family farmer, Caronport, SK, 15 December 2015.

Family farmer, Grenfell, SK, 19 December 2015.

Chris Selness, Regina, SK, vice-president investments – Saskworks Venture Fund, 14 August 2014.

Farm couple, family farm, Parkbeg, SK, 14 December 2015.

Family farmer, Parkbeg, SK, 14 December 2015.

Lyle Stewart, Regina, SK, minister of agriculture, 15 December 2015.

Organic farmers, Kenaston, SK, 16 December 2015.

Family farmer, Elrose, SK, 16 December 2015.

10 *Jordvern* as a Situation of Action: The Material and Non-Material Forces Shaping the Protection of Farmland in Norway

HILDE BJØRKHAUG, KATRINA RØNNINGEN,
AND HEIDI VINGE

Introduction

The concept and phenomenon *jordvern*, directly translated as "farmland preservation," is a particular visible phenomenon both institutionally and discursively in the Norwegian debates over land use. In 2016, 1.11 million hectares, 3.7 per cent of the total land area in Norway, is termed arable, and only one third of this land is capable of growing grain for human consumption. Thus Norway is vulnerable to any losses of agricultural land – even if the figures seem small. If the farmland loss is continued, it will be reduced by 50 per cent by 2050 (Straume 2013). The country has therefore developed a comprehensive system of legislation and planning to ensure the protection of and continued use of land for food production. Following a period of high levels of farmland conversion, 21 per cent of productive farmland lost between 1994 and 2014 (Stokstad and Skulberg 2014), the Norwegian parliament passed a national strategy for farmland preservation in 2015, with an aim to lower the yearly cap on annual conversion of farmland to 400 hectares by 2020 (Storting 2015). Nevertheless, in 2016, 600 hectares of agricultural land was lost (Statistics Norway 2017). Conversion of cultivated and cultivable land to purposes other than agriculture is managed at the municipal level, predicated on the land-use element of municipal master plans, drawn up in accordance with the Planning and Building Act. Conversion of cultivated land to purposes other than agriculture requires permission from the municipality to be exempted from the Land Act §9 (Norwegian Agriculture Agency 2017). Complaints about the permission for exemption must be presented to the regional county authorities, or even at the national level. This chapter asks: How is it that the actual amount of land lost is so much higher than the target, given the existence of a system of laws and regulations, strengthened by a national strategy to protect the land? What forces, material and non-material, are shaping the protection of farmland in Norway?

While objectives for agriculture for decades have been multifunctional, there has been a turn towards a more neo-productivist development (Rønningen, Burton, and Renwick 2012), particularly given the government's objective of maximizing domestic production. Hence the total available area for growing grain has become an important indicator in the Norwegian discourse about food security and food sovereignty (Vinge 2015). Representatives of agricultural interests argue that sustaining this area (and its productivity) is a challenge and should be a priority (Ministry of Agriculture and Food 2011–12). However, the decision to implement and execute measures to preserve agricultural land is also *value-based* and negotiable, and runs contrary to some public interests; it is embedded in cultural valuations of what is in "society's interests" – and individual decisions may seem situational and/or "local." Norway is an interesting case for its well-developed policies and tools to protect farmland, and its obvious failure to exercise these instruments. In this chapter we draw upon the situational approach, developed by Clarke (2005, 2015), to analyse cultural valuations of agricultural land in the Norwegian *jordvern* discourse.

Focus on Increased National Food Production Requires Farmland

Norway renewed its focus on food security and food sovereignty in Norway in the wake of the world food price crisis that began in 2007 and peaked in 2008. This global wake-up call led to serious political and social unrest in both the Global South and North. A series of ongoing developments and some short-term situations have been given as explanations for the crisis: Increasing prices for fossil oils, which in turn raised the prices for agricultural inputs (primarily fuel and fertilizers), a restructuring of agriculture with a shift from food production to biofuel and feed production, a growing middle-class population with a shift towards more meat- and dairy-rich diets, and a decline in the growth of grain production and national grain stocks, combined with several major weather events such as droughts and flooding. These factors gradually and suddenly led to food imbalances and for many, food shortages in the markets. Another major driver, or catalyst in building the crisis scenario, was deregulation within the financial sector. This, according to Brobakk and Almås (2011), led to a rapid influx of financial capital into the food commodity market and contributed to prices increasing more and faster than could be explained solely by supply and demand forces.

The Norwegian government responded with increased attention to land management and food production. The potential impacts from climate change, described by the Intergovernmental Panel on Climate Change (IPCC) in 2007 had already raised awareness (IPCC Core Writing Team, Pachauri, and Reisinger 2007). The Ministry of Agriculture and Food (2008–9) drew up a white paper on climate that discussed how the agricultural sector could contribute to "being part of the solution." Increases in food prices internationally highlighted the increasing shortage of productive agricultural land and led the minister of agriculture and food to state that Norway was experiencing the *positive* effects of global free trade and a deregulated agricultural sector. Thus, the negative externalities of globalized free trade interpreted and translated into a Norwegian context of a protectionist agriculture could imply an easier future for Norway in international trade negotiations than had been experienced during the "multifunctional" epoch. This crisis also rapidly changed the discourse within Norwegian agricultural politics (Ministry of Agriculture and Food 2011–12) and marked a shift from a "multifunctional approach" that emphasized the provision of public goods, to a "food security approach," that emphasized producing enough food within a "food sovereignty approach," and the need for Norway to increase its food self-sufficiency producing food for its own population (Bjørkhaug, Almås, and Brobakk 2012; Vinge 2015).

Farmland is a vital but limited resource that food production depends upon. It is in direct and indirect competition with other land-based activities, and this competition has direct impacts for national and international food security. Hence the *resource* we are studying in this chapter, Norwegian farmland, is *situated* in a discourse where agriculture has survived despite marginal conditions and where the remaining (relatively) small-scale agricultural structure is embedded in a protectionist setting that has the support and cooperation of the public, the state, and agricultural actors (Bjørkhaug and Richards 2008), like a social contract. Even though Norwegian farmland is protected by regulation and laws, and a culture of protectionism prohibits financial speculation, there has been a substantial reduction in productive farmland. Most of the farmland lost is conversion to housing areas around the edges of urban settlement areas (Skog and Steinnes 2016). A substantial amount of land has also been lost to roads and other infrastructure, but also to on-farm developments such as new farm roads, larger or new farm buildings, etc. (Gunnufsen, Øvrum, and Nordal 2015). The latter may be seen as a necessary part of modern food production infrastructure, but the extent of it adds to the many paradoxes of farmland preservation when essential resources are lost with modernization. Another important farmland loss factor is abandonment, mainly of more marginal land in rural areas after farm closures (Vinge and Flø 2015). Speculation in land abandonment to lower agricultural value to promote re-regulation is also an emerging factor in urban areas. The main concern is thus the fact that high-quality land suitable for grain production is disappearing at a high speed.

Jordvern as a Situation of Action

Situational analysis is a methodology developed by Adele Clarke (2005, 2015; Clarke et al. 2003; Clarke, Friese, and Washburn 2018) that builds upon and extends Anselm Strauss and Juliet Corbin's grounded theory (Corbin and Strauss 1990) into what can be called a postmodern mapping tool. According to Clarke, situational analysis "allows researchers to draw together analysis of discourse and agency, action and structure, image, text and context, history and the present moment – to analyse complex situations of enquiry" (Clarke et al. 2003, 554). It allows us to derive (1) situational maps for analyses of relations between actors (human and non-human), discourses, and situations; (2) social worlds/ arena maps that identify the arena(s) of commitment where negotiations take place; and (3) positional maps where positions are taken (or not) (Clarke et al. 2003). For instance, the question of whether or not to preserve farmland is a discursive creation that occurs in texts, talks, mind-sets, and actions. Within a discourse, certain ways of seeing and acting may be perceived as more "normal," taken for granted, or even non-negotiable. This means that some positions or decisions are easier to adopt than others (Foucault 1972).

Discussions and negotiations about land preservation and land use in Norway are embedded within global, international, and domestic discourses and politics. Global trade regimes that relate to agriculture and food (see, e.g., Friedmann and McMichael 1989; McMichael 2009) and the capitalist (free) trade-regime ontology (McMichael 2014) can exert much influence on resolutions that are decisive and domestically irreversible. At the same time, domestic discourses on land use and land preservation, food production and farming exist with ambitions of their own, influencing the discourse on food security and food sovereignty (Bjørkhaug, Almås, and Brobakk 2012; Vinge 2015). Decisions on farmland conversions are handled at local municipality level (see figure 10.3), sometimes appealed by regional or state authorities, and within the context of various types of legislation (see figure 10.2). At the outset the restrictive legislation would deny such conversion. How do competing discourses influence negotiations on the protection of agricultural land and the final, practical decision-making? Situational

mapping allows us to analyse how competing discourses, or even reasoning within specific discourses, influences Norwegian agricultural
land conservation and land use priorities. It permits us to identify the
influences: from the global to the local.

Material and Methods

Our analysis is based on a range of different sources of data. These
include interviews, literature, statistics, documents, and media texts
where *jordvern* is a significant theme. Documents include cases of political decision-making mostly around the country's larger cities (Stavanger, Oslo, and Trondheim) as well as the national policy process (see
also Vinge and Sørensen, this book).

The analysis was performed in two stages. First, an initial discourse –
actor and arena mapping – was performed to name the large discourses
and identify who is involved in producing, supporting, and opposing
them. The public *jordvern* discourse was mapped to identify the elements that appeared most relevant in the situation. Figure 10.1 shows
the rapid growth in media interest around the issue of farmland preservation since 2006. At the start of this period, farmland preservation
came on the political agenda, with the government announcing the
goal of halving the amount of farmland lost annually by 2010.

Figure 10.1. Number of Articles on Farmland Preservation Appearing in the
Norwegian Media 1996–2016

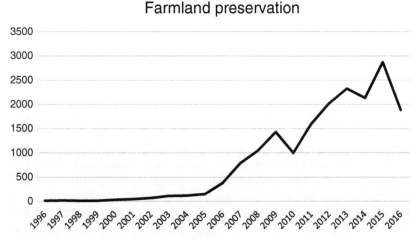

Source: Media Archive Atekst[1] (own analysis)

Our study also involved mapping of official documents describing farmland preservation goals and targets, such as legal texts, white papers, minutes of meetings, and plan documents. Farmland preservation is mentioned as an objective in the Norwegian Constitution §112, the Land Act (Jordloven 1995) and the Planning and Building Act (Plan-og bygningsloven 2008). In addition, current priorities are indicated in the political goals for the maximum amount of farmland that Norway should allow to be converted to other purposes each year. The key legal texts are presented in the adjacent box. Documents from agronomic and agricultural research organizations were also included, providing data for our analysis.

The Land Act §9 (1995)

Cultivated land must not be used for purposes that do not promote agricultural production. Cultivable land must not be used of in such a way as to render it unfit for agricultural production in the future.

The duty to work the land and restrictions on the division of agricultural property seek to ensure both the quality and quantity of farmers' ability to maintain viable agricultural production in the future. This goal is based on the principles of both food security and food sovereignty.

The Planning and Building Act (2008) Chapter I. §1, section 3. Purpose

Ensuring that resources are used in a manner beneficial to society entails taking into account that resources shall be used with a view to the needs of future generations. Land resource management shall be environmentally sound and take into consideration the need to protect the soil as a production factor and the preservation of the land and cultural landscapes as a basis for life, health and well-being for human beings, animals and plants.

Section 11-5. The Land-Use Element of the Municipal Master Plan

The municipality shall have a land-use plan for the whole municipality [the land-use element of the municipal master plan] that shows the connection between future social developments and land use.

National Goal for Maximum Conversion of Farmland

Since 2004, an important policy goal has been to halve the annual rate of conversion of farmland to urban development from a yearly average of 1200 hectares ten years ago to a goal of maximum conversion of 600 hectares of farmland per year. (Ministry of Climate and Environment 2004–5)

National Strategy for Farmland Preservation

A proposed national strategy for farmland preservation was enacted in Parliament 8 December 2015. In this, the goal for the annual conversion was lowered to a maximum of 400 hectares by 2020.

Second, in-depth qualitative interviews were carried out with representatives of local, regional, and national government bodies, government agencies, development, environmental, farmers' and rural organizations – including youth and women's organizations, the agricultural cooperative organization, and a journalist writing on food and agriculture. The following analysis draws primarily on seven in-depth interviews with representatives from the most directly involved stakeholders in the agricultural domain, as shown in table 10.1. These seven actors were chosen as key because their positions were central to the positions in the initial maps. The analysis in this chapter also draws on the insights gained from interviews with the other actors mentioned above.

The topics covered in the interviews included respondents' interest and involvement in discussions on land use and farmland preservation, both generally and in connection to specific cases or conflicts, their reflections on how farmland preservation and interest in the topic has evolved, and previous, present, and potential scenarios. Further subjects included their opinions about laws and regulations, governance, management, and the role and status of different stakeholders and interest groups, including the identification of public and private bodies that play a key role in land use. They also provided insights into how these issues relate to the broader goals of ensuring food security and food sovereignty in Norway.

Following Clarke (2013) we drew an initial positional map of the Norwegian *jordvern* discourse that shows the positions taken (or not taken) and negotiated (figure 10.2). The term is the starting point for the analysis, and its actors, arenas, and discourses are mapped and defined

Table 10.1. Interviews

Interviewee	Interest area
Farmers Union (FU)	Farmers' interests
Federation of Norwegian Agricultural Cooperatives (FNAC)	Food industry interests
Agricultural Purchasing Cooperative (APC)	Food industry interests
Rural Women's Organization (RWO)	Rural development, farming and women's interests
Rural Youth Organization (RYO)	Rural development, farming. and youth interests
County Governor, Agriculture (CGA)	Agriculture institutional interest
Journalist	Farming and food interests

as the situation of action. The map, based on the data sources described above, identifies five major influences on the discourse: (1) global debates or understandings of agriculture and food influencing justification and valuation in land questions; (2) future valuations such as sustainability measurements and considerations for future generations – both challenging ethics and moral questions; (3) the institutional framework of laws and regulations and issues of governance; (4) agriculture's own interests and arguments; and (5) broader societal interests that might conflict with farmland preservation and agricultural interests. The next step was to explore the relations between the identified elements or arenas (Clarke et al. 2003), and how these circulate around all three key analytical areas: justification, culture, and ethics and morals.

Our analysis showed that the representatives of agricultural interests (the focus of this chapter) negotiated farmland around the setting of the sometimes conflicting interests positions shown in figure 10.2 and how stakeholders manoeuvre their justification and make sense of positions and decisions taken in the context of culture and ethics and moral issues. It is within this mapping framework we explore the *jordvern* discourse. In the following, we seek to represent the large discourses that relate to this situation of interest with a goal to reveal the complexity of the *jordvern* situation in Norway today.

To explore the *jordvern* discourse empirically, we ask (1) How is farmland preservation constructed and understood in the agricultural discourse? (2) In what situations is farmland threatened? and (3) When do the agricultural actors see farmland conversion as acceptable? The following analysis explores and discusses these questions.

Figure 10.2. Positional Map of the Norwegian Discourse about Farmland Preservation

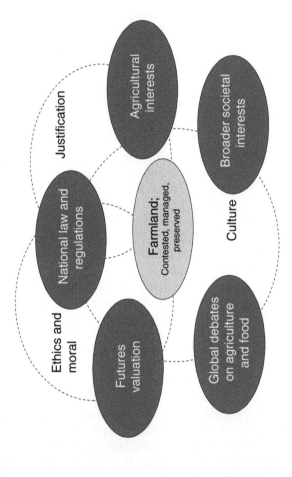

Farmland Preservation in the Agricultural Discourse

We start this section on establishing farmland preservation discourses with the claim that for the actors within the agricultural sector, or arena of interest (see Clarke 2005), perceptions of the value of farmland preservation have developed from merely seeing farmland as an asset for food production, to include a broader recognition of values of farming and agricultural land, and *jordvern* has become more prominent in the agricultural discourse. All interviewees favoured stronger measures to preserve farmland, but they differ in the way farmland preservation materializes in the values they express that underpin the need for preservation.

The interviewees most closely and actively involved in agriculture promote farmland preservation as the ability to "preserve land that has production capacity for food production" (Farmers Union [FU]) and "to maintain Norway's ability to produce food for its own population" (Federation of Norwegian Agricultural Cooperatives [FNAC]). An even broader geographical perspective was presented by the Rural Women's Organization (RWO): "It is about food security and it is about the rights of every country." Such definitions closely resemble the food security and food sovereignty arguments that currently strongly influence Norwegian agricultural policy (Vinge 2015), and the fact that an objective analysis of the vulnerability of Norway's food supply situation is being called for (FNAC). This is strongly connected to the limited availability of agricultural land in Norway, which means that farmland preservation involves "taking care of the scarce land areas, or the scarce areas we have that are suitable for growing food" (Agricultural Purchasing Cooperative [APC]).

It was notable that the agricultural industry interests were careful about explicitly using the food security narrative, as this could potentially be interpreted as a way of "feathering [their] own nests" (FU) and safeguarding their own economic prospects. Our interviewees also saw a broader issue in keeping agricultural land for food production that involved keeping the soil in good shape through good management. From this perspective, farmland preservation goes beyond quantitative material aims, of having and meeting minimum or maximum targets for conversion of agricultural land, and takes on qualitative material aspects, such as soil quality. "I would like to point out that one hectare of soil that has been cultivated for 100 years is, if it has not been ruined by pesticides and fertilisers, full of life. A farmer will produce more from it than if he or she starts cultivating land anew. A farmer needs to build up the soil over many years, to have a good quality, productive soil. So farmland preservation is not just about reducing [the] number of hectares of agricultural land lost to other land-uses{ (County governor, Agriculture [CGA]). This quote introduces the idea of sustainability measurements, an issue also alluded to by the respondent from the Rural Youth Organization (RYO) who spoke of "keeping land fertile for future generations to farm."

Climate change and climate mitigation measurements were also raised as reasons to protect agricultural soil for the future. The interviewee from the Farmers Union emphasized the importance of soil's carbon-binding capacity: "It is obvious that asphalt cover is not good for the climate either.... So I like to believe that those who today are very worried about climate change also recognize that soil protection is also an important part of it" (FU).

Norwegian agriculture is highly structured by and dependent upon economic support offered by the state and upon border restrictions and taxes on imported agricultural goods. This policy is generally supported by the Norwegian population, not only as an agreement between the state and farmers on production of food and fibres and price control, but also as a way of maintaining culturally valued landscapes, amenity values, and biodiversity (Almås 2004; Rønningen, Burton, and Renwick 2012), assigning the farmer the role as a cultural heritage carrier (Daugstad, Rønningen, and Skar 2006). However, this consensus is being challenged politically, as demonstrated by the tensions between (value) conservative farmers in terms of cultural heritage orientation, the rural political party, and parties who favour (neo)liberalization in line with the Conservative party.

"If it becomes cheaper to import, we will lose the focus on managing our own soils well. And on that day ... we lose two things: we lose the benefits of an open and beautiful cultural landscape, and we lose the reason for Norwegian agriculture, that as Norwegians we produce much of our own food on our own land ... the legitimacy of Norwegian agriculture lies in utilizing the land" (APC). In the emerging rift between liberal and conservative political ideology, the issue of safeguarding societal responsibility is mentioned, with strict border controls seen as one way of protecting Norwegian agriculture and its farmland: "Norway must take its share of responsibility in terms of producing food. We know that Norway will need more food in the future, that the world needs more food, and our level of self-sufficiency is lower than ever, historically low. So when people realize that we have a responsibility to produce food they will automatically understand that that means we have to take care of our land. But this, in a way, is what ideologically separates, free trade versus self-sufficiency" (RYO).

Hence farmland preservation is being framed as a value issue that requires a long time frame, and that needs to be sustainably maintained: "Farmland preservation involves taking a long-term perspective. We can't necessarily expect younger people to think very far ahead. So I think farmland preservation should be framed more as a values issue, and values are very important. So one can choose it as, yes, as a value question, simply" (journalist). With this statement the interviewee further points out that there is a difference between sudden threats, such as nuclear bombs and wars, and engaging in a long-term issue, such as farmland preservation. Raising awareness in urban areas about the importance of farming might also increase public support for farmland preservation. Another interviewee touched upon this issue from a different angle, pointing out that the Norwegian public needs this awareness: "It is, of course, about the future security of our own population" (APC).

While all our interviewees agreed that farmland preservation is necessary in itself, the agriculture stakeholders highlighted the tensions between framing both economic viability and the political objective of food sovereignty. The bottom line for farmers is that they run businesses that produce food: "We do not exist as businesses because Norway has the objective to produce food for its own population, no matter how expensive it is. To me that approach is a surrealistic approach" (FNAC). Within this perspective, rationalization is also a necessary endeavour, from the farmers' point of view. A viable agricultural sector also needs to make sense economically.

However, economic considerations can also pose a major threat to farmland preservation. Norwegian farmers are property owners, and their position can create internal tensions over the priority to be given to farmland preservation. "You cannot expect an individual landowner to resist [when there is an opportunity to convert part or all his land for say, housing]. It's a windfall that will economically secure him and two, possibly three, generations in the future. At this point society must take responsibility for farmland preservation. Not the individual landowner" (FU). Here the Farmers Union representative highlights that farmland preservation must be enforced through laws and regulations, and not through prioritizing individual property rights. It was pointed out that many farmers have resisted selling land, only to be forced to do so later by expropriation, receiving lower payments than by voluntary sale. Many "proud and resistant" farmers also have experienced gradually being cornered in by developments, making farming increasingly difficult, without getting compensation.

The construction and changes in the agricultural interest actors' farmland preservation discourse include a cultural turn towards sustainability values. Our analyses do, however, show that farmland owners are found torn between economic pressures and values-based intentions. This leads us to the second part of our analysis, exploring more deeply the situations where farmland preservation is "debated," when there are proposals afoot to convert agricultural land to other purposes.

Farmland Preservation Opponents

In what situations is farmland threatened? As mentioned above, Norway has lost 21 per cent of its farmland in the past 20 years (Stokstad and Skulberg 2014). An analysis of key nodes (see figure 10.3 in discussion section) in our interviews revealed that *roads* and *housing development* stand out as the two most prominent factors (external to agriculture) that currently inhibit farmland preservation. Of the factors internal to agriculture, the *low profitability in agriculture* stood out as the most important. *Societal benefit* (as something overall more important than agriculture) was most frequently used as an argument used by the representatives from agriculture to legitimate converting agricultural land to non-agricultural purposes. *Climate change,* as a discursive term, had both a beneficial and harmful influence on farmland preservation: its influence was harmful when people argued about the need to develop climate-friendly residential/ industrial sites close to existing settlements (see Vinge 2018), but beneficial when the discussion focused, for instance, on carbon sequestration in agricultural land. We will elaborate on these arguments in the following paragraphs.

The construction of roads, houses, and industrial sites is an inevitable consequence of economic development and population growth. Local governments (the municipalities) are obliged to plan these developments in accordance with population projections and economic growth objectives, but doing so can often pose dilemmas: "It's tricky, because we want business development in Norway and we know that houses need to be built ... but the biggest problem ... is that the cheapest, the most economical option is ... often to take agricultural land: be it for road construction, industry, or housing. So in a way we need a little longer-term thinking.... We know that there are alternatives that take much less cultivated land ... So short-term economic gain prevails among local politicians. And that's understandable. If they want business development, then it's hard to see things on a longer-term basis. However, we think that one should" (RYO).

But even for those who do recognize and take it for granted that the country needs more houses and roads, the lack of agricultural land was a pressing issue: "When 97 per cent of our land is not cultivated, then I believe our society must bear the extra cost ... to take care of the non-renewable soil" (APC). The price of land is another thorny issue. Public authorities may, as referred to above, expropriate – i.e., compel the purchase of farmland from landowners at a low price for rezoning, such as for transport purposes. If the land use changes status in local government-planning documents (i.e., from agriculture to housing) the price paid to the owner can be 100 times higher, although there are also regulations in place to keep the price of agricultural land low in order to allow entry for new generations of farmers – if the land keeps its status as agricultural land. This raises tricky questions, as one interviewee pointed out: "Probably really the only possible way to preserve agricultural land in Norway is through laws and political decisions" (APC), even though it is also political decisions that enable building down the land.

Cost and the need for economic development are also key influences on the ability, or lack of it, to preserve agricultural land. The current Norwegian political model seeks to decentralize more decision-making to the local level. Many of our interviewees felt that this works against farmland preservation: "If you leave it to the local government, to municipalities that are struggling economically, they will always look first at saving costs and increasing incomes by creating new jobs and new roads. And so farmland preservation will always be subordinate to this. If we are going to be serious about protecting our soils, then national authorities must take that responsibility and make sure it's done in practice" (APC). Others connect this issue to the (short-term) mandate of local politicians: "It is much easier to argue for what will bring money in at the checkout (the municipal economy) and bring faster results, than to take care of agricultural soils" (RWO). The cost issue can also generate conflicts between local and national interests, particularly when larger road projects, financed and owned at the national or county level, must adopt a specific route through a municipality. Usually in such cases the local government will opt for the cheaper solution, which means building the road on land that is cheaper to develop and doesn't involve the expense of building bridges or excavating tunnels, such as ready cultivated farmland.

Perhaps inevitably, planning processes prioritize planning criteria. The interviewee from the Farmers Union stressed the need to give the conservation of agricultural soil and farmland preservation a higher priority.

> Today they first plan the roads or houses or whatever, and then assess the protection of agricultural land last. But by that point they have gone too far and are almost unable to stop. Farmland preservation must be one of the first criteria to be considered in planning. I have stressed that stricter control over land use changes can actually speed up the development process. There are many developers today who dare not invest in alternative localities, because if another developer manages to convert agricultural land that is most centrally located then he will win the house buyers. If the municipality made it clear that these areas were off limits then the developers would have found other areas. (FU)

This quote highlights the consequences of failure to comply with laws and regulations on farmland preservation. Other interviewees highlighted conflicts with other rules and regulations, with higher compliance becoming a barrier to farmland preservation, giving examples of nature conservation in wetlands, forests, and along coastline and waterways, addressing one of our introductory questions in this book: Are endangered frogs worth more than agricultural land?

With a booming national economy it is very difficult to equate farmland preservation with concerns about food security. Norwegian shops are full of fresh food at relatively low prices. Norwegians spend just 12 per cent of their household income on food, a share that has remained stable for decades (Statistics Norway 2013). While global shocks might transform policies, including agricultural policies (see, e.g., Bjørkhaug, Almås, and Brobakk 2012; Brobakk 2018; Vinge 2015), the main reaction to rising international food prices, as is also the case in Norway, is a craving for ever-cheaper food, as is evidenced by the steady growth of the discount segment among supermarkets (Nielsen 2017), as well as cross-border shopping in neighbouring Sweden (Löfgren 2008).

Even within the agricultural sector, farmland preservation struggles to find a place on the agenda when faced with the other challenges experienced by organizations and industry actors. In a recent strategy-building process the Federation of Norwegian Agricultural Cooperatives ignored farmland preservation as a big challenge.

> So farmland preservation just didn't come into it [our strategy-building]. International commodity prices did, so did volatile prices, climate change, the state of the Norwegian economy. These are all uncertainties. And then there are the certainties: more pressure from markets, to import more, to deregulate (or reregulate), the changing structure of grocery trading that will have a big influence on the future shape of food value chains in Norway. Those are our basic concerns.... And then there is the agricultural side (the political goal to increase domestic food production).... then, we cannot afford to lose any plots of land.... We realize that land will continue to disappear as a result of infrastructure development. It does and we believe that this is necessary. We need to be critical of the negative impacts of infrastructure developments but also recognize that we need infrastructure for business growth. If we do not get that, then we will simply create another problem. (FNAC)

We will further elaborate on this inherent conflict and identify situations where it can be considered legitimate to lose agricultural land.

Justifications for Losing Farmland

When do the agricultural actors see farmland conversion as acceptable? Some of the factors influencing the loss of agricultural land were treated with a certain ambivalence by the interviewees, including the need for business development through providing better infrastructure, and the need to take care of the scarce resources that are fundamental to food production. While some agricultural land can be lost, there are few arguments that can match a discourse based on the "interests of society." Hence it seems that societal concerns are "non-negotiable" (Foucault 1972) within the farmland preservation discourse.

Our interviewees with representatives from the agricultural interests' side claimed that a "nationally important purpose" would be a legitimate reason for converting agricultural land to other uses. Roads and infrastructure for better transport are two such purposes that are considered to be of major national interest. "We have also said that if land is to be converted, it should be for nationally important purposes only, and we see transport infrastructure, for example, as being in that category. And that the degree of utilization should be high. So there are a couple of such requirements that are quite significant. And it is the transport sector that is growing the most in national budgets" (FU).

However, this infrastructure is making increasing spatial demands, given modern expectations and standards for road building. "The problem is this: where we used to build two lanes with a slope of a few metres on each side, we are building four lanes today, and then they'll need a few exits, so there are also a lot of connecting roads. And you also need to build roundabouts on these four-lane roads. So you're seizing an ever-larger area" (FU).

Whilst such national purposes and societal concerns appear non-negotiable, it is also difficult to challenge private property rights, because these are also largely "non-negotiable" (Foucault 1972) within the farmland preservation discourse.

You might say that there are some farmers who are winding down their activities as farmers. They have given up and are planning for generational change. And they foresee that there is going to be local [housing] development and have seen that those who have fought against such developments get incredibly low compensations. So they want to ensure that if the development is really going ahead that they will see some returns from it. But there may also be active farmers who carry on farming, but who might think that they do not want to be the last one standing; the silly old man watching his farm being surrounded by new developments. Then it's better to play an active role in the process and get some returns. If you continue to fight against, fight against, fight against, and you see that everybody is getting much better paid than yourself, then it is quite psychologically stressful. There are some farmers who have been completely destroyed by this. They fight for their land, they fight and fight, but they still lose it by bits and pieces. (FU)

The lack of enforcement of laws and regulations is an obstacle to farmers wholeheartedly supporting the farmland preservation discourse, and it leads some of them to undermine the sustainability of their own industry. However, as the following quote points out, it is hard to blame them. Realistically, when the land may be lost anyway in the longer or shorter term, they may just as well profit from it now, rather than risk their future psychological health. "I have no doubt that family succession would be easier if agricultural land was more effectively protected. And I think there would be less property speculation. Those who want to [continue to] farm would have a bigger chance.... So a really strict enforcement of laws against conversion, and a strict duty to manage the soil is needed. Getting those two things in place would solve a lot of the problems" (FU).

Despite these structural problems, our interviewees identified ethical and moral considerations as promising sources of support for farmland preservation. When it comes to non-monetary valuation, ethics and morals represent sets of values, which are reflected in the public choice to preserve agricultural land. "There's one aspect that is economic and that is hard.... Yet there are other ways to measure the value of that [agricultural land] ... many people think it is important to take care of it [the land], for moral reasons" (RWO).

Similarly, it is hoped that the millennial generation might bring new ideas, based on perspectives of changing futures and global responsibilities that might support the farmland preservation discourse: "I think the new generation is looking at food security as a kind of a future scenario. And they believe that being so dependent on other countries' farmland does not seem right and that it is possible to do something about it. I do not know if they see the connection between wheat production and the Arab Spring and the like, but there is a bit of interest in food security" (journalist).

Discussion and Conclusion

The situation of *jordvern* in Norway today is a strongly contested space with negotiations and power struggles between different knowledge claims. What constitutes, supports, and opposes farmland preservation in this situation? The contested domain is embedded in a context and processes of culture, ethics and morals, and justification of positions and decisions, as figure 10.3 shows. It illustrates the material and

Figure 10.3. Opposing and Supporting Factors for Farmland Preservation in the Norwegian *Jordvern* Discourse

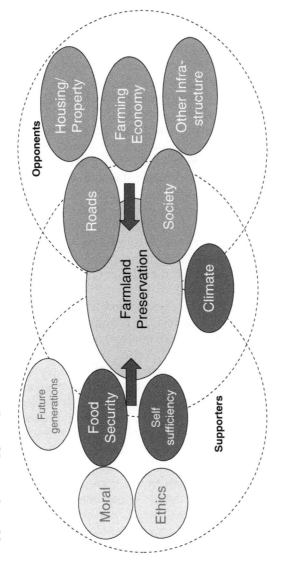

non-material actors (see Clarke 2005) opposing and supporting farmland preservation. The main opposing forces include higher-level actors such as "societal concerns" (an "abstract" force) and those making demands for land for infrastructure, housing, and roads (a "material" force), and lower-level actors, the farmers themselves. Farmers face dilemmas between the low profitability of farming, and farming ethics that can push them to seek windfall gains by converting their private property rights into (sometimes big) cash and improved economic security.

We find that two reinforcing discourses have power as supporting driving forces for farmland preservation in the *jordvern* situation: *the global food security discourse*, and the discourse of *maximizing Norway's self-sufficiency in agricultural products*. These discourses are dominant in important arenas for decision-making such as the annual negotiations between the farmers' unions and the state, and they function as common platforms for agricultural interests and other stakeholders to mount actions and rallies (see McMichael, this book; Vinge and Sørensen, this book). These factors are presently mostly non-material, in the sense that no defined measures of acceptable levels or goals for food security have developed. Adding to these two major driving forces, we find a *moral* and *ethical* discourse, as well as an up-and-coming discourse on the importance of farmland preservations for the right of *future generations* (see Alvarez and Thorseth, this book).

Our analysis shows that farmland preservation has moved from being solely a concern for agriculture and the farming community, and has acquired a broader reach, as a societal interest and part of public discourse. Since the food price spike of 2007/8, there has been a remarkable shift in the public discourse and awareness, and it is now more widely acknowledged that farmland is a scarce and vulnerable resource. Nevertheless, the agricultural sector still finds itself relatively isolated and marginalized in the day-to-day battles for preserving farmland. Also the neo-productivist and neoliberal direction of agricultural policies and development may not necessarily imply that maintaining as much farmland as possible is synonymous with high production levels and food security (see Rønningen's chapter in this book). Traditional farming ethics promoting healthy soils, and the strong connection between land and food production, are thus challenged. Nevertheless, these connections are still strong among most of the stakeholders interviewed.

Farmland preservation in Norway entails regulations that address the farmer as an individual, profit-maximizing actor, and as a steward of the land, managing the soil for future generations. On the one hand, legislation is intended to protect the land from private development. Yet, on the other hand, regulations and legislation oblige him or her to dwell on and operate the farm and to manage it for food production, while there is an established system of price controls, designed to prevent farmland from being turned into an object of speculation. In this sense the legislation is protecting the land and soil from farmers who want to profit from private property rights by selling their land to be used for purposes other than combined farming and dwelling. Nevertheless, it is enforcement that is being questioned.

In the past decades the Farmers Union has partly changed its role from one of protecting farms and farmers taking a property and property-owning perspective, towards a broader role as a champion of farmland preservation, securing it for future generations and for broader societal interests. Although Norwegian farms are relatively small and cover a small fraction of Norway's land area, the farming community is one of the largest property-owning interest groups in the country, as the result of a relatively broad ownership of rural land. Consequently, it appears that they are seeking – and achieving – broader societal legitimacy of agriculture and strategic alliance partners. Particularly interesting is how the youth organization identify national food production in a context of international solidarity. Increased interest in urban farming is also mentioned as a factor here for increased interest and understanding of agriculture as safeguarding social responsibility.

In spite of these trends, agricultural interests point out that city forests, natural areas, waterways, and wildlife, all of which play important roles in providing ecosystem services and recreational opportunities, enjoy stronger protection against development than agricultural land. Inevitably when there are development pressures, different societal actors will choose to defend different interests, and this may mean the preservation of agricultural land becomes minimized as a societal priority. Farmland is mostly privately and individually owned, and most transfers take place within family, allowing few new entrants into farming. This may partly explain why non-farming groups take less interest in preserving agricultural land than they do in other conservation areas. Hence preserving agricultural land has become a "Cinderella" issue with few defenders. This is compounded by the low monetary value of agricultural land (in land-use zoning plans) vis-à-vis agricultural land that has been converted for development for other purposes. Agricultural land preservation is not compatible with pressing societal and private priorities of roads, centralization, housing, and industrial development. And it is hard to get people in a country where such a low share (12 per cent) of income is spent on food to take a passionate interest in food security. In other words, there may be a "missing agenda" among the well-nurtured, general public.

Our situational analysis shows clearly how competing rationales and forces surrounding decision-making about agricultural land lead to ongoing losses of farmland, at a rate faster than the target set by the Norwegian government. While all our interviewees accept the inevitability that some farmland will be lost to other purposes, our findings highlight inherent weaknesses in the decision-making processes. While legislation and planning in principle ought to secure strong protection, the outcome is weak protection.

The FORFOOD project shows that the preservation of agricultural land and the conservation of soil are issues that are being increasingly taken up by other actors, particularly environmental organizations, outside the traditional agricultural domain. Yet the interviewees from within the agricultural sector feel that their voices are rarely listened to in the specific development cases, and that the preservation of agricultural land is often subordinate to other societal interests and private property rights. The only solution that they see to this problem is strong enforcement of conservation laws and regulations, along with defining farmland preservation as a priority criterion in planning. We agree with interviewees who conclude that responsibility for enforcing these laws needs to be elevated to a higher, national level, although this is contrary to Norway's commitment to decentralizing decision-making. Alternatively, it might be necessary to redefine national objectives of food production and food security.

REFERENCES

Almås, R., ed. 2004. *Norwegian Agricultural History*. Trondheim: Tapir Academic Publisher.
Bjørkhaug, H., R. Almås, and J. Brobakk. 2012. "Emerging Neo-Productivist Agriculture as an Approach to Food Security and Climate Change in Norway." In *Rethinking Agricultural Policy Regimes: Food Security, Climate Change and the Future Resilience of Global Agriculture*, edited by R. Almås and H. Campbell, 211–34. Bingley: Emerald Group Publishing.
Bjørkhaug, H., and C.A. Richards. 2008. "Multifunctional Agriculture in Policy and Practice? A Comparative Analysis of Norway and Australia." *Journal of Rural Studies* 24 (1): 98–111. https://doi.org/10.1016/j.jrurstud.2007.06.003.
Brobakk, J. 2018. "A Climate for Change? Norwegian Farmers' Attitudes to Climate Change and Climate Policy." *World Political Science* 14 (1): 55–79. https://doi.org/10.1515/wps-2018-0003.
Brobakk, J., and R. Almås. 2011. "Increasing Food and Energy Prices in 2008: What Were the Causes and Who Was to Blame?" *International Journal of Sociology of Agriculture and Food* 18 (3): 236–59.

– 2005. *Situational Analysis: Grounded Theory after the Postmodern Turn*. Thousand Oaks, CA: Sage Publications.

– 2015. *Situational Analysis in Practice: Mapping Research with Grounded Theory*. Walnut Creek, CA: Left Coast.

Clarke, A., C. Friese, and R.S. Washburn. 2018. *Situational Analysis: Grounded Theory after the Interpretative turn*. 2nd ed. Thousand Oaks, CA: Sage Publications.

Clarke, A., L. Mamo, J.R. Fishman, J.K. Shim, and J.R. Fosket. 2003. "Biomedicalization: Technoscientific Transformations of Health, Illness, and U.S. Biomedicine." *American Sociological Review* 68 (2): 161–94. https://doi.org/10.2307/1519765.

Corbin, J., and A. Strauss. 1990. "Grounded Theory Research: Procedures, Canons and Evaluative Criteria." *Zeitschrift für Soziologie* 19 (6): 418–27. https://doi.org/10.1515/zfsoz-1990-0602.

Daugstad, K., K. Rønningen, and B. Skar. 2006. "Agriculture as an Upholder of Cultural Heritage? Conceptualizations and Value Judgements: A Norwegian Perspective in International Context." *Journal of Rural Studies* 22 (1): 67–81. https://doi.org/10.1016/j.jrurstud.2005.06.002.

Foucault, M. 1972. *The Archaeology of Knowledge and the Discourse on Language*. New York: Pantheon Books.

Friedmann, H., and P. McMichael. 1989. "Agriculture and the State System: The Rise and Decline of National Agricultures, 1870 to the Present." *Sociologia Ruralis* 29 (2): 93–117. https://doi.org/10.1111/j.1467-9523.1989.tb00360.x.

Gunnufsen, E., A. Øvrum, and O. Nordal. 2015. *Tiltak for å styrke jordvernet*. Report 2/2015. Oslo: Alsplan Viak.

IPCC Core Writing Team, R.K. Pachauri, and A. Reisinger. 2007. *Climate Change 2007: Synthesis Report*. Geneva: Intergovernmental Panel on Climate Change (IPCC).

Jordloven. 1995. *LOV 1995-05-12 nr 23: Lov om jord (jordlova)*. Oslo: Ministry of Agriculture and Food.

Löfgren, O. 2008. "Regionauts: The Transformation of Cross-Border Regions in Scandinavia." *European Urban and Regional Studies* 15 (3): 195–209. https://doi.org/10.1177/0969776408090418.

McMichael, P. 2009. "A Food Regime Genealogy." *Journal of Peasant Studies* 36 (1): 139–69. https://doi.org/10.1080/03066150902820354.

– 2014. "Rethinking Land Grab Ontology." *Rural Sociology* 79 (1): 34–55. https://doi.org/10.1111/ruso.12021.

Ministry of Agriculture and Food. 2008–9. *Klimautfordringene: landbruket en del av løsningen*. St. meld. 39. Oslo: Ministry of Agriculture and Food.

– 2011–12. *Landbruks-og matpolitikken. Velkommen til bords*. Meld. St. 9. Oslo: Ministry of Agriculture and Food.

Ministry of Climate and Environment. 2004–5. *The Government's Environmental Policy and the State of the Environment in Norway*. White Paper 21 Oslo: Ministry of Climate and Environment.

Nielsen. 2017. "Dagligvarerapporten 2017." Oslo: Nielsen.

Norwegian Agriculture Agency. (2017). *Omdisponering og deling*. https://
www.landbruksdirektoratet.no/no/eiendom-og-skog/eiendom/
omdisponering-og-deling#omdisponering-av-dyrka-og-dyrkbar-jord.

Plan- og bygningsloven. 2008. *LOV-2008-06-27-71 Plan- og bygningsloven – pbl.
Lov om planlegging og byggesaksbehandling*. Oslo: Ministry of Local Government and Modernization.

Rønningen, K., R. Burton, and A. Renwick. 2012. "Western European Approaches to and Interpretations of Multifunctional Agriculture – and Some Implications of a Possible Neoproductivist Turn." In *Rethinking Agricultural Policy Regimes: Food Security, Climate Change and the Future Resilience of Global Agriculture*, edited by R. Almås and H. Campbell, 73–97. Bingley: Emerald Group Publishing.

Skog, K.L., and M. Steinnes. 2016. "How Do Centrality, Population Growth and Urban Sprawl Impact Farmland Conversion in Norway?" *Land Use Policy* 59:185–96. https://doi.org/10.1016/j.landusepol.2016.08.035.

Statistics Norway. 2013. "Forbruksundersøkelsen." https://
www.ssb.no/inntekt-og-forbruk/artikler-og-publikasjoner/
lite-endring-i-forbruksmonsteret.

– 2017. "Kommunal forvaltning av landbruksarealer." https://www.ssb.no/
kofola.

Stokstad, G., and O.N. Skulberg. 2014. "Fulldyrka areal og kornarealer på Østlandet." R14-14. Ås: Norsk institutt for skog og landskap.

Storting. 2015. "Innst. 56 S (2015-2016) Innstilling til Stortinget fra næringskomiteen. Prop. 127 S (2014-2015) – vedlegg 4." https://stortinget.no/
globalassets/pdf/innstillinger/stortinget/2015-2016/inns-201516-056.
pdf.

Straume, K. 2013. "Monitoring Norwegian Farmland Loss through Periodically Updated Land Cover Map Data." *Norsk Geografisk Tidsskrift / Norwegian Journal of Geography* 67(1): 36–48. https://doi.org/10.1080/00291951.2012.7
59616.

Vinge, H. 2015. "Food Security, Food Sovereignty, and the Nation-State: Historicizing Norwegian Farmland Policy." In *Food Sovereignty in International Context*, edited by A. Trauger, 87–105. Oxon: Routledge.

– 2018. "Farmland Conversion to Fight Climate Change? Resource Hierarchies, Discursive Power and Ulterior Motives in Land Use Politics." *Journal of Rural Studies* 64:20–7. https://doi.org/10.1016/j.jrurstud.2018.10.002.

Vinge, H., and B.E. Flø. 2015. "Landscapes Lost? Tourist Understandings of Changing Norwegian Rural Landscapes." *Scandinavian Journal of Hospitality and Tourism* 15 (1–2): 29–47. https://doi.org/10.1080/15022250.2015.1010283.

11 From Agri-Culture to Agri-Nature: New Alliances for Farmland Preservation in Norway

HEIDI VINGE AND SIRI ØYSLEBØ SØRENSEN

Introduction

Farmland preservation has gained recent attention in Norwegian politics. In 2015 a national farmland strategy was passed in the Norwegian parliament (Stortinget 2014–15), and in February 2018 parliament called the government to update the strategy with more concrete measures in the 2019 budget (Stortinget 2017–18). Protection of arable land has long been considered an important part of Norwegian agricultural policy (see also Bjørkhaug, Rønningen, and Vinge's chapter in this volume). Farmland preservation is even enshrined in the 1814 Norwegian constitution, §110b, and in a special law for farmland, the Land Act, which directs that "cultivable land must not be disposed of in such a way as to render it unfit for agricultural production in the future" (Land Act 1965/1995, nr 23 §9). A compelling reason for this stipulation is that only 3 per cent of Norway's total land area is farmland, which results in a mere 38 per cent of the country's consumed calories being produced nationally (Eldby and Smedshaug 2015).

However, the current sense of urgency to protect farmland is strongly linked to trends in urban development. On the urban fringe, infrastructure and residential development are steadily encroaching on farmland. The significant difference in price between lands that are strongly regulated to preserve it for food production, and land put on the open market for housing or infrastructure development in high-demand areas is approximately six or seven times in favour of the latter. Given a choice, sellers opt for the more lucrative possibility. Thus, in spite of Norway's small amount of agricultural land both per inhabitant and in relation to total land area, and the various parliamentary regulations passed to protect arable land, farmland is being lost to other purposes at a steady pace. Some of the largest cities in the country, most notably Oslo,

Stavanger, and Trondheim, are located in the centre of the country's most important agricultural areas, as might be expected. Good agricultural land in urban-rural fringe areas is therefore under great pressure. Estimates show that if present trends are allowed to continue, almost half of the areas suitable for food production will be lost over the next fifty years (Straume 2013).

This chapter investigates the context for the recent attention to farmland preservation in parliament and explores how the policy field is shaped: who is developing farmland policy in Norway today, and how is farmland conceived of and framed? By exploring these questions we present an examination of new actors entering farmland politics and show how they engage by making sense of it in new ways. Ultimately, the chapter sheds light on strategic alliance formation as a means to influence policy.

The Subject to Policy Regulation: Farmland

Before we get into our discussion of the policy domain, we want to enter the material world to establish the resource that is at the centre of the policy debate: what *is* farmland? While *farmland* generally refers to land suitable for growing food, the more particular biological term for this resource is *soil*, or *humus*. Humus is the rich organic matter that plants grow in and that hosts myriad insects and bacteria. Scientists have no single answer to what humus consists of. When breaking humus down into its constituent parts, they find wide variations – some soils are sandy, while others contain more clay, or a combination of both. These characteristics are contextual, as thousands of years of microclimate in each specific place forms a complex and unique ecosystem. A rule of thumb is that it takes 1,000 years to form one inch of productive soil (Juniper 2013).

Soil is a renewable resource when managed sustainably. Yet when put under asphalt, concrete, or steel, it is gone forever. All over the world, wherever there is urban expansion, municipalities convert farmland into sites for housing and infrastructure and other public purposes. Soil, that is, arable land, is being lost ten times faster than it is being formed over large parts of the United States, while in India and China the rate is estimated to be forty times (Juniper 2013). To a certain extent, this development seems inevitable as more and more people move from rural areas to cities. Much of our most productive soil is found in the vicinity of rapidly growing cities, making it vulnerable to urban expansion. In a property-development mindset, this farmland is seemingly vacant and ready for non-agricultural uses. Focusing on farmland as a fundamental natural resource, however, calls this approach into question.

A recognition of the crucial role of soil and the fact that an increasing amount of the world's farmland is in poor condition has led to growing global awareness of the need to safeguard our prime agricultural resource base (FAO 2015). How is farmland described and interpreted in the latest efforts to preserve farmland in Norwegian politics? In order to approach this question, it is useful to consider theories of policy alliance formation and policy discourses.

Theoretical Perspectives on Alliance Formations and Policy Influence

Organizations can influence policymaking, such as through lobbying, or by voicing their view in public in order to initiate public engagement and elicit democratic pressure to support their objectives. Alliances are crucial to ensure political strength. Theoretical approaches that seek to understand the role of these processes and interaction between actors in a policy field emphasize different aspects of how policy alliances are shaped. In this section, we briefly explain three perspectives on the making of alliances and their potential impact within policy fields: (1) the shared value approach, (2) the pragmatic action approach, and (3) the discursive authority approach. The aim is to enable an analysis that takes into account the complexity of alliance formation and helps us sort out what is going on in the Norwegian policy field surrounding farmland.

Let us start with the shared value approach. Shared values constitute a core in several theoretical approaches to understanding policy alliances and changes in policy over time. The Advocacy Coalition Framework (ACF) proposed by Paul Sabatier and Hank Jenkins-Smith (1993) is based on an assumption that, over time, the actors engaged with any given policy field will join groups on the basis of shared core values, constituting a value system. Changes in group formations and alliances imply a changed value system within the policy field. Therefore the values that policy actors represent are crucial to understanding policy change. The ACF presumes intended and strategic actions based on core values. Other perspectives on the role of shared values in policymaking have focused more on their articulations. Ernesto Laclau and Chantal Mouffe (1985) address them as a process whereby progressive social movements forge connections and alliances with each other. In doing so, they constantly modify their own political identity and their horizon of intelligibility. This approach can add to the understanding of how values are negotiated and become shared, rather than assuming that shared or identical values pre-exist among organizations engaged in a policy field. In this perspective, the potential for policy change lies in establishing "chains of equivalence," or similar articulations voiced by neighbouring social movements. The weakness of alliances is expressed in opposing articulations or disarticulations of shared values.

A second approach to the understanding of alliance formation and policy, which we call the pragmatic action approach, shifts focus from values to actual undertakings that establish associations within the policy field. Actor network theory sees the making of policy alliances as concrete actions taken by engaged actors to establish connections (Latour 2005). Rather than assuming that alliances and policy change result from shared values and how participants act upon and articulate these values, alliance formation and influence are understood as resulting from a series of independent actions, decisions, and initiatives. Of course these actions can express certain values, but the theory suggests that only the actual actions taken by the actors are relevant to making alliances and their influence. Hence the research interest lies in exploring how seemingly arbitrary actions and pragmatic considerations can accumulate connections and associations between actors in ways that result in what we recognize as an alliance, rather than in exploring intentions and values.

While both the values and action approaches focus directly on the *actors* engaged in policy controversies, the third approach we bring into the analysis takes the particular discursive context of policymaking into account. What we call the discursive authority approach draws on the work of Maarten Hajer (2005, 2009). In addition to examining actions and articulations of values, it takes a broader contextual view of alliances and their potential influence. According to Hajer, numerous similar articulations, sometimes called chains of equivalence (see Laclau and Mouffe 1985), do not guarantee change. In this perspective, discourse, defined as "language use conceived as social practice" (Fairclough 1992, 138), is central. Hajer takes up the "mediatization" of politics, as the logics of news media with their dramaturgy influence the way in which power to define policy is produced and reproduced. In order to establish authority and influence in a policy field, one needs to craft storylines that establish an understanding of the situation, the policy problem, and its solution within the span of a sentence.

Following a shared value approach to the understanding of new alliances in the policy field of farmland management, we should expect to find that narratives represent the preservation of farmland as a common core value and, furthermore, that the alliance finds its strength in several similar articulations or utterances voiced by a number of organizations. A strong and potentially influential alliance can be recognized by a unanimous expression of a shared value. On the basis of the pragmatic action approach, however, we should pay attention to the actions of the organizations involved and assume that shared values do not automatically draw actors together. Following the discursive authority approach, we would expect that farmland preservation is constituted as a storyline with specific metaphors that appeal to certain collective fears and define victims and villains.

Summing up, we approach the empirical investigation with three key interests: (1) to examine how values are articulated, disarticulated, and embedded in the alliance, (2) to look into the concrete actions taken by the involved organizations, and (3) to analyse and discuss how an alliance can potentially influence policymaking by means of public communication.

Methodology

The methodological setup of the research conducted followed a situational analysis approach as it is developed by Adele Clarke (2005). Situational analysis is designed for encountering the full complexity of any situation through multi-site investigation. A situation is defined by centring on a particular research object. In our case, this is farmland preservation as a policy issue. Clarke provides several concrete mapping tools to get an overview of actors, positions, and materiality related to the research object. By using different types of analytical maps, the analysis presented in this chapter was first informed by media texts, booklets, and flyers produced by organizations with the theme of farmland preservation, including texts published on organizational websites and opinion pieces published in the Norwegian printed press. The mapping of this material provided important information for the selection of actors for in-depth enquiry. Through mapping we identified a joint opinion piece published in *Stavanger Aftenblad* on 27 February 2014, as a central site of enquiry (Sørum et al. 2014). The article represents a remarkably broad and diverse range of signatories, organizations that in different ways are engaged in the contemporary controversy over farmland preservation.

This chapter is based mainly on the analysis of qualitative interviews with ten persons representing eight different organizations who signed the opinion piece in the *Stavanger Aftenblad* (see table 11.1). The interviews were conducted by the authors as semi-structured conversations covering topics such as land use, agriculture, policy, and strategies for advocacy. We also asked explicitly about policy concerns. Most of the interviews lasted approximately one hour, were recorded, transcribed, and then subjected to thorough thematic analyses.

In the following section the interviewees are referred to by the name of the organization they represent. All quotations are taken from the interviews unless it is explicitly noted that they are not.

Table 11.1. Organizations in *Stavanger Aftenblad* Opinion Piece

Organization	Type of organization
Norwegian Rural Youth	Rural development – youth
Norwegian Society for the Conservation of Nature	Environment
Norwegian Farmers Union	Farmers' interests
The Norwegian Society of Rural Women	Rural women's interests
The Norwegian Cooperative of Grain Producers	Farmers' business interests
Spire, The Development Fund Youth Organization	Development – youth
Nature and Youth	Environment – youth
The Federation of Norwegian Agricultural Cooperatives	Farmers' business interests

Articulations of an Agri-Environmental Policy Field

Our scarce land resources must be preserved for future generations. We join forces to strengthen farmland preservation.

This declaration was introduced in the opinion piece in the regional newspaper, *Stavanger Aftenblad* (Sørum et al. 2014). What is special about this piece is not its focus on farmland preservation per se, but the diversity of the signatories. The article was signed by leaders of a range of civil society organizations, including those concerned with the environment, agrarian interests, rural development, and global solidarity, as well as a number of youth organizations. At first sight, this might seem like an easy assemblage of actors. Looking more closely at them, however, complicates this picture. They can be categorized as either agricultural or environmental organizations. The signatories have stronger or weaker ties to the farmers' movement. The Farmers Union is an interest organization for farmers who, together with other like-minded groups, annually negotiates with the government on farmers' behalf on prices and other central terms for the agricultural sector. Norwegian Rural Youth aims to contribute to viable rural communities and activate and engage rural young people. Strongly tied to the Farmers Union, it focuses on agricultural and policy matters. The Norwegian Society of Rural Women, as its name indicates, is concerned with rural women's issues. Two of the signatories are agricultural industry actors; the Federation of Norwegian Agricultural Cooperatives is an umbrella organization with sixteen member cooperatives, including the Norwegian Cooperative of Grain Producers. The environmental organizations include the Norwegian Society for the Conservation of Nature and Nature and Youth, the youth organization of Friends of the Earth. Spire is an environment- and development-oriented youth organization with increasing engagement in agriculture.

Two specific cases, located in different parts of Norway, seem to have sparked broader engagement with farmland preservation from youth and environmental activists. In Trondheim (the third-largest city in Norway), politicians pressed for housing development on a large area of the highest-quality farmland in 2013 (Vinge 2018). The other incident took place in Vestby in 2015, a small municipality strategically placed at a crossroads in the densely populated and fertile eastern part of the country. In Vestby, the furniture chain IKEA will establish a new warehouse on prime farmland.

When several of our informants talked about how their broader public engagement with the preservation of farmland began, they used a rather diffuse concept of a "certain line" that was crossed to explain why "new forces" entered the field. For example, the secretary of the Norwegian Society of Rural Women said, "It is my experience that agriculture has been alone in this, but that may be changing now…. When you see cases like this [referring to Trondheim and Vestby] that cross certain lines, like the minister of agriculture is doing now, new forces are mobilized." Here "crossing a line" refers to a break with established Norwegian policy, which has long aimed to protect farmland from irreversible change. As a spokesperson for Norwegian Rural Youth said, "They have understood that it is a non-renewable resource we are talking about here."

Pragmatism and Considerations of Legitimacy

The farmers' organizations have long seen farmland preservation as a core area of engagement, varying with different political initiatives and development cases (Vinge 2015). The recent loosening of the general ban against building on agricultural land led to a new mobilization. For agriculturally oriented organizations, the broad media coverage of the proposed IKEA development on high-quality farmland, as well as the coverage of the farmland-devouring Trondheim area plan, were long-awaited opportunities for gaining influence and affecting public opinion. The farmers' organizations take it as a given that they should engage in this matter. We can see pragmatic reasoning in how they talk about their motivation for allying with environmental organizations. An alliance lends greater legitimacy to their cause than standing alone.

Following the actor-network approach, we should also pay attention to the actions and events that constitute the alliance. In this case, the actions taken by the president of Norwegian Rural Youth are worth following. A central arena for her participation was a hearing for a national strategy for farmland preservation. A proposal for a national farmland strategy was first issued by four members of parliament, representing the Liberal party (Venstre)[1] in December 2013 (Stortinget 2013–14). The proposal was discussed in the Committee for Trade and Industry (March 2014), with the committee recommending that the government develop a national strategy for protection of farmland to present for decision in the Storting (Stortinget 2014–15). Prior to the committee statement, the proposal was subject to an open, public hearing on 11 February 2014, which these organizations all attended. This arena gave opportunity for new connections among actors. Leading up to this hearing, several organizations had given statements on how best to safeguard farmland. Seeking to have a greater impact with a broader alliance, the president for the Norwegian Rural Youth organization contacted the different groups at the hearing to undertake a concerted campaign. Noteworthy here is the fact that there was no clearly articulated strategy or plan, but rather a sense of potential. Thus, writing a letter to the regional newspaper seemed to be the first concrete action.

In addition to using an opinion piece to influence the public, pragmatic considerations about which arguments are most effective in promoting the cause of farmland preservation in the current political climate prevailed. Positioning farmland as a *common good* rather than as something that is of interest mostly to individual farmers is one such consideration. In Norway almost all farmland is still owned by family farmers. Farmers' organizations have traditionally been strong advocates of the principle of private ownership of land (Almås 2004). In the case of farmland preservation, however, farmers' organizations have come to the realization that it is in their interest to frame farmland as a necessity for the wider society, not just as something that concerns the agricultural sector or individual farmers. This was a pragmatic consideration: as long as farmland is looked upon as solely the private property of farmers and not as a common good that matters to the whole society, it will lose out when it competes with other societal functions such as infrastructure or housing. In trying to voice this view, however, agricultural organizations have discovered that they lack credibility when talking about farmland preservation as a societal issue. No matter their actual arguments, they are taken as trying to benefit their own members' interests. Forming an alliance with other actors is thus an important strategy. As a leader of the Farmers Union put it, "We try to get others to talk about it instead of us, because we see that when we use it, it is taken as coming from the farmers again, trying to get their hands on a few billion kroner."

Recreational woodlands enjoy a strong normative protection among the general public, whereas farmland is both in real terms and in the minds of urban inhabitants something that belongs to individuals. The Farmers Union want to position farmland as a common good in line with the recreational woodlands: "I think the key to achieving better protection is to give people this sense of ownership," said their deputy leader. He went on, "Maybe not bringing people into the field, but we as property owners must get better at providing paths that can bring people out to the recreation areas."

The Norwegian Society of Rural Women voices the same pragmatism. To increase their impact, they have repositioned themselves as a modern consumer organization, taking a rather large step away from the previous myth about farmwomen who weave and do fundraising. Their goal is to characterize farmland as essential and compelling, and to appeal to people's feelings: "To find creative ways to sell this, to find a way to affect people.... Our normal line of reasoning does not hit its target. So how to crack that code? ... We are marketed as a consumer organization; we try to make sure that people don't think we are the Farmers Union, because we are not. We try to gain a certain trust."

In addition to participating in public debate, all the organizations try to influence politicians more directly. When a conservative government took office in 2013, those politicians increasingly kept agricultural interests at arm's length. Our research shows that environmental organizations find it easy to get meetings with politicians, while those who define themselves as agricultural do not. The minister of agriculture, for instance, declined to meet with the grain producers' organization. According to the spokesperson for the Norwegian Cooperative of Grain Producers, "This was the first time I experienced a minister saying no thanks to a meeting; she is not interested. This is pretty phenomenal, in my opinion. Because then only ideology will be in control, not professional knowledge."

This situation created a need for new arenas to influence policy for the agriculturally oriented organizations and contributed to a push for new alliances based on a realization that action had to be taken in order to make common values visible to other actors in the policy field (Latour 2005).

Discourse: "Global Future" Rather Than "National Economy and Security"

The proposed IKEA store on Norway's best farmland and the magnitude of the Trondheim area plan attracted wide media coverage. This attention offered an opportunity for different actors to gain influence in farmland politics and practice. All the organizations interviewed, albeit in various ways, referred to these incidents when they explained their engagement. Even though these are only two among many other instances of farmland being transformed to serve urban purposes countrywide, the way they have been framed in the media has made them into something larger; they have become important discursive events (Fairclough 1992).

In past debates over farmland preservation, one main rationale has been the importance of safeguarding the national resource base in order to maintain self-sufficiency in agricultural products at a highest possible level (Eldby and Smedshaug 2015). Farmland preservation has been based on an egocentric and economic rationale that is limited by the borders of the nation state. The goal has been communicated as securing Norway's food supply by growing as much grain as possible ourselves and avoiding the importation of agricultural products that can be grown in Norway.

With new actors entering the policy field, a completely different set of values has been positioned at the core of the argument. Even though the cases that sparked engagement with farmland preservation are local, a whole range of *global* concerns are part of the storyline about why soil preservation is important. The national economic and security-oriented self-sufficiency position is replaced by a more ecological and global rationale. Farmers' organizations, for instance, frame it as their duty as stewards of the land to enlighten the public about the importance of farmland, its quality and scarcity. The Society of Rural Women articulated this strong moral commitment to preserving farmland for future generations: "Urban development of farmland is an act of robbery from the future, and the issue must be prioritized in politics."

The thread in the discourse is that food production globally is taking an undesirable direction. The development of mega-farms and the industrialization of food production have become a threat by removing it from its natural resource base. Hence, farmland preservation is inserted into a larger analysis of the direction for food production on a global scale. According to Nature and Youth, "Our fear is that the more you industrialize agriculture, you get more climate emissions, machines, pesticides, everything."

This realization includes a notion that Norway's rather small-scale and family-based agricultural sector is more environmentally sound than its North American counterpart. This line of reasoning proceeds from an environmental point of view; it becomes important to keep agriculture the "Norwegian way," rather than outsource it to the "rest of the world." This storyline implies that an environmental focus does not interfere with farming, but rather strengthens it. The focus then moves towards food production as resource dependent, which sets it apart from the manufacture of other goods. Nature and Youth emphasized that "this is first and foremost a strong agreement about preserving farmland because of its ecology."

A central presumption in this understanding is that farmland is part of nature, rather than being in opposition to nature simply because it is cultivated. As the Norwegian Society for the Conservation of Nature put it, "It is about taking care of one of the most important services that nature offers, and that is food. Nature gives this to us, it is one of the so-called ecosystem services, and safeguarding them is extremely important. And to do that, you depend on diversity in species, right? Why do we have a campaign to save the bumblebee? Because it is incredibly important for our food production."

In the rationale for farmland preservation offered by environmentalist organizations, farmland is framed as a natural resource. The shift of focus from agricultural practices to the resource itself facilitates a perspective that farmers and environmentalists have common interests. This stance represents a significant change, as in the past Norwegian agriculture was a target of environmentalist activism because of the pollution caused by, for instance, chemical fertilizers and imported soy feed concentrates.

Thus, a new opening for an alliance to safeguard the agricultural resource base facilitated the formation of this coalition. Furthermore, it seemed evident from the environmental organizations' point of view that their voice was needed in the policy debate, not only to support farmers, but also to advance the natural resource perspective on farmland preservation. As we shall see, this point of view is increasingly crucial in strengthening the new alliance.

The global perspective follows a narrative starting from the observation that farmland is a scarce resource. It continues: With the acceleration of population growth, climate change, and soil degradation globally, there will be even more need for farmland in the future. Farmland is disappearing at a rapid pace, and even though Norway has a small amount of farmland in proportion to its total land area, the country has a responsibility to protect it. Knowledge claims about soil health, food scarcity, climate change, and population growth are important prerequisites for these arguments. According to the Federation of Norwegian Agricultural Cooperatives, "There is a development now where both politicians and the agricultural organizations in a way turn back to basics towards what really matters – we see dark clouds in the horizon."

Responsibility to *future generations* is also a key aspect of the storyline, and youth organizations are particularly strong in making this argument. Spire, the development-oriented youth group, has a tradition of caring about issues concerning the Global South. They do not have a strong tradition of engagement in domestic issues, but in the case of farmland preservation they have found it important to raise their voice. Spire has launched a proposal for a national ombudsman for future generations, and they see farmland preservation as informing a part of this campaign. This proposed ombudsman would counter what they see as a bias in the political system towards favouring short-term gains at the expense of long-term consequences. The group sees this consideration as especially important in the management of natural resources: "If we can get someone to lift the generational perspective that much too seldom is lifted in the Norwegian debate, this person can show us the faces of our grandchildren."

Most of these organizations assume that people are unaware of the challenge that farmland scarcity represents to the world. Therefore they jointly perceive a need to spread this knowledge. "The market" and "the politicians" are the villains in the story; if the market gains too much power, farmland will be lost, and politicians will allow this to happen.

Possible Disarticulations: *Marka* and Policy Measures as Showstoppers

We have shown that this alliance is based on shared values, pragmatic considerations, and a common discursive framework. At the same time, it is important to highlight the fact that the alliance has certain weak areas; in Laclau and Mouffe's terms (1985), it is fragile and has points of disarticulation. One important point of disarticulation is whether or not housing development should be allowed in the recreational woodlands, called *marka*, that surround many of the largest cities in Norway. Another point is whether farmland should be better protected by law, which would entail a general prohibition against housing development on farmland.

The Norwegian outfields cut across the traditional divide between nature and agriculture, which is a point of conflict between agriculturally and environmentally oriented organizations. This issue is taken off the table because of its disruptive potential. In addition to being a more costly alternative for housing development than flat and drained farmland, the outfields have a strong cultural image and both legislative and normative protection (Lovdata 2009). Farmers' organizations see this law as too rigid and want to soften the total ban against converting recreational natural areas to urban functions, whereas the environmental organizations do not see this as a viable solution to the farmland preservation problem. The deputy leader of the Farmers Union said, "This is what the nature protectors are so scared about. If you give way even a slight bit with regards to the *marka*, it all goes. I agree that the *marka* is important, but building a few houses would still leave plenty of recreational area left. But this has become a symbol; it is like with the carnivores [typically wolves, which kill livestock]: they have become more a symbol than a matter of practical policies. And then it is incredibly difficult to do anything about it. This is why the farmland has to pay the price."

Another major disagreement concerns *how* farmland should be protected. There is strong agreement in the new alliance about the importance of farmland preservation, and it is rather easy to agree on *why* farmland is important. The opinion piece, for example, provides a good indication of why stronger legal protection of farmland is required as the solution to the threat of urban development. Environmental organizations see the Pollution Control Act as a model for such a law (Ministry of Climate and Environment 1981). In the process of recruiting organizations to sign the letter, several actors were positive at first, but later they decided not to join because certain policy proposals were too precise to appeal to a more disparate group. According to a spokesperson from the Norwegian Society of Rural Women, "They unfortunately did not do a good enough job in making it general enough to get everyone aboard. *We* didn't do a good enough job, because we could have included the Norwegian Labour Union, the Confederation of Norwegian Enterprise, and the Norwegian Association of Natural Scientists. We should have been more professional and refrained from saying anything about stronger juridical protection. I think that was where it collapsed."

The alliance signing the joint statement could have been broader, but disagreements about strengthening the juridical protection of farmland got in the way. Farmland preservation as a principle is quite easy to agree upon, but which political measures to apply are not. This alliance will be fragile if it moves beyond raising awareness and spreading knowledge and towards actual policymaking.

Concluding Discussion: From Agricultural Policy to Environmental Policy

In this chapter we have explored two contemporary trends in Norwegian politics: farmland preservation occupying more space on the political agenda, and new pro-preservation alliances taking shape. We have seen that environmental and youth organizations are now increasingly involved in debate and controversies over the inappropriate use, as they see it, of arable land. In the Norwegian context, this engagement is novel. Looking to other countries, such as the United States, we see that environmental interests have been at the forefront of the farmland preservation movement since farmland came on the agenda as part of the environmental awakening in the 1970s (Berg and Zitzmann 1984; Lehman 1995). Farmland preservation was positioned as a means to counter the deleterious effects of urban sprawl, most prominently transportation challenges, costly public infrastructure, and the depletion of nature (Alterman 1997). Agriculture has been described as the ecological nexus connecting humans and nature (Wittman 2009), but the sector has also been targeted by environmental organizations for emissions, pesticide use, and poor animal welfare (Horrigan, Lawrence, and Walker 2002). Michael Bunce labelled the North American farmland discourse *environmentalism*. Resource scarcity was the core discursive theme, communicated in simplistic and crisis-loaded language. Farmers' voices were inaudible (Bunce 1998). More recent studies, however, show that the farmland preservation movement in the United States unites discourses that hold different views of agriculture (Brent 2013). Although the actors here all agreed on the general importance of preserving land, they steered clear of explaining *why* preserving farmland is important, in order to secure the broadest possible support.

In Norway, farmers and environmentalists have a history of both conflict and cooperation. Discursive and practical conflicts have most often been over the preservation versus the cultivation of nature, including forests (Reitan and Holm 2012), and wildlife (Rønningen and Blekesaune 2011). Furthermore, environmental organizations have increasingly focused on the environmental damage associated with large-scale, industrialized agriculture. Alliances have emerged, however, in controversies concerning such issues as genetically modified food (Magnus 2012). Historically in Norway, farmland has been the responsibility of a sectoral system administered through county agricultural boards. The law describing the preservation of farmland, the Land Act, is centrally focused on agriculture. Farmers' organizations have long been the loudest and often the only voice in protests against urban development on arable land in Norway. They have conducted public campaigns to spread knowledge of the importance of farmland, with slogans such as "One square metre of soil equals one bread forever" (Norges Bondelag 2013). Until recently, the main rationale has been farmland's crucial role in maintaining the target of 50 per cent national self-sufficiency in agricultural products. We can thus label the ideology of the Norwegian farmland preservation movement *agrarianism* (Bunce 1998).

Now farmers' and environmental organizations are joining forces. We see a challenge to and alteration of the previous dominant farmland preservation discourse of national self-sufficiency. Our analysis of the Norwegian civil society debate on farmland preservation shows a shift from a storyline that framed farmland preservation mainly as a challenge for agriculture to a storyline that frames it as a crucial challenge for society as a whole. At the same time, we see a shift from an *economic* perspective dealing with the shrinkage of the national agricultural resource base, making farmland development mainly a problem for Norway's self-sufficiency in agricultural products, to an *altruistic* one with a crisis-loaded discourse positioned on a global scale. This storyline centres on the moral responsibility of the Global North, both towards the poor and towards future generations.

In addition to the IKEA building and the Trondheim municipal plan, which were important *discursive events* that served as reference points and elicited greater engagement, these concrete incidents are interlinked with other, seemingly more profound societal dynamics and discourses. These discourses are important to highlight, not only because they contribute to the new alliance analysed here, but also because they affect how important social issues such as farmland preservation are presented, discussed, and assessed. Storylines can create communication networks among actors who otherwise differ in their views on a subject such as agriculture. Global networks of social and symbolic relations influence how farmland and local planning processes are articulated. Seeing farmland as nature, not merely as "cultivated," can change how farmland is treated in political processes.

Our data show that both environmental and agricultural actors deliberately avoid mentioning policy tools in their communication in response to the strong difference of opinion on this question. This may hinder actual commitment in area questions, and development of a better farmland policy at the national level. This study adds insight to the understanding of how policy alliances can become influential, and how shared values, assemblages of actors, and effective storylines are not enough to ensure political action. In addition, to make a policy issue shared, one needs to agree on the tool for protection. Thus we argue that further elaborations on farmland preservation should face the discussion on policy measures.

Still, the protection of Norwegian farmland has recently gained new advocates. This trend represents a shift from the agrarian discourse that has long prevailed. New values and new arguments are central to this shift. To put it bluntly, we see a shift from agri-culture to agri-nature. Presenting farmland as a non-renewable resource contributes to placing agriculture high on the agenda of environmentalist circles. With farmland as nature, the concept of its preservation becomes broader, which also expands its possible support. This shift might pave the way for the integration of farmland preservation in urban development strategies, rather than these two components existing in separate policy spheres, which largely has been the case historically. Can this be a new pivot point for the integration of agricultural and environmental politics in Norway? The policy proposal quoted at the beginning of this chapter aims to introduce a national plan for protection of farmland. Today, decisions about changes in the use of land are made in the local municipality. A national strategy with concrete measures to guide local decision-making thus represents an attempt to protect farmland without interrupting local democracy, so important to Norwegians. The new alliance of actors contributes to the issue of the establishment of farmland conversion as a problem high on the national political agenda. However, there is a long way to go to solve the loss of arable land to urban development.

NOTE

1 André N. Skjelstad, Pål Farstad, Ola Elvestuen, and Abid Q. Raja.

REFERENCES

Almås, R., ed. 2004. *Norwegian Agricultural History*. Trondheim: Tapir Akademiske Forlag.

Alterman, R. 1997. "The Challenge of Farmland Preservation: Lessons from a Six-Nation Comparison." *Journal of the American Planning Association* 63 (2): 220–43. https://doi.org/10.1080/01944369708975916.

Berg, N.A., and W.T. Zitzmann. 1984. "Evolution of Land-Use Policy in the U.S. Department of Agriculture." In *Protecting Farmlands*, edited by F.R. Steiner and J.E. Theilacker, 211–24. Westport, CT: Avi Publishing.

Brent, Z. 2013. "Farmland Preservation, Agricultural Easements and Land Access in California." Food Sovereignty: A Critical Dialogue. International conference, Yale university, 14–15 September, https://www.tni.org/files/download/32_brent_2013.pdf.

Bunce, M. 1998. "Thirty Years of Farmland Preservation in North America: Discourses and Ideologies of a Movement." *Journal of Rural Studies* 14 (2): 233–47. https://doi.org/10.1016/s0743-0167(97)00035-1.

Clarke, A. 2005. *Situational Analysis: Grounded Theory after the Postmodern Turn*. Thousand Oaks, CA: Sage Publications.

Eldby, H., and C.A. Smedshaug. 2015. *Norsk selvforsyning av mat og norsk arealbruk – Tar vi vare på matjorda?* Report 5-2015. Oslo: AgriAnalyse.

Fairclough, N. 1992. *Discourse and Social Change*. Cambridge: Polity.

Food and Agriculture Organization of the United Nations (FAO). 2015. "2015 International Year of Soils." http://www.fao.org/soils-2015/about/en/.

Hajer, M.A. 2005. "Coalitions, Practices, and Meaning in Environmental Politics: From Acid Rain to BSE." In *Discourse Theory in European Politics: Identity, Policy and Governance*, ed. D. Howarth, and J. Torfing, 297–315. Basingstoke: Palgrave Macmillan.

– 2009. *Authoritative Governance: Policy Making in the Age of Mediatization*. Oxford: Oxford University Press.

Horrigan, L., R.S. Lawrence, and P. Walker. 2002. "How Sustainable Agriculture Can Address the Environmental and Human Health Harms of Industrial Agriculture." *Environmental Health Perspectives* 110 (5): 445–56. https://doi.org/10.1289/ehp.02110445.

Juniper, T. 2013. *What Has Nature Ever Done for Us? How Money Really Does Grow on Trees*. London: Profile.

Laclau, E., and C. Mouffe. 1985. *Hegemony and Socialist Strategy: Towards a Radical Democratic Politics*. London: Verso.

Latour, B. 2005. *Reassembling the Social*. Oxford: Oxford University Press.

Lehman, T. 1995. *Public Values, Private Lands: Farmland Preservation Policy, 1933–1985*. Chapel Hill: University of North Carolina Press.

Lovdata. 2009. "Lov om naturområder i Oslo og nærliggende kommuner (markaloven)." https://lovdata.no/dokument/NL/lov/2009-06-05-35.

Magnus, T. 2012. "Den norske diskursen om genmodifisert mat." PhD diss., Norwegian University of Science and Technology, Trondheim.

Ministry of Climate and Environment. 1981. "Pollution and Control Act." https://www.regjeringen.no/en/dokumenter/pollution-control-act/id171893/.

Norges Bondelag. 2013. "Kvadratmeterbrød gikk som varmt hvetebrød." http://www.bondelaget.no/nyhetsarkiv/kvadratmeterbrod-gikk-som-varmt-hvetebrod-article72647-3805.html.

Reitan, M., and F.E. Holm. 2012. "Staten, kommunene og Trillemarka: lokal mobilisering forankret i nasjonale politiske konfliktlinjer." In *Det norske flernivådemokratiet*, ed. M. Reitan, J. Saglie, and E. Smith, 167–95. Oslo: Abstrakt forlag.

Rønningen, K., and A. Blekesaune. 2011. "Redd for rovdyr? Jakten på rovdyrkonfliktens materielle virkelighet." In *Rurale brytninger*, ed. M.S. Haugen and E.P. Stræte, 203–25. Trondheim: Tapir Akademisk Forlag.

Sabatier, P.A., and H.C. Jenkins-Smith. 1993. *Policy Change and Learning: An Advocacy Coalition Approach*. Boulder, CO: Avalon Publishing and Westview.

Sørum, G.J., L. Haltbrekken, N.T. Bjørke, O. Godli, C. Aurbakken, C.B. Jørgensen, E. Enger, M. Gjengedal, A. Vestre, and O. Hedstein. 2014. "Styrk jordvernet!" *Stavanger Aftenblad*, 27 February.

Storting. 1995. The Land Act 1965/1995, nr 23 §9.

Stortinget. 2013–14. "Representantforslag om en helhetlig jordvernplan." https://www.stortinget.no/no/Saker-og-publikasjoner/Saker/Sak/?p=58613.

– 2014–15. "Komiteens merknader." https://www.stortinget.no/no/Saker-og-publikasjoner/Publikasjoner/Innstillinger/Stortinget/2013-2014/inns-201314-149/2/.

– 2014–15. "Prop. 127 c (2014–2015." https://www.regjeringen.no/no/dokumenter/prop.-127-s-20142015/id2413930/#VED4.

– 2017–18. "Representantforslag om en ny jordvernpolitikk som sikrer reelt, nasjonalt vern av matjorda." https://www.stortinget.no/no/Saker-og-publikasjoner/Saker/Sak/?p=69839.

Straume, K. 2013. "Monitoring Norwegian Farmland Loss through Periodically Updated Land Cover Map Data." *Norsk Geografisk Tidsskrift / Norwegian Journal of Geography* 67 (1): 36–48. https://doi.org/10.1080/00291951.2012.759616.

Vinge, H. 2015. "Food Security, Food Sovereignty, and the Nation-State: Historicizing Norwegian Farmland Policy." In *Food Sovereignty in International Context: Discourse, Politics and Practice in Place*, ed. A. Trauger, 87–105. New York: Routledge.

– 2018. "Farmland Conversion to Fight Climate Change? Resource Hierarchies, Discursive Power and Ulterior Motives in Land Use Politics." *Journal of Rural Studies* 64:20–7. https://doi.org/10.1016/j.jrurstud.2018.10.002.

Wittman, H. 2009. "Reworking the Metabolic Rift: La Vía Campesina, Agrarian Citizenship, and Food Sovereignty." *Journal of Peasant Studies* 36 (4): 805–26. https://doi.org/10.1080/03066150903353991.

12 Intergenerational Justice and Obligations to Future Generations: Towards Environmental Rights in Land-Use Policy

ALLEN ALVAREZ AND MAY THORSETH

Introduction

In this chapter we discuss philosophical challenges to the notion that the current generation has an obligation to make agricultural land use sustainable for the sake of future generations. We explore the following philosophical questions: Should we limit the present generation's use of agricultural land in a way that will diminish opportunities to increase their welfare in order to benefit future generations who do not yet exist? Which "future generations" do we need to take into account?

With this approach, we shall argue that there is a need to extend the scope of our obligations beyond national societies, and also beyond the human species – a view that is still anthropocentric but includes nature. The concept of environmental rights supports this approach and is discussed in order to reveal and analyse the complexity of our collective obligations for using agricultural land. Further, we shall argue that our current ethical commitments are connected to our obligations to future generations.

We explore several responses to motivational challenges that undermine any obligation to constrain consumption for the sake of future people, using as our organizing hypothesis Parfit's "non-identity problem" (Parfit 1986, 121–2), and address key aspects of the scope of the obligations problem and the motivation problem. In addition to Parfit, other key authors are Birnbacher (the motivational problem); Hardin (tragedy of the commons); Rawls (overlapping consensus); Cullet and Boyle (environmental rights); and Gewirth, and Meyer (intergenerational justice). Finally, we will also highlight practical implications by discussing why and to what extent we need to constrain agricultural land use for the sake of future generations.

In part 1 we present the problem of moral obligations and responsibilities and the concept of environmental rights and their differing operationalizations. As well we discuss the kind of justice that applies to the present and the future generations and how it can be governed. In part 2 we present the problem of motivation and how it relates to consumption in the present. In part 3 we explore the combination of these in agricultural land-use questions.

1: Accounts of Moral Obligations to Future Generations

Generations: Overlapping Present and Future Cohorts

How can justice apply to relations between generations? *Generations* are social (not familial) groups of birth cohorts whose lifetimes overlap. Birth cohorts refer to individuals born around the same time. Since some birth cohorts overlap lifetimes between the latter years of the earlier cohort and the early years of the cohort that follow, the temporal concept of the "present generation" refers to members of overlapping birth cohorts[1] who have moral obligations to act responsibly for the direct/indirect benefit of future generations.

By referring to overlapping birth cohorts in our definition of generations, we include younger moral agents who will outlive the members of the birth cohort who were born before them. There is a time when all the members of the earlier birth cohort A die but are survived by the younger member of the next birth cohort, B, who will then live to see the birth of later birth cohorts, C, who, in turn, will be part of their present "social generation" – where B will become senior members. Those birth cohorts (A and B and C and so on) that overlap lifetimes are contemporaries in their own generations (see figure 12.1). While members of cohort C are part of the future generation for cohort A (since they do not overlap lifetimes), they are, nevertheless, contemporaries with cohort B as younger members of the present generation as soon as members of cohort B become seniors. In this case, cohort B bridges the gap between cohort A and cohort C. This bridging allows the earlier generation of overlapping cohorts A and B to pass on important land use knowledge, technologies, and resources to the next generation of overlapping cohorts B and C.[2]

Moral Obligations: Pay It Forward or Free Ride

Our understanding of moral obligation may be based partly on the assumption that those who have obligations can reciprocate. The problem with viewing our obligations to future generations is that future generations do not yet exist and therefore cannot reciprocate. Our relations with members of future generations are unidirectional and

Figure 12.1. Overlapping Generations

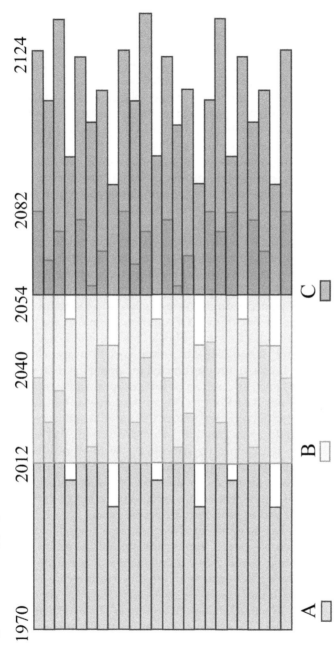

asymmetrical. But moral obligations can still exist without assuming reciprocity. For example, parents have obligations to their children even though their parental obligation does not require that children reciprocate.[3] Strict reciprocity cannot apply to future generations, but a motivating concept equivalent to reciprocity may be appropriate.

While we normally frame our obligations in terms of relations to specific persons and that we reciprocate with these people, we can also give back to a group, so that the target of our obligation is no longer a specific member of that group (since we no longer distinguish individuals or single out specific members of that collective). We "reciprocate" the benefits we received from any member of that group to the whole group – whoever among the members of the group receives our act of reciprocity. To illustrate group-directed reciprocity, consider how mindful we tend to be in cleaning up after we use a common public space such as a bench in a park. When we arrive at the park bench and notice that it is very clean, we can't help but clean up after using it, assuming that we are motivated to give back the cleanliness we enjoyed that resulted from the earlier actions of members of the group who used that bench before we did. Assuming we are so motivated to reciprocate, we feel guilty if we leave our mess behind, despite finding the bench in clean condition, especially if we repeatedly do so. We are inclined to condemn ourselves as freeriders if we do not clean up a common place that we find clean when we arrive. As far as moral obligations are concerned, "group-directed reciprocity" is equivalent to person-specific reciprocity.

Assuming this notion of group-directed reciprocity is reasonable, we can add that the benefit we return to the group must be proportional to what we have received from it. The amount of that benefit must at least be equal to, if not slightly greater than, the benefits we enjoyed. If it is less, we could again feel that we are freeriding. The same ideas about group-directed reciprocity seem to apply to all residents (past, present, and future) of our common planet, Earth. We reciprocate when we conserve natural resources for the sake of future generations, because members of future generations are also members of that group of residents of Earth and users of its natural resources.

"Reciprocity" that is group-directed can also transcend temporal boundaries.[4] When we extend the membership of the group to which we are reciprocating beyond its current members, we include future members as deserving this behaviour. When we reciprocate in this way, we also pay forward the benefits we received in the past. There are reasons for doing so. The first relates to John Rawls's idea of "just savings" for the stability of the basic structure of the society of future generations (Rawls 1971, section 44; see Meyer 2008). The amount should be sufficient for future generations to continue with a society stable enough for members to fulfil their obligations to one another and to contribute to their just savings for their own future generation. If we have enjoyed the benefits of the past generation's conservation, we should do our share of conserving for the stability of the future. A second reason is human survival. If the human species is to survive, we must act in sustainable ways. Finally, given that our generation has benefited from those who preceded us, we must be motivated to avoid freeriding. This is important, as experiments on individuals able to reciprocate show that victims of negative behaviour, such as greed, tend to pay more greed forward, compared to how recipients of generosity pay forward generosity to others (Gray, Ward, and Norton 2014).

Future Generations in Sustainable Development

The question of intergenerational justice is about what current generations owe to future generations. The question is raised against a background of decreasing resources and severe climate change that the current generation is already aware of. The general principle, which has been broadly accepted worldwide, is based on the definition of sustainable development in the *Report of the World Commission on Environment and Development: Our Common Future* (1987): "Sustainable development is development that meets the needs of the present without compromising the ability of future generations to meet their own needs" (World Commission on Environment and Development 1987, part 1). Although this general principle is widely accepted, it remains to be interpreted and implemented. The balance between economic, environmental, and social aspects is commonly agreed upon as a general understanding of "sustainable development." However, several issues are contested, such as the scope, the interaction between human and non-human nature, and diverging economic theories about justice. As an example, it makes a significant difference whether "environments" are conceived in terms of tradable commodities or as a commons. Since *Our Common Future* was published in 1987, an impressive volume of literature has been produced, much of which is outside the scope of this chapter. However, we aim to address environmental rights in the context of sustainable development, as defined above. Environmental rights is a frame for discussing how ethics should inform decision-making about natural resources, including agricultural land use.

Environmental Rights Historically

Environmental rights have been discussed as an integral part of human rights, such as the right to health and food, including a decent quality of life (Cullet 1995, 26). Thus, environmental rights are being interpreted partly as analogous to individual human rights. The rationale for doing so is quite obvious, as the absence of, say, pollution is considered to be a prerequisite for enjoying a healthy life.

There are, however, some drawbacks to individualizing environmental rights and to framing them as individual human rights. The most obvious one is the nature of the environment itself. For example, it does not make good sense to conceive of polluted air in individualized terms, as those responsible for air pollution in a particular area do not themselves necessarily have to be exposed to it. Likewise, people in some particular location may be exposed to pollution or suffer from environmental deterioration caused by others. Industrial pollution is thus not comparable to individual littering. Even though polluted environments are measurable, it is still hard to define their scale and scope in terms of who should be held accountable.

However, there are also good reasons to frame environmental rights as human rights. The complex interdependence between individual humans as well as between humans as a collective and their environment requires that humans preserve the health of the environment on which they all depend for survival and well-being. The resources that our environment provides are necessary conditions for our freedom, well-being, and agency, and all humans should claim access to these resources as rights grounded on such needs (Gewirth 2014, 120). Future generations have the same rights to a healthy environment, and the present generation has the correlative obligations to future generations to preserve the environment for the sake of the latter.[5] To damage the environment is a violation of such rights of future generations, in the same way as it is a violation of the rights of our contemporaries.

A somewhat different but still related point is the problem of ascribing responsibilities for damages for which no particular person can be held directly responsible, because the individual may very well be part of a lifestyle upon which she or he has insignificant influence. This holds true for embedded practices: "The problem arises not because of my actions, but because millions of people like me live a *lifestyle* that involved greenhouse gas emissions, and it is our uncoordinated individual action, which, together, cause harm to the environment" (Moore 2008, 504, as cited in Woods 2015, 99).

Although it is a misconception to talk about *individualized* environmental rights, it still makes good sense to speak of environmental rights in some sense. When we ask what current generations owe to future generations, the environment immediately becomes an issue of the utmost concern. This is because our generation's continuing disregard for environmental issues puts future generations at high risk. One problem of particular interest framed in terms of "the tragedy of the commons" was introduced by Garret Hardin (Hardin 1968). He illustrates the point by imagining herdsmen in a commons who individually try to maximize their own gain by adding more cattle. While each one is acting rationally from an individual perspective, he brings ruin to the commons as the result of overgrazing. Thus, the origin of the tragedy stems from uncoordinated actions when dealing with limited resources. In Hardin's words, "Each man is locked into a system that compels him to increase his herd without limit – in a world that is limited" (1344). The reason we should discuss this as a moral problem involving rights and justice is because the problem is widely agreed to be anthropogenic, that is, brought about by human actions in the first place.

Environmental Rights Today

A present approach to environmental rights has moved away from looking upon environmental rights as analogous to human rights, towards a more collectively based view, including non-human environments themselves. Alan Boyle distinguishes between three perspectives or "generations" of environmental rights, only partly fitting into generations of categories of human rights.

First, environmental rights have to do with civil and political rights, such as giving access to environmental information, judicial remedies, and political processes (Boyle 2007, 1). This is an anthropocentric perspective, focusing primarily on the harmful impact on human individuals rather than the environment itself.[6] Thus, this perspective encourages the "greening" of human rights. The primary role is then empowerment and protection from environmental harm. Second, environmental rights concern economic and social rights, amounting to treating a decent and healthy environment as a basic value and a right comparable to other economic and social rights. Third, consider environmental rights as a collective right. In this account, rights are given to communities of people rather to individuals. This perspective appears to be the most suitable, as rights connected with "the environment" do not seem comparable to individual human rights. A primary reason for proposing this view is that it is difficult to determine who should be held accountable and responsible for environmental damages. Another advantage of this third perspective is that it suggests environmental rights as a quality that has to transcend a purely anthropocentric dimension of human rights.

Here we argue that the environment writ large is a common concern, mainly because any kind of environmental rights depends primarily upon collective relationships between humans and between human

Figure 12.2. Global Environmental Collective

communities and other non-human organisms in their environment. However, it might still be fruitful to speak in terms of rights in connection with the environment as a basic value. The rights in question have a significant range of "stakeholders,"[7] some of which notably disempower people *and* non-human organisms who are not capable of claiming particular rights for themselves. Rather, we should think of the whole environment (or nature) as composed of human and non-human organisms interdependent on each other as a collective. Human stakeholders and non-human organisms, to which human stakeholders are dependent for survival, are all part of an ecosystem sustained by their interdependence. However, a critical difference is that human stakeholders can preserve or destroy non-human organisms and eco-systems. We illustrate this collective interdependence in figure 12.2.

One basic reason for framing environmental rights as collective rather than individual is because environmental damage does not re-strict itself to damaging particular individuals or particular non-human organisms or ecosystems. For example, the result of the destruction of agricultural land through conversion or overuse endangers human stakeholders and non-human organisms elsewhere, and it is difficult to tell which individual in particular is to blame for the damage. This brings us to another assumption that supports a collective view of environmental rights. Such a view would be "less anthropocentric ... [and] it would benefit society as a whole, not just individual victims. It would enable litigants and NGOs to challenge environmentally de-structive and unsustainable development on public interest ground" (Boyle 2007, 32). Thus, environmental rights apply to just governance of agricultural land use. As such, it runs across the division between agribusiness and rural food production.

As pointed out above, damage to the environment seldom results from individual actions. Rather, we can attribute it to the collective lifestyles of our societies that are environmentally detrimental. As an example, it is difficult to delimit the harms that result from particular individuals' ex-cessive consumption when taking intra- and intergenerational perspec-tives into consideration. From this follows another point in favour of the collective view of environmental rights, which is a motivational factor: unless it is possible to identify how each individual action affects the environment, a motivational driving force is missing. If we encourage people to act "green," there is little incentive unless we could tell the dif-ference from acting more or less green. However, those who would miss an individual incentive to change their individual lifestyle may still be encouraged to change their lifestyle on the anticipation that a collective change would make a difference. This brings us to a real obstacle within the frame of liberal democracy, because collective transformation to a different lifestyle is hardly possible unless collectively implemented.[8]

Justice in the Environmental Context

The link between environmental and human rights is the need for protection, and in some contexts conservation, where conservation in particular may apply to endangered peoples, cultures, non-human or-ganisms, and ecosystems that are threatened by extinction due to en-vironmental damage. But there may be other reasons for the quest for conservation, as well, such as an endorsement of particular lifestyles. A dilemma arises if a lifestyle causes damage when available to a large number. This becomes immediately clear to us in trying to explain why individual Chinese people should or should not be allowed to consume the same goods – for example, a private car – as people in less densely populated countries. Most people realize that this is a moral dilemma that cannot be resolved easily at an individualized level. The principle of justice to apply here cannot be based on an individually based theory of human or environmental rights. A key question is whether we still can make sense of environmental rights in a different shape.

Environmental problems are not purely individual or country-specific; they include future generations. When discussing intergenerational justice we should also include an intra-generational dimension, as the principle of justice is equal in both, or so we shall argue, below. For now we shall focus on the collective, that is, the non-individualized dimension of the environment as a basis for our understanding of environmental rights.

The nature of environmental rights is rooted primarily in its irreducibly collective character. This is an empirical dimension, but it also points to the moral dimension of solidarity within and between generations. The solidarity dimension of sustainability is foundational in the Brundtland report, in its appeal to inter-generational equity. One challenge is, however, how to understand "equity." To speak of it in terms of an "equal amount for everyone" would certainly not be relevant when it comes to, for example, the environment as a condition for living a decent life (African Charter, article 24, cited in Cullet 1995, 29). The inequality that results from corrupted environmental rights has little to do with numbers, and a whole lot to do with the commodification of environmental values. More specifically, we could speak of development reduced to economic growth.

To illustrate such a reductionist conception of development, consider the following example: Sardar Sarovar is a developmental project that resulted in displacement of many rural people and in environmental degradation, while urban dwellers profited through an increase in their already high standard of living (Cullet 1995, 33). This project also aimed to provide irrigation water to drought-prone areas of Gujarat, India, as well as electricity to all three states sharing the project. Thus, there were different groups with claims to the same resources. Intra-generational solidarity becomes an issue when, for instance, economic development entails the improvement of someone's environment or quality of life but results in the loss of other resources and deprivation for other people (Cullet 1995). What happened in this case is that the project fed new water-intensive industries near the main urban centres without delivering water to its final destination – after having displaced an estimated 100,000 people who had to be relocated on new land, which is not freely available in India. Many rural people were displaced, causing significant environmental degradation, while urban dwellers already enjoying a comparatively high standard of living benefited. According to Cullet, Sardar Sarovar stands out clearly as a failure to make all people, or at least the least well off, benefit from a development project aimed partly at improving environmental conditions on a regional scale.

In addition to compromising solidarity *within* the same generation, the Sardar Sarovar project also illustrates how sustainable development may still entail an environmental deterioration that is not captured by the prevailing concept of sustainable development. This is a reason why we need to address environmental rights as a kind of collective right across and between generations. In the Sardar Sarovar project there is an intra-generational injustice that is committed against one of several groups with claims to the same resources. This case also illustrates the kind of injustice discussed in Rawls, notably violation of the "difference principle," which allows inequalities of distribution of benefits only if this "difference" or inequality benefits the least well-off in society and does not disadvantage those less privileged (Rawls 1971). With this and similar projects in view, we may now understand environmental rights as collective rights aimed at improving the situation of the less advantaged, now and in the future. How could we make sense of such a concept of environmental rights applying to the huge field of natural resources, arable land included?

Governance of Environmental Rights

On the question whether we should implement environmental rights, that is, a right to a satisfactory or decent environment, we face the question of who should decide in cases where the law would apply. There are a number of options – international courts, national political institutions, local people, or experts (Boyle 2007, 33). There are, however, diverging professional opinions on the legitimating force of these alternatives. As a basic assumption, Boyle argues in favour of the UN International Covenant on Economic, Social and Cultural Rights having "constructive dialogue" with governments rather than litigation in the courts (Boyle 2007, 38). This argument is based mainly on the notion that "since political processes of this kind are inherently multilateral and normally allow for more extensive NGO participation than international courts, they also have a stronger claim to greater legitimacy" (38). Boyle is correct in contending that such political processes would gain greater legitimacy than litigation in the courts. In this way we could anticipate stronger collective commitments to environmental sustainability, including motivation for changing environmentally damaging lifestyles. This would not be a small gain. However, we would still be left with fundamental problems of governance. There are weak international supervisory mechanisms to employ if we put our trust in political processes like constructive dialogue only; national governments remain very important in this file, and they can be unreasonable. In response to this disconcerting fact, the literature has started to discuss "nudges" as a strategy to move collective action in a more environmentally friendly direction (Birnbacher 2015). Nudging uses psychology to create small interventions that influence the way people make decisions. In sustainability contexts it has been argued that this is an acceptable means, as long as the nudging is transparent, we are careful in how we use it, and we avoid substituting individualism for social policy. From an ethical point of view, a counterargument concerns autonomy, as nudges may undermine individual freedom and autonomy, by being illegitimately paternalistic (Birnbacher 2015).

Apart from the motivational challenges, there are barriers to governance of environmental actions. Here we shall look at agricultural land use in particular. In the context of sustainable policies in this field, we need to connect the ethical arguments to global, national, and local levels, as well as to current and future generations. What kind of land use governance would be more sustainable as well as more just? We will return to this in part 3. Now, we shall briefly leave the topic of environmental rights and explain what "rebound effect" means as an obstacle to sustainable development.

The Rebound Effect

The so-called sufficiency rebound tries to explain why it is not necessarily more just development if people in the rich world commit themselves to frugality. The rebound effect may be described as an unintended effect of frugal behaviour in the rich world. This is because frugal behaviour causes new consumption by others (Alcott 2008, 7). The idea of a sufficiency rebound is based on the older idea of an efficiency rebound, which can be expressed as a cost-benefit ratio compared to the expected environmental benefit when holding consumption constant. As an example, technological improvement results in improved fuel efficiency at a lower cost, which in its turn will lead to more consumption as fuel becomes cheaper.

This is a good vantage point from which to discuss why we need to understand how environmental rights can do justice for and between generations, inter alia how the least privileged will not suffer further injustices at the cost of otherwise sustainable development. However, we do not want to conclude that individual frugality is useless. Rather, the point is to show why it does not solve the problem of intra- and intergenerational injustice as long as environmental rights are wrongfully thought of as analogous to individual human rights. One part of the argument relates to the individual/collective dimension of rights, as we have seen, whereas another part concerns sufficiency rebound, having to do with uncoordinated action, and treating environments as a kind of quantifiable commodity. As an illustration of the last point, we draw attention to the possibility of richer countries buying emission quotas from poorer countries, or the possibility of richer countries withdrawing from the accounting of their own emissions when produced abroad.

Frugality by, for example, the purchase of emission certificates is often looked upon as a transfer in the name of equity (Alcott 2008, 15). However, this perception is flawed because there is a lack of transfer in purchasing power. Without such a transfer to either the present or future poor, there will be no sustainable impact upon either intra-generational equity or to intergenerational justice (15). In order to illustrate this point, Alcott mentions that without an explicit transfer, the beneficiary of the income effect could be an affluent neighbour who heats his swimming pool more often. We are sympathetic to this approach to the rebound dilemma, as it gives a fruitful starting point for criticism of a prevailing regime within sustainability discourses.

Alcott's main point is that since a personal shift to frugality does not guarantee either present or intergenerational equality, we need to have a transfer of purchasing power to the poor and to future generations. We add that such action should take account of the collective nature of both governance and the object of our obligations. By that we mean environmental rights need to be extended to non-human organisms and ecosystems as well. Then it becomes obvious that even if it were possible to speak about a transfer of purchasing power, it would still be inadequate when speaking of environmental rights that exclude non-human organisms and ecosystems of the collective. Such collective rights cannot be treated as purchasable commodities. Rather there is a need for another transfer, of the sustainability vocabulary for collective environmental rights.

Part 2: The Problem of Motivation: Moral Consumption for Future Generations

There is a growing consensus that the world population of 7 billion people consuming resources at the current rate is not sustainable.[9] This view, if correct, implies that the present generation should do something to reduce population growth and consumption of natural resources to a level that will correct the current excesses with respect to the earth's capacity to support life. This may be necessary to prevent catastrophic and irreversible depletion of natural resources, especially land needed for producing food and uncultivated land needed for sustaining ecosystems.

Sustainable Consumption Rates

How should consumption rates be evaluated in order to judge if they are sustainable? One prominent definition of sustainability limits consumption to the carrying capacity of ecosystems such that "sustainability is improving the quality of human life while living within the carrying capacity of supporting eco-systems" (IUCN/UNEP/WWF 1991). The Oslo Symposium in 1994 clarified this further by defining *sustainable consumption* as "the use of goods and services that respond to basic needs and bring a better quality of life, while minimizing the use of natural resources, toxic materials and emissions of waste and pollutants over the life cycle, so as not to jeopardize the needs of future generations."[10]

According to the planetary boundaries report[11] published by a group of environmental scientists (Steffen et al. 2015), the consumption of the present generation has already crossed important limits in four of nine planetary boundaries, including climate change, loss of biosphere integrity, land-system change, and altered bio-geochemical cycles. At the time the report was first published in 2009, land-system change had not yet been crossed.

Attempts to measure sustainable human consumption, such as the Environmental Performance Index of 2014, show how different countries are performing (Yale Center for Environmental Law & Policy & Center for International Earth Science Information Network at Columbia University 2014). Even if there are good reasons to imply that global consumption rates need to be reduced, the economic consequences of such reduction is still a major challenge to effective mitigation.

Doubts about Our Ability to Harm Future People and the Search for Deep Norms to Radically Motivate Action

What does it mean to harm future people? If members of the present generation are responsible for causing harm to future people by the way they consume resources, what is the nature of this responsibility? One attempt to analyse this responsibility has raised doubts about our responsibility in harming specific future people. An example is the difficulty of identifying exactly which future people we can harm because two opposite ways of using natural resources (unconstrained consumption versus conservation) lead to the existence of different future people who are *nonidentical* to each other. Unconstrained consumption (or depletion) will cause one group of future people to exist, and conserving resources will cause another group of people to exist. Thus, if by harming we mean causing a person to be worse off than she could have been by our action, we cannot really harm the people who will exist if we deplete resources, because they will not exist at all if we do the alternative of conserving natural resources.[12] Conserving resources will lead to a different set of future people who are not identical to the ones who would exist if we deplete resources. This doubt about our ability to harm two non-identical sets of future people has been known as Parfit's non-identity problem (Parfit 1986).

If we try to solve this non-identity problem by saying that it makes *no difference* whoever comes to existence in the future, and that what matters is the aggregate well-being of one set of future people compared to the other group who will exist if we take another course of action, it would imply that having more future people equally living with very low levels of well-being is better than having fewer future people with high levels of well-being. Why? Because the aggregate well-being of so many people taken together, even if low, is greater than the aggregate well-being of a very few people, even if their well-being is very high. This seemingly *repugnant* implication requires us to rethink how we should compare the well-being of future people and people of the present generation as well.[13] Mere aggregation of the well-being of a group of people will conceal the relative levels that the worse-off in each group suffer. We also value basic cognitive and physical abilities that are *noncomparative* or *absolute thresholds* of well-being that should not be deprived from anyone. Aggregating the low well-being of the deprived of their basic needs together with others who are well off seems morally problematic.

It seems reasonable to think that we can avoid harming any member of future generations if we adopt conservation policies. Those alternative people who would come into existence as a result of our adopting the depletion policy would have a state of well-being that is so low that their suffering would be worse than not existing at all. However, Parfit assumes that the lives of these less well-off future people would be worth living even if this very low state of well-being is caused by their predecessors' depletion of natural resources. If the present generation's loss of agricultural land leads to a decreased capacity of future people to produce the food that they need to survive, then they are harmed in a morally significant way by virtue of the deprivation from which they will suffer.

Is the Low Level of Well-Being of Future People Caused by Unconstrained Consumption Really Better?

The reason Parfit's account of the non-identity problem is not as problematic as we discussed in the previous section is because the well-being level of the people that Parfit assumed would exist (if we do not constrain consumption) is still much higher than we have now.[14] Parfit also assumes that relevant technologies that increase human well-being will be developed four centuries after the depletion choice has been made. Contrary to that assumption, there is some consensus among environmental scientists that climate change by 2400 would bring a lot of suffering and death to people at that time.[15] If we ignore what proponents of constrained consumption call a sufficiency threshold below which well-being becomes extremely low and life intolerable, then we will probably not see the serious effects of choosing unconstrained consumption.

A sufficiency threshold is missing in Parfit's account because he seems to subscribe to a view that well-being is a matter of comparison. However, if we adhere to an alternative non-comparative view of well-being where – below a certain threshold – well-being must be valued in an absolute (non-comparative) sense, then we will see that what matters is that one has enough resources or abilities and not how much one's share of resources compares with others'.[16] Such a view can even accommodate an egalitarian perspective by proposing two thresholds: preference satisfaction threshold (where equality matters as a principle of distributive justice), and a subsistence threshold, where basic cognitive and physical abilities are at risk if deprived of the means to reach this minimum level. Assuming Parfit sees the level of well-being of the present generation as above the minimum subsistence threshold, then unconstrained consumption indeed does not harm anyone. But if unconstrained consumption causes future people to fall below the minimum threshold after three centuries (see figure 12.3), then these people are harmed. They are harmed because to exist with a very low level of well-being is worse than not existing at all.

From Aggregate Utility to Sufficiency of Abilities

Rather than defining well-being or welfare as simply preference satisfaction (or utility, happiness) and quantify it from 0 to some higher number, we can instead define well-being as having some baseline level of cognitive and physical abilities to value certain functionings (*doings* and *beings*; see Sen 1991, 1999) and pursue these functionings.[17] Viewing well-being this way may avoid falling into repugnant conclusions[18] such as to prefer

Figure 12.3. Parfit's Depletion Graph with Sufficiency Level Revealed

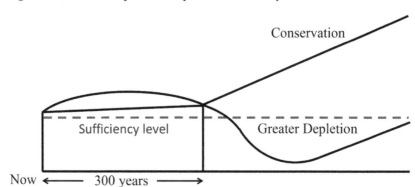

a future where we have more people who suffer from very low levels of well-being because their aggregate well-being exceeds that of a smaller population that enjoys high levels of well-being per capita. By setting an absolute threshold level[19] that protects basic abilities, the problems associated with aggregation, such as repugnant conclusions, may be avoided.

Consumption-Harm Threshold

Freedom to achieve valued functionings (see Sen 1991, 1999) can be adversely affected by lack of resources and climate change, and related extremely dangerous environments, as, for example, being prone to flooding and erratic/unusually extreme weather caused by previously unsustainable policies and consumption. The present generation should constrain itself from such activities and implement policies on a level of intensity sufficient not to breach the harm threshold for future generations. Constraint involves some degree of self-deprivation. Up to what level should we deprive ourselves of consumption? One way to determine such a limit is to set the bottom threshold of consumption for what is needed to secure our basic functionings, such that we avoid depriving ourselves to the point of losing our basic functionings. We may consume more than subsistence, but not to the extent of causing future generations to be deprived of the means to secure their basic functionings.

Ideal Consumption Levels That Take Future Generations into Account

If members of the present generation have a responsibility to give future generations the opportunity to have consumption levels on a par with their own, they need to account for their level of consumption so that it will not deplete resources. One view proposes a chain of obligation between present and future generations linked by the direct obligation of parents of the present generation to their children, who, in turn, will have direct obligation to their own children, and so on.[20] Since the lives of the children of the present generation will overlap with the lifetime of a future generation, a chain of obligations obtains where each generation is required to keep its consumption at a level that allows resources to be passed on to children who, in turn, have the same obligations to pass sufficient resources to their own children, enabling them to keep their own obligations, and so on. According to this view it is unfair to leave children with resources insufficient to fulfil their own parental obligations. Each generation is obligated, therefore, to pass on a larger share of resources to its successors. This chain of obligations view is based on three premises:[21]

- P1: Principles of justice require a uniform distribution of resources between contemporaries if each individual would derive similar benefits given equivalent life opportunities.
- P2: It is wrong to place others in a position where they are unable to fulfil their moral obligations to third parties.
- P3: It is wrong to cause individuals to come into existence whose lives are not worth living.

Furthermore, the collective nature of these obligations, as we have argued in part 1, requires collective action. As the proverb says, "It takes a village to raise a child." In the same way, this parental chain of obligations can be fulfilled only if we recognize that we are part of the greater collective where the future generation is connected to us.

Part 3: Environmental Rights, Agricultural Land Use in Future Generations

In this section we shall turn to an applied level of argumentation in the context of land use. We will draw upon some of the conclusions from the previous sections, most importantly those connected with environmental rights. This is mainly because we think obligations to future generations ought to be part of a scheme that includes both rights and obligations. In order to make sense of this, we must include the environment in this scheme. In doing so, we support the widening of human rights to include the right to a healthy environment. This extension enables us to broaden the perspective of human rights, as well as to strengthen the importance of access to a healthy environment, mainly as an integral part of human rights, but also to the environment that comprises the human and non-human collective.

In part 1 we established that environmental rights are *anthropocentric* in the sense that only humans are capable of being proper rights-holders. Since, however, human interdependence with the environment is decisive in establishing such rights, we need to include the interaction itself in the very concept of rights and corresponding duties to future generations. This brings us to a second important aspect of environmental rights, as they are directed not only to future generations. Rather, environmental rights are equally for *intra-generational* relations. A third essential characteristic of environmental rights is the fact that they can be conceived of only in the plural, that is, as *collective* rights. Integral to this aspect is also the importance of *solidarity*. The very rationale for speaking of rights in the first place is that the particular context in view makes a strong appeal to values that are shared between us humans across local and national borders. The values in view are considered to be *commons*, in contrast to values in commodities. Hardin's well-known worry about the tragedy of the commons (Hardin 1968) makes the case, particularly when speaking about scarcity of natural resources. As such, land use is about the kind of resources referred to by Hardin. In our context the particular resources are identified as, inter alia, bears, wolves, reindeer, sheep, and healthy ecosystems in rural environments. As an example, we have to deal with conflicts between different stakeholders and proponents of conflicting values.

Here we want to point to conflicts both between and among different claimants and users of the commons. Some of the most basic conflicts do, however, offer a basis for new alliances across the traditional divide between rural and urban stakeholder interests. On the basis of the following outline of these conflicts and new alliances, we will point out the potential for overlapping consensus between parties who were previously in conflict with each other. Two outstanding kinds of conflicts underlie the new alliances between farmers on the one hand and environmentalists like Nature and Youth and Spire on the other, both of which concern the need for conservation of soil and arable land. One conflict has to do with a global concern for sustainability of nature, including arable land, whilst the other is a criticism of a neoliberal commodification and industrialization of farmland. Both have led to new and promising alliances (Bjørkhaug, Rønningen, and Vinge; and Vinge and Sørensen, this book). Let us present the conflicts and new alliances.

CONFLICT 1: BETWEEN NATURE/WILDLIFE AND FARMING
Traditionally, media and others have framed the conflict between wildlife and farming as one between different stakeholders, notably

wildlife proponents and farmers. However, as the empirical analyses in Bjørkhaug, Rønningen, and Vinge, as well as Vinge and Sørensen show in this volume, there is a growing common concern among these parties for conservation of soil and arable land. The common enemies are industrialization and downsizing of soil and arable land as a commons. These parties further share a concern for future generations, although their reasons for doing so may differ, ranging from global to more individualized perspectives. Thus, there is only seemingly a conflict between urban and rural interests.

CONFLICT 2: *BETWEEN NEOLIBERAL ECONOMY/INDUSTRIALIZATION OF FARMLAND, AND ECOLOGICAL/ENVIRONMENTALIST CONCERNS*
This is a conflict about commodification of soil and farmland as a non-renewable natural resource. Wildlife proponents and farmers join forces to strengthen farmland preservation, most notably with a common appeal to future generations and scarce resources. We may interpret this new alliance as a pragmatic alliance for policy reasons (see Vinge and Sørensen, this book), as the different parties of the alliance also have their own, partly divergent reasons. As an example, some farmers frame farmland as a necessity for the wider society, like the environmentalists, while toning down their own private interests. Thus, conflict *and* new alliance exists within and across the urban/rural divide.

Based on the empirical analyses of the Norwegian context undertaken by Bjørkhaug, Rønningen, and Vinge, as well as Vinge and Sørensen in this book, we may now point out the following:

1 The types of conflicts described may be described only partly as a rural/urban divide.
2 There are new alliances between wildlife and farming joining forces against industrialization and commodification of arable land as a commons.
3 There is a common concern for future generations across the traditional conflicting division lines (i.e., wildlife/farming, rural/urban).

As we can see, the conflicts correspond only partly to a rural/urban divide. Interestingly, we see potential new alliances between proponents of wildlife and farmers, in taking a common interest across the cultivated/uncultivated divide. We will not be particularly concerned about this divide here, although there seem to be interesting new alliances that cross it (Rønningen and Flemsæter 2013, 4–5).

The parties in these new alliances join forces in supporting and framing common concerns, although for partly different reasons. Here we have focused on conservation as one such common concern. The parties have varying reasons to support conservation and protection of arable land, some of which overlap. We may here only briefly offer a list of their reasons: ecological sustainability; concern for future generations; focus on commons in a global perspective; protection against a neoliberal economy and industrialization of farming; inclusion of farmland as part of nature; and soil and arable land seen as a non-renewable resource. The plethora of divergent reasons supporting the same overarching values points us in the direction of Rawls's theory of overlapping consensus.

Turning to Rawls's (1985) concept of *overlapping consensus* when analysing these kinds of new alliances, we may see that conceiving of arable land as a commons subject to environmental rights might even make it easier to obtain overlapping consensus. We do not believe it is possible to refute the opposing stakeholders by reducing the conflicts to one common concern for all. Rawls's idea of an *overlapping consensus* entails accepting that people are embedded in different comprehensive values, but may, at a political level, still agree to the policies, albeit for different reasons. There is a need to face these conflicts by accepting their presence, while also making a strong appeal to *reflective judgment,* or a *broadened way of thinking* – the need for looking upon one's own interests from the perspective of everyone else (Kant 1952, 32; Arendt 1968, 220).

In the case of new alliances across the rural/urban and wildlife/farming divides against commodification and industrialization of the commons, we see a possible overlapping consensus in everyone's concern for promoting and improving collective human well-being. The three ideologies (wildlife, farming, industrialization) value well-being but differ on how it might be promoted and/or enhanced. Classical neoliberalism believes that industrial development will lead to more wealth, thereby increasing societal well-being. That wealth could then finance technological development, which could mitigate the effects of industrial pollution. Defending the value of agricultural smallholders is another strategy to promote the well-being of those who produce food in sustainable ways, which will benefit everyone, since we all need food to be well and survive. Those who promote wildlife preservation think in terms of ecosystem services such that destroying untouched nature means wasting the very valuable resources that are part of the system that sustains people who depend upon the stability of such systems.

Conflict between these competing conceptions of how well-being may be promoted is similar to tension between conflicting traditions and cultures. Whereas the particular ways of valuing traditions may be considered private (e.g., comprehensive value), particular ways of valuing natural resources are also "private" to those who adhere to that ideology, even though the content of each of the three ideologies actually concerns the well-being of everyone in society.

In the context of this chapter, we are looking for ways to strengthen environmental rights. In speaking of intergenerational justice and obligations to future generations, we need to include current living people, as well. Sustainable land use is subject to limited commons. As such it is a challenge both now and in the future. Across and within generations we need to appeal to reflective judgment and overlapping consensus. From an anthropocentric perspective on environmental rights, we would have liked to believe that there is sufficient rationality between current living people to make common ground for what it takes to share limited resources in a reasonable way. As bringing about agreement between opposing stakeholders is probably a futile effort if done by itself, we will most certainly also have to look in the direction of self-imposed limitations (see Birnbacher 2015, 163). An interesting place to start looking is in the new alliances between farmers and environmentalists that seem to materialize in some land-use contexts (see Vinge and Sørensen's chapter).

Conclusion

We have analysed a modest conception of *obligations to future generations* in terms of *environmental rights* and discussed how they apply to agricultural land use. This obligation is collectively conceived, as opposed to being observed from more individualistic perspectives. We have shown that the corresponding duties that will fulfil collective environmental rights are not too demanding and do not undermine the urgency of helping the worse off in the *present* generation, as pointed out by those who criticize the future generation discourse for being a luxury concern. In fact, a kind of collective obligation constitutes our concern for our own survival as human beings (thus anthropocentric), but at the same time it genuinely protects the survival and conservation of other species and the environment. In other words, our concern for our collective well-being as members of the current generation includes our concern for the well-being of our children, who will be the bearers of the next generation.

We have shown that contending approaches to promoting and enhancing our collective well-being may seem intractable (or irreconcilable), but they actually converge, not only in their concern for well-being but also in the concern for the interests and well-being of future generations. The challenge is to find ways by which these convergences may be translated to ethical and effective policy for agricultural land use and to explore other concerns on which these contending approaches may overlap.

NOTES

1 The way we conceptualized overlapping generations in this chapter is parallel to how the so-called overlapping generations were modelled in economics (see Samuelson 1958). Generations overlap between old and young. All generations will have earlier and later periods of their lifetimes that will overlap with the periods of the lifetimes of their predecessors and those who will be born later.

2 This account reduces the complexity of tracking lifetimes of members of different generations by assuming, for the sake of simplicity, that global birth cohorts will live about the same length of time – 70 years average (the 2012 estimated average life expectancy at birth for Monaco is 89.68 years and 48.69 for Chad; see CIA 2012).

3 On the view that moral principles apply only to persons who can recipro- cate harm and benefit, Parfit adopts Barry's objections to the reciprocity view (Parfit 1986, 357). Parfit uses the example of parental obligations to their children to defeat the reciprocity view of moral scope. See also Barry (1978).

4 There are ways to analyse reciprocity as sources of moral motivation for conserving natural resources for the sake of future generations. Gosseries (2009) evaluated three models of reciprocity to future generations without espousing these views himself.

5 Gewirth discussed the correlative duty to preserve the beauty of the envi- ronment that will have the same effect to fulfil the rights of future gener- ations to have their basic needs "to know, to satisfy curiosity, to fulfill the profound desire to understand the world" (Gewirth 2014, 121–2).

6 In this view, damage to the environment deprives access for other humans (future generations) to resources they need to fulfil their rights to freedom and well-being (Gewirth 2014).

7 "Stakeholder" is used here in a way analogous to its use in corporate social responsibility (CSR) literature. The transition from referring to "sharehold- ers" to talk about "stakeholders" is based on the opinion that it offers a more adequate account of the kind of interest of the parties in view in the CSR context. The same applies to the context of environmental rights, as some- thing is at *stake*, which transcends the question of what (and how) to *share*.

8 This is an important point, but we will not discuss liberal democracy fur- ther here.

9 Some claim that current consumption has already overshot the earth's capacity (see Brown 2012). Carrying capacity is the amount of resources available versus what is needed by a given size of population. The resources available should be greater than the need, and population size should be small enough that its needs will not exceed the resources available. Human technology has and can continue to modify carrying capacity such that the impact (I) of human consumption on the earth's carrying capacity can be equivalent to the population (P) multiplied by affluence (A), or human consumption per capita, and technology (T); thus I = PAT (see Ehrlich and Holdren 1971; Mitchell 2012). An alternative measure of human impact on the earth's biocapacity that avoids speculations about the limits imposed by the earth's carrying capacity is called ecological footprint. Even using this ecological footprint concept as a metric, it has been found that in 1999 human demand had already exceeded the earth's biocapacity by 20 per cent (see Wackernagel et al. 2002).

10 Oslo Roundtable on Sustainable Production and Consumption 1994.

11 Rockström et al. (2009). See especially table 1, page 473.

12 Parfit calls this the person affecting view of harm.

13 Derek Parfit looked for a theory X that would solve this problem. Many think that this is the result of insisting on the utilitarian doctrine of maximizing utility, and that no utilitarian theory on this issue will lead to a morally plausible answer (see Arrhenius 2012, as cited in Huseby 2012, 190–1).

14 Tännsjö points this out in his argument that there is nothing wrong with the well-being of even those in the low well-being outcome people in Parfit's repugnant conclusion, since they live a life worth living and their level of well-being is even higher than we have today. See Tännsjö (1997). We do not know if a higher level of well-being than we have now would actually result from choosing a depletion policy as shown in Parfit's projection of well-being levels resulting from depletion policies (Parfit 1986, 362).

15 Breaching the limits of the earth's bio-capacity, for example, could result in such suffering and death. See Rockström et al. (2009).

16 As Harry Frankfurt puts it, "What is important from the point of view of morality is not that everyone should have *the same* but that each should have *enough*" (Frankfurt 1987, 21).

17 For a similar sufficientarian approach to this problem, see Huseby (2012).

18 How do ordinary people view and/or interpret the so-called repugnant conclusion? One view that does away with the unpleasantness of the repugnant conclusion is to claim that the lives of those living in low levels of well-being are not miserable but their lives are worth living (see Tännsjö 1997, 251). But what makes the repugnance work is the idea that the level of well-being is so low as to make it miserable enough to be repugnant. A life worth living is worth living only when compared to non-existence, but

actually it is a miserable life. Such misery could perhaps be construed as so low that it breaches the threshold level of a life worth living. That level may be so low, making it not worth living at all, such that not existing is better if such suffering is to be avoided.

19 This harm threshold level has two lines: minimum threshold of subsistence (basic minimum rights) and maximum threshold of preference satisfaction (capabilities). One sufficientarian interpretation proposes that no individual should have well-being lower than the minimum but could allow increases up to the maximum, so long as no one is caused to fall below the minimum.

20 See Howarth (1992). This view proposes an algorithm that computes the proportion of consumption levels between generations. Dieter Birnbacher refers to parental concern that extends to future generations as indirect motivation: "What motivates us to care for the (distant) future" (Birnbacher 2015). See also Howarth (1995).

21 See Howarth (1992). The formula proposed in this chain of obligations view is as follows:

$$c^* = [n/(1 + n)]S_t$$

Where c^* is the optimal consumption level for period t, n is the renewal rate of natural resources S at period t, and S is the available resources at any given period t.

Note that the applicable formula for the current generation 0 is $c^* = [n/(1 + n)]S_0$. So if the rate of renewal n of resources in period 0 is 4.25 and the amount of available resources S is 42 units, the optimal consumption rate c^* should be $[4.25/(1 + 4.25)]42$ units $= (4.25/5.25)42$ units $= 34$ units.

REFERENCES

Alcott, B. 2008. "The Sufficiency Strategy: Would Rich-World Frugality Lower Environmental Impact?" *Ecological Economics* 64 (4): 770–86. https://doi.org/10.1016/j.ecolecon.2007.04.015.

Arendt, H. 1968. "Crisis in Culture." In *Between Past and Future: Eight Exercises in Political Thought*, edited by H. Arendt. New York: Meridian.

Arrhenius, G. 2012. *Population Ethics: The Challenge of Future Generations*. Oxford: Oxford University Press.

Arrhenius, G., J. Ryberg, and T. Tännsjö. 2010. "The Repugnant Conclusion." Stanford Encyclopedia of Philosophy. http://plato.stanford.edu/entries/repugnant-conclusion/.

Barry, B. 1978. "Circumstances of Justice and Future Generations." In *Obligations to Future Generations*, edited by R.I. Sikora and B. Barry, 204–48. Philadelphia: Temple University Press.

Birnbacher, D. 2015. "Some Moral Pragmatics of Climate Change." In *The Politics of Sustainability: Philosophical Perspectives*, edited by D. Birnbacher and M. Thorseth, 153–73. Abingdon, UK: Routledge.

Boyle, A. 2007. "Human Rights or Environmental Rights: A Reassessment." *Fordham Environmental Law Review* 18:471–511.

Brown, L. 2012. *World on the Edge*. Hoboken: Taylor and Francis.

Central Intelligence Agency (CIA). 2012. "Country Comparison: Life Expectancy at Birth." https://www.cia.gov/library/publications/the-world-factbook/rankorder/2102rank.html.

Cullet, P. 1995. "Definition of an Environmental Right in a Human Rights Context." *Netherlands Quarterly of Human Rights* 13 (1): 25–40. https://doi.org/10.1177/016934419501300103.

Ehrlich, P.R., and J.P. Holdren. 1971. "Impact of Population Growth." *Science* 171 (3977): 1212–17. https://doi.org/10.1126/science.171.3977.1212.

Frankfurt, H. 1987. "Equality as a Moral Ideal." *Ethics* 98 (1): 21–43. https://doi.org/10.1086/292913.

Gewirth, A. 2014. "Human Rights and Future Generations." In *Environmental Ethics*, edited by M. Boylan, 118–22. 2nd ed. Chichester, UK: Wiley-Blackwell.

Gosseries, A. 2009. "Three Models of Intergenerational Reciprocity." In *Intergenerational Justice*, edited by A. Gosseries and L.H. Meyer, 119–46. Oxford: Oxford University Press.

Gray, K., A.F. Ward, and M.I. Norton. 2014. "Paying It Forward: Generalized Reciprocity and the Limits of Generosity." *Journal of Experimental Psychology: General* 143 (1): 247–54. https://doi.org/10.1037/a0031047.

Hardin, G. 1968. "The Tragedy of the Commons." *Science* 162 (3859): 1243–8. https://doi.org/10.1126/science.162.3859.1243.

Howarth, R.B. 1992. "Intergenerational Justice and the Chain of Obligation." *Environmental Values* 1 (2): 133–40. https://doi.org/10.3197/096327192776680124.

– 1995. "Sustainability under Uncertainty: A Deontological Approach." *Land Economics* 71 (4): 417–27. https://doi.org/10.2307/3146707.

Huseby, R. 2012. "Sufficiency and Population Ethics." *Ethical Perspectives* 19 (2): 187–206.

IUCN/UNEP/WWF. 1991. *Caring for the Earth: A Strategy for Sustainable Living*. Australian National University. https://portals.iucn.org/library/sites/library/files/documents/CFE-003.pdf.

Kant, I. 1952. *The Critique of Judgement*, translated by J.M. Meredith. Oxford: Clarendon.

Meyer, L. 2008. "Intergenerational Justice." Stanford Encyclopedia of Philosophy. http://plato.stanford.edu/entries/justice-intergenerational/.

Mitchell, R.B. 2012. "Technology Is Not Enough: Climate Change, Population, Affluence, and Consumption." *Journal of Environment & Development* 21 (1): 24–7. https://doi.org/10.1177/1070496511435670.

Moore, M. 2008. "Global Justice, Climate Change and Miller's Theory of Responsibility." *Critical Review of International Social and Political Philosophy* 11 (4): 501–17. https://doi.org/10.1080/13698230802415946.

Parfit, D. 1986. *Reasons and Persons*. Oxford: Oxford University Press.

Rawls, J. 1971. *A Theory of Justice*. Cambridge, MA: Belknap of Harvard University Press.

– 1985. "Justice as Fairness: Political Not Metaphysical." *Philosophy & Public Affairs* 14 (3): 223–51.

Rockström, J., W. Steffen, K. Noone, A. Persson, F.S. Chapin, E.F. Lambin, T.M. Lenton et al. 2009. "A Safe Operating Space for Humanity." *Nature* 461 (7263): 472–5. https://doi.org/10.1038/461472a.

Rønningen, K., and F. Flemsæter. 2013. "Arealpress i utmarka." *Forskningsglimt* 2. Bygdeforskning, Trondheim.

Samuelson, P.A. 1958. "An Exact Consumption-Loan Model of Interest with or without the Social Contrivance of Money." *Journal of Political Economy* 66 (6): 467–82. https://doi.org/10.1086/258100.

Sen, A. 1992. *Inequality Reexamined*. New York: Russell Sage Foundation.

– 1999. *Development as Freedom*. Oxford: Oxford University Press.

Steffen, W., K. Richardson, J. Rockström, S.E. Cornell, I. Fetzer, E.M. Bennett, R. Biggs et al. 2015. "Planetary Boundaries: Guiding Human Development on a Changing Planet." *Science* 347 (6223): 1259855. https://doi.org/10.1126/science.1259855.

Tännsjö, T. 1997. "Doom Soon?" *Inquiry* 40 (2): 243–52. https://doi.org/10.1080/00201749708602449.

Wackernagel, M., N.B. Schulz, D. Deumling, A.C. Linares, M. Jenkins, V. Kapos, C. Monfreda et al. 2002. "Tracking the Ecological Overshoot of the Human Economy." *Proceedings of the National Academy of Sciences* 99 (14): 9266–71. https://doi.org/10.1073/pnas.142033699.

Woods, K. 2015. "Climate Justice, Motivation and Harm." In *The Politics of Sustainability: Philosophical Perspectives*, edited by D. Birnbacher and M. Thorseth, 92–109. Abingdon, UK: Routledge.

World Commission on Environment and Development. 1987. *Report of the World Commission on Environment and Development: Our Common Future*. http://www.un-documents.net/wced-ocf.htm.

Yale Center for Environmental Law and Policy, and Center for International Earth Science Information Network at Columbia University. 2014. "Environmental Performance Index 2014." https://sedac.ciesin.columbia.edu/data/set/epi-environmental-performance-index-2014.

13 Land and the Value Calculus: Towards a Reculturalization of Farmland

PHILIP MCMICHAEL, HILDE BJØRKHAUG,
AND BRUCE MUIRHEAD

Introduction

During the past few decades, there has been an increasing global interest in agricultural land as an asset for cultivating more food, but also in associated possibilities for profit-making. New concepts describe the phenomenon, such as land grabbing and farmland financialization, the former being a broad and critical conceptualization of a new occupation of land for production, conservation, or development, while the latter encapsulates financial interest in land as an asset for derivative trading and profiteering. Academic interest accelerated with the food crisis of 2007–8, which the literature reflects. From fewer than ten publications on land grabbing written each year before 2009, the number increased to twenty in 2010 and peaked with seventy-five in 2013.[1] Even more clear are numbers for publications focused on financialization – prior to 1991, there were none, ten in 2006, twenty in 2007, and eighty in 2009. Six years later, an astounding 249 were published.

In focusing on factors in land use decisions, this book highlights the ongoing contention between a globalizing culture of economism and a more situated socio-ecological commons culture. While the former views land as a financial asset to be acquired for industrial or speculative purposes, the latter views land as embedded in living cultures. Tashunka Witko (Crazy Horse), a leader of the indigenous Lakota people of the Great Plains of North America, perhaps best reflects that position when he remarked, "One does not sell the land upon which the people walk" (Edwards 2011). To view land as a financial asset, as it is now seen in an age of market uncertainty, loses sight of the fact that much of the land being commandeered today is a common property resource and/or represents a livelihood for millions of small producers, including farmers, pastoralists, fisherfolk, and forest-dwellers.

How do we balance a financial asset with a human right to a situated livelihood/material culture? Further, how do we temporally position financial investment in land? In this concluding chapter, we present some of the drivers for the increasing assetization and financialization of farmland and will note opportunities for reversing this trend. Finally, we will propose the culturalization of farmland as a concept that recognizes cultural valuation and potentially more democratic input on decisions on farmland management.

From Cultural to Financial Farmland

The FORFOOD project is focused on factors that influence decisions on the destiny of agricultural land. This book presents a collection of empirical and theoretical work on conflicting approaches to land among agricultural, environmental, and financial interests and how negotiation on valuation evolves, who "wins" and who "loses," and mechanisms proposed to better protect farmland and how those who depend on the land can be empowered. We have explored the position of culture, values, and ethics in decision-making related to agricultural land in the recent past, the present, and in the future, and across geographical spaces and governance structures.

Even though there has been a recent rush to land globally, the competition for agricultural land is not new (Cotula 2012; McMichael 2014). Cotula, for example, has pointed out that the drivers for the latest phenomenon are financial as well as so-called market forces in a classical supply–demand relationship, with both situated in the economic sphere. In a review of land acquisitions, Cotula finds that many transfers occur on a national scale. New owners, lessees, investors, or developers are often citizens of the country in which this is occurring, or members of the diaspora. However, the size of these acquisitions is sometimes difficult to estimate as the result of transaction fluidity (Ouma 2014). Some pass "under the radar" of those monitoring such transactions, as Geoffrey Lawrence, Sarah Ruth Sippel, and Nicolette Larder show in this book, using mediators that make geographical boundaries imprecise. How land acquisitions are interpreted differs by culture – some investors are interpreted as more "foreign" or "unfriendly" than others (see, e.g., Larder, Sippel, and Lawrence 2015), or gain more media attention than warranted by their investments (Cotula 2012).

How do we balance a financial asset with a human right to a situated livelihood/material culture – what has been called "customary rights"? Further, how do we temporally position financial investment in land? For both questions, displacement of farming communities is a recurring outcome of contemporary land deals. Oxfam claims more than 1,500 large-scale land deals have been signed since 2000, and that "we're entering a new and even more dangerous stage of the global land rush. The frenzied trade in millions of hectares of forests, coastlines and farmlands has led to murder, eviction and ethnocide. Land contracts are being signed and projects are breaking ground without the full consent of the communities living there" (Oxfam 2016, 5).

Such land deals threaten eviction of rural and Indigenous inhabitants, who, if adequately supported, are capable of protecting landscapes and waterways. Again, according to Oxfam, "Half of the world's landmass is home to Indigenous peoples and local communities that are its traditional owners. But they have no formally recognized ownership to 80% of this land ... often considered fair game for plunder, typically under the guise of 'economic development ... There is a long list of benefits to securing people's rights to these lands. It would protect more than 5,000 human cultures, and 4,000 different languages, as well as 80 per cent of the planet's biodiversity" (Oxfam 2016, 5).

Critically, as land deals spread industrial agriculture, which contributes up to 30 per cent of greenhouse gas emissions, eliminates biodiversity, and chemically contaminates the environment, the seven planetary boundaries are threatened: climate change, ozone depletion, ocean acidification, biodiversity, freshwater, global nitrogen, and phosphorus cycles. Thus far, climate change, nitrogen, and acidification are over or at a threshold beyond which nonlinear feedbacks may kick in. So how land is now managed is critical for the future of Earth and its inhabitants. And it challenges short-term financial thinking to recognize and address longer-term planetary thresholds. This contention between economic and socio-ecological cultures defines the current moment in world history and its significance for long-run survival.

Animating this debate is the modernist assumption that common property resources and small farming systems are inefficient uses of land, especially for "feeding the world." But when up to 70 per cent of the world's food is produced by small-scale producers (ETC 2009), and when about 50 per cent of land recently acquired is for biofuels, feed crops for affluent animal protein consumers, and speculation, it is unclear how the world might be fed, even with intensification of industrial agriculture. In addition, it is by no means certain that industrial agriculture, even with "sustainable intensification," can be as ecologically efficient as those small-scale biodiverse farming systems geared to reproducing soil fertility, hydrological cycles, and healthy food staples (Hart et al. 2015; Rockström et al. 2017).

Industrial agriculture has experienced declining biophysical productivity, with soil depletion and falling efficiency of nitrogen use from 60 to 20 per cent from the 1950s to the 1990s (Ploeg 2010, 100). The costs of "biophysical override" have risen with prices of agro-inputs amplified by rising energy costs and agribusiness conglomeration (Weis 2007). In consequence, agribusiness migrates offshore to take advantage of cost-reducing investments in Southern land, water, and labour, and the prospect of untapped markets for agro-inputs provided by newly recruited out-growers (McMichael 2013). This contributes to the universalization of a model of agriculture whose technologies are commercially standardized rather than culturally place-based. As Sophia Murphy observes, conventional agro-industrial emphasis is on agricultural output, rather than function, focusing on developing capacity for (external) seeds and fertilizer inputs. The alternative conception of raising productivity is as "food output per acre rather than yield per plant" where farming is diverse, with investment situated in "ecologically sound and socially just technologies" (Murphy 2008).

As a 2008 joint study by the UN Conference on Trade and Development (UNCTAD) and the UN Environment Program (UNEP), Organic Agriculture and Food Security, found that "organic agriculture outperformed conventional production systems based on chemical-intensive farming and is thus more conducive to food security in Africa." Analysing 114 projects across twenty-four African countries, the study showed yield doubling where organic (or near-organic) practices were used, and "strong environmental benefits such as improved soil fertility, better retention of water, and resistance to drought in these areas" (UNCTAD and UNEP 2008, 236).

Conventional expectations of the demise of rural cultures and their farming systems is built into the modern development model, which assumes a linear movement of peasants and small farmers off the land, providing "unlimited supplies of labor" for urban jobs (Lewis 1954). As we are now learning, such a singular linear temporality has serious consequences. First, it erases connection with continuing ecological practices deemed obsolete and rejected as impractical for a techno-future. Second, development's linear temporality now threatens present and future, via accumulating greenhouse gases. As Malm emphasizes, "For every year global warming continues and temperatures soar higher, living conditions on earth will be determined more intensely by the emissions of yore, so that the grip of yesteryear on today intensifies – or, put differently, *the causal power of the past inexorably rises*, all the way up to the point when it is indeed 'too late.' The significance of that terrible destiny, so often warned of in climate change discourse, is the final *falling in of history on the present*" (Malm 2016, 9).

While such a historical force cannot be avoided, it can be tempered. Thus, a responsible initiative to divest from fossil fuels, reduce monoculture, and shift to land use patterns mimicking bio-diverse natural cycles would protect and draw upon *extant* farming cultures with ecological practices to reduce such historically rooted effects in the present and the future.

Land Questions in the Twenty-First Century

Questions of land use gathered urgency in the first decade of the twenty-first century following three decades of increasingly unregulated agro-exporting operations encircling the globe, institutionalized by the 1995 WTO trade and investment protocols in the name of "feeding the world." The consequences included dismantling public supports for national farm sectors, privileging transnational agribusiness, spreading agro-industrial monoculture, disregarding ecological integrity, and displacing small-scale producers and local farming systems with commercial food dumping (Rosset 2006).

In consequence, in 2005 the UN's Millennium Ecosystem Assessment (MEA) reported that the last half-century of economic development "resulted in a substantial and largely irreversible loss in the diversity of life on Earth." Furthermore, the MEA observed that "existing national and global institutions are not well designed to deal with the management of common pool resources, a characteristic of many ecosystem services," and poverty reduction strategies "have not taken into account the importance of ecosystems to improving the basic human capabilities of the poorest" (United Nations 2005, 1, 20). In other words, modern political economy elides ecological relations and their significance for rural cultures. In 2007 the UN Environment Programme claimed the planet's water, land, air, plants, animals and fish stocks were all in "inexorable decline" (quoted in Vidal 2007), and in 2008 the International Assessment of Agricultural Science and Technology for Development (IAASTD) observed, "Business as usual is no longer an option," in the context of multiple crises (energy, climate, food) at the start of the twenty-first century. It questioned industrial agriculture and transgenic foods as solutions (to food insecurity, climatic emergency, ecosystem degradation, and slum expansion), noting that markets fail to adequately value environmental and social harm (IAASTD 2008, 20).

In the same year, in the context of a serious "food crisis" precipitating a World Food Summit in Rome at the UN's Food and Agriculture

Organization, the International Planning Committee for Food Sovereignty (IPC) proclaimed a "Platform for Collective Action" at the accompanying Terra Preta Forum: "The serious and urgent food and climate crises are being used by political and economic elites as opportunities to entrench corporate control of world agriculture and the ecological commons. Actions by some governments and top UN leadership at the High Level Conference on World Food Security, Climate Change and Bio-Energy (the FAO Summit) constitute an assault on small-scale food providers among whom women and Indigenous People are in the forefront, and the natural commons" (Indigenous Environmental Network 2008).

The 2008 Rome contention foreshadowed a new politics concerned with what came to be known as the global "land grab." In his chapter in this volume, Philip McMichael analyses articulations of local and global land management in the deliberations of the Civil Society Mechanism and questions the utility of the UN system in addressing land use for the future. Across the world, particularly in the Global South and Eastern Europe, investors grabbed land in response to food inflation and biofuel subsidies. Fuel crops replaced food crops, accounting for almost 50 per cent of the rise in food prices (McMichael 2010). Borras et al. noted, "The World Bank report on land grabs (or, as the Bank calls it, agricultural investment), released in September 2010, estimated this global phenomenon at 45 million hectares" (Borras et al. 2011, 209). According to the Grass Roots Anti-Imperialist Network (GRAIN), since the "food crisis" some land deals have "backfired or failed for different reasons," such as water scarcity, lack of investor farming expertise, civil resistance, volatile financial and currency markets, unstable governments, and legal ambiguities regarding land tenure (GRAIN 2016). However, GRAIN reports many new deals are underway "to expand the frontiers of industrial agriculture," and beyond gaining access to food supplies, oil palm expansion beyond Southeast Asia into Africa complements "a broader corporate strategy to profit from carbon markets, mineral resources, water resources, seeds, soil and environmental services" (GRAIN 2016). A further effect, addressed in Jacob Muirhead's chapter, is where land grabbing occurs by default as smallholders, unable to meet the private standards of certification systems, forfeit their land to private interests associated with global retailers.

In addition to acquiring land by private financial investment, Siri Granum Carson notes sovereign wealth funds have followed suit, raising serious ethical questions where pension funds in particular are involved – such as the Norwegian Government Pension Fund. Her chapter discusses the potential impact of such funds in encouraging private investments to consider more sustainable land use investments.

This parallels the debates regarding "responsible agricultural investment," addressed by Jennifer Clapp, whose chapter reviews the soft power limitations of voluntary guidelines regarding responsibility to the land and its producer cultures. And the question of responsibility informs the final substantive chapter by Allen Alvarez and May Thorseth, who ask whether and to what extent future generations as well as other species deserve consideration in tempering the economic calculus with an ecological calculus.

In this "land grab" moment the lines were drawn on a global scale between two visions of addressing the combined food and climate crises: one involved intensifying industrial agriculture and its infrastructures, and the other protected local farming systems and their shared ecosystems. These visions represent distinct cultural values. The former promotes a private financial calculus of "economic efficiency." The latter promotes biodiverse systems of "ecological efficiency" embedded in social networks of seed sharing and local markets (see Holt-Giménez 2006; Perfecto, Vandermeer, and Wright 2009).

Broadly, these distinct visions constitute alternative ontologies, meaning they envision practices that are alternative ways of organizing land use, centred on distinctive agricultural systems (McMichael 2014). In relation to these distinguishing features, the chapters by Hilde Bjørkhaug, Katrina Rønningen, and Heidi Vinge, by Jostein Tapper Brobakk and Bruce Muirhead, and by Geoffrey Lawrence, Sarah Ruth Sippel, and Nicolette Larder, survey the shifting strategies for land-use decisions in Norway, Canada, and Australia, respectively, and their agricultural implications. The extent of Norway's agricultural landscape is quite limited, enabling a close look at local cultural priorities for land use, within a food security framework. Australia, with its long history of foreign investment in natural resources, now faces financial intensification of large-scale land deals by investors and sovereign wealth funds in the name of global food security. Under such conditions, as addressed in the chapter by Jostein Tapper Brobakk and Bruce Muirhead, land deals are generating substantial political contention over who has access, or not, to agricultural land (foreign or local investors) and associated methods of land use. And, as argued by Hugh Campbell and David Reynolds, the question of land ownership transfers associated with the ongoing "land grab" increasingly overshadows prior contention over the impact of trade agreements and associated food imports on agrarian cultures. Katrina Rønningen's chapter contrasts earlier European initiatives in multifunctionality, securing rural communities and environments, with a more recent focus on food security via "neo-productivism," expelling farmers as land holdings consolidate. Heidi Vinge and Siri Øyslebø Sørensen empirically show the formation of new alliances, and Allen Alvarez and May Thorseth discuss how new alliances can create a potential for overlapping consensus in land questions between parties with previous conflicts. A recent report by The Greens/European Free Alliance in the European Parliament notes, "The rush for land in Europe has a different character than for instance in Africa. Ordinarily, the concentration of land in the EU takes place legally.... [But] land has increasingly become an investment and an object of speculation and is no longer primarily the basis of small-scale farming. At the same time, agriculture is becoming more intensive and farms are getting bigger. This is a threat to biodiversity, the groundwater, our rural social structures, and the quality of food. Soil, grassland, and arable land are not a commodity but the livelihood of farmers" (Heubuch 2015, 3).

Rønningen notes that these trends are nevertheless triggering local alternatives, favouring organic food and questioning centralized decision-making regarding how land is to be used. And this phenomenon informs the research of Elisa Da Vià, who examines reproduction practices and sharing of farm-saved seeds by farmer networks in Italy, Spain, and France, promoting agro-ecological alternatives to conventional industrial agriculture, to enhance agricultural resilience and secure livelihoods on the land. This involves the extraordinary rise of collaborative relations among farmers regarding seed use and exchange as an active method of co-production of farming knowledge, and, in turn, integrative relations with food preparers and consumers (Da Vià 2012).

By contrast, a financial calculus for land use by agribusiness or land dealers can discount social needs in the service of private interest. This is clear in the recent phenomenon of "flex crops," involving substitutability of food, feed, and fuel crops (Borras et al. 2012). Here "financial speculation renders land and crops increasingly fungible as governed by the price form – at the expense of a rational farming of the land for social and ecological sustainability" (McMichael 2012, 684). As Diana Henriques (2008) has noted, "The spectre of a hungry world is being used to push the agenda for industrial agriculture, but in reality, the majority of the land is used for producing animal feed and agrofuels, as well as land speculation, rather than food crops. A World Bank report on land acquisitions shows that only 37% of this land is used to grow food."

Alternatively, an ecological calculus applied by farming communities to land use focuses on managing the natural fertility of soils, durable hydrological cycles, and ecosystem integrity as the foundation of resilient farming cultures. Whereas industrial agriculture is a heavy energy consumer and greenhouse gas emitter, ecological farming is an energy converter and provider. The ultimate value of non-industrial farming is that to preserve human civilization and its ecological base, farming the land sustainably means expanding carbon sinks via agro-forestry and bio-diverse practices, adopting agro-ecology as a method of rebuilding soil carbon, thereby reducing atmospheric carbon and regenerating nature in the process. Integral to this calculus is the increasing recognition of the importance of agricultural landscapes as multifunctional spaces that combine food provisioning with improving rural livelihoods and protecting healthy ecosystems (Hart et al. 2016).

Towards a Reculturalization of Farmland?

As suggested, there is key tension between a broadly practised low-input ecological calculus and a politically dominant financial calculus. The latter is represented by powerful financial conglomerates, reinforced by the discursive influence of the market model, and publicly supported, given government needs for debt financing and receptiveness to powerful financial lobbies. A striking example is the Ethiopian government's recent sponsorship of "de-territorialization" via long-term land rental agreements to foreign investors to modernize production of an unspecified range of exportable crops. Opposition politicians view these agreements to be less about the land and its produce, and more about government brokering of international influence via secret deals, so that "the party in power is an intermediary without which no one can get a piece of the action" (Liberti 2013, 24). States regularly alienate land and resources via the complicity of local chiefs or community leaders (Vermeulen and Cotula 2010). African lands with customary tenure are easily targeted for state appropriation because of "legal manipulations, which deny that local indigenous (customary) tenures deliver property rights, thereby legalizing the theft of the lands of the poor or subject peoples" (Wiley 2012, 751). Thus, in Tanzania land designated as the property of the local village has been redefined by the government as "general" land to lease to biofuel companies (Vermeulen and Cotula 2010, 174–5), and in Mozambique, where community boundaries are imprecise, land law manipulations "have generally weakened communities' ability to protect their land from a government that favours an influx of foreign investors" (Friends of the Earth 2010, 13), including World Bank–supported Jatropha crops, for biofuels.

Here, indebted states and local elites mortgage public authority to private ends to capture foreign exchange or investments, and territory is redefined as a source of present and future income – thereby alienating control of habitat to investors or conservation organizations with no relation to national territory other than a financial calculus. A case in point is MacDonald's account of conservation organizations whose members "become ontologically complicit with the knowledge categories of the institutional field ... that structures and provides the material resources and legitimacy needed to support the organization's existence" (MacDonald 2013, 241). His ethnography of the International Union for Conservation of Nature (IUCN) observes that, from a distance (without field experience), the IUCN accumulates selective knowledge of conservation sites across the world – the goal being "to rationalize and then modify situated knowledge or practice within ideological boundaries of understanding subscribed to by transnational organizations" (235). While this process may be resisted and/or modified, it illustrates global landscape planning via a financial calculus, reducing meanings, practices, and processes of human/nature interaction – culture – to a standardized price form.

The value tension between financial, ecological, and cultural calculi informs each chapter one way or another. The question generally comes down to who should inherit the land? Which "who" generally implies a particular modus operandi. Those interests promoting food security via an economistic view of agriculture – as an input-output operation modelled on industrial production – stand in opposition to *extant* farming communities whose livelihood and culture depend ultimately on ecological viability. Given recent decades of neoliberal regulations, such communities have been confronted with withdrawal of public supports and market pressures from larger agribusiness concerns, enabled by forms of market rule (e.g., WTO protocols privileging transnational corporate investors and traders).

Accordingly, farming communities have lost ground, so to speak. But there remain countless examples of continuing agro-ecological experimentation across the world as small-scale producers cling to their rural culture and values of land stewardship (see Pionetti 2005; Ploeg 2009; Fitting 2011; Kerssen 2012; Da Vià 2012; Baker 2013; McKeon 2015). Furthermore, these communities are often connected through their membership in the 200 million–strong international peasant coalition, La Vía Campesina (LVC). As a founding member of LVC claimed, "It's a movement of people of the land who share a progressive agenda. Which means we share the view that people – small farmers, peasants, people of the land – have a right to be there. That it's our job to look after the earth and our people. We must defend it and we have to defend it in the global context" (Nettie Wiebe, quoted in Desmarais 2007, 98).

LVC champions agro-ecology in anticipation of a deepening crisis of industrial agriculture, claiming, "To feed future populations, we must nurture the land." Accordingly, LVC is developing agro-ecological schools and networks to assist farmers in conversion to or consolidation of ecological farming, and publicly advocating for reorientation of research and extension systems to support agro-ecological innovation and scaling up via farmer organizations. At the same time, small producer practices include constant innovation for survival on the land under conditions of climatic change.

For example, a report on the Deccan Plateau of South India by Carine Pionetti shows how seed saving minimizes risk, increases crop diversity and nutrition, provides "self-reliance and bargaining power within the household" for women (Pionetti 2005, xiv), allows women to select seeds to meet specific individual, environmental, and climatic needs, allows planting at appropriate times, and provides assets (seeds constitute a currency, particularly among women with few resources). Seeds constitute the security of a "knowledge commons" – a democratically organized defence against agribusiness and states under pressure to transform farming into a singularly commercial venture. Once farmers join "value-chains," they become dependent on a production chain "where the choices of inputs and the use of the harvest are predetermined by agro-chemical and food-processing firms" (xv). Here a financial calculus would replace an ecological calculus with considerable impact on local cultural values.

Nevertheless, there is considerable pressure from states to counter "de-commodification," as is evident in recent formulations of regional trade rules, which generally favour allowing foreign investment in domestic farmland, outlawing seed saving and sharing by farmers, and allowing global retailers to compete in local markets (GRAIN 2017). The current involvement of public authorities in alienating common property resources and subsidizing private agribusiness in the name of global food security deepens the commodification of nature and farming. As a financial calculus gains traction, it further conditions policymaking and how the future is to be managed. And this has the effect of foreclosing the possibility of managing landscapes for the public good and an ecological calculus.

These developments represent a contemporary struggle between minority private interests and the majority world's attempts to protect, preserve, and develop self-organizing systems at a human scale commensurate with ecosystem sustainability. Presently the amount of food produced and exchanged informally among local networks in Europe outstrips the amount of food produced by what we call conventional, modern commercial agriculture (see Da Vià 2012). This is a world-wide pattern, surfacing in community-supported agricultures, farmers' markets, urban gardening, slow food networks, and so on. As much as 40 per cent of the population of some African cities and up to 50 per cent in some Latin American cities engage in urban or peri-urban agriculture (Cohen and Garrett 2009, 8). Much of this activity is under the official statistical radar, but it implicitly recognizes the growing importance of communities exercising their cultural priorities to address imme-diate food insecurities and protect landscapes in a time of ecological uncertainty.

Conclusion

This book explores how culture, values, and ethics influence arguments and justifications in decision-making on the management of agricul-tural land in the recent past, the present, and the future. In short, it highlights the moral and ethical responsibilities of land use. It presents a collection of empirical and theoretical work on conflicting approaches to land among agricultural, environmental, and financial interests and how negotiation on valuation is evolving, who "wins" and who "loses," and mechanisms proposed to better protect farmland and how those who depend on the land can be empowered. In the process, the collection has provided insights into how "resource hierarchies" are culturally constructed, as different interests and agendas compete for this finite resource: how do agricultural interests, environmental inter-ests, and financial interests imply different and potentially conflicting approaches to land? As these chapters have demonstrated, pressures on land are multiple and complex, and with the purported imperative to feed and house a growing population, generate wealth through re-source extraction and financial speculation, the non-trade values of land, like its cultural dimensions, are easily sidelined to the detriment of a wider society. As a number of these chapters have implicitly asked, can the centre hold, or will financial considerations run roughshod over long-term agricultural sustainability?

Will it be the case that the global food regime, associated with the overproduction of food, over-exploitation of resources, rising food commodity and land prices, as well as growing environmental degra-dation direct us to a future that no one really wants? At the heart of this question are contestations over land use, as diverse social actors articulate multiple and competing understandings of human/nature relationships and associated land use. Such conflicts often result in out-comes that come at the expense of public goods such as environment, biodiversity, and cultural amenity, as has been demonstrated through-out this collection. Authors have pointed to the necessity of an epis-temic shift to secure both the environment and its food-producing capacity into the future. To that end, we suggest that a situated cultural valuation of land, a socio-ecological commons culture, represents an alternative ontology and counterforce against the globalizing culture of economism in land use questions.

This collection's research questions were focused on exploring the multiple ways in which contestations over land use are materializing from a variety of different perspectives as well as their implications. For example, the first section of the book addresses policy and public discourses on agricultural land and competing resources, and property and community rights that animate conversation and inform the activ-ities of stakeholders. The second section investigates what we style as regulations and certification schemes, followed by moral and ethical questions, and governance implications. The book also examines land regulatory issues at the national level, using Australia, Canada, and Norway as the test cases and informing that discussion through refer-ence to civil society responses to land questions. In addition, all chap-ters in one way or another point to the consideration of ethical questions about the various interests involved in land governance or exploita-tion. The final section explores the existential question of humanity's responsibility to environmental sustainability and the rights of future generations of humans and other species to land for food production.

Ultimately, as this collection suggests, the issues and questions raised are inherently imbued with cultural meaning, differentiating cultural priorities of agricultural, environmental, and financial interests. These are not necessarily mutually exclusive interests, as farmers may have distinctive environmental concerns in order to sustain their ecologi-cal capital, and financiers may favour investments in "ecosystem ser-vices." However, given the current critical threshold in world history, concerning ecosystem sustainability and climatic stability, and given unequal power relations affecting access to private resources and pub-lic support, it is, as we have outlined in this book, important to distin-guish these interests to examine their respective cultural appeal and social impact.

NOTE

1 Scopus search 2017: https://www.elsevier.com/solutions/scopus.

REFERENCES

Baker, L.E. 2013. *Corn Meets Maize: Food Movements and Markets in Mexico.* Boulder, CO: Rowman and Littlefield.

Borras, S.M. Jr, J.C. Franco, S. Gómez, C. Kay, and M. Spoor. 2012. "Land Grabbing in Latin America and the Caribbean." *Journal of Peasant Studies* 39 (3–4): 845–72. https://doi.org/10.1080/03066150.2012.679931.

Borras, S.M. Jr, R. Hall, I. Scoones, B. White, and W. Wolford. 2011. "Towards a Better Understanding of Global Land Grabbing: An Editorial Introduction." *Journal of Peasant Studies* 38 (2): 209–16. https://doi.org/10.1080/03066150.2011.559005.

Cohen, M.J., and J.L. Garrett. 2009. "The Food Price Crisis and Urban Food (In)Security." Human Settlements Working Paper Series. London: iied/UNFPA. http://www.iied.org/pubs/display.php?o=10574IIED.

Cotula, L. 2012. "The International Political Economy of the Global Land Rush: A Critical Analysis of Trends, Scale, Geography and Drivers." *Journal of Peasant Studies* 39 (3/4): 649–80.

Da Vià, E. 2012. "Seed Diversity, Farmers' Rights, and the Politics of Depeasantization." *International Journal of Sociology of Agriculture and Food* 19 (2): 229–42.

Desmarais, A.A. 2007. *Globalization and the Power of Peasants: La Via Campesina.* Halifax: Fernwood Books.

Edwards, S. 2011. "Pain's Simple Sounds." Mill Swamp Indian Horse Views, 13 November. http://msindianhorses.blogspot.com/2011/11/pains-simple-sounds.html.

ETC. 2009. "Who Will Feed Us?" ETC Group Communiqué. https://www.etcgroup.org/content/who-will-feed-us.

Fitting, E. 2011. *The Struggle for Maize: Campesinos, Workers, and Transgenic Corn in the Mexican Countryside.* Durham, NC: Duke University Press.

Friends of the Earth. 2010. *The Jatropha Trap: The Realities of Farming Jatropha in Mozambique.* No. 118, September. https://www.foei.org/wp-content/uploads/2010/09/19-foei-jatropha-eng-lr.pdf.

GRAIN. 2016. "The Global Farmland Land Grab in 2016: How Big, How Bad?" 2 June. https://www.grain.org/article/entries/5492-the-global-farmland-grab-in-2016-how-big-how-bad.

– 2017. "How RCEP Affects Food and Farmers," 19 June. https://www.grain.org/article/entries/5741-how-rcep-affects-food-and-farmers.

Hart, A.K., P. McMichael, J.C. Milder, and S.J. Sherr. 2015. "Multi-Functional Landscapes from the Grassroots? The Role of Rural Producer Movements." *Agriculture and Human Values* 33 (2): 305–22. https://doi.org/10.1007/s10460-015-9611-1.

Henriques, D. 2008. "Food Is Gold, so Billions Invested in Farming." *New York Times*, 5 June. http://www.nytimes.com/2008/06/05/business/05farm.html.

Heubuch, M. 2015. *Land Rush: The Sellout of Europe's Farmland.* Greens/ European Free Alliance. https://www.greens-efa.eu/files/doc/ docs/19abd146a6f61773450e58f438b3d287.pdf.

Holt-Giménez, E. 2006. *Campesino-a-Campesino: Voices from Latin America's Farmer to Farmer Movement for Sustainable Agriculture.* Oakland, CA: Food First Books.

Indigenous Environmental Network. 2008. "Now Is the Time for Food Sovereignty." http://www.fao.org/fileadmin/user_upload/foodclimate/ statements/powless.pdf.

International Assessment of Agricultural Knowledge, Science and Technology for Development (IAASTD). 2008. "Executive Summary of the Synthesis Report." http://www.wecf.eu/download/2008/SR_Exec_Sum_130408_ Final.pdf.

Kerssen, T.M. 2012. *Grabbing Power: The New Struggles for Land, Food and Democracy in Northern Honduras.* Oakland, CA: Food First Books.

Larder, N., S.R. Sippel, and G. Lawrence. 2015. "Finance Capital, Food Security Narratives and Australian Agricultural Land." *Journal of Agrarian Change* 15 (4): 592–603.

Lewis, W.A. 1954. "Economic Development with Unlimited Supplies of Labour." *Manchester School* 22 (2): 139–91. https://doi.org/10.1111/j.1467-9957.1954. tb00021.x.

Liberti, S. 2013. *Land Grabbing: Journeys in the New Colonialism.* London: Verso.

MacDonald, K.I. 2013. "Nature for Money: The Configuration of Transnational Institutional Space for Environment Governance." In *The Gloss of Harmony: The Politics of Policy-Making in Multilateral Organizations,* edited by B. Müller, 227–54. London: Pluto.

Malm, A. 2016. *Fossil Capital: The Rise of Steam Power and the Roots of Global Warming.* London: Verso Books.

McKeon, N. 2015. *Food Security Governance: Empowering Communities, Regulating Corporations.* London: Routledge.

McMichael, P. 2010. "Agrofuels in the Food Regime." *Journal of Peasant Studies* 37 (4): 609–29. https://doi.org/10.1080/03066150.2010.512450.

– 2012. "The Land Grab and Corporate Food Regime Restructuring." *Journal of Peasant Studies* 39 (3/4): 681–701. https://doi.org/10.1080/03066150.2012 .661369.

– 2013. "Value-Chain Agriculture and Debt Relations: Contradictory Outcomes." *Third World Quarterly* 34 (4): 671–90. https://doi.org/10.1080/ 01436597.2013.786290.

– 2014. "Rethinking Land Grab Ontology." *Rural Sociology* 79 (1): 34–55. https://doi.org/10.1111/ruso.12021.

Murphy, S. 2008. "Will Free Trade Solve the Food Crisis?" *Food Ethics Council* 3 (2). https://www.foodethicscouncil.org/uploads/publications/food_ethics_summer08(web).pdf.

Ouma, S. 2014. "Situating Global Finance in the Land Rush Debate: A Critical Review." *Geoforum* 57:162–6.

Oxfam. 2016. *Custodians of the Land, Defenders of Our Future: A New Era of the Global Land Rush*. Ottawa: Oxfam.

Perfecto, I., J. Vandermeer, and A. Wright. 2009. *Nature's Matrix: Linking Agriculture, Conservation and Food Sovereignty*. London: Earthscan.

Pionetti, C. 2005. *Sowing Autonomy: Gender and Seed Politics in Semi-Arid India*. London: IIED.

Ploeg, J.D. vander. 2009. *The New Peasantries: Struggles for Autonomy and Sustainability in an Era of Empire and Globalization*. London: Earthscan.

– 2010. "The Peasantries of the Twenty-First Century: The Commoditisation Debate Revisited." *Journal of Peasant Studies* 37 (1): 1–30. https://doi.org/10.1080/03066150903498721.

Rockström, J., J. Williams, G. Daily, A. Noble, N. Matthews, L. Gordon, H. Wetterstrand et al. 2017. "Sustainable Intensification of Agriculture for Human Prosperity and Global Sustainability." *Ambio* 46 (1): 4–17. https://doi.org/10.1007/s13280-016-0793-6.

Rosset, P.M. 2006. *Food Is Different: Why We Must Get the WTO out of Agriculture*. Halifax: Fernwood.

United Nations. 2005. *Ecosystems and Human Well-Being: Millennium Ecosystem Assessment* Washington, DC: Island.

United Nations Conference on Trade and Development (UNCTAD) and United Nations Environment Programme (UNEP). 2008. *Organic Agriculture and Food Security in Africa*. New York: United Nations.

Vermeulen, S., and L. Cotula. 2010. "Over the Heads of Local People: Consultation, Consent and Recompense in Large-Scale Land Deals for Biofuels Projects in Africa." *Journal of Peasant Studies* 37 (4): 899–916. https://doi.org/10.1080/03066150.2010.512463.

Vidal, J. 2007. "Global Food Crisis Looms as Climate Change and Fuel Shortages Bite." *Guardian*, 7 November. https://www.theguardian.com/environment/2007/nov/03/food.climatechange.

Weis, T. 2007. *The Global Food Economy: The Battle for the Future of Farming*. London: Zed.

Wiley, L.A. 2012. "Looking Back to See Forward: The Legal Niceties of Land Theft in Land Rushes." *Journal of Peasant Studies* 39 (3–4): 751–75.

Contributors

Allen Alvarez is a philosopher who works in the field of bioethics and has done research and education on health-care ethics, ethics of technology, distributive justice, and research ethics. He holds a PhD in philosophy from the University of Bergen and did postdoctoral research at the Norwegian University of Science and Technology in Trondheim and at the Centre for Applied Ethics at the University of British Columbia. He has published on the place of sufficiency thresholds in moral reasoning about health-care resource allocation as a matter of distributive justice, articulating the argument that basic capacity is fundamentally important. That work has informed the discussion included in this volume on the rights of future generations to access resources essential to their well-being. Allen's earlier work on the role of empirical research in bioethics highlighted the need to investigate empirical assumptions we make or imply in value-based moral reasoning. This focus on empirical ethics re-emerged in his most recent work on the role of embedded philosophizing in health care, particularly in clinical situations when facing life-and-death decisions.

Hilde Bjørkhaug is associate professor in sociological theory at the Norwegian University of Science and Technology and research professor at Ruralis: Institute for Rural and Regional Research in Trondheim, Norway. Her research interests include agricultural restructuring, family farming, and the role of small and medium-sized farms in food and nutrition security. She also studies changes in the agri-food value chain, including questions on ethics, power relations, policy, and financialization. Her most recent co-edited book, with colleagues Geoffrey Lawrence and André Magnan, is *The Financialization of Agrifood Systems: Contested Transformations* (Routledge, 2018). She is an active member of the European Society for Rural Sociology and is secretary/

treasurer of the executive board of the International Sociological Association's Research Committee 40 (the Sociology of Agriculture and Food).

Jostein Tapper Brobakk is a senior researcher at Ruralis: Institute for Rural and Regional Research, with a PhD in political science from the Norwegian University of Science and Technology. His research is centred upon the impact of climate change on agricultural policy and farmer perceptions, policy regime development, and governance in the agri-food sector. He has been a visiting researcher at the University of Waterloo, Ontario, Canada, doing fieldwork on land-related developments in Saskatchewan, Canada. His most recent publication is a book chapter on ethics in public financialization in Norwegian sovereign wealth funds in an edited volume on financialization of agri-food systems, Bjørkhaug, Magnan, and Lawrence eds, *The Financialization of Agri-food Systems: Contested Transformations* (Routledge, 2018).

Hugh Campbell is professor of sociology at the University of Otago in New Zealand. His main research interests are the impact of neoliberalization on farming, trade policy, and attempts to generate alternatives to mainstream agri-food systems. From 2000 to 2010 he was director of the Centre for the Study of Agriculture, Food and Environment undertaking transdisciplinary research into agricultural sustainability and the impact of new forms of agri-food governance in New Zealand. His current research activities are exploring farming ontologies and modernity.

Siri Granum Carson is an associate professor of philosophy at the Programme for Applied Ethics at the Norwegian University of Science and Technology, with a particular focus on globalization, corporate social responsibility, and business ethics. She is director of the research programme HAVANSVAR – Humanities Ocean Initiative – as part of the strategic research area NTNU Ocean. Carson is also associate professor II at the University of Bergen, connected to the UNESCO chair for Sustainable Heritage and Environmental Management, Nature and Culture.

Jennifer Clapp is a Canada Research Chair in Global Food Security and Sustainability and professor in the School of Environment, Resources and Sustainability at the University of Waterloo, Canada. She has published widely on the global governance of problems that arise at the intersection of the global economy, the environment, and food security. Her most recent books include *Speculative Harvests: Financialization, Food, and Agriculture* (with S. Ryan Isakson, Fernwood Press, 2018),

Food, 2nd ed. (Polity, 2016), *Hunger in the Balance: The New Politics of International Food Aid* (Cornell University Press, 2012), and *Corporate Power in Global Agrifood Governance* (co-edited with Doris Fuchs, MIT Press, 2009).

Nicolette Larder is a lecturer in human geography at the University of New England, Australia. Her research interests span urban food systems, food sovereignty, and financialization of the food system. She is a lead investigator on the DAAD-funded project, Understanding the Role of Finance in Australian Agriculture. Upcoming research will explore the economic geography of the craft beer sector in Australia and New Zealand.

Geoffrey Lawrence is emeritus professor of sociology at the University of Queensland, Australia. His research spans the areas of agri-food restructuring, neoliberal globalization, financialization, and food security. During his academic career Geoff has published some twenty-five books and over 500 peer-reviewed journal articles and book chapters. His most recent co-edited book, with colleagues Hilde Bjørkhaug and André Magnan, is *The Financialization of Agri-food Systems: Contested Transformations* (Routledge, 2018). He was president of the International Rural Sociology Association (2012–16) and is an elected fellow of the Academy of Social Sciences in Australia.

Philip McMichael is professor of development sociology at Cornell University. He is author of *Food Regimes and Agrarian Questions* (Fernwood, 2013), *Development and Social Change: A Global Perspective*, 6th ed. (Sage, 2016), and the award-winning *Settlers and the Agrarian Question* (Cambridge, 1984); and has edited *Contesting Development: Critical Struggles for Social Change* (Routledge, 2010), and *Biofuels, Land and Agrarian Change*, with Jun Borras and Ian Scoones (Routledge, 2011). He works with the Civil Society Mechanism in the UN Committee on World Food Security, and has consulted with UNRISD, the FAO, La Vía Campesina, and the IPC for Food Sovereignty, and IPES-Food.

Bruce Muirhead is associate vice-president, Research Oversight and Analysis in the Office of Research at the University of Waterloo, and a professor in the Department of History. He has written extensively on Canadian trade negotiations since the Second World War, as well as Canadian politics, diplomacy, and economic development. His more recent work has focused on the evolution of Canadian agricultural policy, and especially dairy and egg supply management. He is the Egg

Farmers of Canada Chair in Public Policy, where his research centres on the relevance and usefulness of supply management by comparing the Canadian system with those found in comparable sectors in Australia, New Zealand, the United Kingdom, and the United States.

Jacob Muirhead is a PhD candidate in comparative public policy at McMaster University, Hamilton, Ontario, Canada. His research focuses on the regulation of transnational agricultural value chains through private standards and legal contracts. Muirhead is the co-author of "Traceability in Global Governance" published with *Global Networks: A Journal of Transnational Affairs* (2019). He is also a 2019 recipient of a Social Sciences and Humanities Research Council of Canada Post-Doctoral Fellowship that will fund his project exploring the regulatory potential of commercial contracts in transnational agri-food governance.

David Reynolds has researched the political, social, and environmental aspects of food, working with researchers at the University of Otago, in the Centre for Sustainability, the Department of Sociology, Gender and Social Work, and the Department of Food Science. He is undertaking a PhD at the School of Social Sciences, Monash University, in Melbourne, Australia.

Katrina Rønningen is a rural geographer working on agricultural, environmental, and rural resources and policies at Ruralis: Institute for Rural and Regional Research. She holds a Dr.polit in geography from the Norwegian University of Science and Technology and a master's in land-use planning from the Norwegian University of Life Sciences. *Multifunctionality of agriculture, cultural landscapes, climate change*, and *farmland preservation* are keywords for her agriculturally orientated research. As well, she studies commodification and marginalization in rural areas, conservation and land-use questions linked to aquaculture, large carnivores, wind energy, land use rights, and land use pressures in Indigenous reindeer herding.

Sarah Ruth Sippel holds a PhD in geography and is a senior researcher at the University of Leipzig, Germany, and an honorary senior research fellow with the School of Social Science at the University of Queensland, Australia. She leads a four-year research project on imaginations of land, funded by the German Research Foundation. She has worked intensively on the interlinkages between export agriculture, rural livelihood security, and labour migration in North Africa and the Western Mediterranean. Her current research explores the nexus between global food security and financialization of natural resources, especially in the Australian context, as well as emerging forms of solidarities within global agri-food systems.

Siri Øyslebø Sørensen is associate professor in the Department of Interdisciplinary Studies of Culture at the Norwegian University of Science and Technology. She specializes in gender studies and social studies of science and technology. Her research interests include studies of policymaking and organizations with a primary interest in how inequalities, difference, and categorizations are produced and changed.

May Thorseth, professor of philosophy in the Department of Philosophy and Religious Studies at the Norwegian University of Science and Technology, is also director of NTNU's Programme for Applied Ethics. Current research projects include BIOSMART: Managing the Transition to a "Smart" Bio Economy, funded by the Norwegian Research Council, as well as BINGO: Bringing Innovation to Ongoing Water Management – a better future under climate change. For an EU-Horizon 2020 project, Strategic, Tactical, Operational Production of water Infrastructure against cyber-physical Threats (STOP-IT), Thorseth is its ethics advisor.

Heidi Vinge is a researcher at Ruralis: Institute for Rural and Regional Research, Norway. She is completing her PhD dissertation in sociology at the Norwegian University of Science and Technology, where she investigates the relationship between knowledge and power in farmland politics and planning, and how these configurations are embedded in structures of climate-change mitigation measures and neoliberal ideals.

Index

The letter *f* following a page number denotes a figure and the letter *t* denotes a table.

Lightning Source UK Ltd.
Milton Keynes UK
UKHW010758170320
360469UK00011B/231